Constructivism and International Relations

Alexander Wendt and his critics

This new book unites in one volume some of the most prominent critiques of Alexander Wendt's constructivist theory of international relations and includes the first comprehensive reply by Wendt.

Partly reprints of benchmark articles, partly new original critiques, the critical chapters are informed by a wide array of contending theories ranging from realism to poststructuralism. The collected leading theorists critique Wendt's seminal book *Social Theory of International Politics* and his subsequent revisions. They take issue with the full panoply of Wendt's approach, such as his alleged positivism, his critique of the realist school, the conceptualisation of identity, and his teleological theory of history. Wendt's reply is not limited to a rebuttal only. For the first time, he develops his recent idea of a quantum social science, as well as its implications for theorising international relations.

This unique volume will be a necessary companion to Wendt's book for students and researchers seeking a better understanding of his work, and also offers one of the most up-to-date collections on constructivist theorising.

Stefano Guzzini is Senior Researcher at the Danish Institute for International Studies, Copenhagen, and Professor of Government at Uppsala University, Sweden.

Anna Leander is Associate Professor in the Department of Political Science and Public Management at the University of Southern Denmark, and Associate Professor of International Political Economy at Copenhagen Business School, Denmark.

The New International Relations

Edited by Barry Buzan, *London School of Economics*
and Richard Little, *University of Bristol*

The field of international relations has changed dramatically in recent years. This new series will cover the major issues that have emerged and reflect the latest academic thinking in this particularly dynamic area.

Constructivism and International Relations

Alexander Wendt and his critics

Edited by
Stefano Guzzini and Anna Leander

Routledge
Taylor & Francis Group

LONDON AND NEW YORK

First published 2006
by Routledge
2 Park Square, Milton Park, Abingdon, Oxon OX14 4RN

Simultaneously published in the USA and Canada
by Routledge
270 Madison Ave, New York, NY 10016

Routledge is an imprint of the Taylor & Francis Group

Transferred to Digital Printing 2006

Typeset in Baskerville by
Book Now Ltd

British Library Cataloguing in Publication Data
A catalogue record for this book is available from the British Library

Library of Congress Cataloging in Publication Data
Constructivism and international relations: Alexander Wendt and his
critics/edited by Stefano Guzzini and Anna Leander.
  p. cm.– (The new international relations)
Includes bibliographical references and index.
1. International relations–Sociological aspects. 2. International relations–
Philosophy. 3. Wendt, Alexander, 1966– I. Guzzini, Stefano. II. Leander,
Anna. III. Series.

JZ1251.C66 2006
327.1'01–dc22   2005014086

Publisher's Note
The publisher has gone to great lengths to ensure the quality of this reprint
but points out that some imperfections in the original may be apparent

ISBN10: 0–415–33271–0 (hbk)
ISBN10: 0–415–41120–3 (pbk)

ISBN13: 978–0–415–33271–2 (hbk)
ISBN13: 978–0–415–41120–2 (pbk)

Für Else

Contents

Contributors

Andreas Behnke teaches international politics at Towson University, Maryland. He has published in *Alternatives, Cooperation & Conflict, Millennium: Journal of International Studies*, and *Zeitschrift für Internationale Beziehungen*. His research interests include International Relations theory, critical security studies, political geography, and the concept of the political in contemporary international politics.

Lars-Erik Cederman is Professor of International Conflict Research at the Swiss Federal Institute of Technology, Zurich. He obtained a PhD in political science from the University of Michigan in 1994 and has since taught at the Graduate Institute of International Studies in Geneva, Oxford, UCLA, and Harvard. He is editor of *Constructing Europe's Identity: The External Dimension* (Lynne Rienner, 2001) and the author of *Emergent Actors in World Politics: How States and Nations Develop and Dissolve* (Princeton University Press, 1997). He is also the author and co-author of articles in scholarly journals such as the *American Political Science Review, European Journal of International Relations, International Organization, International Studies Quarterly, Journal of Conflict Resolution*, and *Proceedings of the National Academy of Sciences*. His main research interests include computational modelling, International Relations theory, nationalism, integration and disintegration processes, and historical sociology.

Dale C. Copeland is author of *The Origins of Major War* (Cornell University Press, 2000), which examines the link between the rise and decline of great powers and the outbreak of devastating system-wide wars and the crises that increase the risk of such wars. He is currently working on a second book entitled *Economic Interdependence and International Conflict*. This project considers the conditions under which inter-state trade leads to either war or peace. Other research interests include the origins of economic interdependence between great powers, the realist–constructivist divide, and the logic of reputation-building. Among his recent articles are: 'A Realist Critique of the English School' (*Review of International Studies*, June 2003); 'Economic Interdependence and War' (*International Security*, Spring 1996); and 'Trade Expectations and the Outbreak of Peace' (*Security Studies*, autumn 1999–winter 2000). He is the recipient of numerous awards, notably MacArthur and Mellon fellowships and a post-doctoral fellowship at the Center for Science and International Affairs, Harvard University.

Christopher Daase is Professor of International Relations at the Geschwister Scholl Institute of Political Studies, Munich University, Germany. He previously served as Director of the Programme in International Conflict Analysis at the Brussels School of International Studies. He received his PhD from the Free University Berlin for a dissertation on 'Small Wars: How Unconventional War Changes International Politics'. His teaching and research interests centre on International Relations theory, international security and conflict regulation.

Petr Drulák is Director of the Institute of International Relations in Prague. He has published on theory of International Relations, European integration, and EU enlargement in a number of Czech and international publications (including *Journal of International Relations and Development* and *Journal of European Public Policy*). He is the author of the first Czech textbook on theories of International Relations (2003). In 2003–4, he was Jean Monnet Fellow at the European University Institute in Florence.

Stefano Guzzini received his doctorate from the European University Institute, Florence. He is Senior Researcher at the Danish Institute for International Studies and Professor in the Department of Government at Uppsala University, Sweden. He previously taught at Central European University, Budapest (1994–2002), and worked at the late Copenhagen Peace Research Institute (2000–3). He is the author of *Realism in International Relations and International Political Economy* (Routledge, 1998) and is currently working on *Power and International Relations* (Cambridge University Press). Together with Milan Brglez he edits the *Journal of International Relations and Development*.

Friedrich Kratochwil studied classics, philosophy and political science in Munich and received as a Fulbright scholar an MD in international politics from Georgetown University (1969) and a PhD from Princeton (1976). He taught at Maryland, Princeton, Columbia, Delaware, and Pennsylvania, before returning (1995) to Germany and taking the chair in International Politics at the European University Institute in Florence (2002). He has published widely on International Relations, social theory, international organization, and international law in US and European journals. His latest book (edited with Edward Mansfield) is entitled *International Organization and Global Governance* (New York: Pearson Longman, 2005). Presently he is working on a manuscript entitled *The Practice of (Inter)national Politics*.

Anna Leander is Associate Professor in the Department of Political Science at the University of Southern Denmark, Odense, and Associate Professor of International Political Economy at Copenhagen Business School, Denmark. She received her PhD from the European University Institute, Florence, worked at Central European University, Budapest (1995–2003), and at the late

Copenhagen Peace Research Institute (2000–4). She is the author of a number of articles in refereed journals. Her current research focuses on private authority in world politics.

Katalin Sárváry recently received her PhD in International Relations from the Central European University, Budapest. Her research examines the promise of a dialogue on diplomacy between classical and constructivist theories of practice.

Hidemi Suganami is Professor in the Department of International Politics at the University of Wales, Aberystwyth. His major publications are *The Domestic Analogy and World Order Proposals* (Cambridge University Press, 1989) and *On the Causes of War* (Oxford University Press, 1996). With Andrew Linklater, he has recently completed a book-length project on the English School of International Relations.

Alexander Wendt received his PhD from the University of Minnesota in 1989. His research interests lie at the intersection of International Relations, social theory, and philosophy of social science. He is the author of *Social Theory of International Politics* (Cambridge University Press, 1999) and a number of articles in refereed journals. He is currently Professor at the Ohio State University, and taught previously at the University of Chicago, Dartmouth College, and Yale University.

Maja Zehfuss is Senior Lecturer in International Relations at the University of Warwick. She is the author of *Constructivism in International Relations: The Politics of Reality* (Cambridge University Press, 2002). She currently works on war, memory and the politics of ethics.

Series editor's preface

The debate around Alex Wendt's *Social Theory of International Politics* has been a centrepiece of theoretical thinking in IR since the book was published in 1999. The book brought into focus, and intensified, discussions that were already under way in response to a series of influential articles by Wendt, a series he has continued since Social Theory came out. This book offers a major extension of that process, though given the energies and implications in play, and Wendt's continued development of his own thought, no doubt not a culmination of it. Unlike Waltz, and his 'Theory of International Politics', with which Wendt and his 'Social Theory' are frequently compared, Wendt does not see his theory as a full and closed creation. Whereas Waltz has been content to defend his bastion from within, Wendt continues to sally forth, opening up new fronts, and engaging with his critics in a sustained attempt to refine his theory and put it on firmer foundations. This book gathers together nine critiques of Wendt that build on both his book and his subsequent work, and allows him a generous space to reply. It displays critical debate at its best, not (for the most part) as a simple destructive attempt to pull the house down, but (if I may say in this context) as a constructive one in which the critical dialogue stimulates the development of the theory.

The fact that Wendt and some other constructivists have sought to position their work in the middle ground of IR theory shapes this debate in interesting ways. Waltz's theory, and the neo-neo position that has evolved from it, occupied one end of the theoretical spectrum and could only easily be attacked from one side. The attempt of Wendt and the constructivists to challenge the neo-neo hegemony wins quite wide support amongst the critics even where they find flaws in the argument, and even those who disagree with Wendt in one way or another often credit him with advancing the theoretical debate. But the middle-ground positioning of Wendtian constructivism means that it is subjected to attack from both sides – neo-neo rationalist materialism, and postmodern, 'ideas all the way down' thinking. Basic military strategy, and the German experience in the twentieth century, suggests that two-front wars are difficult to win. The only hope of success is a good offence, and that seems to be the approach that Wendt is taking.

In line with the current fashion in IR theory, it is the philosophical side of Wendt's theory that has attracted the most comment. That remains true in this volume, though there is also plenty of engagement with the IR theory side of

Wendt's thinking. One audience for this book will be those who believe that progress in IR theory can only be achieved by getting the whole enterprise onto a firmer foundation in philosophy of knowledge – though which foundation of course remains contested. For those engaging with this debate for the first time, the essays collected here provide a good overview of many of the core issues. For those already part of the debate, they provide a further extension of it, detailed replies by Wendt to the main points, and a new contribution by him. In this volume he even takes the opportunity to join his critics, standing outside his theory for a while and proposing an alternative philosophical platform for it in quantum social theory. For many in IR this move will take them onto entirely unfamiliar ground, forcing them to think hard and in detail both about the philosophy underpinning the natural sciences and about the implications for social science of the strong levels of analysis division found there between the classical (Newtonian) physics of the solid material world we see around us and the uncertain and mysterious quantum physics of the micro-world that underpins the classical one. Wendt provides as clear and engaging an account of this as one is likely to find in the social sciences, exposing the implicit and explicit Newtonianism of both neo-neo and post-modernist thinkers. He invites his audience to engage with the social implications of not just an analogy with the structural uncertainties of the quantum physics world, but a kind of merger with them. Doing so, he argues, provides a whole new way of confronting the problem of consciousness that is the essence of the social world. The good general Wendt finds here an attack that should disorientate his enemies on both fronts, and force the more energetic and creative of them back to their books for some overdue cross-disciplinary re-education. This is 'new International Relations' with a vengeance.

Barry Buzan

Preface

Alexander Wendt's work has rapidly become one of the main reference points of the theoretical debate in International Relations (IR). *Social Theory of International Politics* was acclaimed and contested even before it was published in 1999. Since then, it has been the issue of special panels at many conferences, of a forum in the *Review of International Studies* ('Forum on *Social Theory of International Politics*' 2000) and in *Cooperation and Conflict* (Jackson 2001; and Behnke, chap. 3 this volume), to name just two. It became the object of an interminable series of book reviews, including a paragraph in *The Economist* (3–9 March 2001: 89), an event perhaps unique for any theoretical treatise in IR.

Wendt's book is part of a trend in IR, visible ever since the 'Inter-Paradigm Debate' or 'Third Debate', to acknowledge that meta-theoretical and theoretical reflections are necessarily connected. In his book, he consequently first develops his position in the philosophy of science and social theory (part 1) before establishing an IR theory of inter-state politics (part 2). Given this prominent place of meta-theoretical matters, Wendt's version of constructivism is usually understood as one of the most abstract ones, little concerned with actual empirics or politics.

The impression of a perhaps overly abstract endeavour will certainly be reinforced by Wendt's more recent developments. He did return and clarify part 2 of the book. But this update of his IR theory came in the version of a theory of history (Wendt 2003), again raising the stakes of abstract thought. Similarly, his reply to this volume is a move to a higher level of theoretical abstraction. Here, Wendt is pushing for a discussion of the metaphysical underpinnings of social theorising, a part 0 or preface, as it were, to be added before the book starts. In a very daring and ambitious move, he asks social scientists to consider the possibility of a quantum social science.

But exactly this movement to higher abstraction indicates perhaps another way of fruitfully approaching Wendt's version of constructivism. Instead of starting from the abstract 'downwards', as the book does for logical reasons, one could proceed from his dissatisfaction with the state of world politics 'upwards'. Indeed, strange as it may seem to some, politics is also an initial trigger for Wendt. From early on, one of his basic questions is the possibility of change or learning in world politics. This topic will find him at odds with neorealism, which leaves little room for change, i.e., the very possibility of international politics. The end of the Cold

War created a window of opportunity to put politics and social learning into the limelight of IR theory again. For Wendt as for many others, international affairs being of a social nature, this historical event showed that there was nothing 'natural' in the state of world politics.

If the international system is a social fact which allows for the possibility of social learning, then Wendt needed to understand reflexivity in the social world, i.e., the link between the 'common sense' in international affairs (mostly realist materialism) and the way it not only understands but also constructs the actual state of world politics. Even though Wendt uses Waltz's neorealism as a foil to launch his own theory, realism's main importance resides not primarily in its alleged explanatory power, but in the political effects of providing the common language in which world politics takes place. Realism is a *social fact in world politics* itself. It was arguably these shared meanings in IR and its link with practice which prompted Wendt to think about the underlying assumptions of power politics as a practice and realism as 'its' theory.

Questioning underlying assumptions takes Wendt's critique of realism as practice and theory to the philosophy of social science and now ultimately metaphysics. His recent piece on the teleology of history again shows how politics and metaphysics are related. He explores the conditions for the possibility of a liberal Kantian world. This requires a rethinking of the common sense in world politics. It also prompts a reflection on IR theory which must be able to conceptualise historical reflexivity (social learning), which Wendt achieves by arguing for a more interpretivist philosophy of science (keeping the old German idealist link between progress and a version of philosophical realism, so that 'reason' can play its role). Hence, his reflections on the conditions for the possibility of a Kantian learning push him to a qualified interpretivism. And now, in turn, he adds an account of the conditions for the possibility of interpretivism through his proposed theory of quantum consciousness. Put in this way, it makes perfect sense to link his political vision in his history of progress (Wendt 2003) directly to his present proposal of a social science quantum theory.

For this is the challenge of theorising à la Wendt: all levels of the theory are intrinsically connected. Changing one can affect all the others. IR theory stays in direct relation to the philosophy of science and indeed to philosophy more generally. According to Wendt, theoreticians simply cannot afford to leave any of these levels out if they want to provide a coherent theory of international politics.

Whether theoreticians in IR will pick up this gauntlet remains to be seen. There are many more specific threads in IR theorising that need to be taken up right now, not the least for constructivists themselves, as many of the following pages show. Also, even if one does share a more comprehensive ambition, Wendt's project might lack a sense of 'epistemological modesty', as Colin Wight put it in his discussion of an earlier version of Wendt's reply at the annual conference of the International Studies Association in New Orleans in 2004.

Yet, we believe that, exactly for this comprehensive ambition, engaging Wendt's version of constructivism has been fruitful for advancing in a series of theoretical issues, not the least about the different ways of doing theory. Focusing on the connected facets of Wendt's project, the contributors of this volume had to clarify their concepts and sharpen their own approach, whether constructivist or not. And so did Wendt in his reply. We hope readers will experience a similar challenge and inspiration.

Stefano Guzzini and Anna Leander

Acknowledgements

It all started in 1999. We had organised a summer school at the Central European University in Budapest on 'The Sociological Turn in Theories of International Relations'. Scholars from Central and Eastern Europe interested in theories of International Relations (IR) found a forum to meet and to debate contemporary IR theory, an event which was, and perhaps still is, too uncommon in the 'region'. The guest speakers included Lars-Erik Cederman, Peter Katzenstein, and Friedrich Kratochwil for the week on IR, László Bruszt, Colin Crouch, and Ronen Palan for the second week in international political economy.

Based on a core of participants, but not limited to them, we then decided to prolong this experience by making a series of workshops which would develop the theme of the summer school. To some extent, a discussion of Alexander Wendt's just published theoretical treatise *Social Theory of International Politics* was an obvious choice. In its holistic component, it is one of the most 'sociological' approaches to IR so far. Moreover, he clearly showed the connection that exists between a meta-theoretical and a theoretical framework, developing both. Finally, his entire theorising is an attempt to draw together different traditions, which makes him relatively open to them – and to their critiques.

Two workshops were held, in Budapest (June 2000) and Copenhagen (March 2001), in which we discussed topics and different drafts, having Andreas Behnke joining the last workshop as discussant. The project became one of the few genuinely cross-European projects in IR theorising. At some point, Zlatko Šabič, then editor of the *Journal of International Relations and Development* (JIRD), gave us the idea of submitting the result for publication as a special issue. Some papers were selected and finally presented to an international audience at the fourth Pan-European conference of the ECPR/SGIR in Canterbury (September 2001). Our special issue appeared in December 2001 in *JIRD*.

While writing our piece for the special issue, we contacted Alexander Wendt for comments on our draft. His reaction was so positive that we then decided to ask him whether he would agree to a full book on his work in which the special issue would be complemented by other articles. When he agreed, we discussed different possibilities for the final selection of articles. This is surely a difficult task for every volume of this kind. Wendt's theory had provoked much heated debate. We decided to focus on articles which were entirely dedicated to his work and to which he had not already replied. We eventually decided to drop an introduction to save space. But even with these criteria and conditions, there were more articles which could have been included, some appearing when we had started submitting our book proposal. All this to say, that in a world of longer books, we would have included more and sincerely hope that the book encourages readers to relate to the wider Wendt discussion which we simply could not accommodate here.

The selection combines a chronological and logical sequence. Although starting from the debate on Wendt's book, it now reaches beyond this. The first three chapters are early general analyses of Wendt's *Social Theory of International Politics*, ranging from Dale Copeland's realist critique to Friedrich Kratochwil's constructivist and Andreas Behnke's more radical critique (we are not sure we dare to say 'poststructuralist' without this being superficially taken against the author). These are followed by Hidemi Suganami's and our own critique of the book, which reflect on this first round of discussion and make the link to the last four chapters which deal with significant specific issues of Wendt's theory. Maja Zehfuss's chapter as well as that by Lars-Erik Cederman and Christopher Daase deal with the difficult theorisation of identity.[1] The last two chapters analyse Wendt's underlying theory of change. For the special issue of *JIRD*, Katalin Sárváry and Petr Drulák had already 'pre-empted' that topic. When Wendt published his more explicit theory of history in 2003, it was only natural to return to them and ask them to update their earlier contributions in the light of this new material. Alexander Wendt's reply to the critics concludes the book.

We are grateful to a number of publishers and academic journals for permission to reprint material which appeared elsewhere in this or an earlier version. Copeland's chapter is reprinted with permission from *International Security* and MIT Press (vol. 25, no. 2, 2000, pp. 187–212). Kratochwil's chapter appeared first in *Millennium: Journal of International Studies* (vol. 29, no. 1, 2000, pp. 73–101). Suganami's chapter is a revision of an earlier publication which appeared in the *Review of International Studies* (vol. 28, no. 1, 2002, pp. 23–37), printed here with permission of Cambridge University Press. Our own chapter is a slightly edited version of an article which appeared under another title in the *Journal of International Relations and Development* (vol. 4, no. 4, 2001, pp. 316–38). Sage and NISA granted permission for the reprint of Andreas Behnke's chapter, which appeared in *Cooperation and Conflict* (vol. 36, no. 1, 2001, pp. 121–34). The chapters by Zehfuss and Cederman and Daase were both originally published in the *European Journal of International Relations* (respectively, vol. 7, no. 3, 2001, pp. 315–48, and vol. 9, no. 1, 2000, pp. 5–35) and are reprinted with the permission of Sage. The last three chapters are first published here.

In the long gestation of this issue, we have incurred many debts. We acknowledged earlier the help we received in the preparation of the special issue. At this stage, we want to extend our gratitude to the contributors of the volume, and to the staff at Routledge who have made this possible.

We want to dedicate our contribution to this volume to the memory of Else, Stefano's mother and our children's grandmother, who died in October 2004.

---

1 Incidentally, Behnke, Cederman and Daase, and Zehfuss had presented earlier versions of their research on Wendt at the same workshop-panel of the third Pan-European conference of the ECPR/SGIR in Vienna (September 1998).

1 The constructivist challenge to structural realism

A review essay[*]

Dale C. Copeland

For more than a decade realism, by most accounts the dominant paradigm in international relations theory, has been under assault by the emerging paradigm of constructivism. One group of realists – the structural (or neo-/systemic) realists who draw inspiration from Kenneth Waltz's (1979) seminal *Theory of International Politics* – has been a particular target for constructivist arrows. Such realists contend that anarchy and the distribution of relative power drive most of what goes on in world politics. Constructivists counter that structural realism misses what is often a more determinant factor, namely, the intersubjectively shared ideas that shape behavior by constituting the identities and interests of actors.

Through a series of influential articles, Alexander Wendt has provided one of the most sophisticated and hard-hitting constructivist critiques of structural realism.[1] *Social Theory of International Politics* provides the first book-length statement of his unique brand of constructivism (Wendt 1999).[2] Wendt goes beyond the more moderate constructivist point that shared ideas must be considered alongside material forces in any empirical analysis. Instead he seeks to challenge the core neorealist premise that anarchy forces states into recurrent security competitions. According to Wendt, whether a system is conflictual or peaceful is a function not of anarchy and power but of the shared culture created through discursive social practices. Anarchy has no determinant 'logic', only different cultural instantiations. Because each actor's conception of self (its interests and identity) is a product of the others' diplomatic gestures, states can reshape structure by process; through new gestures, they can reconstitute interests and identities toward more other-regarding and peaceful means and ends. If Wendt is correct, and 'anarchy is what

*   For their valuable comments on earlier drafts of this essay, I thank Spencer Bakich, Eric Cox, John Duffield, Kelly Erickson, Mark Haas, Jeffrey Legro, Len Schoppa, and Dennis Smith. Portions of this essay were drawn from the paper 'Integrating Realism and Constructivism', presented at the annual meeting of the American Political Science Association, Boston, Massachusetts, in September 1998. For insightful comments on that paper, I thank Michael Barnett, Miriam Fendius Elman, Iain Johnston, Andrew Kydd, Randall Schweller, Jennifer Sterling-Folker, and Alexander Wendt.

1   See, *inter alia*, Wendt (1987; 1992a; 1994; 1995).

2   References to Wendt's book are given in the text, enclosed in parentheses.

states make of it', then realism has been dealt a crushing blow: states are not condemned by their anarchic situation to worry constantly about relative power and to fall into tragic conflicts. They can act to alter the intersubjective culture that constitutes the system, solidifying over time the non-egoistic mind-sets needed for long-term peace.

Notwithstanding Wendt's important contributions to international relations theory, his critique of structural realism has inherent flaws. Most important, it does not adequately address a critical aspect of the realist worldview: the problem of uncertainty. For structural realists, it is states' uncertainty about the present and especially the future intentions of others that makes the levels and trends in relative power such fundamental causal variables. Contrary to Wendt's claim that realism must smuggle in states with differently constituted interests to explain why systems sometimes fall into conflict, neorealists argue that uncertainty about the other's present interests – whether the other is driven by security or nonsecurity motives – can be enough to lead security-seeking states to fight. This problem is exacerbated by the incentives that actors have to deceive one another, an issue Wendt does not address.

Yet even when states are fairly sure that the other is also a security seeker, they know that it might change its spots later on. States must therefore worry about any decline in their power, lest the other turn aggressive after achieving superiority. Wendt's building of a systemic constructivist theory – and his bracketing of unit-level processes – thus presents him with an ironic dilemma. It is the very mutability of polities as emphasized by domestic-level constructivists – that states may change because of domestic processes independent of international interaction – that makes prudent leaders so concerned about the future. If diplomacy can have only a limited effect on another's character or regime type, then leaders must calculate the other's potential to attack later should it acquire motives for expansion. In such an environment of future uncertainty, levels and trends in relative power will thus act as a key constraint on state behavior.

The problem of uncertainty complicates Wendt's efforts to show that anarchy has no particular logic, but only three different ideational instantiations in history – as Hobbesian, Lockean, or Kantian cultures, depending on the level of actor compliance to certain behavioral norms. By differentiating these cultures in terms of the degree of cooperative behavior exhibited by states, Wendt's analysis reinforces the very dilemma underpinning the realist argument. If the other is acting cooperatively, how is one to know whether this reflects its peaceful character, or is just a façade masking aggressive desires? Wendt's discussion of the different degrees of internalization of the three cultures only exacerbates the problem. What drives behavior at the lower levels of internalization is precisely what is not shared between actors – their private incentives to comply for short-term selfish reasons. This suggests that the neorealist and neoliberal paradigms, both of which emphasize the role of uncertainty when internalization is low or nonexistent, remain strong competitors to constructivism in explaining changing levels of cooperation through history. And because Wendt provides little empirical evidence to support his view in relation to these competitors, the debate over which paradigm possesses greater explanatory power is still an open one.

The first section of this essay outlines the essential elements of Wendt's argument against the backdrop of the general constructivist position. The second considers some of the book's contributions versus existing theories within the liberal, constructivist, and realist paradigms. The third offers an extended critique of Wendt's argument against structural realism.

Overview: constructivism and Wendt's argument

Three elements make constructivism a distinct form of international relations theorizing. First, global politics is said to be guided by the intersubjectively shared ideas, norms, and values held by actors. Constructivists focus on the intersubjective dimension of knowledge, because they wish to emphasize the social aspect of human existence – the role of shared ideas as an ideational structure constraining and shaping behavior.[3] This allows constructivists to pose this structure as a causal force separate from the material structure of neorealism.

Second, the ideational structure has a constitutive and not just regulative effect on actors. That is, the structure leads actors to redefine their interests and identities in the process of interacting (they become 'socialized' by process). Thus, unlike rationalist theories such as neorealism and neoliberalism, which hold interest and identities constant in order to isolate (respectively) the causal roles of power and international institutions, constructivism considers how ideational structures shape the very way actors define themselves – who they are, their goals, and the roles they believe they should play.[4]

Third, ideational structures and actors ('agents') co-constitute and co-determine each other. Structures constitute actors in terms of their interests and identities, but structures are also produced, reproduced, and altered by the discursive practices of agents. This element allows constructivists to challenge the determinacy of neorealism. Structures are not reified objects that actors can do nothing about, but to which they must respond. Rather structures exist only through the reciprocal interaction of actors. This means that agents, through acts of social will, can change structures. They can thereby emancipate themselves from dysfunctional situations that are in turn replicating conflictual practices.[5]

For constructivists, therefore, it is critical to recognize that an actor's reality at any point in time is historically constructed and contingent. It is the product of human activity – historical social practices – and thus can, at least in theory, be

---

3 See Klotz and Lynch (1998: 4–5), Checkel (1998), Wendt (1992a), Adler (1997), Finnemore (1996: chap. 1).
4 See Onuf (1989: chap. 1), Klotz (1995), Klotz and Lynch (1998: 7), Hasenclever *et al.* (1997: 158–67), Katzenstein (1996a), Jepperson *et al.* (1996), Wendt and Duvall (1989), Ruggie (1998a: chap. 1), Bukovansky (1997), and the special issue ('Special issue on the origins of the national interest' 1999) of *Security Studies*. For a broader discussion of the rationalist-constructivist debate and for further references, see Katzenstein *et al.* (1999).
5 Hopf (1998: 172–3), Wendt (1992a; 1994), Adler (1997: 338–40), Klein (1994: chaps 1–2), Reus-Smit (1997), Finnemore (1996: chap. 1).

transcended by instantiating new social practices. This process of cultural change may be slow; after all, agents are sometimes coming up against thousands of years of socialization. But even the most embedded structures can be altered by acts of will (and the requisite social mobilization). The neorealist presumption that there are universal laws of international politics that work across space and time, driven by the given reality of structure, must therefore be discarded or at least highly qualified.[6]

Social Theory of International Politics moves beyond this core constructivist framework. For Wendt, constructivism in its different strands is simultaneously too extreme and too limited in its attack on neorealism. It is too extreme when it claims that it is 'ideas all the way down', namely, that all aspects of human reality are shaped by socialization through discursive practices.[7] Material forces do exist and may have independent causal effects on actor behavior. Moreover, the state is a real, self-organized actor that has certain basic interests prior to its interaction with other states. Yet, according to Wendt, constructivism is too limited when it simply tests ideas as causal factors against realist variables such as power and interest, without exploring the degree to which these apparent 'material' variables are really constituted by ideational processes. If much of what scholars take to be material causes is actually the product of historical social practices, then realism explains far less in international relations than is commonly assumed.

Social Theory of International Politics is a complex work of both social philosophy and social science, one that justifies multiple readings to absorb its subtleties.[8] Its core argument, however, can be summarized as follows. The book's target is Waltzian neorealism. The overarching goal is to do for constructivism what Waltz did for realism, namely, the building of a parsimonious systemic theory that reveals the overarching constraining and shaping force of structure – this time from an ideational perspective. (Thus the title's twist on Waltz's masterwork – '*Social* Theory of International Politics'.)

As with neorealism, Wendt's argument is founded on the notion that states are the primary actors in world politics. States are self-organized units constructed from within by the discursive practices of individuals and social groups. As units that exist in the collective knowledge of many individuals, they are not dependent on the thoughts of any one person. Moreover, as self-organized entities, each possesses a 'corporate' identity as a sovereign actor, an identity not tied to inter-action with other states.[9] Even more controversial for extreme constructivists,

6 Berger and Luckmann (1991 [1966]: 60), Ashley (1986 [1984]), Wendt (1992a: 410), Der Derian (1995), Hall (1997), Koslowski and Kratochwil (1994).

7 In earlier work, Wendt himself comes close to this more extreme constructivist line (Wendt 1992a: 401; 1995: 73). On the idea that material structures gain their meaning only through discursive practices, see Bukovansky (1997: 218), Finnemore (1996: 6, 128), and Dessler (1989: 473, 461).

8 For a recent discussion on the more philosophical aspects of the book, see the forum on Alexander Wendt ('Forum on *Social Theory of International Politics*' 2000).

9 Going beyond his previous work, and borrowing from James D. Fearon, Wendt also includes another form of identity that is intrinsic to the state – its 'type' identity as a particular form of sovereign actor (e.g., being a 'democracy', a 'fascist' state, etc.). See Fearon (1997).

Wendt also suggests that states possess certain essential needs that arise from their nature as self-organized political units: needs for physical survival, autonomy, economic well-being, and collective self-esteem – namely, the group's need to feel good about itself (see chap. 5, especially 207–9, 224–6, 235–6).

Wendt argues that it is only with this starting point – the state as a 'pre-social' actor with certain basic needs – that we can see the impact of interaction at the system level on the interests and identities of states. If states were solely a product of interaction, there would be no independent things upon which interaction could have its effect. Moreover, the state could never act as a free-willed agent employing rational deliberation to change its situation; it would be little more than a cultural automaton (198, 74, 125–30, 179–82, 244). Wendt also contends, contrary to more extreme constructivists, that the state, at least initially, has a tendency to be egoistic in its relations with others. Wendt acknowledges that members of groups, as social identity theory has shown, almost always show favoritism toward each other when dealing with members of the out-group. This means that, in the initial stages of a state-to-state interaction, egoistic self-help behavior is likely to be exhibited (306, 322–3).[10]

Wendt's apparent concessions to the neorealist paradigm, however, do not mean that egoistic orientations will always be dominant, that states cannot learn to be more other-regarding and cooperative. Drawing from symbolic interactionism, Wendt argues that interaction with other states can lead actors to significant redefinitions of self. In the process of interacting, two states, designated as 'Ego' and 'Alter', take on certain roles and cast the other in corresponding counter-roles. Such role-taking and alter-casting, depending on the type of behavior exhibited (egoistic vs. other-regarding, militaristic vs. cooperative), can lead to one of two results: a reproduction of initially egoistic conceptions of self and other, or a transformation of the shared ideational structure to one that is more collective and other-regarding (327–36). The critical point for Wendt is that a structure has no reality apart from its instantiation in process. Structure, he stresses, '*exists, has effects, and evolves only because of agents and their practices*' (185, emphasis in original; see also 313). Hence, if egoistic and militaristic conceptions of self and other continue, it is only because of the interactive practices that sustain those conceptions. Likewise, discursive practices are the source of any transformation in interests and identities. By casting the other in a non-egoistic light, and acting toward it from an other-regarding standpoint, actors can begin to build collective identities that include the other as part of the definition of self (chap. 7, especially 336–42, 368–9).

The book begins its sustained critique of neorealism in chapter 3. Wendt argues that behind Waltz's explicit model of international politics, emphasizing anarchy and the distribution of material capabilities as primary causal factors, lies an implicit model focusing on the distribution of interests across states. That is, neorealism cannot explain variations in international outcomes without implicitly invoking different types of states – some of which seek only to maintain what they

---

10 On social identity, see Mercer (1995).

have (status quo states) and some of which seek to change the system through force (revisionist states). Systems consisting only of status quo states constitute 'one kind of anarchy', while systems with revisionist states constitute another. Foreshadowing his later discussion, Wendt suggests that status quo states should be relatively peaceful (anarchies of a Lockean or perhaps Kantian kind), while revisionist states will be conflictual, with states always on the edge of elimination (anarchy with a Hobbesian culture). This argument implies that anarchy, as a mere absence of central authority, has no one 'logic'. Rather the way a particular anarchy and distribution of power plays itself out will depend critically on the distribution of interests in the system – 'what states *want*' (106, emphasis in original).[11]

Waltz's neorealism is therefore underspecified: a hidden variable, the distribution of interests (status quo vs. revisionist), is doing most of the explaining. Any material structure, in fact, will have no effect except insofar as it interacts with the ideational structure that is the distribution of interests. Concrete interests, moreover, are not simply given by the system. Socialized beliefs about what kinds of objectives are worth pursuing or avoiding will shape each state's actual interests. So, while individuals and states may have certain basic needs (such as needs for survival, esteem, and autonomy), how these needs are manifest in particular actors will be a product of social discursive practices (113–35).

Building on this foundation, in chapter 6 Wendt lays out what he calls the three 'cultures of anarchy' that have characterized at various times the past two thousand years of international relations. In each culture, states play certain types of roles vis-à-vis each other, complete with specific behavioral norms. In a Hobbesian culture, which according to Wendt dominated world affairs until the seventeenth century, states cast each other in the role of 'enemy': the other is a threatening adversary that will observe no limits on the use of violence. Violence must therefore be employed as a basic tool for survival. In a Lockean culture, which has characterized the modern state system since the Treaty of Westphalia in 1648, states view each other as rivals that may use violence to advance their interests, but that are required to refrain from eliminating each other. In a Kantian culture, which has emerged only recently in relations between democracies, states play the role of friends, that is, states do not use force to settle disputes and work as a team against security threats (258, 260–2, 279–80, 298–9).

The behavioral norms for each culture are known by the actors and are thus 'shared' to at least a minimal degree (a minimal requirement for a culture). These norms, however, can be internalized to three degrees. In the first degree, consistent with neorealism, compliance to the norm is solely a function of coercion: the actor complies because of the threat of punishment founded on the relative superiority of the other actors. In the second degree, closer to the neoliberal view, actors conform to the norm not because they see it as legitimate, but merely because

---

11 Wendt's argument here extends earlier work by Schweller (1996), Moravcsik (1997), and Stein (1990).

they think it is in their self-interest. Acceptance at both the first and second degrees is therefore purely instrumental, and when the costs and benefits of complying change, behavior should also change. At the third level, consistent with constructivist logic, states have internalized the behavioral norms as legitimate, as part of who they are. They identify with the other's expectations, incorporating the other within their cognitive boundaries. Only at this level does the norm really 'construct' states by shaping their core interests and identities as actors (chap. 6, *passim*, esp. 250).

Given that there are three forms of culture, depending on the norms followed by the actors, and three degrees of internalization of these norms, Wendt portrays international systems as being in any one of nine possible modes at any particular time. On the horizontal axis, moving from left to right, is the 'degree of cooperation' represented by the Hobbesian, Lockean, and Kantian cultures respectively. On the vertical axis, from bottom to top, are the three 'degrees of internalization' (see 254, Figure 4). This three-by-three grid offers some advantages. It allows us to see conflictual Hobbesian systems as a product of shared internalized ideas at the third degree (a social construction) and not just as a product of material forces (the realist view). Moreover, high degrees of cooperation (a Kantian culture) can be a product of pure self-interested compliance resulting from the threat of punishment (first degree) or the simple benefits of cooperation (second degree). Conflict does not confirm realism, just as cooperation does not confirm liberalism or constructivism. It all depends on the degree of internalization – *why* the actors acted in a conflictual or cooperative fashion, *why* they treated each other as enemies, rivals, or friends.

Wendt's key assertion is that the culture in which states find themselves at any point in time depends on the discursive social practices that reproduce or transform each actor's view of self and other. Anarchy is what states make of it. A Hobbesian system will be sustained only if actors continue to act toward each other in egoistic, militaristic ways. Such a culture is not the inevitable result of anarchy and the material distribution of power, as neorealists would have it. Rather, because egoistic, violent mind-sets are maintained only by egoistic and violent processes, a culture of realpolitik can become a self-fulfilling prophecy. If actors gesture differently, showing that they are casting the other in a less self-centered manner, then over time a Hobbesian culture can move to a Lockean and possibly a Kantian form. We must never forget, Wendt reminds us, that cultures are not reified givens, but products of historical social processes. Today's 'common sense' about international relations – that it is a self-help world of egoistic states – is itself a product of historically contingent ideas and not a true reflection of the intrinsic nature of states (296–7). By engaging in new practices, states can instantiate new ideational structures that help actors transcend collective-action problems and historical mistrust. The constructivist move of regarding egoism as always an ongoing product of the social process helps us see that self-interest is not some eternal given driving actor behavior, but an ongoing product of the system. As Wendt asserts, 'If self-interest is not sustained by practice, it will die out' (369).

Wendt's constructivist challenge

The next two subsections consider some of the implications of *Social Theory* for the three most important approaches in international relations theory: liberalism, constructivism, and structural realism. My focus is on the strengths and weaknesses of the argument against structural realism, given this theory's importance as the primary and constant target of Wendt's analysis.

Contributions of Wendt's argument

The contributions of *Social Theory* to modern liberalism are significant. The book cuts against the grain of recent liberal and neoliberal developments by drawing inspiration from traditional 'idealist' arguments of the interwar period. Wendt offers a socially scientific underpinning for the idealist claim that diplomacy can fundamentally change the way states think about themselves and others. Recent liberal theory focuses on the impact of domestic-level forces in the formation of state preferences.[12] Neoliberal institutionalism adopts realist assumptions about rational actors with exogenous preferences to consider how institutions further cooperation by solving problems of informational uncertainty.[13] Against liberalism, Wendt poses the causal and constitutive role of systemic ideational structure on the preferences of states, independent of domestic-level processes.[14] Against neoliberal institutionalism, Wendt's work challenges the assumption of exogenous preferences, particularly the assumption of egoistic, absolute gains-maximizing states. If egoism is sustained only by process, as Wendt claims, then new, more other-regarding practices can reshape the shared ideational environment, moving states to levels of cooperation not explained by neoliberalism.

The book also pushes the constructivist paradigm to a new level of sophistication. Strong constructivists will be frustrated by Wendt's acceptance that states and individuals have basic needs that are independent of social interaction, by his assertion that these actors are predisposed by nature to be egoistic (at least initially), and by his view that states are indeed actors with corporate identities that exist prior to interaction. Yet Wendt shows convincingly that, without these baselines, social processes at the international level would have nothing to act upon. The extreme constructivist position – that it is ideas all the way down – leaves the theorist with all structure and no agents. Indeed, if actors were to be wholly constituted by structure, then the constructivist program would fall apart. Agents would be purely puppets of the ideational environment in which they find themselves – in George Herbert Mead's terms, each would exist simply as a socially conditioned 'Me', without the free-willed 'I' capable of resisting the socialization process.[15] In such a situation, there is no possibility for transformation of the

---

12 See Moravcsik's (1997) summary.
13 Keohane (1984), Krasner (1983), Hasenclever *et al.* (1997), Rittberger (1993).
14 In doing so, Wendt is also challenging domestic-level constructivists.
15 Mead (1934: chap. 3). On Mead's significant influence on Wendt's thinking, see Wendt (1999: 327–36, 170–1, 264–5; and 1992a).

structure through the actions of agents. The system would continually reproduce itself, and change across time resulting from discursive practices would be impossible – except through exogenous material shocks outside of the model.[16]

Wendt's critique of neorealism offers three main contributions. First, he goes beyond liberal and constructivist theorists who treat power and interests as factors covered by realism, and who then seek simply to show that 'ideas matter' as a separate causal force. Such theorists, by not asking whether power and interests are constituted by social interaction, give away too much to realism; they are reduced to performing mop-up operations for phenomena not explained by 'realist' variables. Wendt shows that, to the extent that ostensibly material variables such as power and interest are actually shaped by social practices, they should more properly be considered ideational variables consistent with a constructivist view of world politics.

Second, Wendt helps improve all systemic theorizing – whether neorealist, neoliberal, or constructivist – by providing the most rigorous philosophical justification yet produced for treating the state as an actor. Most systemic theorists view the state-as-actor assertion as a reasonable assumption for the purposes of theory building, and go no further. This leaves them vulnerable to unit-level theorists who counter that only individuals and social groups exist, and that there-fore processes within the state must be the theoretical focus. Wendt demonstrates that the state is a real self-organizing entity that, being held in the collective memories of many individuals, is dependent for existence on no particular actor (just as other social groups are, for that matter).

Third, and most important, with his claim that 'anarchy is what states make of it', Wendt offers the boldest critique of realism in the field. Against the realist assertion that anarchy forces states to worry constantly about survival and therefore about relative power, Wendt seeks to show that spirals of hostility, arms racing, and war are not inevitable in an anarchic system. If states fall into such conflicts, it is a result of their own social practices, which reproduce egoistic and militaristic mind-sets. Anarchy does not compel them to be conflictual. It is an empty vessel with no inherent logic (249). To explain behavior and outcomes, this vessel must be filled with varying interests and identities – status quo or revisionist states whose characteristics are at least in part a function of international interaction. Such an analysis helps to overcome the pessimism inherent in many realist arguments.[17] If states can transcend their past realpolitik mind-sets by

16 On the conditions for change in collective ideas, see Legro (2000).

17 The primary target here is Waltz (1979), but also implicitly offensive realists such as Mearsheimer (1994–5) and Labs (1997). Scholars in the defensive realist camp of structural realism are typically less pessimistic, because they believe that certain forms of soft-line diplomacy can mitigate, although not eliminate, the security dilemma. See especially Glaser (1994–5), Lynn-Jones (1998), Jervis (1999), Walt (1987), and Van Evera (1999). On the debate between offensive and defensive realists, which Wendt does not discuss, see Lynn-Jones and Miller (1995), Frankel (1996), and Jervis (1999: 48–50).

instantiating new, more other-regarding practices, then hope for the future can be restored.

Weaknesses of Wendt's argument against structural realism

Wendt's critique of structural realist theory suffers from problems of misspecification and incompleteness. Although it is true that states trained to think aggressively are more likely to be aggressive, Wendt's point that realism cannot explain behavior and outcomes without implicitly relying on a hidden variable – the distribution of interests – goes too far. It is based on a misunderstanding of how structural realist arguments are set up to make predictions. Structural realists are not naïve. Like all theorists – whether liberal, constructivist, or classical realist – they recognize that states may exist that, because of domestic- or individual-level pathologies, have interests extending far beyond mere security. Such states tend to destabilize a system, because they are constantly seeking opportunities to expand through force. Yet structural realists build their theories from the starting assumption that all states in the system are presently only security seekers, that they have no nonsecurity motives for war.

The reason for beginning with this assumption is straightforward. It is easy to show that states with pathological unit-level characteristics are often aggressive. But if realists can explain why systems may move from cooperation to conflict, depending on the material conditions, even when all states are security seekers, then the paradigm offers a powerful baseline for theory development. By withstanding the hardest possible deductive test, realism shows the tragedy of world politics – that good states may do bad things, even against other good states. The initial assumption of a system of security seekers can then be relaxed to demonstrate how systems will be even more conflictual once states with unit-level pathologies are introduced.

To show how purely security-seeking states can still conflict, structural realists point to prudent leaders' uncertainty about two temporal dimensions – first, the present intentions of the other and, second, and even more critical, the future intentions of the other.[18] Both of these dimensions are at the heart of the realist understanding of the security dilemma. In a two-actor security dilemma, states A and B are both seeking only their own survival. But, given the difficulty of seeing the other's motives (the 'problem of other minds'), state A worries that B currently harbors nonsecurity motives for war. Hence, if B takes steps only for its own security, these steps may be misinterpreted by A as preparations for aggression.

---

18 For ease of exposition, below I use the terms 'intentions' and 'motives' largely synonymously. Although intentions is the more commonly used term, motives more accurately captures what is at stake, namely, whether states differ in their core reasons for acting – either for security or for nonsecurity objectives. See Glaser (1992).

State A's counter-efforts, in turn, will likely be misinterpreted by B as moves to aggression, sparking a spiral of mistrust and hostility.[19]

Even more intractable for systemic realists is the problem of future intentions. Even when states A and B are both fairly certain that the other is presently a security seeker, they have reason to worry that the other might change its spots some years later as a result of a change of leadership, a revolution, or simply a change of heart resulting from an increase in its power.[20] The fear here is not that the present 'distribution of interests' contains states with innately aggressive intentions, but that the future system will contain such states.

In short, systemic realists understand that inherently aggressive states are possible. But they do not require the system in the present moment to contain such states for it still to fall into conflict. Contrary to Wendt's claim, therefore, anarchy and distributions of power can have effects that do not depend on assumptions about the real, current distribution of interests (even if the possibility of evil states down the road is important). Realism only needs states to be uncertain about the present and future interests of the other, and, in anarchies of great powers, such uncertainty may often be profound.

The question of uncertainty is critical to understanding the differences between structural realism and constructivism, and where Wendt's analysis misses the mark. Consider, first, uncertainty regarding the other's present intentions. Wendt is aware that this kind of uncertainty challenges his point that the current distribution of interests drives the way anarchy plays itself out. He counters that, at least in the modern environment, the 'problem of other minds' is not much of a problem. States today can indeed learn a great deal about what the other is doing and thinking. That knowledge may not be '100 percent certain', Wendt argues, 'but *no* knowledge is that' (281, emphasis in original). To assume a worst-case scenario and to treat the other as hostile may be more dangerous than adopting a conciliatory policy, because it creates a self-fulfilling prophecy of mutual mistrust (281, 107–9, 360).

This counter-argument has serious flaws. In essence, it is an effort to assume away the problem – that there really is no problem of other minds – and it is weak on three grounds. First, Wendt's view that states typically know a lot about the other's motives is an unsupported empirical statement based only on a reading of the contemporary situation. Even if it were true for the majority of states today – and it certainly does not capture the reality between the states that count, such as the United States and China – his point cannot be retrofitted into the previous five

---

19 See, *inter alia*, Jervis (1978) and Glaser (1997). As Andrew Kydd (1997b: 125–6) notes, uncertainty over the other's motives is an essential component of any structural argument drawn from the security dilemma.

20 Jervis (1976: 62), Jervis and Art (1985: 3), and Mearsheimer (1994–5: 10). Defensive realists tend to put more emphasis on uncertainty about present intentions, whereas offensive realists stress the problem of future intentions and the consequent need to increase power as a hedge against future threats. Compare especially defensive realists such as Glaser (1994–5) and Walt (1987) with offensive realists such as Mearsheimer (1994–5).

centuries that constitute the focus of Wendt's analysis. In sum, if uncertainty about present intentions was rampant during these five hundred years, it (along with shifts in relative power) may explain a great deal about changes in conflict and cooperation over time.

Second, Wendt's view is inconsistent with his recognition that states often do have difficulty learning about the other. The very problem Ego and Alter have in first communicating is that 'behavior does not speak for itself'. It must be interpreted, and 'many interpretations are possible' (330). This point is reinforced by Wendt's epistemological point of departure: that the ideas held by actors are 'unobservable' (chap. 2). Because leaders cannot observe directly what the other is thinking, they are resigned to making inferences from its behavior. Yet in security affairs, as Wendt acknowledges, mistakes in inferences – assuming the other is peaceful when in fact it has malevolent intentions – could prove 'fatal' (360).

Wendt accepts that the problem facing rational states 'is making sure that they perceive other actors, and other actors' perception of them, *correctly*' (334, emphasis in original). Yet the book provides no mechanism through which Ego and Alter can increase their confidence in the correctness of their estimates of the other's type. Simply describing how Ego and Alter shape each other's sense of self and other is not enough.[21] Rational choice models, using assumptions consistent with structural realism, do much better here. In games of incomplete information, where states are unsure about the other's type, actions by security-seeking actors that would be too costly for greedy actors to adopt can help states reduce their uncertainty about present intentions, thus moderating the security dilemma.[22] Wendt cannot simply argue that over time states can learn a great deal about other states. It is what is not 'shared', at least in the area of intentions, that remains the core stumbling block to cooperation.

Third, Wendt's position that the problem of other minds is not much of a problem ignores a fundamental issue in all social relations, but especially in those between states, namely, the problem of deception. In making estimates of the other's present type, states have reason to be suspicious of its diplomatic gestures – the other may be trying to deceive them. Wendt's analysis is rooted in the theory of symbolic interactionism, but he does not discuss one critical aspect of that tradition: the idea of 'impression management'. Actors in their relations exploit the problem of other minds for their own ends. On the public stage, they present images and play roles that often have little to do with their true beliefs and interests backstage.[23]

21 Consider Wendt's statement that 'Ego's ideas about Alter, *right or wrong* are not merely passive perceptions of something that exists independent of Ego, but actively and on-goingly constitutive of Alter's role vis-à-vis Ego' (335, emphasis added). His subsequent discussion offers no insights into how Ego would be able to learn that its ideas about Alter were indeed right or wrong.

22 See Fearon (1995), Glaser (1994–5), Kydd (1997a; 1997b: 139–47), and Copeland (1999–2000). When discussing game theory, Wendt's book considers only games of complete information, in which actors are certain about the other's preferences and type (106–7, 148, 159–60, 167, 183, 315).

23 See especially Goffman (1959: chap. 6).

In laying out his dramaturgical view of Ego and Alter co-constituting each other's interests and identities, Wendt assumes that both Ego and Alter are making genuine efforts to express their true views and to 'cast' the other in roles that they believe in. But deceptive actors will stage-manage the situation to create impressions that serve their narrow ends, and other actors, especially in world politics, will understand this.[24] Thus a prudent security-seeking Ego will have difficulty distinguishing between two scenarios: whether it and Alter do indeed share a view of each other as peaceful, or whether Alter is just pretending to be peaceful in order to make Ego think that they share a certain conception of the world, when in fact they do not.[25] Wendt's analysis offers no basis for saying when peaceful gestures should be taken at face value, and when they should be discounted as deceptions.[26] When we consider the implications of a Hitlerite state deceiving others to achieve a position of military superiority, we understand why great powers in history have tended to adopt postures of prudent mistrust.

The problem of future intentions – which Wendt's book does not discuss – is even more intractable. The problem is rooted in the possibility of domestic changes in the other that occur despite efforts to maintain cooperative relations. Wendt brackets off domestic processes to focus on the effect of interaction between states. This approach fails to consider the implication of liberal and domestic-constructivist arguments on the conclusions of Wendt's systemic constructivism. States do not form a conception of themselves only through interaction with other states. Socialization processes internal to a state can change the state's identity and interests independently of such interaction. Wendt captures this point in his discussion of the four forms of identity: 'corporate', 'type', 'role', and 'collective'. The first two develop through processes within the state, reflecting the self-organizing aspect of the unit, and do not require the recognition of other states for their meaning.[27] Role and collective identities, on the other hand, are constituted only through interaction between states.[28]

These distinctions have profound implications for the potential impact of security dilemmas in Wendt's framework. If the nature of the other's domestic

24 These actions are what game theorists would call efforts at 'strategic misrepresentation'. On the instrumental manipulation of norms for self-interested reasons, see Kowert and Legro (1996: 492–3).
25 This problem is especially pernicious in Wendt's Lockean and Kantian worlds, where states do seem to be following norms of self-restraint. But even in a Hobbesian world, it is highly likely that Ego may believe that Alter is an 'enemy' even when Alter does not accept this assessment. It is not enough for Wendt to say that they both intersubjectively share the view that the other is an enemy (260–3). In fact, in a spiraling security dilemma, there are two separate beliefs that do not overlap: Ego thinks Alter is an aggressive enemy, when Alter knows that it is not; and Alter likewise thinks Ego is an aggressive enemy, when Ego knows that it is not. Again, it is what is *not* shared – the uncertainty in the system – that is problematic.
26 Costly signaling games in rational choice game theory again provide a mechanism by which states can evaluate valid versus potentially deceptive gestures.
27 See Wendt (1999: 224–33) and (1994).
28 For Wendt's earlier twofold distinction between corporate and role identities, see Wendt (1994).

regime can change independently of international interaction, then, even when Ego is confident that Alter is currently a security seeker, it must worry that Alter might *become* pathologically hostile later on. This worry will be particularly intense if Ego faces an exogenous decline in relative power that would leave Alter preponderant later, should it acquire nonsecurity motives for war.[29]

This discussion reveals a deep irony in the constructivist take on international relations. It is constructivism's very emphasis on the mutability of interests and identities, when taken down to the domestic level, that reinforces why anarchy compels states to be on guard. States know that diplomacy alone will rarely be enough to ensure the long-term peaceful nature of the other (consider the difficulties that Washington faces today in stabilizing Russia's democratic institutions). This problem is heightened by a fact of which Wendt is aware: that domestic processes are typically far more 'dense' than international ones (2, 13, 21, 27–8, 107–8). Wendt believes that this fact makes his argument for a systemic constructivism a 'hard case'. But he overlooks the more profound point: that the independence of domestic processes undermines his effort to show that material structures do not constrain and shape state behavior except by way of ideas rising through international interaction. If states know that the nature of the other is mostly a function of its own domestic processes, then they must pay great attention to their present and future material capability, in order to guard against a situation in which the other becomes aggressive later on.[30] Thus domestic-level constructivism reinforces the value of a systemic realist view of world politics, at least as a baseline starting point for theory building.

Reinforcing the dilemma of changing future intentions is the critical difference between a systemic realist conception of structure and Wendt's notion. Wendt stresses repeatedly that structure is always a function of interaction: that structure exists, has effects, and evolves only because of agents and their practices. Structures cannot be considered given realities independent of process. This is the mistake of actors reifying structures and then forgetting that they are historically contingent, that they are sustained or transformed only by human activity (150, 185–6, 313, 340, 364, 368). In previous work, Wendt takes Waltz to task for his statement that international structures, like economic markets, 'are formed by the coaction of their units'. If this is so, and structures are not exogenously given but are generated and sustained by coaction, then actors can set about changing the structures that reinforce competitive and violent behavior.[31]

The problem here is that Waltz's economic analogy does not really capture what systemic realists mean by 'structure'. For such realists, structure is a function of the *potential* for coaction among units. In anarchy, states have to worry more about

---

29 See Copeland (2000: chaps 1–2), Van Evera (1999: chap. 5), and Levy (1987).

30 This problem is reinforced by the fact that intentions can change 'overnight' (as a result of a coup or revolution, for example), whereas significant changes in relative power take many years to effect. Allowing oneself to fall behind in power, hoping that the other will always stay peaceful, is thus fraught with risks.

31 Wendt (1992a: 401–2, 406–7, 410) and Waltz (1979: 91).

what the other might do tomorrow or in ten years than about what it is presently doing or has done in the past. The economic markets of Waltz's analogy, it is true, are not generated until there is buying and selling activity. This is simply because markets are designed to improve the utility of individual actors versus the non-cooperative outcome, and no improvement can be made unless there is exchange (that is, interaction). Structures in international politics are different. The actors are not trying to increase their utility per se, but to avoid harm. Hence present and past interaction is not the core issue; the potential of others to do harm in the future is. This means, among other things, that actors in anarchy must worry about exogenous decline in their material basis for survival, and the probability that the other will be aggressive after such decline.[32]

The distinction between Wendt's focus on structure as the coaction (interaction) of units, and a realist focus on structure as the potential for coaction, is neither semantic nor trivial. It reflects a fundamentally different conception of the role of time in international politics. For Wendt and other constructivists, it is the past that matters – how interactions and gestures in the historical process have socialized actors toward certain conceptions of self and other. Realists certainly do not dismiss the ways that past interaction shape current beliefs.[33] Most fundamentally, however, realism is a forward-looking theory. States are rational maximizers of their security over the foreseeable future. Hence they remain constantly vigilant for any changes in their external situation that might damage their chances for survival later. Reduced to five words, then, the divide between constructivism and systemic realism is all about past socialization versus future uncertainty.[34]

This analysis has a straightforward implication: there is no need for any interaction in the present or past for a constraining structure to exist. Power structures – the relative distribution of material resources – are not generated by social practices (even if practices can sometimes change the distribution over time). Structures exist by the mere presence of the other, and its potential to do harm in

---

32 Note that actors here are not automatically assuming 'worst case', namely, that policies must reflect the mere possibility that the other might later aggress. Rather security maximizers, if they are rational, will always calculate according to the *probabilities* of certain undesirable things coming to pass. Given uncertainty, however, estimates of these probabilities will often be high. Cf. Brooks (1997). For a model of rational decision-making that develops this defensive realist notion, see Copeland (2000: chap. 2).

33 As noted, realists employ costly signaling models to show how actors can rationally update their estimates of the other's character and motives, based on its past behavior.

34 This does not mean that constructivism does not deal with the problem of uncertainty. But it does so by looking at how socialized notions of self and other shape actors' views of the future possibilities. The causal story remains one of historical discursive practices molding current mind-sets; actors see the future only through the strong filter of past socialization (see Adler and Barnett 1998: chaps 1, 2, 13). The realist view of the future focuses on the things that might occur independent of an actor's past interaction with the other. So while realists accept that historical interaction can reduce uncertainty about the other's character and motives, they argue that prudent actors can never ignore the many exogenous determinants of the other's future behavior. The security dilemma can be moderated, but never eliminated.

the future – its potential to 'coact' by invading, if you will. Hence, in anarchy, even when a state has no relations with the other, even if the other does not know that the state exists, the state is forced by the situation to contemplate future scenarios in which the other could do it harm. When scouts returned to ancient Assyria with the first reports on the Egyptian empire and its phenomenal resources, Assyrian leaders would have been imprudent not to have at least considered the possibility of an Egyptian invasion. No interaction was required for Egypt's relative power to have a constraining effect on Assyria's behavior.[35]

The pernicious issue of uncertainty helps us appraise the value of Wendt's discussion of the three 'cultures' of anarchy and their three degrees of internalization. Wendt uses his three-by-three grid in chapter 6 – Hobbesian, Lockean, and Kantian cultures on the horizontal axis, and first, second, and third degrees of internalization on the vertical – as a visual tool to show that interaction can socialize states away from conflictual to more cooperative forms of behavior. States in each of the nine boxes, he argues, share at least a basic notion of what the behavioral norms are in the system. In terms of the question of present and future intentions, however, there are two problems.

First, Wendt assumes that a state knows not only which of the nine boxes it is in, but which box the *other* is in. If Ego, for example, knows that it is in the top right box, where it follows and has deeply internalized the Kantian norm of not using violence to settle disputes, it may still be uncertain about Alter's true disposition. If Alter is following the norm in terms of its behavior, does this reflect its strong internalized belief in the norm (third degree), or just its induced compliance because of fear of punishment or loss of benefits should it defect (first or second degrees)? For Ego, this question is critical, because, if Alter is only conforming to the norm for fear of punishment or expectation of benefits, Ego has every reason to fear that Alter's behavior will not be so cooperative should the material conditions that shape costs and benefits change.[36] Yet Wendt does not explain how states are supposed to know whether the other has deeply internalized a norm or not. Thus we are still in the dark as to how state uncertainty about present and future intentions is to be overcome.

This problem is compounded by the fact that the three cultures, as Wendt lays them out, are distinguished from each other in terms of behavioral norms. Which culture a system is in at any point in time, as Wendt's discussion reveals, is known only by the degree to which states follow, in terms of their external behavior, the norms Wendt specifies: in a Hobbesian culture, whether they observe no limits in their violence; in Lockean, whether they use violence but refrain from killing one

---

35 Note that this is not even a 'first contact', because Egypt does not yet know of Assyria's existence (cf. Wendt 1992a: 403–7).

36 See Wendt (1999: 303–5) where he notes that Kantian cooperative behavior at the first and second degrees is purely instrumental. States are treating each other as 'friends' only in form, not in substance: 'For egoistic states friendship might be nothing more than a hat they try on each morning for their own reasons, one that they will take off as soon as the costs outweigh the benefits, but until that happens they will be friends in fact even if not in principle' (305).

another; and in Kantian, whether they do not use violence to settle disputes (258; see also 260–1, 268, 279–80, 283–4, 298–9). Thus in his three-by-three grid (254, Figure 4), the horizontal axis, which details the three cultures, is defined by the degree of 'cooperation', with Hobbesian cultures showing the most conflictual behavior and Kantian the most cooperative. Wendt thus uses behavioral/outcome measures to classify the changes in the world system over time. In the seventeenth century, the system moved from a Hobbesian to a Lockean culture, he argues, because even though many states were being eliminated before that time, few were after (279, 284, 323). Yet when the system experiences large-scale warfare, Wendt sees this either as an indication of a Hobbesian culture or as a sign that the system is shifting back into one (259–60, 270, 279, 314). That Wendt uses behavior to define culture is also shown by the fact that states could be in a Kantian culture even if they are only at the first and second degrees of internalization – that is, even if they comply with the behavioral norm not to use violence to settle a dispute only because of fear of punishment and narrow self-interest (303–6).

If behavioral compliance defines the culture one is in, leaders are thrown right back into the problem of other minds that underpins the security dilemma. They are forced to rely on inferences, in the form of probabilistic estimates, of the other's true motives and strategic objectives based on the other's behavior. But inferences are a weak substitute for direct knowledge. The chances for misinterpretation within anarchic systems – perceiving the other's actions as reflecting hostile motives, even if they are not intended that way – remain high.

Wendt's practice of measuring culture by the level of cooperative behavior exhibited by states also poses a methodological problem. In essence, Wendt collapses the thing he wants to explain – why the system has apparently become more cooperative over time – into the causal factor he wants to triumph, namely, the instantiation of new ideas about self and other through interaction. This makes it hard to know what would falsify his argument. Whenever behavior turns conflictual, Wendt can argue that the culture has become Hobbesian; whenever the behavior becomes more cooperative, the system is moving toward a Lockean or a Kantian culture.

The deeper problem here is Wendt's willingness to call any system where states know and follow norms at the first and second degrees of internalization a 'culture'. States at these levels are acting only because they are compelled by coercive threats (the first degree) or seeking to maximize their net benefits (the second degree). Wendt argues that as long as they share at least a basic knowledge of the behavioral norms, they share a culture. This is an extremely thin definition of culture, one having nothing necessarily to do with the typical constructivist emphasis on actors' interests and identities. Indeed the term 'internalization' is a misnomer for these first and second degrees. At these levels, there is no need for any internalization of the behavioral norm, but only for some knowledge that the norm exists. By Wendt's definition, therefore, an opportunistic state that joins a collective security system just to buy time for a secret military buildup is 'sharing' in a Kantian culture simply by virtue of knowing the norm not to use violence. If the term 'culture' is to be used for any knowledge of phenomenon X that two actors have in common, whether or not they incorporate this knowledge into their value systems, then culture serves little value in social scientific analysis – it means almost everything, and therefore nothing.

Even more important, however, Wendt's explanations of behavior at the first and second degrees are driven precisely by what is not shared between the actors. As Wendt notes, for the first degree in the Hobbesian world, a state complies 'only because [it] is forced to, directly or by the threat of certain, immediate punishment'. Its behavior 'is purely externally rather than internally driven'. Thus 'it is private meanings plus material coercion rather than culture which does most of the explanatory work' (269). One might add that, in these scenarios, it is private meanings and material incentives that do essentially all the explanatory work. Given this, and given the fact that actors are not internalizing the norm but only at most knowing of its existence, what value is gained by calling the first and second degrees 'cultures'?

The above analysis indicates that Wendt's three-by-three grid is not a framework of three cultures and three degrees of internalization. Rather it is a typology that shows on the horizontal axis the dependent variable to be explained – the degree of cooperative behavior in a system at any particular time – and on the vertical axis the three main ways this variable can be explained: by the effect of threats and punishments (coercion in realist literature); by potential external benefits of cooperation (neoliberal arguments); or by the internalization through interaction of interests and identities that shape the way actors view strategies and outcomes (the constructivist view). Shifting to a focus on the degree of cooperative behavior in a system, and what factors explain it, allows us to see the real potential value of Wendt's constructivist argument. Only at his 'third degree' is his cultural explanation operating, and such an explanation can be posed against the primary realist and neoliberal *counter-explanations* that involve self-interested actors calculating the costs, benefits, and risks of action. Then, when we see a shift in the level of cooperation, we do not automatically assume a shift in 'culture'. Instead we look for evidence that could confirm or refute the three alternative theories.

This recasting of Wendt's framework, however, shows us how far he has to go empirically to convince us of his thesis. Even if we accept that the international system has become more cooperative over the last two decades, Wendt has provided little evidence that this cooperation reflects an increasingly deep internalization of other-regarding values. Moreover, he must show that this increasing stability is not simply the result of a self-interested adjustment by the remaining great powers to the reality of nuclear weapons, the benefits of global trade, and a reconnaissance revolution that has made surprise attacks less viable.[37]

---

37 Wendt's empirical task is complicated by his assertion that the recent shift to cooperation was furthered by such 'master variables' as interdependence and common fate (344–53). These variables are largely material in nature – depending as they do on globalization, increased trade, and the destructive qualities of modern weaponry (especially nuclear weapons). Wendt lays out a two-stage process toward cooperation: initially, states respond to the external conditions out of self-interest, but later they may move beyond this to more other-regarding stances (345–6, 350, 360–1; see also 303 and 311). Yet Wendt offers little evidence that cooperation between modern great powers such as the United States, China, and Russia has gone beyond this self-interested first step.

The problem is even more pronounced with regard to Wendt's ability to explain the shifts in relative cooperation over the last five hundred years. Because behavioral changes do not necessarily mean cultural changes, it is up to Wendt to show that conflictual periods were the result of the internalization of conflictual interests and identities, and not adjustments induced by changing external conditions. To do so, he must plunge into the documents, which ultimately are the only means to reveal why the actors did what they did. Staying at the realm of behavior makes it impossible to sort out whether realism, liberalism, or constructivism provides the best explanation for the results observed.

Conclusion

Social Theory of International Politics provides an important starting point for further debate and constructivist empirical analysis, but only a starting point. Wendt has not shown that anarchy tied to changing distributions of power has no logic, only that constructivist variables can perhaps, under certain conditions, moderate actors' level of uncertainty about others' intentions. Yet constructivism is inherently an argument about how the past shapes the way actors understand their present situation. By its very nature – its focus on historical process – constructivism has trouble analyzing how rational, prudent leaders deal with the pernicious problem of future uncertainty. And this uncertainty is given by the human condition. Human beings are not born with the ability to read the minds of other actors, and they have only limited means for foreseeing the future. Moreover, human beings, as constructivists emphasize, are mutable – they can be changed through interaction. Yet if much of this interaction takes place at the domestic level and is independent of diplomatic interaction, then prudent states must be worried. They know that the other may become aggressive despite all diplomatic efforts to instantiate other-regarding values and to communicate their own non-aggressive intentions. The material distribution of power then becomes critical to their calculations. It represents the other's potential to do harm in the future. Hence, if power trends are negative, a declining state must worry that the other will turn aggressive after it achieves preponderance, even if it seems peaceful right now.

The task ahead lies in testing the propositions that fall out of Wendt's constructivist argument. In explaining variations in the level of cooperation over the past two millennia, there are three main competing arguments – Wendt's systemic constructivism, systemic realism, and neoliberalism – to which we could add a fourth, namely, a more domestic-constructivist argument (one that shades into unit-level liberalism). Systemic constructivism (or what might be called 'neo-constructivism') focuses on interstate interactions as the source for new, or reproduced, conceptions of self and other, which in turn affect state propensities to fall into conflictual or cooperative behavior. Systemic realism predicts changes in the levels of cooperation based on changes and trends in the distribution of material power over time, set against a baseline of actor uncertainty about the future. Neoliberalism, accepting the neorealist foundation of rational actors worried about the future, stresses the role of institutions as mechanisms that reduce the uncertainty that can lead to conflict. Finally, domestic constructivists and unit-level liberals emphasize changes within particular states that alter aggregated state interests and identities. When domestic processes produce states with motives beyond mere security, we should expect more conflictual behavior, all things being equal.

None of these positions needs to reject the causal factors highlighted by the alternative approaches. Indeed, as I have argued, systemic realists recognize the domestic-constructivist/liberal point that internal processes can change the nature of the opponent over time, and they use it to show how a system of purely security-seeking states can still fall into conflict and war. But instead of trying to collapse these different theories into one model of 'culture', as *Social Theory* does, we need to recognize that each of these approaches focuses on separate and often independent causal variables. In this way, we can see that egoistic and militaristic mind-sets are sustained and transformed not only by international interaction, as Wendt claims. They may be, but how often and to what extent is a question for empirical analysis. And because Wendt's book does not offer such an analysis, the debate is still very much an open one. Sometimes egoism and militarism will be caused by domestic processes alone (e.g., if an aggressive ideology triumphs through revolution). Sometimes they will result from prudent fears of the future, especially during periods of dynamic change in the relative power balance. Sometimes they will reflect a lack of institutional mechanisms for learning about the other state, and thus rational misjudgments about the other's type.

Although the road ahead for Wendt's neoconstructivism is still long, *Social Theory of International Politics* provides a solid constructivist vehicle for traveling it. The book allows scholars to differentiate clearly between truly material and ideational explanations, and between accounts that emphasize the role of states as actors and those that incorporate transnational forces and divisions within polities. It has reinforced the importance of diplomacy as a tool for reducing high levels of misunderstanding that can impede cooperation. Yet by bracketing off domestic processes, Wendt has overlooked the irony of constructivism: that the mutability of human ideational structures at the domestic level reinforces leaders' great uncertainty about future intentions at the interstate level. The security dilemma, with all its implications, is real and pervasive. It cannot be talked away through better discursive practices. It must be faced.

2 Constructing a new orthodoxy?

Wendt's *Social Theory of International Politics* and the constructivist challenge*

Friedrich Kratochwil

Assessing 'progress' in the scientific study of international politics faces several difficulties. There is initially the issue of the objects of study and how the subject matter shall be delineated. Subsequently, there is the issue of the criteria by which we can produce warranted knowledge. One position argues that true knowledge can only be gained by following a particular method. Popular since Descartes, this stance is nowadays best represented by the unity of science position whereby anything claiming to have scientific status has to follow a specified method. An alternative contention proposes that, first of all, 'knowledge' should not simply be identified with one mode of knowing, particularly since even within science there exist many different warrants that cannot be reduced to one criterion.

The story told so far treads on familiar ground in that the first problem is one of ontology, while the second deals with problems of epistemology and method. Consequently, two solutions seem to exist. Either we can now privilege ontology and assume that the world discloses itself by affecting our senses and that, therefore, we have to come to some primitive or basic observational statements which 'tell it like it is'. Alternatively, we can take the sceptic's objection to the reliability of sense data seriously – after all the oar is not broken when immersed in water and optical theory clearly shows why this 'misperception' occurs – and doubt the primacy of sense perception and even of ontology. In such a case, we would rely on method as our only hope for providing the necessary warrants.

But, whatever position we take, even this sketchy account suggests that matters are even more complicated since there are certain interaction effects between these two issues. Epistemological and ontological levels might not be that independent of each other, but are probably 'tightly linked through the mediating lens of the linguistic/conceptual structure' of the discourse in a field (Layder 1985: 261).

These difficulties are further exacerbated when the objects of our theoretical inquiries are not the 'things' in the world but when they are, as in the social sciences, characterised by recursivity. Social objects are not simply describable in terms of purely observational categories or measurement procedures. Rather their

* I gratefully acknowledge the help and criticisms of Rodney Hall, Oliver Kessler, and Jens Steffek who read earlier versions of this paper.

descriptions must make reference to the shared representations underlying the actions of actors that allow us, for instance, to identify the marks on a piece of paper as a 'signature'. Different from an 'autograph', a signature might bind those having attached it to a document. If we could do with simple descriptions, then there could be no difference between some marks on a paper, an autograph, or a signature, since observationally all descriptions entail more or less the same movements and marks.

Most recently, these controversies have been revived in IR by the constructivist critique of logical positivism. But a similar challenge has been mounted by the rational choice approach, which has become a major contender for bestowing the coveted warrant of 'science' to a piece of research. Constructivists can be found not only in the cultural sciences. Indeed, some of its most prominent exponents have been biologists (Maturana and Varela 1992) who, in turn, influenced an entirely new system theory in sociology (Luhmann 1984, 1997). Nonetheless, there is more than an elective affinity between constructivists and those who have focused on 'meaning' in the past. Many constructivists have been influenced by ordinary language philosophy and speech act theory, even if such an orientation is not a necessary precondition for research in the constructivist mode.

Given these elective affinities it is, therefore, rather surprising that the recent *magnum opus* of a leading constructivist attempts to provide a new solution to the old dilemmas through some radical compromises (Wendt 1999). Alexander Wendt not only claims to be a scientific realist, i.e., he puts ontology first and method second, but he also espouses some form of the unity of science position despite his acknowledgement of the ontological differences between natural and social objects. While I think Wendt's attempt is not as successful as claimed, there is no doubt in my mind that this is a work of outstanding scholarship. His work is far more comprehensive and sophisticated than most 'theory' discussions in IR that start with the usual three approaches and then either degenerate quickly into the counting of hands (on the one hand, on the other hand) or privilege one approach, such as 'realism', to continue with a demonstration of how much (or little) of the 'variance' the other approaches are able to explain. Wendt's avoids such gambits and engages his critics and intellectual friends at a much more principled level of social theory and philosophy of science.

It is, therefore, quite instructive to take on Wendt on this principled level and see why and how his attempt at steering a middle course between the major existing schools of thought runs into heavy weather despite his tranquil exposition of the explosive issues involved. In a way, I am more worried that, instead of remaining a provocative and fruitful new departure, true to its constructivist premises, the 'reasonable middle ground' that emerges from Wendt's engagement with unreconstituted Waltzian realists, with the somewhat disoriented political scientists of the mainstream, and with rational choice believers, might actually succeed in becoming the new orthodoxy. Precisely because I think that Wendt has done a yeoman's job in sensitising us to the complexities in building better social theories, it is important to call into question some of his conclusions, and reopen some controversies which have been papered over.

We all profess to like debate and controversy, relying in due course on John Stuart Mill (1975 [1859]) and Karl Popper (1994), who extolled the necessity and virtue of debates for the growth of knowledge. But as even the example of the latter shows, we do not always practise what we preach.[1] Despite our alleged love for debates, we seem to like the quiet of certitude even more and prefer the monologue of instruction rather than the arduous give and take of serious engagements with those who disturb our self-assuredness. After all, mathematicians do not argue, they demonstrate!

The conception of science as a set of 'true', atemporal, and universal statements clashes with the notion of science as a praxis, in which all insights are preliminary and debates about the meaning of 'tests' and the allocation of the burdens of proof, rather than demonstration, are the important elements. We feel understandably uneasy with the jurisdictional metaphor, considering 'truth' as the result of certain procedures, and abandoning the foundational idea that 'truth' is a property of the 'world'.

In this context, I shall argue that, because Wendt's *Social Theory* is based on a particular version of 'scientific realism', it relies on some problematic foundationalist notions (although he protests this several times). I suggest that the 'representational' dimension of such foundational theories is convincing only on the basis of rather unreflected conventional wisdom and experience. Here, metaphors become exceedingly important, but also misleading. We feel that there has to be some foundation on which the edifice of science is erected. Only then are we able to square the preliminary character of our knowledge with the representational theory of truth by simply depicting it as 'coming closer to' the line which once and for all determines facticity. Below, I shall argue that these spatial metaphors are misleading and that some other ways of thinking about 'progress' in science might be more helpful. I suggest that the image of a crossword puzzle or of playing Scrabble provides a better analogy to science as a practice than the idea of erecting a house on some 'rock bottom' (materialist, of course, given the current fashion!). On the basis of this argument, I then explore the notion of science as an argument in which coherence and various strategies of shifting the burden of proof are taken as criteria for leading to both legitimate and final determinations, even though both criteria can seldom be satisfied together (I am partially influenced here by Laurence BonJour 1985).

The argument proceeds as follows: I provide an overview of Wendt's *Social Theory*, followed by some criticisms that are largely internal to Wendt's argument and concern clarifications or the repair of inconsistencies. In the subsequent section, I address the question of what can be learned from Wendt's truly impressive attempt as well as from its shortcomings: where might we look for further enlightenment when no secure foundations in the 'observables' or in some *a*

---

1 Popper did not mince words when he and his opponents disagreed and he did seldom 'learn' from his enemies who had refuted some of his tenets. See the useful discussion of Paul Diesing (1991: chap. 2).

priori method can be discovered? While I obviously cannot provide some firm resting place which ends all debates by pointing to 'God's' view of the world – precisely because such a view 'from nowhere' (Nagel 1986) is not available to us – I address the allegation of 'relativism' that such a negation entails and the anxieties it engenders. In the absence of firm foundations it is not true that 'anything goes' nor that this 'anti-anti-relativism' entails, as the result of this double negative, the proof of the primacy of ontology upon which everything else must be founded.

Wendt's *Social Theory*

For Wendt, the problem of a theory of IR entails substantive 'first order' questions, but also 'second order' problems of social theory. To that extent, Wendt is well aware of the interdependence of the two issues above. Indeed, Wendt claims not only that IR theory would greatly benefit from systematically raising such second order issues, but also that such a mode of inquiry would result in a considerably deeper social picture of the international arena. In using Kenneth Waltz's structural theory as a foil, Wendt argues that there is not one single logic of anarchy but rather several, depending on the nature of the actors who populate the international system, i.e., whether they approach the Hobbesian, Lockean, or Kantian ideal-types. Instead of the usual threefold division of theories in IR texts, Wendt's trichotomy is not introduced *ad hoc* by looking around what is available, but instead is carefully derived from some theoretical concepts, i.e., from roles by which states represent themselves and each other (Wendt 1999: chap. 4).

This time around Wendt has resisted deducing his argument of 'anarchy is what the states make of it' from a hypothetical situation of a 'first encounter' between some space aliens and humans.[2] In Wendt's previous work the assumption of a common signalling system allowed for the non-violent resolution of the rather scary situation. These predispositions or external factors not only served as the means by which people made sense out of their choice situation, but also suggested that factors remaining external to the theory did most of the explaining.

The role of ideas

Wendt's present innovation consists in the explicit inclusion of a common system of meanings (culture) and a more stringent derivation of interests from both conceptions of the self and the identification with others. Such moves allow him to dismiss some traditional red herrings, such as the dichotomy of explanation by 'material interests' as opposed to 'ideas'. Insofar as power and interest are constituted by ideas, Wendt renders ineffective the tactic of neoliberals, rational choicers, and realists alike of treating power and interests, even institutions, 'as idea-free base-lines against which the role of ideas is judged' (Wendt 1999: 94). He maintains

---

2 For Wendt's construal of a first encounter with extraterrestrials, see Wendt (1992a); for a principled critique of this position, see Zehfuß (1998).

what makes a theory materialist is that it accounts for the effects of power, interests, or institutions by reference to 'brute' material forces – things which exist and have certain causal powers independent of ideas, like human nature, physical environment, and, perhaps, technological artefacts. The constitutive debate between materialists and idealists is not about the relative contribution of ideas versus power and interest to social life. The debate is about the relative contribution of brute material forces to power and interest explanations. Materialists cannot claim power and interest as 'their' variables; it all depends on how the latter are constituted.

(Wendt 1999: 94)

This argument disposes quickly of the sterile debate about the 'role of ideas' that has been limping along in IR circles. It also clearly puts Wendt, in terms of the predominant taxonomy, in the 'idealist' camp. Wendt is careful not to be identified with a 'radical' form of idealism that claims it is only ideas that count ('turtles all the way down') but embraces some 'rump materialism' (Wendt 1999: chap. 3). Although this commitment is allegedly 'rooted in scientific realism's naturalistic approach to society', Wendt has to admit that this 'rump' does not do much of the explaining (ibid.: 136), thus explicitly alerting us to the dangers of conflating the 'objective' with the 'material' (ibid.: 95). In this context, 'emergence' or 'super-venience' – taken up later in the book – play a crucial role. Wendt's warnings could not be clearer:

When Neorealists offer multipolarity as an explanation for war, inquire into the discursive conditions that constitute the poles as enemies rather than friends. When Liberals offer economic interdependence as an explanation for peace, inquire into the discursive conditions that constitute states with identities that care about free trade and economic growth. When Marxists offer capitalism as an explanation for state forms, inquire into the discursive conditions that constitute capitalist relations of production . . . Enmity, inter-dependence, and capitalism are to a large extent cultural forms and to that extent materialist explanations that presuppose those forms will be vulnerable to . . . idealist critique.

(Wendt 1999: 135–6)

In short, as in the case of language – which is only possible when individuals are capable of making some noises for which moving one's tongue is causal – there is not much that can be learned from such a study of causality. If we are interested in communication, we had better get involved in the deciphering of the structure of language and of the meanings that are connected with certain utterances. As a matter of fact, not much remains of 'rump materialism' (making some noises) when we realise that we can communicate even without such 'noises', as reading and writing demonstrates. Although we might need some material marks on a paper, these preconditions are again different from the formerly mentioned causes. This argument, in turn, suggests that neither of them can be the necessary or sufficient cause and, therefore, the true 'fundament' for communication.

The last issue raises two further important problems for social theory. First, whether all explanations have to be causal in nature, as the unity of science position seems to suggest. Second, how are we to conceptualise the common understandings that are part of the idealist explanation? Given the commitment to methodological individualism, it seems that this common knowledge among actors has to be the aggregate of the ideas individuals have. To that extent, any hope for a holistic social theory that also wants to be based on some notion of scientific realism seems to be illusory.

In an analysis of great subtlety and persuasiveness, Wendt's answer to the first question is *not* that causal accounts are privileged because they represent the true 'scientific' form. Yet, he does not endorse the notion that non-causal accounts are the proper way of analysing social phenomena either, as adherents of the autonomy of the cultural sciences claim. Instead, he shows that, in both the natural and the social sciences, at least two different types of questions and of explanations are used: there are 'causal' statements that answer 'why' questions. And there are 'what' and 'how possible' questions that are inquiries into the constitution of things. The latter takes a different form than explaining the occurrence of an event by its efficient (antecedent) causes. In causal accounts both cause and effect have to be independent of each other, while in the case of a constitutive relationship no such independence is implied.

The request in constitutive explanations is rather for explicating the structures that constitute the phenomenon in the first place (e.g., 'what is sovereignty?', not 'what "causes" it?'). Wendt shows that some of the most important explanations in the natural sciences, such as the kinetic theory of heat or the double helix model of DNA, fall into the constitutive category. Since both questions are logically irreducible to each other (despite some conceptual links), and since both are occasioned by different interests that cut across the nature/culture divide, neither can be automatically privileged.

Such a view also quickly disposes of the problem that any explanation has to satisfy the subsumption model familiar from Carl Hempel and Popper. For them the conjunction of the initial conditions with universal laws leads to a singular hypothetical statement (prediction) that is derived via a logical inference. Because of the logical equivalence of prediction and explanation in this model, singular statements could be used to falsify the universality of 'laws' by means of the *modus tollens*.[3] Wendt acknowledges the problematic nature of this position popularised by logical positivism. He sides with those who accept 'theories' in which explanations do not exhibit the logical equivalence of prediction and explanation (the theory of evolution is the best example). Furthermore, he points out in true 'scientific realist'

---

3 If p, then not q, q therefore not p; whereby p represents the alleged universal law and q the singular hypothetical statement.

fashion that the identification of a *causal mechanism*, rather than the logical sub-sumption, does the explaining in any case.[4]

Taking the democratic peace argument as a foil, Wendt suggests:

> subsumption under a law is not really explanation at all, in the sense of answering *why* something occurred, but is simply a way of saying *that* it is an instance of a regularity. In what sense have we explained peace between the US and Canada by subsuming it under the generalization that 'democracies do not fight each other'? When what we really want to know is why demo-cracies do not fight each other, to answer that question in terms of still higher order laws merely pushes the question one step back. The general problem here is failing to distinguish the grounds for expecting an event to occur (being an instance of regularity) with explaining why it occurs. Causation is a relation in nature not in logic.
>
> (Wendt 1999: 81, emphasis in original, references omitted)

Clearly, this outlined position is very critical of the traditional unity of science position, endorsed by most 'mainstream' approaches to IR. But most 'theoretical' debates in the field are seldom aware of the complexity of these problems. Political scientists happily take parts and pieces from Popper and Hempel, fit some Thomas Kuhn with it, enhance it by some elements of Imre Lakatos, add perhaps a little Milton Friedman (the 'as if' character of basic assumptions is here truly a favourite), while holding on to the idea of testing against reality which is entirely incompatible with any of these elements. To his credit, instead of proceeding in this fashion, Wendt provides a controversial but independently articulated alternative that is sensitive to these differences.

Equally controversial to many will be Wendt's answer to the second question above: how to conceptualise the beliefs that give meaning to our actions and allow us to engage in cooperative ventures, limit conflicts, justify claims, and make demands on each other. Most members of our cohort decisively opt for the individualist notion that such 'common knowledge' has to be explained by aggregating the individually held beliefs. But this procedure poses the further problem of how these beliefs 'got in there', i.e., the heads of the actors and why these beliefs happen to coincide.

Furthermore, issues of selection and of socialisation make, in turn, a discussion of social structure and of the interdependence of agency and structure necessary. Thus, Wendt's exchange with Waltz (1979) is more than a rhetorical ploy. The aspiration to provide some final answer ('theory is . . .', 'a system is . . .') is common to both theories. Wendt claims that his theory is clearly the wider one; his approach is systemic, cognitive, and interactionist, instead of structural, materialist, and static. Wendt's approach also allows for a more comprehensive analysis of change

---

4 For an argument for social mechanisms instead of covering laws, see Elster (1989). For a more recent discussion, see the anthology assembled by Peter Hedström and Richard Swedberg (1998).

instead of reducing IR to the alternatives of hierarchy versus anarchy, or to positional changes within the system. Such an alternative necessitates fundamental changes in the analytical instruments, in the selection of criteria of reductionism, and in the evaluation of interaction as an important theoretical concern. I can focus here only on a few themes which seem to me the most important and innovative.

Individualism versus holism

Let me start with the debate on individualism and holism in social science. It is here that Wendt provides some interesting evidence that 'culture' is indeed something different than the individualist notion of common knowledge in game theory. The nature of common knowledge has already inspired a remarkable set of exchanges in the German *Zeitschrift für Internationale Beziehungen* between adherents of rational choice and constructivism.[5] But that exchange emphasised the distinction between strategic and communicative rationality and the (im)possibility of reducing the latter to the former. In *Social Theory* the issue of individualism versus holism provides the background and organising axis for Wendt's treatment. Thus, his discussion is ultimately devoted to the demonstration of the importance of social structures which are systemic but cultural rather than materialist. These structures link micro-level and macro-level through both constitutive and causal effects that can be observed in actual interactions. Wendt distinguishes in this context between (minimal) social situations, in which interaction takes place without mediation by common knowledge, and those where common knowledge shapes such interactions.

The term 'social action' is used by Wendt in the traditional sense in that an action is viewed from the actor's perspective and possesses a strategic dimension, i.e., the interacting 'other' is taken into account. Thus, to take Wendt's example, when the Aztecs and Spaniards in 1519 encountered each other, they both possessed some knowledge of how to treat the other, which informed their actions. The Aztecs probably 'mistook' the Spaniards as gods whose arrival had been prophesied, while the Spaniards dealt with them as 'savages'. As in the 'original encounter' it would have been surprising if such a meeting could have evolved without degeneration. While the interaction between these two parties was 'social', it was informed neither by 'common knowledge' nor by shared meanings (culture). Only the latter provides the taken-for-granted knowledge of, for instance, modern international politics that frames interactions in the state system. Thus, what a 'state' is has to be 'known', and actors have to understand the implications of 'sovereignty' for their practices. Indeed,

---

5 See the debate between Harald Müller (1994), Gerald Schneider (1994), Otto Keck (1995), and Rainer Schmalz-Bruns (1995).

compared to the situation facing Cortez and Montezuma, this represents a substantial accretion of culture at the systemic level, without an understanding of which neither statesmen nor neorealists would be able to explain why modern states and state systems behave as they do.

(Wendt 1999: 158)

These puzzles suggest that collective representations are something different from the common knowledge of game theory. Wendt argues that the relationship between the collective structures of meaning and individual beliefs is one of 'super-venience and multiple realizability' (Wendt 1999: 162). To that extent 'culture', as the shorthand for collective representations, cannot exist or have effects apart from the beliefs of individual actors, but is not reducible to them. As in the case of language, it exists only insofar as it is used by individual speakers but cannot be conceptualised as the 'private' possession of each speaker. Drawing on Emile Durkheim, Philip Pettit, and Margaret Gilbert, Wendt argues:

> Structures of collective knowledge depend on actors believing *something* that induces them to engage in practices that reproduce those structures; to suggest otherwise would be to reify culture, to separate it from knowledgeable practices through which it is produced and reproduced. On the other hand the effects of collective knowledge are not *reducible* to individuals' beliefs ... Indeed, as Margaret Gilbert points out, we can ascribe beliefs to a group that are not held personally by *any* of its members, as long as members accept the legitimacy of the group's decision and the obligation to act in accordance with its results.
>
> (Wendt 1999: 162–3, emphasis in original, references omitted)

The latter point is of particular importance as it explains Wendt's often criticised state centrism (Wendt 1999: chap. 5). It is not that Wendt does not 'see' other actors populating the international arena, or that he wants to deny their influence. Instead he is interested in the reproduction of the state system and, therefore, states and their constitution have to be at the centre of his attention. If one wants to criticise Wendt here, one has to do this via his conception of politics, as it is 'protection' that defines the state's 'essence'. Thus, it is not a neutral conception of politics as, for instance, the formal definition of making collective choices, or of representation, or as an even more substantive notion such as the Aristotelian good life. Wendt's definition comes rather close to the Hobbesian (and perhaps impoverished) notion of politics, which holds that no other social relations are possible unless they are 'compatible with the "forces" and especially the "relations of destruction" ' (ibid.: 8, see also 198).

Without organisation and social cooperation, however, the 'forces of destruction' cannot even be conceptualised, since war is, after all, a social phenomenon that presupposes groups and politics. Consequently, it cannot serve as the foundation of all politics even if force plays an extremely important role. Thus, 'the war of all against all' which supposedly lies at the 'bottom' of the social contract is an impossible construction, both historically (as Hobbes was well aware)[6] and logically. It is surprising to see how easily Wendt falls into the Hobbesian trap (for a further elaboration of this point, see Kratochwil 1989: chap. 4). This understanding of politics unites him with the (neo)realists but it does not make much sense if one espouses a constructivist approach. Let me be clear about this: the reason is not that constructivists believe in the inherent goodness of man or have peace as a political project, as opposed to realism's preoccupation with security and defence. The reason is rather that there are no simple givens for constructivists, such as 'structures' or 'forces' that are not again results of particular actions and 'constructions' that require further explanations.

Similarly, Wendt's attribution of intentions, desires, and beliefs to 'states' might seem like strange anthropomorphism, but it is not much stranger than the everyday acceptance of corporate personality. In that case too, we make important distinctions between shareholder rights and the rights of the corporate entity itself, and we assert their irreducibility.[7] We may not be convinced by Wendt's neo-Weberian emphasis on centralisation of the coercive means as the state's essence. The story of the growth of nationalism and popular legitimacy is at least as important here. Yet, Wendt is certainly correct by following Weber:

> that individuals' actions have to be 'oriented' toward the corporate Idea does *not* mean that everyone in the group must have this idea in their heads [*sic*] . . . What matters is that individuals accept the obligation to act jointly on behalf of collective beliefs, whether or not they subscribe to them personally.
>
> (Wendt 1999: 219)

A new systemic theory?

All this sets then the stage for Wendt's new systemic theory and his take on the agent/structure debate. Wendt cannot subscribe to a systemic theory recognising only capabilities and systematically neglecting interactions. As he suggests:

> The debate is not between 'systemic' theories that focus on structure and 'reductionist' theories that focus on agents, but between *different theories of system structure* and how structures relate to agents.
>
> (Wendt 1999: 12, emphasis in original)

He therefore not only abandons Waltz's unhelpful conceptual grid, but takes issue with the entire account of structures reproducing themselves across time.

---

6 Hobbes (1968 [1651]: 187) explains that 'It may preadventure be thought, there was never such a time, nor condition of warre as this . . . [*bellum omnium contra omnes*] . . . But though there had never been any time, wherein particular men were in a condition of warre one against another . . .'

7 See, for example, the discussion of the *Barcelona Traction Case* of 1970 (*Belgium v. Spain*), in *Reports of the International Court of Justice* (The Hague, 1975).

Without going into Wendt's detailed (but rather meekly voiced) criticism of Waltz, it is important to note that he clearly opts for an explanation of 'sameness' in terms of *cognitive structures*.

Furthermore, he argues *contra* Waltz that social structures affect not only 'behaviour' but the actors' very identities. In short, social structures have not only behavioural effects but also 'property effects'. Furthermore, these effects cannot be reduced to simple causally efficient influences. The latter presuppose independence between the entities concerned, but 'property effects' obviate such independence. To that extent, any 'theory' based on radical individualism cuts itself off from analysing this constitutive influence of ideas as they affect properties. It also automatically reduces the agent/structure problem to one of co-determination or interaction, rather than one of mutual constitution and *conceptual dependence*.

Wendt wishes to steer clear of the Scylla of postulating some mysterious 'group mind' and the Charybdis position of pure methodological individualism, in which any idea can only be a 'subjective' representation. Thus, Wendt introduces George Mead's distinction between 'I' and 'Me', and between *individuality per se* and the *terms of individuality*. The latter term (Me, or the 'terms of individuality') refers to those properties of an agent's constitution that are intrinsically dependent upon culture. The 'I', or the 'individuality per se', designates an agent's sense of the 'self' as a distinct locus of thought, choice, and activity (Wendt 1999: 182).

Wendt then distinguishes between four types of identity, a move that is somewhat problematic, since he tries to graft his ideas to the scheme of Jim Fearon. The first, the personal or corporate identity, seems to correspond to the 'I' in the above discussion. The second involves a 'type identity' which seems based sometimes on nothing more than classificatory rules, such as age. Third are 'role identities', which 'are not based on intrinsic properties and as such exist only in relation to others' (Wendt 1999: 227). And, finally, there is the 'collective identity', in which the boundary between self and other is blurred through identification, i.e., the self is categorised as 'other'. Collective identification is never total, as otherwise the extinction of the 'self' would result, and there are apparently powerful psychological mechanisms at work that prevent total identifications. Nevertheless, to view, for example, an attack on a 'friend' as an attack on oneself is one of the basic facts of international life on which even the famous 'inherent' right to 'collective *self-defence*' [*sic*] is founded (see United Nations Charter, art. 51).

With these conceptual instruments in place, Wendt can attack the core of neorealism's main tenet: the 'logic' of anarchy. He argues that three distinct macro-level structures develop out of the permissive environment of anarchy, depending on how 'others' are conceptualised. These structures could be called in accordance with their most prominent theorists: a Hobbesian, Lockean, or Kantian system of anarchy. Wendt's interesting next step is then to free the notion of 'culture' from too close an identification with the internalisation of norms, a mistake commonly made. Thus, the Hobbesian world is believed to be one in which norms are followed because they are 'guaranteed' by a credible enforcer. If norms are better internalised, as is traditionally mantained, they give rise to a

Lockean system. Here 'rivalry' and 'cost-calculations' channel conflicts. Finally Wendt suggests the Kantian perspective represents the deepest level of internalisation; no longer are force or price calculations determinative, but the legitimacy of the norms represent the dominant motive.

This conceptualisation, however, leads to the conflation of two distinct problems: that of the existence of norms and their internalisation on one hand, and that of 'political order' or the possibility of inducing large-scale cooperation on the other. For Wendt, the existence of a stable Hobbesian culture in certain periods seems to indicate that certain norms and expectations have been thoroughly internalised without opening a path towards greater cooperation. Such a 'stickiness' depends also on a process and the 'lock-in' of certain assumptions about the relationship of self and other. If more and more members of a system represent each other as enemies, there comes a point at which these representations define 'reality':

> At this point actors start to think of enmity as a property of the *system* rather than just of individual actors and so feel compelled to represent all Others as enemies simply because they are part of the system. In this way, the particular Other becomes Mead's 'generalized Other', a structure of collective beliefs and expectations that persists through time even as individual actors come and go and into the logic of which actors are socialized.
>
> (Wendt 1999: 264, emphasis in original, reference omitted)

Consequently, Wendt holds that change at the macro-level requires above all a redefinition of the posture of the self to the other, in particular with respect to force as a strategy of pursuing one's goals (Wendt 1999: 258). Thus, violence among 'rivals' is self-limiting as total wars are prevented by the accepted right of the 'other' to exist. To the extent that the right to life and liberty are non-controversial, conflicts are limited largely to 'property' issues. Finally, in a Kantian world the threat of force has receded and the presumption of non-violent dispute-settlement in such a 'security community' is the dominant maxim.

This thesis leads to two surprising results: first, the logics of anarchy are not dependent upon how deeply a culture is internalised:

> Hobbesian logics can be generated by deeply shared ideas and Kantian logics by only weakly shared ones. Each logic is *multiply realizable*: the same effect can be reached through different causes.
>
> (Wendt 1999: 254, emphasis in original)

Second,

> Realist pessimism notwithstanding, it is easier to escape a Hobbesian world, whose culture matters relatively little, and harder to create a Kantian one based on deeply shared beliefs. It is Realists who should think that cultural change is easy, not constructivists, because the more deeply shared ideas are – the more they 'matter' – the stickier the structure they constitute will be.
>
> (Wendt 1999: 255)

With this Wendt has provided some strong arguments for the ideational notion of social structures, and for the thesis that these structures are instantiated by the roles and representations of self and other. Wendt clearly considers the Lockean version of international politics as the most apt description since the Westphalian settlement. He also interprets the subsequent low death rate of states as a persuasive proof that *cultural*, not natural, selection, advanced by imitation and learning, provides the best analogy for the exploration of systemic change. Cultural selection occurs through changes in the mechanism of 'reflected appraisal' rather than through (re)distribution of capabilities. Since he has argued that fundamentally different systems emerge depending upon whether the actors conceive of each other as enemies, competitors, or friends, his last chapter is devoted to the investigation of how the actors 'learn to see themselves as a reflection of how they are appraised by significant Others' (Wendt 1999: 341). The self still has to take, reject, or modify the identity which the others have 'cast' for it, but his interactionism leads Wendt to identify the representational practices of others – rather than the actual choice of an identity by the actor – as the important puzzle. Wendt realises of course that in determining the options powerful states will have significantly more influence than weaker ones. Nevertheless, he is (strangely) uninterested in both problems, i.e., in how powerful states influence the menu of available choices and in the 'final choice'.

Since 'we are – or become – what we do', Wendt reverts to a general discussion of 'collective identity formation' and to the master variables that govern that process (interdependence, common fate, homogeneity, and self-restraint). The first three are termed 'efficient causes', the last a 'permissive cause'. Under conditions of interdependence the incentives for cooperation – in the sense of making for extended identifications – are checked by fears of exploitation. The situation of 'common fate' depends on the perception that the survival or welfare 'depends on what happens to the group' (Wendt 1999: 349). While this might seem like a strong identification, Wendt argues that common fate perceptions (usually provided by an 'external threat') have not prevented states from not cooperating because of the fear of exploitation (ibid.: 353). One might ask then what purchase 'identifications' have.

The last of the efficient causes is 'homogeneity', or likeness. Categorising others as being similar to oneself does not necessarily lead to 'identification'. But Wendt claims that homogeneity reduces conflict that otherwise could arise out of differences in corporate and type identity. In short, recognising that someone is like us is an inducement to treating him alike (Wendt 1999: 354). Finally, self-restraint, i.e., knowledge that the other is unlikely to resort to force, engenders 'trust'. In choosing the assurance the citizens of the Bahamas have concerning a US invasion, Wendt elaborates:

> When Bahamian foreign policy makers wake up each morning, they *know* that the United States is not going to conquer them, not because they think the US will be deterred by superior power, not because they think that on that day the US will calculate that violating the norms of sovereignty is not in its

self-interest, but because they know that the US will restrain *itself*. Like all knowledge this belief is not 100 percent certain, but it is reliable enough that we would think it irrational for the Bahamians to act on any other basis.

(Wendt 1999: 360, emphasis in original)

There is certainly something to this stress on 'routines' and 'discipline' in social life. But whether or not this example can carry the weight placed upon it depends on the assessment of the theory as a whole. It is to this problem that I want to turn in the next section.

Clarifications, criticisms, and disagreements

A work of such scope and complexity is likely to engender a series of questions that arise from ambiguities in the argument, or out of mistakes in logic or fact. One prime candidate for theoretical elaboration or correction is Wendt's assertion concerning the respective advantages of rationalist and constructivist models. Wendt argues (correctly) that the former are useful for analysing decisions in which interests and identity are stable, while the latter are more appropriate for longer-term change. There is a certain plausibility to this argument, but the juxtaposed 'lesson' does not follow, that is, that 'rationalism is for today and tomorrow and constructivism for the *longue durée*' (Wendt 1999: 367).

First of all, anyone familiar with Fernand Braudel's work will realise that the *longue durée* is the domain for structural explanations precisely because identities and interests do not matter, since they 'wash out' over long periods. Someone who changes the priorities has to show why his version of the *longue durée* should be accepted. Second, the reader who has just worked through a rather demanding text of some 300-plus pages which emphasise process over structure and actors and their ideas over material factors, and who also remembers the unravelling of the former Soviet bloc within a few years, might question Wendt's judgement. Since rationalist models – through their simplifying assumptions concerning interests and identities – can be shown to be a special case of constructivist models, their relationship is not one that can be described in terms of their fitness for short-versus long-term types of analysis. Rather the problem consists in deciding whether by the introduction of simplifying assumptions, problems of interest-formation, roles, and identities can be neglected in a concrete case.

Further, such an assessment will have to go beyond traditional risk-analysis since, by definition, new identities and interests change the type of actor and, thus, also the 'known' universe on which the frequency distributions and probabilities relied. What makes such events as the French Revolution or even the Cuban missile crisis so frightening is that the 'roles' used as yardsticks for assessing actions are no longer valid. This brief discussion alone suggests that the conceptualisation of long versus short run is seriously misleading and does not do justice to the problems involved.

Similarly, Wendt's 'proof' that, despite significant differences between natural kinds and social kinds, the same methods are applicable to each is less than *mostrum*

convincing, particularly since it is based on a simple *non sequitur*. After explicitly acknowledging the reflexivity of social life, i.e., that actors can come to understand themselves as the authors of their structures and thus transcend the subject/object distinction, Wendt admits that social scientific theories alone have the potential to become part of the 'world'. Consequently, 'such transformations violate the causal theory of reference, since reality is being caused by theory rather than vice versa' *Bullshit* (Wendt 1999: 76). After one further sentence, Wendt presents his conclusion: 'In sum, the ontology of social life is consistent with scientific realism' (ibid.). This conclusion, however, does not follow; having postulated the primacy of ontology, having furthermore acknowledged the important difference between natural and social kinds, the surprising conclusion is that none of all this matters!

Now let us examine the Bahamian example more closely. Despite its intuitive appeal it seems that too much is claimed. After all, given the absence of a concrete conflict of interest, even hardened realists would not claim that an attack has to follow necessarily from structural givens.[8] The 'indifference' that arises out of isolation is, for Rousseau, the nostrum that minimises violence in the state of nature, even if the actors' motivation is no longer that of the *amour de soi* but of the *amour propre*. Wendt is certainly right in holding that many decisions (or rather non-decisions) do not result from explicit cost/benefit analyses. But in order to show the 'mechanisms' at work here, one needs something like 'hidden faces of power' or the 'disciplinary' understandings of Michel Foucault, in which the limits of sense are not a neutral description of the things, but are recognised as being part of a disciplinary program according to which actors fashion themselves. Similarly, Pierre Bourdieu's concept of 'habitus' might be illuminating.

This is (I hope) not a criticism of the kind 'why did you not write the book I wanted you to write?'. Rather it raises the more principled question of whether problems of political practice can be reduced to questions of 'reflective appraisal', altercasting, or identification, or whether an interactionist perspective might not be too narrow. After all, many practices and habits are formed in which the processes *false* Wendt relies upon do not seem to be involved. A lot of what goes on in 'moral training' relies on examples and the demonstration of how simple rules provide short-cuts for resolving otherwise potentially interminable 'internal' discussions of what one should do.

Wendt (re)discovers scientific realism

I have already mentioned in passing that Wendt's interactionist perspective seems to neglect the 'final choice' of why and how an actor takes the role in which he or she is cast. In the discussion above, the factors internal to the actor remained obscure as role and expectations were emphasised. Now I want to add a more

---

8 See Hobbes's (1968 [1651]: 185) explicit argument, 'For warre consisteth not in Battell only, or the act of fighting; but in a tract of time wherein the Will to contend by Battell is sufficiently known.'

→ *Deterrence?*

principled criticism of the neglect of language's role in social life. This omission has various implications, ranging from simple anomalies and blind spots to methodological commitments strangely at odds with constructivism.

Obviously, the last remark flags something more than mere criticism which might even fall into the category of deep-seated and irresolvable disagreements. Let me be clear that this criticism is not part of some contest concerning who is the 'better' or 'truer' constructivist, in which self-designations and quotes from others ('he or she also says x and he or she is a constructivist') are persuasive. Important theoretical and metatheoretical problems are at stake. The issue is not whether somebody says or believes she or he is a constructivist, but whether or not such a (self-)identification makes sense in view of some of the tenets defining constructivism.

In this context Wendt's commitment to, and version of, 'scientific realism' can be questioned on two counts. First, whether his rendition of this perspective is indeed appropriate and, second, whether his version of 'realism' is compatible with constructivism as a metatheoretical orientation. Given the rather different emphases among scientific realists concerning methodological and ontological issues, one can indeed doubt whether 'realism' is a well-defined philosophy that can serve as a foundation and carry the weight Wendt places upon it.[9] Moreover, the virtually complete neglect of the *social* component of scientific realism, most notably in the work of Roy Bhaskar, on which Wendt often relies, is especially surprising. Bhaskar emphasises 'science' as a communal practice rather than as a simple finding and 'testing' of theories. My point is not simply that this common-sense view of realism, and of testing against reality, is naïve. Neither Wendt nor the scientific realists actually espouse it. By picking and choosing certain parts and tenets and neglecting others, one might establish a position acceptable to all parties. But one accomplishes this feat only by equivocations and by suppressing differences that ought to be examined. Again, my objection is not to the 'picking and choosing' per se. We all develop our positions by relying on bits and pieces of various traditions. The question is one of justifying these choices by providing a perspective that is coherent rather than merely acceptable to 'the profession'.

This brings us back to the dilemma of the apparent incompatibility of two standards for knowledge – truth and consensus – and the strategies by which we mediate these tensions. The most obvious strategy is the attempt to make consensus dependent upon truth, based on the hope that either logic or reality, if properly questioned, will adjudicate. But most problems cannot be solved that way because they belong to the category of 'undecidable' questions. Thus, neither the logical tool of the 'excluded middle' (bivalence principle) nor the test against reality is applicable. The second strategy is to assert that truth is a function of consensus in a scientific community sharing criteria of what represents 'good science'. Results are considered 'true' as they emerge from particular procedures and practices. Truth is then not only contingent on some theoretical framework and some

---

9 See here also Martin Hollis and Steve Smith's (1991) warnings.

taken-for-granted or background knowledge (measurement) but is also derived from argumentative procedures. The arguments among the practitioners centre on the importance or meaning of tests, on the justifications for calling something an anomaly (rather than a refutation), an error (rather than a 'discovery'), and so forth. In other words, reaching the final decisions is based on some legitimate procedure that allocates burdens of proof.

Interestingly, such a perspective dethrones science as a paradigm of knowledge since it undermines foundational claims of the scientific method to show things as they really are. Instead, the choice between finality and legitimacy of a decision arises. Given the fact that these two criteria often point in different directions, it is more appropriate to use the analogy of a court and its formal procedures to 'establish' the truth, rather than making the notion of truth a function of representing reality. The fact that scientists have even asked for such a 'court', and that many scientific associations and enterprises increasingly use quasi-judicial procedures,[10] suggests a deep-seated change both in the practice of science and in the public's acceptance of scientific statements as self-justifying instruments of 'truth'.[11] Wendt's attempt to found not only *a* social theory, but *the* (generic) 'social theory', seems, therefore, somehow old-fashioned, hardly compatible with his own constructivist perspective, and curiously out of sync with some of the most important developments in 'science'.

Since much depends on the assessment of 'scientific realism', its further examination is in order. The first thing to notice is that, despite Wendt's claim, the term scientific realism applies to people with rather disparate epistemological orientations; it seems rather difficult to fathom what Bhaskar's 'realism' has in common with David Lewis's realism. In the title of one of his books, Lewis challenges the normal conception of 'reality' by arguing for the 'plurality of worlds' (Lewis 1987), and Rom Harré suggests that there is a *variety* of realisms.[12] Thus, there is considerably more debate and controversy among these philosophers of science than the rather unified position Wendt invokes when grounding his social theory in this school. But be this as it may, scientific realists according to Wendt share certain commitments, such as the following:

1   the world is independent of the mind and language of individual observers;
2   mature scientific theories typically refer to this world;
3   even when it is not directly observable.

10 On the federal advisory apparatus, see Primack and Hippel (1974). For an interesting discussion of the general problems involved, see Matheny and Williams (1981).
11 See, for example, Kantorowitz (1975); see also the attempts to establish a 'court' for good scientific practice: US Department of Commerce (1977), which reports on the results of a conference in which the Commerce Department, the National Science Foundation, and the American Association for the Advancement of Science participated with the purpose of vetting the proposals for a science court.
12 See Rom Harré's (1986) excellent introduction to various schools of thought and the issues involved.

I am not sure whether this rather general characterisation is apt for Wendt's purposes. That there are 'unobservables' in every theory is hardly controversial, strict empiricists excepted. Such a view is shared by pragmatists, postmodernists (whatever that means), constructivists, and logical positivists alike. Instead, the controversies centre on the meaning of the two other statements. Here again, hardly anyone – even among the most ardent constructivists or pragmatists – doubts that the 'world' exists 'independent' from our minds. The question is rather whether we can recognise it in a pure and direct fashion, i.e., without any 'description', or whether what we recognise is always already organised and formed by certain categorical and theoretical elements. Thus, Kant's 'thing in itself' is 'there', but it is unrecognisable and as such uninteresting until and unless it is brought under some description. Consequently, there remain two problems that need further clarification: first, whether this 'naming' is indeed a function of the congruence of our concepts and the 'things', as this provides the yardstick for 'truth'; or, second, whether 'truth' is a matter of the conditions governing the justifiability of *assertions* rather than a matter of the 'world'.

Most 'realists' not only believe in natural kinds and some essence that 'correctly' names the things in the world, but they must also hold some form of 'iconic' theory of truth. As the latter has come increasingly under attack, Wendt (1999: 58) explicitly states that his 'theory' does not imply such a foundational stance (since theories are always tested against other theories and not against 'the world'). However, I cannot see how such an argument can be squared with his emphasis on 'essences' and natural kinds. Even more astonishing is Wendt's argument 'that "truth" does not do any interesting work' in the realist philosophy of science. While pragmatists, who rely on usefulness rather than truth, can espouse such a position, this stance is incoherent for a scientific realist (see, for example, the various essays in Rorty 1991). As Wendt (1999: 65) himself argues elsewhere, 'science is successful because it gradually brings our theoretical understanding into conformity with the deep structure of the world out there.'

Thus, the suspicion mounts that several incompatible things are being bolted together. There is first of all the problem that too much is made out of the 'miracle' theory of science which allegedly justifies scientific realism. While the success of science is no problem, the inference that it is owing to its 'correct' apprehension of reality is a difficulty. After all, a theory can be successful without necessarily referring to something real. Thus, contrary to the conception of a Popperian 'Third World', where all these true entities are housed, one might wonder where all these entities such as atoms, phlogistons, even elements such as fire – about which even Kant was still writing a dissertation – have gone.

Furthermore, how do we know that we have got nearer to the truth instead of only substituting one theoretical concept with some other? The new concept allows us to ask interesting questions, but they might lead us again down a blind alley, while a former allegedly refuted truth might suddenly provide some new starting point. As the history of science has shown, these are not imaginary examples (see, for example, the studies by Popper's own disciple, Joseph Agassi [1975]). Instead, they correct the view that 'science' can be described as a simple process of monological demonstration in which, by conjectures and refutations, a self-correcting process of progress commences. Although Wendt does not base his account on Popper and his followers, he still shares much of their 'plot' and 'rational reconstruction' of the history of science. Without wishing to enter the discussion about Popper's intellectual development, it is important to realise that he increasingly moved away from his original monological understanding of science by stressing the importance of exchanges among scientists. This adjustment was important since it united Popper's philosophy of science with his political theory.

As Popper suggested: 'Rational discussion is central to the open society and to science. In both, the purpose of rational discussion is to criticise and refute' (as quoted in Agassi 1975: 34). This argument shows the constitutive character of debate and criticism for scientific knowledge and thus dethrones 'demonstration' and purely logical criteria from their position as guarantors of truth. As Popper proposes, unanimity – the goal of logical demonstration – is not 'fruitful' and might actually be the death of science. This idea is most explicit in his last book, *The Myth of the Framework* (Popper 1994). There Popper not only tried to show that there is virtue in disagreements, and that fruitful communication among scientists is not dependent upon a shared framework, a late answer to Kuhn's notion of incommensurable paradigms. Rather scientific inquiry is based on the respect of certain *ethical* principles that govern arguments and the allocation of burdens of proofs in the debates.

Regardless of whether one is persuaded by Popper's strategy, it was certainly one of the most discussed epistemological issues during the past two decades. Even realists like Bhaskar have emphasised the importance of this 'social' component of knowledge. This component is not some part of a sociology of knowledge that can be neglected in a rational reconstruction of science.[13] It is rather intrinsic to 'science' as a practice, even if it does not fit some problematic rational recon-struction of scientific progress. The virtual omission of this entire dimension of scientific activity and of two decades of epistemological debate by Wendt, his implicit embrace of the 'monological' ideal buttressed by the bivalence principle of logic (either the world is so, or not so), is all the more surprising as this neglect centrally touches upon important issues of theory-building. As the scientific realist Rom Harré has pointed out, realism has to answer to the criticisms

---

13 See, for example, Bhaskar's (1975: 9) argument, 'To see science as a social activity, and as structured and discriminating in its thought, constitutes a significant step in our understanding of science.' Similarly: 'What the orthodox tradition omits from its account of science is the nature of scientific activity as work; or when, as in transcendental idealism, it does recognise it, it considers it only as intellectual and not as practical labour. Accordingly, it cannot see knowledge, or at least the achievement of a closure as a transient social product' (Bhaskar 1979: 19).

made during the last few decades,[14] and can be reconstructed only in a more modest form that is close to scientific practice and avoids previous fatal errors (Harré 1986: 5).

> The account of science to be set out . . . is based on the thought that science is not a logically coherent body of knowledge in the strict, unforgiving sense of the philosophers' high definition, but a cluster of material and cognitive practices, carried on within a distinctive moral order, whose main character-istic is the trust that obtains among its members and should obtain between that community and the larger lay community with which it is interdependent . . . The idea of a philosophical study of the moral order that obtains in the scientific community is not new. But the significance of admitting it to the centre of our interest has rarely been acknowledged. I hope to show that science has a special status, not because it is a sure way of producing truths and avoiding falsehood, but it is a communal practice of a community with a remarkable and rigid morality.
>
> (Harré 1986: 6)

Given this perspective, Wendt's *Theory* looks curiously old-fashioned. Although he repeatedly emphasises that science is not logic and that real 'causal mechanisms' rather than logical implications have to be investigated, he misses entirely the larger point addressed by Popper and Harré.

One can only guess why Wendt, who is certainly familiar with this literature, has chosen to pass over this problem. One reason could be that the audience he tries to persuade to embrace his position as the new middle-ground is deeply committed to the notion that logical closure and deductive rigour are the characteristics of good science. After a prolonged period of mindless empiricism, the recent insistence of some stringency in the argumentation seems like an important corrective. Unfortunately, the stridency with which this new ideal is advocated and the questionable nature of the claims involved suggest that it is not 'science' but success in terms of power within the 'profession' that is the motive for such a dogmatic attitude.

As Wendt is patient with the neorealists of yesteryear by engaging them on the

---

14 'Many realists have based their defences of scientific realism on the doctrine (one might almost say, the dogma) of bivalence, the principle that most theoretical statements of a scientific discourse are true or false by virtue of the way the world is . . . Other realists have persisted with the idea that the essence of scientific discourses and material practices, such as experimentation, is some abstract logical framework. Sceptics had little difficulty in demonstrating that no real scientific research program could come anywhere near realising the bivalence principle in practice, nor have they had much trouble in showing that real scientific thinking could make little use of logical schemata if its cognitive and material practices were made explicit. It looks as if the work of a scientific community can be rational only at the cost of being impossible, while, on the other hand, the extreme sceptical reaction offers nothing but a caricature of what we know the scientific achievement to have been' (Harré 1986: 3).

level of the Waltzian orthodoxy – even if it is confusing and does perhaps more harm than good for getting his own message out straight – so does he also patiently accept the current predilections of 'rigour' (rational choice), of 'empirical testing' (empiricism), and truth (which unites all, because who could be against truth?). While these conceptions and their combination are ambiguous, they fit quite well with mainstream social science even though this agglomeration is based on a concept of science that most 'scientific realists' have long abandoned.

The failed marriage: scientific realism meets constructivism

Now there remains the question of whether and to what extent 'realism' and constructivism are compatible. This involves not only the status of ideas as opposed to natural forces – a problem that I think Wendt solves quite nicely – but also the problem of the status of 'social kinds' and of 'essences', as adumbrated above. Even if we do not consider 'essences' to consist in a single feature or property that differentiates an object from all others, there is the assumption that objects have to fall under one description which is fitting or correct, as opposed to (all?) others.[15] Thus, Wendt (1999: 49) somewhat ironically contrasts his essentialist account with those of some postmodernists, who suggest that even observable entities such as 'dogs and cats do not exist independent of discourse'. Elaborating on a 'dog', Wendt (1999: 73) argues that: 'Human descriptions and/or social relationships to other natural kinds have nothing to do with what makes dogs dogs.' This seems clear enough and well in tune with our common-sense understandings. However, a moment's reflection shows that the matter is a bit more complicated.

The first thing we notice is that defining man's essence in terms of some biological properties commits a category-mistake of the first order. The fact of a certain genetic endowment clearly locates humanity within the 'animal kingdom' and shows us that some of the human capacities, such as speech or reflexivity, are related to biological features such as a movable tongue or a well-developed cortex. But these facts do not entitle us to assume that such an essentialist description is particularly helpful for answering our questions concerning humankind's social life and for investigating the symbolic structures upon which social orders are based. Thus, humanity's essence is not a question about some unique feature only, but is crucially related to the questions we are interested in asking. Focusing on some unique feature might not be helpful at all. For instance, it is certainly true that 'man' is the only featherless biped, but this characterisation is very useful neither for biology nor for the analysis of social order. To that extent, it is correct that we have to be interested in the 'generative' aspect of 'essential' characterisations rather than on some unique feature. Nevertheless, essentialism must hold that there is one and only one 'true' description of a thing.

This leads us to a second difficulty with Wendt's argument: his insistence not only that the existence of things is independent of our descriptions, but that our

15 See, for example, the attempt to proceed with such a definition of 'essence' in Sayer (1997).

descriptions of the things are independent from particular frames of reference. That the second argument does not follow from the first should be clear, especially to constructivists. Contrary to Wendt, and without necessarily embracing the postmodern position, the problem constructivism raises in a big way *is not* the one of *existence* but of recognising *what* the existing thing is. In other words, we cannot talk about 'things in themselves', but need descriptions; these descriptions are not neutral and somehow objective but embrace all types of social practices and interests that then make the things into what they are called or referred to. Thus, while 'dog' might be a name for an animal, it is not a description which is appropriate under all circumstances. Part of what defines a 'dog' for us is not only its zoological characteristics, but a socially significant property such as 'tameness', which brings a dog under the description of 'pet'. When we encounter an animal that lacks this property we are entirely justified in calling it something different, such as 'dingo', even if its genetic code is the same as that of a dog!

Similarly, it is difficult to say what a fork or a broom 'is' unless we understand the uses and the roles of these instruments in our practices. Why do we a perceive a 'broom' in the corner, and not some elongated piece of wood with some bristles on top, held together by a wire, and how do I decide which of these properties or materials is its 'essence'? Similarly, would a 'fork' be a fork if we did not use it for holding food but rather think it is an instrument for gouging one another's eyes, as some knights in the play by Thomas Becket apparently thought when this new-fangled instrument was introduced? The object itself certainly cannot tell us!

In short, what is at issue is not the existence of the 'thing in itself' but its recognition as 'something' which can only be established by bringing it under a description. Thus, a table *is* different depending on whether I bring it under the description of a physicist, or a chemist, or avail myself of the common-sense language in referring to it. It is, therefore, pretty useless to argue in the abstract (i.e., without specifying the interests and purposes) which of these descriptions is the 'true' one, as it should be clear that 'truth' is not a function of the 'things', or of the 'world', but of assertions that are made within certain frames and descriptions. Short of taking a position of extreme reductionism, i.e., that all descriptions and frames can be reduced without loss to one description – the favourite game of 'materialists' who want to hit 'rock bottom' somewhere, as well as of Platonists who claim for themselves God's view of the world – the talk about 'essences' seems pretty sterile. Wendt (1999: chap. 3) himself is right when he resists this turn in his discussion of 'rump materialism'. But his argument makes it then all the more unintelligible why he hangs on to some of its red herrings. Whatever merits different versions of essentialism have, be they material or ideational, it is certainly no accident that the growth of science occurred only after we had given up on the idea either that the world could speak for itself, or that it can be comprehended from a Platonic perspective.

Similarly, if social systems are not simply 'there' but arise as the result of construction, then one of the interesting questions is that of the boundaries of such systems: how they are drawn and how they mediate between the environment and the system. Thus, Luhmann's systems theory has fruitfully taken a stance that analyses the operations by which a system draws its boundaries and reproduces itself, instead of focusing on the elements of the system (Luhmann 1997). Even if one does not share Luhmann's decentred approach, the problem of boundaries and their maintenance is an important issue that cannot be aborted by some ontological fiat.[16] Thus, it is more than disappointing that such questions are practically ruled out by Wendt's insistence on the ontological priority of the state (see, e.g., Wendt 1999: 198, 240). He also cuts himself off from the analysis of the shifting boundaries of the political, as exemplified by the debates in political economy (see, e.g., Stubbs and Underhill 1994; Cerny 1995). He thereby excludes the possibility of engaging with crucial issues of inclusion and exclusion that animate the discussion of citizenship and the state's capacity to act, and from the analysis of secular changes by which systems and actors get reconstituted, as Rodney Hall (1999) has so nicely shown. To deal with such interesting and important questions by definitional exercises or apodictic statements (e.g., a system is . . . the state is ontologically prior to the system, etc.) is to dismiss them and needlessly to impair the heuristic power of a systemic theory of international politics, particularly when the dismissal is based on a mistaken analogy.[17]

Finally, there seem to be different conceptions of 'system' at work in Wendt's book. On the one hand, there is the residual Waltzian notion of a system as a sum of states positioned vis-à-vis each other. In other words, Wendt retains a conception of system (even if enriched by interaction) that comes close to a natural system. In chapter 4, though, the concept shifts, as the system is now understood as a combination of material factors, ideas, and interests (*vide* the discussion of 'rump materialism'). Finally, in chapter 6 we arrive at the virtual conflation of 'system' with culture. But, as Jens Steffek has asked, can one define a social structure simply by 'culture'? Usually, when we talk about structures, we do distinguish them from the more encompassing notion of 'culture' (that might house or be compatible with several structures).[18]

Moralité, or what can be learned from it

If we cannot rely on a firm foundation, then we seem to question the existence of 'truth', along with 'science' as a method of arriving at it. This raises the problem of

---

16 For an interesting treatment of boundaries and their role in social systems and international politics, see Albert *et al.* (2001).

17 See Wendt's (1999: 198) claim: 'states are ontologically prior to the state system. The state is presocial to other states in the same way that the human body is presocial.' First, the question is not whether one or the other state is 'prior' but what the relationship between systems and states is. Second, there is the question whether the state, which is not a natural kind, can be likened to a 'body' and thus whether the priority claim makes any sense, and third, the question whether such a biological priority tells us anything interesting about the specific social character of man (aside from his extreme dependence in infancy and thus the need for particular care in early developmental phases).

18 Jens Steffek, communication to the author, 8 February 2000.

relativism and often engenders the charge of nihilism. While a more critical perusal of my argument indicates the unjustifiability of such an inference (as only a dogmatic epistemology and conception of science is called into question) there is clearly some uneasiness in dispensing with notions of secure foundations. Admitting that forgoing such foundational claims might be painful, the more interesting question is what can be done given our predicament.

As I tried to show, there are various attempts to 'fox' these issues, such as recognising the force of the sceptics' criticisms while holding on to the notion of a truth which we approach, but never reach. Similarly, we might claim to dispense with foundationalism while keeping the 'realist' vocabulary and conceptual framework intact. All these gambits are problematic responses to the crisis. As a first step it may be useful to offer some middle position, counteracting the fears both of hopelessness (nihilism) and of arrogance that comes from the alleged possession of 'truth'. As a second step, however, it is necessary to reflect critically on such a middle position and perhaps embark on a different strategy, especially when it becomes clear that the 'middle' course has no particular virtues but many of the disadvantages of the positions it tries to mediate.

I believe that turning away from foundational notions, such as the bivalence or the rationality principles, and interpreting the question of decidability as one of a fair procedure, provides a more honest approach. Here, some ethical principles rather than demonstration and deduction are critical. Basically, this amounts to the recognition that finality and legitimacy of a judgement coincide only in logic. These criteria point to different directions not only in practical matters, but also in science. The problem of fairly allocating the burdens of proof is therefore not as simple as suggested by Lakatos (1970), who distinguished between naïve and sophisticated falsificationism and progressive and degenerate problem shifts. Nevertheless, ethical reflections provide scientists in such situations with some standards. As Paul Diesing, when summarising the debate about 'research programs', points out:

> there is no rule that says that scientists ought to abandon a degenerating research program and shift to a progressive one. Two or three rival programs may develop side by side for a long time, each striving to produce the novel facts that mark it as progressive, and their fortunes might fluctuate several times. The only rule Lakatos suggests is that each program should keep an honest score.
>
> (Diesing 1991: 46)

In this context, Wendt's (1999: 373) rather apodictic statement that scientific study depends on 'publicly available evidence and some possibility of falsification' is trivial. It does not address issues of judgement, of the criteria that govern the weighing of the evidence, or of the discharge of one's responsibility for either sticking to one's (possibly refuted) theory or of abandoning it. The core controversy is usually *not* about evidence at all, as Jervis correctly points out, but rather about assigning strategic burdens of proof.[19] It is the 'default position' that usually invites controversies of a quite different and serious kind than problems of evidence or of the formal adequacy of some model or theory (for an interesting treatment of this problem in law and science, see Gaskins 1992). The emphasis on ethics points precisely to these difficulties. It brings to the fore the silent presuppositions, invites us to reflect critically upon them, and establishes the importance of practical reason and judgement (not only of deduction and theoretical reason). These considerations also provide the strongest possible rationale for pluralism, not as the 'second best' but as the most promising strategy for advancing our knowledge.

Nevertheless, ultimately the loss of foundations is unsettling precisely because foundations promise (however falsely) some security. In this way, we keep our bearing and are assured that our questions will somehow come to a rest. One way of dealing with the loss of the 'metaphysical comfort' is to inquire into the reasons why we felt such comfort in the first place, why certain metaphors such as that of a chain, of a circle, or of a fundament provided such persuasive power, despite the realisation that the hopes built upon them will be disappointed.

Consider in this context the notion of coming nearer to truth while never quite arriving there. Here, the idea of successive polygons used for determining the content of a circle gives some plausibility to this stance. The problem is, however, that in the case of the circle we do have the perimeter given, while the entire problem of scientific knowledge is that there is no way in which we can know its limits. Progress in the latter case consists in being able to ask questions which were not even thinkable before, even while there is no perimeter from which we could determine whether we have come closer to truth. In this respect, the notion of knowledge as a procedure analogous to exhausting the interior of the circle does no longer make much sense.

Furthermore, the metaphor of the circle seems to be a double-edged sword. When we focus on the perimeter instead of the interior, the fear rises that we might get caught in a circle that turns 'vicious'. Consequently, recursivity becomes suspect and the generative capacity of the circle metaphor has to give way to that of a chain, or that of a foundation. Both the chain metaphor and the 'ground' metaphor suggest an absolute 'beginning' (or end), as Aristotle shrewdly observes.[20]

19 As Robert Jervis (1998: 975) suggests, 'we should not adopt the Whiggish stance that the fate of a research program is predominantly determined by the extent to which it produces propositions that anticipate and fit with empirical facts. Programs – and even more, their first cousins paradigms – are notoriously difficult to confirm or disconfirm. Not only do they shape what counts as a fact at all, but there are so many steps between the assumptions and outlooks on the one hand and empirical findings on the other that neither in social nor natural science can the evidence ever be unambiguous.'
20 Aristotle, *Nicomachean Ethics* 1095b31; actually, after Aristotle has discussed his famous chain of goals and has arrived at the notion of a supreme good for which everything else is being done, he then distinguishes the procedure as to inquiring into the nature of this good either by proceeding from the facts to the good or from the good to the facts, like runners 'run either from the judges' stand to the far end or in the reverse direction'.

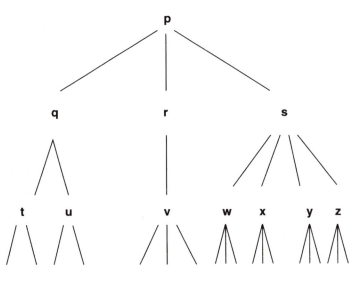

Figure 2.1

Both rely on rudimentary spatial experiences for their suggestive power. The 'ground metaphor' implies that our knowledge is structured like a building, in which the upper echelons receive support from lower ones. To that extent, the image of 'justified belief' (or warranted knowledge) resembles the figure of a pyramid (see Figure 2.1). (For a further discussion of the problems of such a 'foundationalist' account, see Haack 1993: 24.)

At some point, we have to assume some basic beliefs that are justified not by further beliefs but by some immediate perceptions. Unfortunately, this problem led to the downfall of strict empiricism. Besides, without changing the architectural metaphor, we realise that not all beliefs need independent support. As the image of an 'arch' suggests, it is the 'mutual support' of the parts that can carry great weight. While this example shows that independence of beliefs is too demanding a criterion, it is the 'solid ground' or rock bottom, as experienced by gravity, that gives this metaphor its generative power. When, with the change in the view of the world as a disc, such notions as 'above' and 'below' lost their naïve ontological status, the answer to the new insecurities and conceptual puzzlements was the construal of an absolute point of view. In this 'view from nowhere', space became a system of coordinates within which everything could be located.

The metaphor of the 'chain', on the other hand, supports our naïve version of scientific progress as a sequence of discoveries of cause and effect that is somewhere anchored in reality. This image is also well in accordance with some textbook version of the 'path' of science. But, as the physicist John Ziman pointed out, this metaphor is seriously misleading as an account of scientific progress:

> This point is of the greatest importance, since it explains so much of the strange sense of unreality that scientists feel when they read books on the

philosophy of science. It is abundantly obvious that the overall structure of scientific knowledge is of many, many dimensions . . . The initial path to a new discovery may be apparently one-dimensional with no more reliable authority than a simple causal chain. But the strategy of research is to seek alternative routes, from other starting-points, to the same spot until the discovery has been incorporated unequivocally into the scientific map.

(Ziman 1991: 84)

The interesting point of these observations is not only that a new metaphor is proposed, but also the realisation that, by choosing the metaphor of a 'map' rather than that of a circle, or that of a pyramid, the fears engendered by the previous metaphor vanish. In addition, former fears are actually turned into strengths; mutual support is no longer seen as vicious, but *as proof of superiority*!

But even the map might not be the most fruitful metaphor. After all, it presupposes a 'land', pre-given and virtually unchanging, that has to be discovered and mapped. It is, therefore, still beholden to the notion of representation. But if in at least some part of science the aim is not the discovery of something 'pre-existing', as, for example, some experiments in high-energy physics suggest, but an endeavour in which 'the process to be observed has never occurred before in the history of the Universe: God himself is waiting to see what will happen!' (Ziman 1991: 62), then notions of representational accuracy quickly lose their usefulness. Similarly, when we accept the thought that we cannot get in between the 'things' and our description of them, but that, in true constructivist fashion, their 'ontology' depends on the purposes and practices embedded in our concepts, then we no longer need to hold on to the 'thing in itself' as an anchor. We are finally free to address the question of how to go about our inquiries.

Perhaps the metaphor of a game of Scrabble provides then a better image. We begin with a concept that makes certain combinations possible. In criss-crossing we can 'go on', and our additions are justified by the mutual support with other words and concepts. Sometimes, we cannot proceed as our attempts of continuing get stymied. Then we begin somewhere else, and might, by circuitous routes, reach again some known terrain. Potentially there are innumerable moves, and no two games are identical since moves at different times will have different consequences. On the other hand, no move of them is free in the sense that 'anything goes'. But none could have been predicted by the 'view from nowhere'. Without making too much of this metaphor, because like all metaphors it eventually breaks down, I think it captures our predicament in generating knowledge and of the constructivist challenge (for a similar view of constructivism as a metatheoretical commitment, see Guzzini 2000a). To that extent, no new middle ground, no new orthodoxy is needed.

3 Grand Theory in the age of its impossibility

Contemplations on Alexander Wendt

Andreas Behnke

What exactly *is* international politics? As Stefano Guzzini (1998) has demon-strated, this question has haunted the theoretical and meta-theoretical debates of this field of study since its inception. The inability to produce a set of authoritative answers to this question has led to a rather paradoxical situation. On the one hand, international politics has always been a fragmented, diversified, and incoherent endeavour, having ambiguous boundaries with related disciplines in the social sciences and a less than firm idea of what constitutes its proper subject matter. On the other hand, there has always been a desire for, and a fascination with, Grand Theory, with attempts, that is, to overcome the fragmentation and diversity and to turn the field of study into a proper discipline with generally accepted method-ological rules and a firm delineation of International Relations (IR) subject matter. This way, scientific progress and cumulative knowledge could replace the perennial debates between more or less incommensurable positions on how to study international politics. Hans Morgenthau's *Politics Among Nations* (1948), Morton Kaplan's *System and Process in International Politics* (1957), and Kenneth Waltz's *Theory of International Politics* (1979) are arguably the relevant bookmarks in the history of international politics. Yet, while each of these books left its distinctive mark on the intellectual development of the field, each one also, in a sense, failed to establish IR as a discipline. In fact, each book can be said to have contributed to the state of fragmentation and contestation within IR. To take but the last of these *opera magna*, Waltz's attempt to define and delineate international politics in terms of rigid scientific standards and a clear-cut theory of power-balancing served for the longest time as the convenient strawman for the formulation of critical and poststructuralist approaches. If there is anything positive to be said about his *Theory of International Politics*, it has to be this inadvertent contribution to a more meta-theoretically reflexive field of study – and an even deeper chasm between main-stream and critical approaches in the field.

I raise these issues here as I believe that Alexander Wendt's *Social Theory of International Politics* (henceforth, *STIP*) should be understood within this context, as yet another attempt to provide some discipline for an unruly field. The title itself of course is a straightforward indication that this book is meant to be a follow-up to Waltz's *Theory*. Moreover, the methodological and meta-theoretical discussion that occupies the first half of the book operates as an update of neorealism by absorbing

Blaney 1996

some of the critical insights formulated by constructivists, postmodernists, and critical theorists. Yet in the last instance, the basic assumption of neorealism – the definition of international politics as the behaviour of states under the condition of anarchy – remains mostly intact. Wendt's modification of Waltzian neorealism is ultimately a very limited one. 'Anarchy is what states make of it': no causal power can be granted to the absence of supreme authority in the international system (Wendt 1992a). However cleverly phrased, this insight does little to revolutionize the field. As Inayatullah and Blaney (1996) have demonstrated, Wendt's basic theme remains the behaviour of pre-existing states in a social 'state of nature'. Anarchy itself, in other words, is not a social construction but simply the quasi-natural condition under which ontologically given states conduct their business. What Wendt adds to this set-up is the proposition that, in the absence of a structural imperative, states can 'construct' their identities in processes of symbolic interaction. Whether states relate to each other as friends or enemies is decided in these processes. From a meta-theoretical point of view, Wendt's move adds a thin layer of "subjectivist ontology" to the study of international politics, but avoids the more radical hermeneutics suggested by critical and poststructuralist approaches. States are states; politics only starts when they begin to negotiate their outward social identities.

In other words, in terms of its basic assumptions, Wendt's shot at Grand Theory is scarcely different from its predecessor. This of course forces the question of whether it will fare any better in its ambition to provide a disciplinary structure for international politics. After all, Wendt casts his net quite wide. In order to establish a methodological regime, he even includes 'postmodernism' as a source of potential insights into the study of international politics, which raises the expectation that his version of Grand Theory can avoid the excessive rigidity that characterized the previous attempt by Waltz.

If the response of the field so far is anything to go by, it would seem that *STIP* is destined for the same fate as its predecessors. There is on the one hand the expressed desire and appreciation for a Grand Narrative. *STIP* was the topic of a special Roundtable at the 2000 ISA Convention in Los Angeles and the publication of a special 'Forum on Alexander Wendt' in the *Review of International Studies* (and, for that matter, a special seminar in the Political Science Department at Stockholm University). Whatever the immediate purpose of these academic rituals, they served to establish the book as a new point of reference, a work towards which the field has to orient itself. Representatives of both the 'rationalist' and the 'reflectivist' camp were invited to comment on the book, thus confirming its claim to a theoretical scope that transcends these boundaries – Grand Theory indeed, with its appeal to disciplinary coherence, unity, and identity.

Yet at the same time, and despite coming from very different backgrounds, the reviews seem to agree on one central point: that, as an attempt to offer an authoritative disciplinary guidebook to IR, *STIP* is a failure. Its conceptualizations and definitions are confusing and contradictory (Doty 2000), its basic assumptions about international politics misguided (Krasner 2000), its meta-theoretical discussion misleading and contradictory (Smith 2000; Doty 2000), its ambition old-fashioned and out of sync with recent developments (Kratochwil, chap. 2 this volume), and the theoretical and substantial questions it raises perhaps simply irrelevant (Alker 2000; Keohane 2000). The celebratory gestures made towards the book and its author are, it must be said, not in keeping with the extremely critical substantial comments and objections of the respective reviews. If anything, it seems that the responses so far re-emphasize the differences between the camps rather than accept *STIP*'s claim to disciplinary unity. For virtually all the reviewers, *STIP* provides a convenient backdrop against which they once again assert the distinctiveness of their preferred meta-theoretical commitments, rather than an opportunity to establish common ground.

The reception of the book therefore indicates that the goal of establishing *STIP* as the Grand Theory for international politics will not be accomplished. This point deserves further elaboration, as I consider this failure to be embedded in the very structure of the book, rather than the outcome of individual scholars' preferences. There are, I would argue at least three 'impossibilities' within *STIP*:

- the impossibility of reconciling constructivism and 'science';
- the impossibility of assuming the position of detached meta-theoretical arbiter;
- the impossibility of formulating a substantive Grand Theory of international politics in the age of globalization.

I will deal with these three issues in turn.

Constructivism as science?

How can we study the art of diplomacy and international politics in a scientific fashion without being distracted by idealistic dreams and metaphysical contemplations? Any Grand Theory of IR provides its answer to this perennial question. For Morgenthau, the answer rested in the fundamental truths of human nature. For Waltz, the distinctive structural features of the international system defined the positive reality about which IR has to accumulate knowledge. For Wendt, the reality of international politics is defined as the social construction of the international system via social structures in which ideas and symbolic interactions define the way states relate to each other.

Perhaps the most relevant comment on Wendt's attempt to render social constructivism commensurable with a commitment to a unitary notion of science, based on epistemic realism, was written three years before *STIP* was published. Erik Ringmar pointed out, in the first comprehensive assessment of Wendt's work, that Wendt might be a constructivist, albeit 'a highly reluctant one, and curiously enough the constructivism which he defends takes the form of a *substantive* theory of international politics and not the form of a philosophical argument' (1997: 282). In other words, Wendt reduces constructivism to an argument about the significance of ideas for the conduct of international politics, yet avoids the epistemological critique that is immanent in this perspective. This tension, as Steve Smith's (2000) review argues in detail, persists in *STIP*. According to Wendt, representational constructions and ideas are the stuff that matters to states and, based on different configurations, states behave differently towards each other. Yet states themselves and the world around us also contain material realities, knowable and accessible to our minds without the mediation of 'ideas' and representational constructions.' After all, cats are cats, dogs are dogs, and pigs can't fly, no matter what our ideas about them are (Wendt 1999: 49–56). Yet despite this call to arms for common sense, Wendt remains unable to establish the relationship between the material and the ideational realm of reality. This is the gist of Smith's critique (Smith 2000: 153–6), to which I have little to add, except that in a sense the question about the relationship between the material and the ideational is a phoney one, as it avoids the more significant matter of the condition of possibility for distinguishing between material and ideational stuff in the first place. In order to make that distinction, both ideas and material matter must be objects independently available for the researcher to assess and evaluate in a detached fashion. In Wendt's version, constructivism is thus reduced to a contribution to the subject matter of IR – ideas matter too (Ringmar 1997: 282). Yet constructivism in its various expressions is usually offered as a philosophical critique of knowledge (Berger and Luckmann 1991 [1966]; Schmidt 1987). And, *pace* Wendt, it usually denies the possibility of establishing firm grounds within ontology (e.g., Berger and Luckmann 1991 [1966]: 67). From such a perspective, the role of representations and ideas cannot be limited to the impact they have on states' behaviour. As a philosophical critique, constructivism applies also to the status of scientific knowledge itself. In other words, constructivism shows Wendt's own theory to be but another narrative, another construction of reality, and no claim to scientific standards and respectability can deflect this critique (Wendt 2000: 165). The constant reference to these standards is necessarily a mere ritual, their relation to epistemic (or scientific) realism simply reiterated and never fully explored. As soon as the full implications of constructivism are acknowledged, Wendt's attempt to render constructivism as 'science' becomes an impossibility.

Arbitration or adaptation?

Authors of Grand Theory assume a rather peculiar position. Positioning themselves above the fray of contending schools of thought, approaches, and methods, they arrogate to themselves the ability to decide upon the respective merits and limitations of these fragments that have yet to be integrated into a proper discipline. Their own contributions therefore have a tendency to intimate the absence of any problematic metaphysical assumptions. Any such acknowledgement would in turn bring their theories back into the fray of philosophical dispute and methodological contestation. This, of course, is what happened to all the previous attempts at Grand Theory, as they provide rewarding targets to demonstrate the inevitability of meta-theoretical commitments.

Wendt's position as the author of *STIP* is based on the arrogation of the role of arbiter between contending meta-theoretical claims that have developed in the wake of Waltz's *Theory of International Politics*. For Wendt the question is which of these fragments of a discipline can be fitted together and which can be discarded as falling outside the disciplinary boundaries. In other words, to what extent can the contending schools be reconciled under the theoretical roof offered by his Grand Theory, and where does his razor need to cut off excessive realist rigidity and exaggerated epistemological scepticism? To tackle this question, Wendt has to introduce a number of ultimately problematic assumptions. Firstly, his position as arbiter assumes, or rather stipulates, the commensurability between different and often explicitly contentious approaches. In *STIP*, much of this debate is structured in terms of 'realism' versus 'postmodernism'. In order to bridge the schism between these approaches, Wendt basically offers two arguments: postmodernists are positivists too (1999: 67; 2000: 173), and (as discussed above) social constructions are susceptible to positivist research. I dealt with the latter argument in the previous section; the former deserves a brief discussion. Wendt's argument here is that 'postmodern' scholars such as David Campbell and Roxanne Doty also base their work on evidence and work by 'amassing data and developing the best narrative [they] can to make sense of them' (Wendt 2000: 173). While I have to admit that I cannot quite make out what the logic of Wendt's argument is here, the gist of it seems to revolve around the fact that 'postmodernists' too collect data for their research. Now if this is meant to prove that 'postmodernists' face certain tasks, such as providing evidence for their conclusions and answering questions of representativeness and reliability in their analyses (albeit in a different fashion than positivists would), this should not come as much of a surprise. Critical discourse analysis is after all an empirical approach (Milliken 1999). Where 'postmodernists' differ from 'positivists' of course is in the treatment and analysis of the material they gather. For the latter, empirical material contains data and information about reality 'out there' which can be extracted via proper operationalization and careful analysis. In other words, textual 'data' for positivists is always indicative of something else, namely a reality of which it tells us. For 'postmodernists', however, textual data is that very reality, in the sense that discourses, narratives, and other structures of signification are textual phenomena as such. Texts are therefore not indicative of a reality beyond themselves; they are productive of that reality. To amass large amounts of data is therefore a way not to gather reliable knowledge about reality, but to prove the reiterative and repetitive nature of discursive representations in order to establish their dominant character.

Wendt's interpretation of 'postmodern' research methodology in terms of its positivist counterpart here is characteristic of an overall problem in his argument about the commensurability of contending schools. Based on their stipulated compatibility, the opposing approaches are strung out as dichotomies, ostensibly rendering their different assumptions and substantive commitments a matter of respective degree. *STIP* is indeed full of such dichotomies: ontology versus epistemology, materialism versus idealism, agency versus structure, holism versus individualism, micro-structures versus macro- structures, internal versus external, constitution versus causation, corporate identity versus social identity, and, as discussed above, 'realism' or 'mainstream IR' versus 'postmodernism'. Everything matters. The question Wendt has to arbitrate is: how much?

Yet on close inspection Wendt's answers to these questions are anything but 'empirical' decisions (Wendt 2000: 166). In fact, Wendt consistently privileges one pole of the theoretical dichotomies over the other, assessing the contribution of the latter always in terms of the former. Much of the content of Wendt's decisions is therefore already given on the pre-empirical, meta-theoretical level. Ontology dominates over epistemology, as the pre-social identity of cats, dogs, states, and human beings is simply stated to be unproblematic. Materialism is privileged over idealism, as the former defines the 'rump' of states, their identity and interests, rendering the latter an addendum, useful, but not critical for the explanation of states' behaviour. In fact, in times of crisis, ideas are useless at best, and misleading at worst, as Montezuma and the Polish cavalry of the Second World War had to experience (Wendt 1999: 56; 2000: 166–7). 'Internal' precedes 'external': states are constituted or constructed predominantly 'internally' via certain essential properties, with the states system relegated to a secondary role, as it does not contain the same density of institutional and normative structures that we find inside the state. Moreover, the system is itself only secondary to its units. 'There cannot be a states system without states any more than there can be a (human) society without people. The units make their respective systems possible' (Wendt 1999: 194). Finally, 'realism' provides the rendition of 'postmodernism' in terms of its useful contribution of the role of ideas to international politics and its useless epistemological scepticism that unduly limits the scientific nature of international politics.

None of these decisions is a stable one. Each deconstructs itself as soon as we let the inferior position play out its logic, thus making Wendt's position as the arbiter of IR an impossible one. The possibility of distinguishing between material and ideational matter becomes problematic once we realize that this very distinction is an 'idea' itself. We might add to the instability of this decision by pointing out that any definition of the 'material' identity of entities is very much contextual and therefore based on social conventions (Kratochwil, chap. 2 this volume, pp. 41–2). For genetic engineers, 'man' might very well be a self-organizing genetic structure. For a political scientist, for an artist, or for an aeronautical engineer, such a description would be irrelevant.

To argue that states are (mostly) constructed or constituted internally and that the international system plays only a secondary role builds in itself on a problematic anthropomorphization. But the argument is even more peculiar than that. It reveals itself to be virtually nonsensical when we ask about the condition of possibility for differentiating between the internal and external, domestic and systemic construction of the state. In order for this to be possible, the boundary between the domestic and the international obviously already has to be in place. The problem is that this boundary is only drawn in the production of the state itself. Domestic, after all, is what is going on within a state, and the international realm is the one beyond states' borders. Thus the argument about the internal constitution of states assumes, before the state is constructed, what only the state itself can construct. This, of course, also undermines Wendt's peculiar distinction between internal and external sovereignty (Wendt 1999: 206–9). Again, these realms are produced through the recognition of sovereign statehood and cannot therefore precede it.

Finally, Wendt's rejection of 'radical' constructivists and 'postmodernists' and their insistence on the ultimate 'deconstructibility' of statehood (rendered in Wendt's version as 'ideas all the way down') produces a peculiar tension between his normative commitment to the state as the preferred political institution and a research agenda which cannot address the changing historical forms of statehood. We might very well agree with Wendt that the state is 'the dominant form of subjectivity in contemporary world politics' (1999: 9). Furthermore, there may be good reason to prefer states over other actors in world politics, as the former are 'the only democratically-accountable institutions we have today to provide security and political order' (2000: 174). The point here is not to quibble with the empirical correctness of this statement, although it seems to be a somewhat problematic generalization, given the recent experiences in, for instance, the Balkans, Africa, and Indonesia. The point is rather to pose the question about the ability of the state to fulfil all these functions under the significantly changing conditions in contemporary world politics. Given the recent discussions about globalization and internationalization, these questions take on a particular salience if we are to understand how statehood is to be accomplished or 'performed' under these novel circumstances. This is not to say that statehood was ever an unproblematic given. As Istvan Hont (1994) pointed out some time ago, the modern nation-state has always been 'in a crisis' and its persistence therefore needs to be understood as a political accomplishment. One does not necessarily have to be a radical constructivist or poststructuralist to acknowledge this insight. Yet within the field of IR it appears that these approaches have done the most to highlight and analyse the social and political processes through which states are enacted and reproduced under different historical conditions (e.g., Campbell 1998; Weber 1998). The problem is therefore not to avoid any confusion between states and football teams (Wendt 1999: 70), but to be able to analyse the political and social processes through which states can maintain or modify their institutional structure. Simply to assume the existence of states is therefore anything but an unproblematic, pre-theoretical ground from which to judge alternative approaches.[1]

The point here is not to criticize Wendt for basing his own theoretical framework on a number of ontological and methodological assumptions. This is simply unavoidable. What is problematic, however, is his attempt to assess and judge alternative approaches as if his framework would provide him with a neutral ground. The result is, as many of his reviewers noted, the necessary misrepresentation of these alternative approaches, be they 'rationalist' or 'postmodern'.

---

1 Wendt's counter-argument that *STIP* is concerned not with the construction of states but with the construction of the state system (2000: 174) is of course not a way out of his conundrum. States cannot meaningfully be conceived of as ontologically preceding the state system. Hence the production of states and the state system are two sides of the same coin.

Thick book – thin theory?

The question that still deserves some reflection is then what *STIP* actually contributes to our understanding of world politics. Most of the reviewers so far, while providing very detailed engagements with the meta-theoretical arguments, have astonishingly little to say on this aspect of the book. One exception is Hayward Alker, who articulates the suspicion that *STIP* might not be all there is to the study of global politics. In those parts of the world where international politics is experienced in a very different fashion from the point of view of the Anglo-American world, *STIP* might offer very little in the way of an adequate understanding of its political dynamics (Alker 2000: 149–50). I would agree with Alker's observation, except that I find it difficult to see why the substantive limitations of *STIP* should not also produce a problem in comprehending politics of the Anglo-Saxon world.

Allow me to respond to Wendt's caricature of 'postmodernism' in kind by offering a caricature of the substantive theory he offers in *STIP*. At the end of the day, the critical question in contemporary global politics is whether states hate each other, respect each other, or really, really like each other. Cooperation and conflict are to be explained by the anthropomorphized 'state of mind' of states, which, as Wendt asserts, 'are people too' (1999: 194). Suffice it to say that there are significant issues of conflict and cooperation in contemporary global politics that do not lend themselves easily to this exceedingly restrictive model. As for conflict, let us start with the observation that, according to the *SIPRI Yearbook 2000*, only two out of twenty-seven major armed conflicts in 1999 were still interstate wars. The rest of these conflicts took place within states. We might then point to Mary Kaldor's (1999) recent analysis of new forms of political violence, in which she aptly demonstrates that the traditional monopoly and control over the use of force and the conduct of war is moving away from the state level through simultaneous processes of localization and globalization. Armed conflict, her case study suggests, now cuts across the (state) boundaries that traditionally defined the structure of war in the international system. Whether states hate or respect each other seems to offer little explanation for this development.

As for international cooperation, it seems fair to say that, for instance, the creation of supranational structures of governance within the European Union cannot be reduced to the question of whether states are sufficiently fond of each other to subject parts of their sovereign prerogatives to such structures. Questions of legitimacy, democracy, and authority arise exactly at the point where Wendt's statist model ceases to offer any analytical and conceptual grip. At stake is precisely what form of political organization and authority can be institutionalized in response to transformations in the international capitalist economy. To forego the answer by once again pointing as a matter of fact to the state and to reduce the complex economic and political dynamics in this process to states' 'frame of mind' is therefore hardly a satisfactory response.

No conclusions

To briefly summarize the above argument, *STIP*, as the latest attempt at defining and disciplining international politics, is a failure. Firstly, it cannot reconcile constructivism with a (rather old-fashioned) commitment to 'science'. Secondly, its assessments of contending theories and approaches rest on particular, yet in this context unaddressed, meta-theoretical commitments which produce a biased and often misleading representation. Thirdly, for all its meta-theoretical and philosophical elaborations, *STIP* provides disappointingly little in the way of understanding world politics in late modern times.

The fact that globalization and internationalization have significantly changed the logic and structure of global politics is today a matter found in IR textbooks and 'Introduction to IR' courses (Baylis and Smith 1998). That these developments might render it difficult or indeed impossible to formulate a Grand Theory in international politics seems to be an insight that is not as easily accepted. Yet, as the boundaries between inside and outside, state and non-state, private and public, domestic and international are becoming increasingly difficult to draw through facile gestures, Grand Theory, because of its reliance on such clear-cut boundaries, finds the conditions of its own possibility evaporating.

The continued fascination and preoccupation with Grand Theory in the field of IR is a peculiar anachronism. It remains committed to the ideal of a disciplinary unity that in fact no longer finds any correspondence in the subject matter of which it claims knowledge. Alexander Wendt's *Social Theory of International Politics* is ample testimony in this case, as it demonstrates the price to be paid for formulating Grand Theory. As I have tried to argue, from both a methodological and a substantive point of view, *STIP* produces inconsistencies and contradictions that create the conditions of its own impossibility.

It would therefore be counterproductive once again to give in to the temptation of grand theoretical edifices that rest on clay feet, even if it is by way of a critique. As Roland Bleiker argues, by 'articulating critique in relation to arguments advanced by orthodox IR theory, the impact of critical voices remains confined within the larger discursive boundaries that were established through the initial framing of debates' (1997: 58). (There is of course some irony in the fact that I concur with this argument at the end of a critique of Wendt.) If we instead understand and accept that the intellectual and academic strength of IR lies in its diversity and plurality of perspectives and approaches, precisely because this plurality and diversity is in a sense a reflection of an increasingly multifaceted subject matter called 'world politics', the anachronistic nature of Grand Theory might sink in a bit faster. For Bleiker, the alternative to the desire for Grand Theory is made possible by a Nietzschean *Vergessen* of IR theory – not as a self-inflicted case of collective amnesia, but as a productive process through which new 'thinking spaces' are no longer confined or closed off by the need for ritualized deference to books such as *STIP*. In this sense: forget Wendt.

4 Wendt, IR, and philosophy
A critique[*]

Hidemi Suganami

Introduction

Alexander Wendt's *Social Theory of International Politics* has been discussed widely. Its reception ranges from wildly enthusiastic (Alker 2000) to intensely negative (Behnke, chap. 3 this volume). Some reviews are well researched (e.g., Zehfuss, chap. 6 this volume), erudite (e.g., Kratochwil, chap. 2 this volume), and thought-provoking (e.g., Campbell 2001); others are not quite so well executed.[1] None of the existing works, however, subjects to a close philosophical scrutiny the precise internal logic of Wendt's extensive argumentation regarding his work's location in the field – in particular, how it relates to, and differs from, the American 'rationalist' orthodoxy in IR, comprising neorealism and neoliberalism. The purpose of this chapter is to fill this gap.

In the following, I concede that Wendt's empirical hypotheses regarding collective identity formation are sufficiently plausible in their own right to warrant historical case studies by those who wish to explore such an avenue, and will also help us speculate on the transformative potentials of the contemporary international system. I argue, however, that his philosophical argumentation, by means of which he tries to demonstrate his work's distinct location within the American IR orthodoxy, but away from its individualist core, is unpersuasive. First, I wish to outline the substantive contention of his book.

Wendt on collective identity formation

Stripped to its core, Wendt's view is that there is no such thing as *the* logic of anarchy; that how states interact with each other depends on what kind of international political culture they live under; that, broadly speaking, there are three such cultures, Hobbesian, Lockean, and Kantian; and that each culture defines for the states what their social identity or role should be – so that they are 'enemies', 'rivals', or 'friends', respectively. Where the existing international culture is deeply

---

* This is based on Suganami (2002). I am grateful to Cambridge University Press for permitting me to publish a revised version.
1 Smith (2000) and Palan (2000) were also helpful for my purpose.

internalised by the states, it will be difficult, though not impossible, for them to alter their identities. This happens, according to Wendt, along a symbolic interactionist path, in which states under anarchy not only learn to cooperate in spite of the free rider problem, but, in so doing, also alter their conceptions of Self and Other in the direction of developing a collective identity. Wendt dedicates an entire chapter (Wendt 1999: 313–69) to spelling out the details of how this may occur, which I summarise below.

In the beginning, according to Wendt, when states first form a system, they do so in a context free of institutional constraints, and this tends to make states that adopt aggressive, egoistic identities prosper at the expense of those which are more other-regarding. Because there is nothing to prevent it, the system would be dragged down to the level of the most self-interested. This process of selection is reinforced by that of learning: an egoistic and manipulative stance adopted by a state towards another is likely to be reciprocated. As hostile interactions continue and come to prevail within the system, enmity comes to be treated as the name of the game, an attribute of the system itself rather than of particular states (Wendt 1999: 264). This is how an international system comes to acquire the Hobbesian culture.

Wendt's story so far is a hypothetical one – about what would happen if states encountered one another in a quasi-state of nature – and he does not have in mind any particular historical period or case to explain, though he would welcome having his hypothesis tested against history (Wendt 1999: 82). He does not, however, complete his hypothetical picture by giving an account of how an international system may move from the Hobbesian culture of enmity to the Lockean one of rivalry. Instead, he explores how the Lockean culture might be transformed into the Kantian one of friendship, suggesting that this is the problem faced by the international system *today*, because '[w]hether or not international politics has been Hobbesian for most of history, states managed to escape that culture *some years ago*' (ibid.: 339, emphasis mine; cf. Wendt 2003). However, Wendt's exploration of the paths from the Lockean to the Kantian culture turns out also to be a hypothetical one, pointing to a few factors which may contribute to bringing about such a transformation, and not aimed at explaining any specific case of transition.

In his discussion, Wendt notes three familiar factors which would, under appropriate conditions, contribute to the process of transformation from a more individualistic culture to a culture of collectivity. These are what he calls 'three master variables' – interdependence, common fate, and homogeneity. They are presented by Wendt, not simply as factors contributing to cooperative behaviour, but more specifically as factors which help reshape the identity or role of states from 'rival' to 'friend'.

Interdependence would help cultivate collective identity, especially if 'someone had the bright idea of portraying the situation as one of interdependence' (Wendt 1999: 347). Then a discourse may begin about what 'we' should do. Wendt adds that collective identity is more likely to result from interdependence where interaction between states is more dense, leading to the formation of '"core areas," around which concentric circles of identification might then develop' (ibid.:

347–8). He acknowledges that interdependence would not lead to cooperation where the fear of exploitation is pronounced, but suggests that in the Lockean culture such a fear would be less serious than in the Hobbesian one, making it more likely for interdependence to contribute to the creation of a cooperative scheme. Where a fear of exploitation is not very intense, common fate, too, is said by Wendt to contribute to the emergence of a 'We who should work together' (ibid.: 352), although he adds that, where the threat is not so acute, the emergence of perceptions of common fate may depend on much ideological labor by '"entrepreneurs" and/or "epistemic community" who take the lead in reframing how actors understand themselves' (ibid.: 352–3). As for homogeneity, or mutual alikeness, Wendt rightly acknowledges a number of reasons why it is not by itself sufficient to produce prosocial behaviour, but suggests that it may contribute to increasing the ability of Self and Other to see themselves as members of the same group. Where, prompted by these three master variables, cooperation and collective identity begin to prevail in the interactions of states within a system, a tipping point will again be reached, and friendship, as opposed to rivalry, will come to be seen as the attribute of the system itself. This is how the system comes to live under the Kantian culture.

But none of this would happen, Wendt acknowledges, if states could not trust that a prosocial behaviour would be reciprocated by others. How do states come to know that other states would be self-restraining? Here Wendt suggests three plausible scenarios. First, through repeated compliance with the norms enjoining the peaceful settlement of international disputes, states gradually internalise the institution of the pluralistic security community. By observing each other's habitual compliance, states gradually learn that others can be trusted. Second, some states – democratic states in particular – are strongly predisposed to settle their disputes with each other by peaceful means. This only needs to be appreciated among such states for them to realise that they would be self-restraining. Third, a state may reach a moment of reflexivity, in which it is realised that other states' hostility towards it is to some extent because of its own hostile attitude towards them. If, as a result, the state in question unilaterally resorts to policies of self-binding or sacrificing, as did the Soviet Union under Gorbachev's 'new thinking', then it might succeed in signalling to the others that it could be trusted.

Wendt realises that '[i]n most situations the best that can be expected is concentric circles of identification, where actors identify to varying degrees with others depending on who they are and what is at stake, while trying to meet their individual needs as well' (Wendt 1999: 364). Still, he believes that, while such a progressive transformation is not inevitable, it is likely in fact to be irreversible – barring severe 'exogenous shocks' (ibid.: 312). This is because, Wendt believes, '[w]ith each "higher" international culture states *acquire* rights – to sovereignty in the Lockean case, freedom from violence and security assistance in the Kantian – that they will be loathe [*sic*] to give up, whatever institutions they may create in the future' (*ibid.*).

What Wendt has here is a set of causal hypothetical sketches of collective identity formation in interstate relations. His substantive contribution is to have enabled us to conjecture a number of possible scenarios, based on various combinations and permutations of these sketches, of the process through which the dominant international political culture, states' conception of themselves, and their behaviours all become increasingly less egoistic. It is not my purpose to engage in empirical testing of Wendt's substantive hypotheses. Suffice it to express my appreciation here that they point to some plausible transformative potentials of the contemporary international system and help undermine neorealism's immutability thesis (see Linklater 1996); and further that Wendt's approach, based on structurationism and symbolic interactionism, offers a somewhat more comprehensive picture of the 'evolution of cooperation' than the well-known Axelrod (1984) version.

I am troubled by the fact that a few key features of contemporary world politics which will have some bearing on the growth of international cooperation – the inequalities of power among nations, the presence of a variety of agents in world politics, and the multiplicity of identities that they may claim or acquire in constituting themselves as agents – are absent or largely absent from Wendt's considerations (see Suganami 2001). It is not my aim here, however, to try to formulate more plausible empirical hypotheses than those contained in his work. My focus is to expound and criticise the very complex philosophical argumentation by means of which Wendt tries to carve out for himself a distinct territory within the contemporary disciplinary boundaries of International Relations. This is not an insubstantial critique of Wendt's book inasmuch as about a half of the volume is dedicated to a detailed attempt to locate itself in relation to the existing approaches.

Very simply put, his contention in this respect is that, like neorealists and neoliberals, he is on the side of science, but that, unlike them, he is not an individualist. In connection with the first part of this contention, he expresses his allegiance to scientific realism, which, as I shall try to argue in the next section, is redundant – at least for his main purpose of demonstrating the reality of the state. In connection with the second part, he invokes the distinction, which he does not in fact explicate well, between causal and constitutive relationships, on the basis of which, as I shall explain in the subsequent section, he mistakenly thinks he can demonstrate the fundamental inadequacy of the individualist ontology presupposed in neorealism and neoliberalism. There follows a brief section in which I argue that, because of his own concession to the individualist ontology, the difference between his position and the other two he is criticizing is only a matter of degree.

Scientific realism and the ontological status of the state

Concerning those entities, such as subatomic particles, which are not observable directly by our senses but which scientists invoke to explain physical phenomena, there are, Wendt explains, two standard positions to which philosophers of science subscribe: empiricism and scientific realism. Because these entities cannot be observed directly, empiricists do not accept that they can be said to exist. By contrast, scientific realists, according to Wendt's understanding, argue that it is reasonable to infer the existence of these entities as the cause of certain observable effects, given that the theory invoking their existence, independently of our knowledge-claims about them, is our best satisfactory explanation for those effects. If every unobservable thing invoked in scientific theory were nothing but a fiction, scientific realists say, the success of science would be an unintelligible miracle (see Wendt 1999: 47–91). Wendt calls this 'the Ultimate Argument', which, for him, is a strong enough ground to make one subscribe to scientific realism (ibid.: 64–7). In addition, Wendt rejects the covering-law model of scientific explanation in favour of the view that scientific explanation consists in presenting a plausible causal mechanism underlying the phenomenon in question (ibid.: 81–2). This view is also associated with, or treated as an aspect of, scientific realism.

I do not subscribe to empiricism, in Wendt's version, because I consider that reducing the criterion of existence solely to direct observability is silly. It unduly narrows the range of things that can legitimately be said *to exist*: I see no good reason why the verb '*to exist*' cannot be extended to cover a host of other things – 'the English language', 'the proof of Fermat's last theorem', 'the UN', just to list a few candidates as they come to mind. In any case, the idea of *direct observability*, which underlies empiricism, is itself problematic. And, I accept, there is a challenging problem of how to explain the success of science for which scientific realism offers a solution (see Newton-Smith 1990). Furthermore, like Wendt, I, too, reject the covering-law model of scientific explanation and consider that scientific explanation consists in presenting a plausible causal mechanism underlying the phenomenon in question.[2]

There are, however, two points at which my position diverges from Wendt's. One concerns the way he defends scientific realism, which I do not find entirely persuasive; the other relates to the use he makes of the doctrine in defending the belief in the reality of the state, which I find unnecessary. Below, I shall elaborate these two criticisms in turn.

As was noted, Wendt subscribes to scientific realism on the strength of what he calls the Ultimate Argument. According to this, it is reasonable to infer the existence of unobservable entities as the cause of certain observable effects, given that the theory invoking their existence, independently of our knowledge-claims about them, is our best satisfactory explanation of those effects. If every unobservable thing invoked in scientific theory were nothing but a fiction, it is argued, the success of science would be an unintelligible miracle.

In my, admittedly rather limited, understanding, science is a process of redescribing nature in such a way that myriads of what might otherwise be seen as

---

2 I should add here that by 'causal mechanisms' I have in mind generative potentialities which, if we wish to make sense of what happens in the world, it would seem reasonable to suppose are embedded in it. Or, to put it in the way I most prefer, if we want to make sense of the world as we experience it, it is reasonable to subscribe to the conception of 'the world' according to which 'potentialities', though we do not experience them unless they are realised, are components of it.

unintelligible miracles are increasingly (a) found not to have been miraculous after all (because science reveals them to have been governed by the laws of nature) and (b) rendered less and less unintelligible (because science gives an 'intelligibilifying' representation of what underlies the regular sequences of events governed by the laws of nature) (see Harré 1985). In this process, science has invoked and given descriptions of many kinds of entities which are not 'directly observable' by us. In my understanding, these entities are meant (in the practice of science) to be present in the world, and the descriptions of these entities are intended (in the practice of science) to be descriptions of the relevant aspects of the world as it is. But there exists a gap between (1) acknowledging this, as I do, and (2) asserting, as does Wendt, that it is reasonable to assume the presence of such entities in the world on the ground that their presence is assumed in the currently best scientific explanation. I do not in fact understand why it is necessary to go beyond simply acknowledging that a particular entity, under certain descriptions, is invoked in the currently best scientific explanation, and simply leave it at that. After all, an entity which scientists invoke in their currently best explanation of nature may be rejected by science at some future point. And this is how I find Wendt's defence of scientific realism not entirely convincing (though I must add I am not an empiricist as defined by Wendt).

Moving on to my second criticism, I find it very hard to grasp why it is necessary to invoke the (to me less than entirely problem-free) doctrine of scientific realism to justify a perfectly (and to me quite independently) sensible view that states, though unobservable by our senses, are really existent. Yet this is the line Wendt follows when he argues for the reality of the state. The following passage should be read carefully:

> If on June 21, 1941 we had attributed to 'the German state' the intention to invade the Soviet Union the next day, we would have correctly predicted the behavior of millions of individuals on the 22nd. Without that attribution it would have been difficult, even impossible, to predict and make sense of what was going on. The challenge for nominalists [or those who reject scientific realism] is to explain why this is the case. If the concept of state agency is merely a useful fiction, *why* is it so useful as to seem almost indispensable? The realist has a ready answer: because it refers to a real but unobservable structure. Drawing on the Ultimate Argument for the reality of unobservables discussed in chapter 2, the realist could argue that it would be a 'miracle' if a concept that predicted observable behaviour so well did not refer to something real. Like quarks, capitalism, and preferences, we know that states are real because their structure generates a pattern of observable effects, as anyone who denies their reality will quickly find out. If John refuses to pay taxes on the grounds that the US state is merely a fiction, then he is likely to experience consequences just as real as he does when he stubs his toe on a table. The reasoning here is abductive: positing a structure that is capable of intentional action is 'an inference to the best explanation' for the patterns of behaviour that we observe. In the realist view, any system, whether biological or

corporate, whose behaviour can be predicted in this way counts as an intentional agent.

(Wendt 1999: 216, reference omitted)

There are a few problems here. First, Wendt conflates the question of whether the state, though unobservable, is none the less *real*, and that of whether the state, though seemingly different from a real person, is *really an intentional agent*. Second, regarding the latter question, the hypothetical case that he uses to demonstrate the inadequacy of nominalism is not a relevant test for nominalism as such. Third, and most importantly, Wendt does not in any event need to invoke scientific realism to argue his case that states can and do cause things. Of these, the first needs only to be noted, and so let me focus on the other two.

Regarding whether the state is really an intentional agent, I consider nominalism to be correct; my view is that the idea of a state as an intentional agent is at best a useful fiction. Why this fiction can ever be 'so useful as to seem almost indispensable' is simply that, in those cases where the fiction appears so useful, the states concerned are highly effective. Of course, not all states are as effective as was Nazi Germany at a moment of its highest effectiveness, when Hitler's decision to invade another country was being implemented, as in Wendt's example. Clearly, however, the US state is effective enough in collecting taxes, and in a number of other areas, to make John, in Wendt's example, suffer the consequences of his non-payment. In the circumstances, refusing to pay taxes on the ground that the US state is merely a fiction would make John not just a nominalist, but a foolish one. And, importantly, it is for his foolishness, and not for nominalism, that he is punished – for if he had been a sufficiently prudent nominalist, he would have noted the usefulness of going along with the fiction that the United States, like a real person, was an intentional agent, and would have paid his taxes. Wendt's example of John therefore constitutes a test of prudence, not of nominalism as such.

But Wendt would retort: 'How could a state, an effective one, get its effectiveness if its status as an intentional agent, as you say, were a mere fiction? Though unobservable, it must surely be real to the extent that it is effective (or causative).' This should not have troubled him at all, however. What cannot go unnoticed in this context is that Wendt's own concept of causation allows him to say that '[n]orms are causal insofar as they regulate behavior' and '[r]easons are causes to the extent that they provide motivation and energy for action' (1999: 82). Clearly, neither 'norms' nor 'reasons' are the sorts of things that Wendt would wish to call observable structures. So, according to Wendt's own idea of causation, unobservables can and do cause. If so, he should have no difficulty in saying that the state can and does cause, and he should be able to do this without a complex detour into the realist philosophy of natural science.

Now, the most important thing to notice about 'the ontological status of the state' (Ringmar 1996) is that the state belongs to the realm of institutional facts, and, as with any social institution, the existence of any particular state is necessarily a historical one. Grounded in historically continuous collective consciousness, a state (an effective one) presents itself as a historical, societal, given – or reality – to all individual persons, inside and outside the state, even though it would be true to say that the state would not exist, or continue to do so, if no individual ever held seriously the belief that it existed (see Searle 1995). What is striking about Wendt's discussion of this subject is that he appears to accept all these propositions (Wendt 1999: 24, 215–21), yet he is much exercised about the supposedly metaphysical nature of the idea that unobservable structures can have effects.

My argument against Wendt here would fail if it were the case that, without subscribing to scientific realism as explained and defended by him, we could not say that norms could be causal or that reasons could be causes. It would also obviously fail if it were the case that, without committing ourselves to scientific realism as explained and defended by him, we could not say that the state existed or affected our lives. I fail to see how either could be the case. I therefore conclude: Wendt's invocation of scientific realism is unnecessary in the context of discussing the real existence of the state; *all that he needs to do here is to point to the causal potentials of collectively held ideas*; and to this the discussion of the reasonableness or otherwise of the belief in the knowledge-independent existence of quarks, which is Wendt's example, is irrelevant.[3] I should add that this conclusion does not presuppose my having been right in my criticism of Wendt's defence of scientific realism.

Causation, constitution, individualism, and holism

One does not have to uphold the philosophical doctrine of scientific realism to believe that international relations should be studied scientifically. But Wendt professes to do the latter (Wendt 1999: 39), and his subscription to scientific realism can be seen as part and parcel of this scientific orientation on his part. Wendt's scientific orientation itself requires some explanation in that, as I argued elsewhere, he could have been a historian of collective identity formation – that is, if he were genuinely interested in the processes of collective identity formation as such. I say this because what he offers in his book in substance is a set of hypothetical narrative sketches that pay attention to all the key ingredients of standard historical

---

3 Smith (2000: 163) rightly remarks that Wendt's scientific realism 'seems largely to drop out in the second half of the book when he analyses international politics, where symbolic interactionism underlies the argument.' In his comments on an earlier draft of this chapter, Wendt alerted me to the fact that his 'concern to grant the reality of unobservables pertains not only to the state, but also (and if not more so) to the deep structure of the states "system" ' and questioned if my argument about the state applies there also. If by 'the states system' Wendt means its 'structure', then, to the extent that his 'structure' is 'cultural', and 'culture' is a system of collective beliefs, my argument does seem to apply there as well. See also Kratochwil's (chap. 2 this volume) erudite engagement with Wendt's book, in which he casts serious doubt on Wendt's understanding of scientific practice and his rendition and employment of scientific realism, and characterises Wendt's combination of scientific realism and constructivism as a failed marriage. My discussion here has focused more narrowly on the internal logic of Wendt's own argumentation regarding the need to embrace particular aspects of scientific realism in order to make it possible to entertain the thought that states and the states system are causally efficacious.

explanations – background conditions, mechanistic processes, contingent circum-stances, and volitional acts of the key agents (see Suganami 2001).

Be that as it may, by proclaiming to be on the side of science, Wendt has positioned himself within mainstream American International Relations, at the core of which lie neorealism and neoliberalism. But it is also Wendt's wish to transcend these two closely interrelated positions, and he pictures himself as doing so through his rejection of the individualist ontology presupposed by these positions. My view is that, while Wendt's approach, based on structurationism and symbolic interactionism, does produce hypotheses that go beyond those stemming from neorealism and neoliberalism, the way in which he tries to distinguish his position categorically from these two contains a number of problems. In this section, I hope to demonstrate this step by step.

Wendt's reasoning[4]

The gist of Wendt's complex reasoning, aimed at undermining neorealism and neoliberalism in favour of his own position, is as follows. These doctrines are both fundamentally unsatisfactory because they are based on individualism. Indi-vidualism is in turn inadequate because it assumes that the agents's properties – or identities and interests – are logically or conceptually independent of the social structure. In fact, the identities and interests of the agents are *not* independent of the social structure logically or conceptually. This is because there is a *constitutive* relationship between them. In a *causal* relationship, the cause and the effect are logically or conceptually independent of each other; but, by contrast, a constitutive relationship entails the presence of a logical or conceptual linkage between that which does the constituting and that which is thereby constituted. Thus, the presence of the structure's constitutive impact on the agents' properties means that the agents are not logically or conceptually independent of the structure, and this, according Wendt, reveals the inadequacy of individualism and, with it, the fundamental unsatisfactoriness of the two doctrines concerned. Central to this line of thinking is the distinction between causation and constitution, based on the belief that a logical or conceptual linkage is absent from the former, but present in the latter.

I sympathise with Wendt's desire to undermine the two dominant paradigms of IR at a stroke. It would be exceedingly satisfactory for a meta-theorist of a par-ticular discipline if she or he could come up with anything like a single conceptual distinction the neglect of which can be shown to have helped false doctrines to flourish, and Wendt's strategy here is of that sort. However, I do not think it works and want to show why. For this purpose, I wish first to analyse the nature of 'causation' and 'constitution' in some depth as I find Wendt's own explication in need of an overhaul.

4 The reconstruction of Wendt's reasoning here is based on my reading of his entire book in which relevant aspects of his thinking are scattered. In particular, see Wendt (1999: chaps 1, 2, 4, 6, 8, but esp. pp. 77–88 and 165–84).

Causation and constitution

In his discussion of causation, Wendt does not clearly separate an analysis of causal *relations* from that of causal *statements*. The former requires us to speculate on *what goes on in the world*, independently of us, when what we call, or rightly recognise as, 'causing' goes on; it asks for a rationally defensible interpretation of what 'causation' as such is (to which one possible answer of course is that it is 'nothing' – for 'causation', or 'causal *necessitation*', is all in the mind, according to this 'causal irrealist' view). The latter, by contrast, requires us to explicate our understanding of *what it means to say* that something causes or caused something (see Mackie 1974). Wendt does not in fact say much about the first subject, but suggests in passing that causal processes are mechanistic ones producing effects, somewhat analogously to the workings of machines (1999: 81–2). He gives more space to the second subject, and states as follows: 'In saying that "X causes Y", we assume that (1) X and Y exist independent of each other, (2) X precedes Y temporally, and (3) but for X, Y would not have occurred' (ibid.: 79).

I have two objections to this analysis. First, Wendt should have clarified whether this is meant to be an analysis of a singular causal statement, regarding the occurrence of particular events in succession, or that of a general one, regarding a regular causal sequence. Second, he should have drawn attention to the danger of using symbols such as 'X' and 'Y' in this context, which is to obscure the fact (a) that the events thereby represented are describable in many ways and (b) that it is only under certain (causally relevant) descriptions that a causal relationship can be seen to obtain between two events. Point (a) is particularly pertinent because, apparently unnoticed by Wendt, the cause-event and the effect-event can, under some descriptions, be seen to have a logical or conceptual relationship – as can be noted, for example, if we are to say 'the heat hitting the reflector at the back caused it to be projected forward'. This reveals that Wendt's independence requirement, stated in (1) above, is not in fact reducible to the claim that there should not be any logical or conceptual connection whatsoever between the cause-event and the effect-event, or, more precisely, that there should not be any descriptions available of the two events, such that, under these descriptions, the two are seen to be logically or conceptually linked. This realisation would lead to the view, to which I subscribe, that the independence requirement should be interpreted to mean, rather innocuously, that the cause-event and the effect-event are simply *different* events. It is always 'something *else*' that 'something' causes. It is not precluded that these events, under suitable descriptions, have a logical or conceptual link – as suggested by the reflector example above (see Mackie 1974: 32; Davidson 1963: 698). Wendt seems oblivious of these issues.

As for 'constitution', Wendt (1999: 83ff.) suggests that there are a variety of constitutive relationships, but in his book he draws special attention to the holist variety with respect to the social world whereby 'social kinds' are constituted by, or embedded in, 'discursive structures'. He offers some helpful examples: '"treaty violations" are constituted by a discourse that defines promises, "war" by a discourse that legitimates state violence, "terrorism" by a discourse that delegitimates non-state violence' (ibid.: 84). Such constitutive relationships are on the plane of socially accepted ideas, and the presence of such a relationship can be appreciated when and only when the logical or conceptual connection, accepted within the society, between the items so connected is understood.

The discussion above points to a more satisfactory way of distinguishing a causal from a constitutive relationship than I find in Wendt's analysis: whereas the former is a mechanistic relation of production, the latter is a relation of logical enablement. For my part, I would add that causal relations also obtain when agents perform intentional acts to bring about some consequences. Wendt will not object to this, given his conception of an intentional, 'auto-genetic', agent, which I shall discuss later. In short, a causal relationship has to do with *mechanistic coming about or intentional bringing about of an effect-event (under a relevant description)*, whereas a constitutive relationship has to do with *making a particular description of something logically possible*.[5] The two kinds of relationships are thus quite incommensurate and cannot be contrasted, as is done by Wendt, along the single axis of the presence or otherwise of logical/conceptual connections.

Now, Wendt gives much prominence to a constitutive relationship in his discussion because he believes, and wants to show, that the agents' identities and interests are constituted by the social structure, and because for his purpose it is imperative, he thinks, that the relationship could be demonstrated to be of a constitutive kind as he defines it. For if the social structure can be shown to have a constitutive relationship with the agents' identities, then individualism (which, for Wendt, implies the absence of such a relationship) can be shown to be an inadequate doctrine; and with this demonstration neorealism and neoliberalism (both based on individualism) can be shown to be in need of transcendence by Wendt's type of approach, which, while remaining scientific, goes beyond the two positions by rejecting individualism (in favour of structurationism).

As he moves to a more substantive discussion of international politics in the final chapters of his book, Wendt identifies three cultures of anarchy, or three discursive structures under which states may find themselves. These, as we saw, are labelled Hobbesian, Lockean, and Kantian. It is his key contention that these cultures not only causally influence the lives of states living under them or coming into contact with them, but that they each constitute for the states their identities, or roles, distinctive of each culture. Thus, the Hobbesian culture is said to constitute states as enemies, the Lockean culture as rivals, and the Kantian culture as friends (see Wendt 1999: chap. 6). I will try to show, however, that, over and above the causal relationships that Wendt accepts obtains between cultures and identities, there is nothing of any substance to discuss.

5 This is the most lucid interpretation I can make of the distinction between the two kinds of relationship *that Wendt invokes at key junctures in his argument*. Wendt's category of 'constitutive theorizing' is in fact wider than is suggested by the way the distinction is explicated here. See Wendt (1999: 83ff.). But this does not seem to me to affect the argument that follows.

Mutual constitution or equivalence

Here I will focus on Wendt's contention that the Hobbesian international culture has a constitutive relationship with a state identity of enmity; the same argument as I develop below applies to the other cultures/identities also. I take it that in the present context 'the Hobbesian international culture' and 'state identity of enmity' are shorthand expressions, respectively, for (a) 'the international system having the Hobbesian culture (and neither of the two other cultures)' and (b) 'states having enemyhood (and neither of the two other roles) as their identity'. Wendt's contention is that (b) is constituted by (a), which entails that (b) logically presupposes (a). For an endorsement of this move, consider Wendt's aforementioned example, that 'treaty violations' are constituted by a discourse that defines promises. One central meaning of this is that without that discourse there logically cannot be such a thing as 'treaty violations', i.e., something being conceivable as a case of treaty violation logically presupposes the presence of a discourse that defines promises. So, by the same token, I take Wendt to be saying that (b) logically presupposes (a), or that the state identity of enmity is logically inconceivable without the Hobbesian international culture.

We should note, however, that, according to Wendt (1999: 171, 180, 259, 260), the constitutive process works in the opposite direction as well. So Wendt's contention can be restated as follows: no state identity of enemyhood without the Hobbesian international culture and no Hobbesian international culture without the state identity of enemyhood, logically. This is Wendt's thesis of mutual constitution.

But what precisely is this thing called the relationship of mutual constitution in this case? I submit that (a) and (b) are in fact two different descriptions of one and the same situation, just as 'A becoming the wife of B' and 'B becoming the husband of A' are two different – one male-centric, the other female-centric – descriptions of one and the same event, their wedding. Not only that: I could not locate in Wendt's book any explicit attempt to define (a) independently of (b), or (b) independently of (a). I conclude therefore that the expressions (a) and (b) denote one and the same social situation and suspect also that the two are one and the same concept expressed differently. I am not making a generalized claim that structural and agential properties are identical, or that the relationship of mutual constitution is always the same as that of identity. But, in this instance, I fail to see any difference between (a) and (b), which strike me as two ways of making the same point – one at the system level, the other at the unit level. The Hobbesian international culture *is* states having enemyhood as their identity and states having enemyhood as their identity *is* the Hobbesian international culture. What we have here then is not a case of mutual constitution, but equivalence.

Back to causal relations

It may be noted that, if the Hobbesian international culture and state identity of enmity are one and the same thing under different descriptions, there cannot be a causal relationship between them because, as we saw, such a relationship demands that the cause and the effect be different events (or situations). However, it is a reasonable causal hypothesis that the presence or dominance, in a given international system, of the idea that under anarchy states are inevitably in the Hobbesian state of 'war of all against all' would tend to make states think of themselves as enemies and behave in a hostile way towards each other, make it difficult for them not to do these things, and encourage those entering the system to follow the pattern. Would we have to abandon this reasonable causal hypothesis?

Fortunately not. We can hold on to the view that the Hobbesian international culture and state identity of enmity are identical and yet, without contradiction, subscribe to a causal hypothesis that the Hobbesian idea (that under anarchy states are inevitably enemies all against all), if present or dominant in an international system, tends to make states think of themselves as enemies and behave in a hostile way towards each other, make it difficult for them not to do these things, and encourage those entering the system to follow the pattern. This causal hypothesis, it will be noticed, relates, as it should, two items which are not one and the same thing: on the one hand, the presence or dominance, within a given system, of a general idea about the consequences of anarchy; and, on the other, the tendency of the individual units to act out the scenario.

Over and above this plausible causal hypothesis, which Wendt himself also entertains, there is, I submit, nothing of any substance to consider. It is entirely consistent with this assessment that, when he moves to flesh out his allegedly constitutive thesis regarding the relationship between international political cultures and state identities (1999: 274ff.), what he ends up offering is a number of straightforwardly *causal* narratives. He could not have done otherwise, in my view.

Wendt's concession to individualism

Wendt's strategy has been to undermine neorealism and neoliberalism by demonstrating individualism to be inadequate and to do so by pointing to the constitutive relationship between the existing cultural structure of the international system and the states' role or identity associated with the culture. In my view, this strategy fails. But I now want to draw attention to two other things. First, Wendt (1999: chap. 7) is reasonably persuasive in his portrayal of how in the course of interaction states may be caused to alter not only their behaviour but also their identity. Since this is a significant contribution to our understanding of the mechanisms of the evolution of cooperation between states (neglected by the neorealists, and only partially understood within the neoliberal paradigm), Wendt does not have to drive himself quite so hard to cause further damage to the two theoretical positions which his own in substance supersedes. Second, his drive in this regard to criticise the individualist basis of neorealism and neoliberalism is misplaced because, notwithstanding his stress on holism, he makes very important concessions to the individualist ontology himself. In this section, I want to say a few words about this last point.

Wendt on individualism and holism

In a clearly formulated passage, Wendt contrasts individualism and holism as follows:

> The individualist hypothesis is in effect that all identities are personal identities, all interests personal interests, all behaviors meaningful because of personal beliefs. Nothing in or about the actor or his behavior logically or conceptually presupposes other actors or culture. The holist hypothesis is that culture constitutes role identities and their corresponding interests and practices. Regardless of the thoughts in one's head, one cannot be a certain kind of agent, or engage in certain practices, unless these are recognized by others. If holists are right then it will be impossible to reduce society to independently existing idiolects, as required by the individualist view that thought is logically prior to society. Individualist approaches to social inquiry may still be useful for some questions, but will be inherently incomplete insofar as they presuppose irreducible societal facts. If the holist is right, in other words, we will have to revise our conventional view of intentional agency, which is rooted in individualism, if not jettison it altogether.
>
> (1999: 178)

While being critical of individualism, Wendt is equally unwilling to subscribe to radical holism, according to which 'intentionality is merely an effect of discourse' (1999: 178), or 'motive and intentionality [far from being causes of behaviour] actually refer to the public criteria by which we make behavior intelligible, by which we make *ascriptions* of motive' (ibid.: 179; emphasis in original). What Wendt prefers is a moderate holism, which means the same as a moderate individualism. It is 'not that culture does not help constitute the meaning of an agent's desires and beliefs, but that agents have a role to play in social explanation which cannot be reduced to culture' (ibid.: 181). But, in coming to terms with the need to accommodate individualism, Wendt argues as follows, which is worthy of attention:

> [It is possible to distinguish] between individuality *per se* and the social *terms* of individuality. The former refers to those properties of an agent's constitution that are self-organizing and thus not intrinsically dependent on a social context. Some of these properties are material: individuals live in genetically constituted bodies that do not presuppose other bodies, and have minds in virtue of independent brains. Others are cognitive: agents exist partly in virtue of their own thoughts, which they can continue to have even if they are marooned on a desert island. Both kinds of properties are essential to intentional agency, and, even if they are caused by society, they exist independent of them. They give the Self an 'auto-genetic' quality, and are the basis for what Mead called the 'I', an agent's sense of itself as a distinct locus of thought, choice, and activity. Without this self-constituting substrate, culture would have no raw material to exert its constitutive effects upon, nor could agents

resist those effects. The intuitions that sustain individualism are rooted in this aspect of individuality.

(1999: 181–2)[6]

What is striking in the above passage is Wendt's apparent subscription to the view that we have a sense of ourselves as a distinct locus of thought, choice, and activity, and that we have a pre-societal individuality which enables us to be intentional agents. Unlike rocks, he says, human beings are intentional agents that 'exist partly in virtue of *their own thoughts*' (1999: 181, emphasis mine; see also 225). It seems to me, however, that if Wendt is willing to make this degree of concession to individualism, then his effort to undermine neorealism and neoliberalism because of their rootedness in individualism begins to lose its edge. The difference between Wendt, on the one hand, and Waltz and Keohane, on the other, is a matter of degree. For Wendt the difference is no doubt highly significant; for the more radical holists it is less so.[7]

There is, however, a noteworthy passage later in Wendt's book, which indicates that his social constructivism may go deeper than is suggested by his quasi-Cartesian argument that our self-awareness of our own thoughts is a ground for believing in pre-societal individuality. He states:

> It is only in certain cultures that people are treated as intentional agents with identities, interests, and responsibility, the capacities most of us today associate with being an individual person. The fact that human beings have these capacities naturally does not always mean they have them *socially*.

(1999: 52, emphasis in original)

It may be that here he goes some way towards the idea of the social construction of the agent, though, not clearly – for his belief may be that human agential capacities are not so much socially constructed as recognised, or fail to be recognised, socially. But if Wendt is to oppose individualism in such a manner that it makes sense for him to distinguish himself categorically from neorealists and neoliberals, he will have to start arguing that our self-conception as a locus of

---

6 The penultimate sentence here is puzzling. If a constitutive relationship is, as Wendt says, one of logical or conceptual enablement, not like a billiard ball hitting another, it makes no sense to talk of the constituting element *exerting* effects upon the element thereby to be constituted, or the latter *resisting* the effects exerted by the former. 'Exertion' and 'resistance' may be appropriate metaphors in some causal relationships, but are not possible in logical or conceptual relationships. Wendt's reference here to 'exertion' and 'resistance' would seem to reveal that, at least part of the time, he is not distinguishing the two kinds of relationships clearly. Likewise, Smith (2000: 156, 157) says that he is 'troubled by his [Wendt's] notion of causal and constitutive theories', that, in his view, 'Wendt's view of constitutive theorizing is very different to the dominant use of the term "constitutive" in the social sciences, where it tends to be contrasted to explanatory theory', and he considers 'Wendt as seeing constitutive theory as a form of causal theory'.

7 The individualist basis of symbolic interactionism, followed by Wendt, has been noted by Palan (2000).

thought, choice, and activity too must have come from society, even though human potentials for such things may be rooted in our biological makeup.

Conclusion

My critical engagement with Wendt's book has focused on the way it characterizes itself, rather than on its substantive contentions about international relations. As far as the latter goes, it is my view that Wendt's exploration of transformative potentials in the contemporary international system places him above Waltz and Axelrod. But, in the course of my detailed engagement with the self-characterization of the book, I hope to have eliminated some confusions in the argument and pointed out some mistakes in its logic.

My contentions against Wendt can be summarised by the following seven points:

1   Wendt's defence of scientific realism is not entirely convincing.
2   In any case, his invocation of this doctrine is unnecessary for his purpose of ascertaining the reality of the state.
3   His comparative analysis of causal and constitutive relationships requires an overhaul.
4   When this is done, these relationships can be seen to be quite incommensurate; they cannot be contrasted along the single axis of the presence or otherwise of logical connections in them.
5   His assertion of the specifically constitutive, as opposed to causal, relationship between a given international political culture and the corresponding identity of the states is unpersuasive.
6   His strategy – to undermine neorealism and neoliberalism by pointing to the constitutive relationship between the existing cultural structure of the international system and the states' role or identity associated with the culture – therefore fails.
7   His castigation of individualism as the main source of the inadequacies of neorealism and neoliberalism is marred by important concessions he makes towards it.

In short, the very complex philosophical argumentation through which Wendt tries to distinguish his work from that of others is unpersuasive, but the dubiousness of some of his key philosophical moves in this connection does not appear to undermine the empirical plausibility of his substantive hypotheses.

5 Wendt's constructivism

A relentless quest for synthesis[*]

Stefano Guzzini and Anna Leander

Against its usual portrayal as a *via media* (Wendt 2000), or as an attempt at bridge-building (Palan 2000), this chapter claims that Alexander Wendt's ultimate project is synthesis strongly understood. In the world of scholars, Wendt is not a hunter, but a gatherer. Yet he is a gatherer of a kind. He is not simply striving to establish a list of collector's items, a 'golden mean' combination of the 'best of' different other positions. Rather, Wendt wants to abstract, reconfigurate, indeed sometimes 'assimilate' (Wendt 2000: 180) apparently antagonistic theoretical positions within one (his) social theory of IR. Constructivism comes into play since it allows this second-order meta-solution. Perhaps more than any other, Wendt's project exemplifies constructivism's 'almost frightening potential as meta-theory subsuming all others' (Wæver 1997: 25).

Wendt's synthesis wants at times to overcome but also to preserve existing contradictions at a higher level. Often, it resembles the way Einstein embedded Newtonian physics: for much of our daily life the latter is perfectly good enough. Yet Wendt is uncomfortable using this higher level actually to 'dissolve' all the tensions into a new unitary thought. He instead plays with an idea of complementarity which one could liken to the dualism of particles/waves in twentieth-century physics: in some moments light behaves like particles, in others like waves, without there being an overriding idea which could synthesise it (for this idea in a normative IR context, see Guzzini *et al.* 1995: 427–30).

This project of a synthesis comes with a purpose. Wendt targets the theoretical orthodoxy in international relations, most explicitly its underlying materialism and individualism. Yet he makes his argument for a theoretical heterodoxy by consciously staying within the *disciplinary* orthodoxy. For Wendt accepts the narrow confines for the discipline erected by Kenneth Waltz, as well as the narrow

* This is a slightly edited version of Guzzini and Leander (2001). We are very grateful to the many people who then had generously provided us with comments, suggestions and criticisms, namely Emanuel Adler, Alexander Astrov, Andreas Behnke, Milan Brglez, Chris Browning, Barry Buzan, Lars-Erik Cederman, Petr Drulák, Anja Jetschke, Peter Katzenstein, Mette Lykke Knudsen, Friedrich Kratochwil, Richard Little, Ian Manners, Michael Merlingen, Heikki Patomäki, Frank Schimmelfennig, Trine Villumsen, Jutta Weldes, Alexander Wendt, Antje Wiener, Colin Wight, Ole Wæver and Maja Zehfuss. The usual disclaimers apply.

borders of the classical self-understanding of international society itself. In other words, to undermine more legitimately two key theoretical positions in IR, methodological and ontological individualism and materialism, he consciously stays within the identity-defining parameters of the discipline, including its reference to states as the main organising principle.

This unusual mix of orthodoxy in terms of disciplinary self-understanding and theoretical heterodoxy, so we claim, is responsible for some of the main tensions within the project. For, as canny as it is for being able legitimately to speak to and attack the mainstream of IR research, we claim that such a choice of a grand synthesis such as his *Social Theory* comes paradoxically with risks of closure exactly because it is done within this disciplinary orthodoxy. His strategy risks becoming hijacked by this orthodoxy: his theory must reproduce it. He updates the self-understanding of the discipline exactly at a time when it is again challenged. Through his statist theory, he reproduces the embedded understanding of politics of a narrowly defined international society – which might appear rather out of touch with world politics. In other words, his synthesis, as opening and challenging as it is within IR, runs the risk of reifying a specific historical stage of both the discipline and international politics.

This chapter will show how one can make sense of Wendt's approach as a synthesis combining disciplinary orthodoxy and theoretical heterodoxy. In a first step, we analyse how Wendt's project is self-consciously inscribed into the disciplinary identity of IR, a choice which makes the constant reference to (neo-)realism necessary. Then, we examine three different synthesising moves within his meta-theory and his theory. On both levels, it allows him to encompass different versions of rationalist approaches and of realism and liberalism respectively, as special cases of his own. Here we argue that, however Wendt or his defenders and critics want to call his final synthesis, it has little to do with 'positivism' as it is commonly understood in the discipline. Finally, we spell out some of the tensions of Wendt's project, when his theoretical synthesis has to function within the disciplinary identity from which he starts.

Wendt's orthodoxy in the disciplinary identity of IR

Throughout its history, the discipline of IR has been plagued by a problematic identity. War and peace formed the early subject matter but, except for political reasons, it was not self-evident why this would need an extra discipline. Conflicts, whether armed or not, have been of interest to lawyers, psychologists and sociologists alike. The domestication of violence was crucial for all sciences of the state, as political science often used to be called (and in some places still is). Nor was there any special methodology to set IR aside, as marginal utility calculus did for economics.

The first demarcation happened with regard to international law, in whose backyard IR used to be. Morgenthau (1936), himself a lawyer, argued that one needed to radicalise legal positivism, and based its argumentation not on the internal logic of law, but on its context. This tension between law and reality became an evergreen for IR debates. This move, however, placed IR (and Morgenthau) squarely within political science.

To allow for a second demarcation not only from law, but also from political science, the IR discipline had to insist that there was a significant difference between domestic and international politics. The notion of 'anarchy' satisfied this quest. Whereas domestic politics had indeed domesticated violence through the state, the international realm was experiencing a form of the 'state of nature' before the Leviathan. According to Aron, had states escaped this state of nature in their relations, there would no longer be a theory of international relations (Aron 1962: 19).

Whereas politics at home can look at a variety of purposes, international relations, so the story goes, were caught in a security dilemma. Without an arbiter above the parties who could enforce order, actors have to look after themselves (including cooperation and building coalitions). Having no guarantees when trust is not reciprocated, they have to be on guard. Everybody being relentlessly on guard might end up in an arms race whose security effects could be negative.

The starting point of anarchy and the security dilemma can be found in all sections of the classical tradition. It does not demarcate 'realism' from 'idealism', but IR from political science. What distinguished 'realism' is a further assumption: its cyclical view of history. Whereas, in principle, an 'idealist' position would not exclude the possibility of the international system becoming 'domesticated' (although not necessarily in the same way as in domestic politics), realism would insist that, whatever improvement there is, it can only be temporary. We are bound by and will inevitably return to the security dilemma in one guise or another.

Adding the assumption of a cyclical view of history had the invaluable side-effect of cementing the differences of IR and hence at least temporarily 'resolving' the identity problem of IR. At the same time, it made the self-definition of realism and the legitimate boundaries of IR coincide.

The overlap of the self-identification of a discipline and the assumptions of realism had two logical consequences. First, any attempt to redefine the borders of the discipline was immediately seen as an attack on realism. Vice versa, there has been the tendency to see the many attacks on realism as attacks on the legitimate independence of the discipline as such, which would call for significant reactions by IR scholars more widely. In the so-called second debate waged in IR, realists mistook an attack on the methodology of the discipline, part of its identity so far, as an attack against realism. Bull's (1966a) defence of a more traditionalist approach was based exactly on the substantial difference which set IR apart. However, later studies seemed to show that the majority of 'scientific' writers had never given up basic realist assumptions (Vasquez 1983). When the transnational paradigm was launched, it again undermined the classical boundaries of IR – and was therefore perceived as a critique of realism, although Keohane and Nye (1977) had repeatedly pointed out that their approach did not invalidate realism in all, or even necessarily the more significant, circumstances.

Waltz's *Theory of International Politics* (1979) acquired its status in the discipline not because it said anything new or because it had a theoretical sophistication unparalleled elsewhere. Waltz's work has become paradigmatic for the new (reductionist) twist he gave to the self-identification of realism-cum-IR. Challenged in its boundaries by the emerging liberal or transnationalist research, the *Theory of International Politics* redefined what the subject matter of an IR theory could be. It was a balance of power theory under anarchy that set the international system apart from hierarchical systems. This again made IR coincide with a very restrictive (and materialist) view of realism, now dubbed neo-realism (for a more detailed discussion, see Guzzini 1998: 125–41). For Waltz, other approaches could well be perfectly legitimate, but were a form of 'reductionist' theorising or foreign policy analysis – that is, not international relations proper.

Wendt is aware of the possible conflation of the boundaries of IR and realism. Indeed, he comes close to making the same conflation when he writes that 'there should continue to be a place for theories of anarchic inter-state politics, alongside other forms of international theory; to that extent, I am a statist and a realist' (Wendt 1992a: 424), as if the two last things were necessarily connected.[1] Yet, one can perfectly well be a statist without being a realist, as some institutionalists would be quick to point out; and a realist and not a statist, as testified by realist scholars in international political economy (IPE) such as Susan Strange.[2]

With good knowledge of this potential confusion, Wendt chooses to embed his theoretical challenges against the mainstream of IR (including realism) within a very orthodox definition of the subject matter of IR. This choice is cunning. Given that earlier debates were haunted by the conflation of realism and the identity of IR, assuming *disciplinary orthodoxy* might be a more effective way of making realists understand that their *theory* is wrong. And, for Wendt, realism must remain the main target since it is closest to the self-definition of practitioners and hence most prone to damaging self-fulfilling prophecies in international politics. Seen in this way, it is perhaps less surprising that he uses the last paradigm of realism-cum-IR, Waltz's *Theory of International Politics*, as a foil, although by this time this enterprise entailed a serious effort of 'reanimation', as it were. Indeed, the real interlocutor often seems to be Buzan, Jones and Little's and reworking of neo-realism, which shares with Waltz and Wendt a similar spirit of looking for 'a wide-ranging and integrative general theory of international relations' (Buzan *et al.* 1993: 65).

Wendt's disciplinary boundaries are set in a narrow and orthodox way. He has little doubt that international politics is first and foremost about inter-state relations. He tells us that this is so because 'states are still the primary medium through which the effects of other actors on the regulation of violence are channelled into the world system' (Wendt 2000: 174). In response to critics who point to this state-centrism, Wendt simply answers that accusing a theory of international politics of state-centrism is like accusing a 'theory of forests for being tree-centric' (Wendt

1 But observers also react in this way. In an early typology (Jaeger 1996), Wendt's statism earned him the label of a 'realist constructivist, as opposed to 'liberal-institutionalist constructivists' such as Müller (1994; 1995) and Risse-Kappen (1995b).
2 For an assessment of Strange's idiosyncratic mix, see Guzzini (2000b) and Leander (2001a).

1999: 9). Moreover, in orthodox realist fashion Wendt assumes unified action capacities of states and even anthropomorphises states by giving them purposes and intentions.

Wendt's state-centrism and his essentialising of states have been among the most contested issues of his theory, as he anticipates in the book himself. Suffice it to say at this point that, by giving Waltz such a central place in his disciplinary reconstruction, Wendt makes Waltz's narrow definition of the IR discipline stand for classical IR at large. In other words, Wendt's starting point in Waltz reads Waltz's narrow understanding of IR backwards onto the IR tradition.[3] Waltz's theory has the place of the 'previous synthesis', although Waltz's project was a completely different one from Wendt's, namely defining IR by narrowing it down. Instead of starting with defining politics first, as arguably some (including Morgenthau) in the classical tradition did, Wendt finds his subject (matter) already made up for him. As we discuss in the last section, this feature will inevitably produce tensions with his constructivist approach. Before moving to this discussion, we want first to show how his synthesis proceeds to embed contrasting meta-theories and theories as special cases of his own.

Wendt's heterodox social theory of IR: a project of manifold synthesis

Within this disciplinary orthodoxy, Wendt situates his theoretical challenges. He gives theoretical predominance to inter-state relations and anarchy – but only in order to redefine both. Whereas the security dilemma seems a logical necessity, Wendt argues that anarchy is foremost a social construct. Instead of having a logic of anarchy, he establishes cultures of anarchy. Once states are understood as sharing a culture, their very identity is open to conceptualisation, and not only their utility calculus.

For it is here that Wendt places his two most daring challenges to the discipline. He criticises existing theories for being too individualistic. He wants a theory to include a truly holistic component. He argues for a dualist ontology that takes both agency and structure seriously (Wendt 1987), and he proposes an idealist understanding of structure, and of politics (Wendt 1992a). His version of constructivism is the encompassing framework within which this takes place.

Wendt consciously bases his theory on the primacy of ontological choices. In his opinion, the excessive focus on questions of knowledge and truth has contributed to the big schisms in IR. According to him, these antagonisms have led to many mutual misunderstandings and eventually to a block on communication. For Wendt, this is a threat to his entire project. For if theoretical debates are again relegated to the realm of 'ideology', of unbridgeable assumptions, theoretical debate can never command a cross-paradigmatic audience. Wendt's ambition to

---

3 We are indebted to Alexander Astrov for this point, which will be taken up again in the concluding section.

'wrap up' IR by offering an encompassing approach would be killed at its inception. Indeed, the very need for further theoretical discussion would be undermined. And, however difficult it might be to classify Wendt, he is surely a convinced theoretician.

In other words, for his project Wendt must avoid a return to the days when the 'Third Debate' (Lapid 1989) or the 'rationalist–reflectivist' divide (Keohane 1989 [1988]) was said to be a non-starter since, to put it in Kuhnian terms, paradigms were 'incommensurable' (Holsti 1985; Krasner 1985). This superficially received argument about incommensurability legitimised 'business-as-usual at the price of a pre-defined pluralism' (Guzzini 1993: 446), since it was a welcome excuse not to bother too much about what other people had to say (Wight 1996). A specific stage in the development of IR debates was reified (Guzzini 1998: 108–22), cutting short a self-reflection in the discipline which would upset existing research programmes and scientific cultures. Hence, in his own understanding Wendt needed to 'rewire' IR debates to make his ambitious theoretical enterprise possible.

Moreover, putting two fundamental ontological choices first was to permit him a strategy of synthesising apparently contradictory positions on both the metatheoretical and the theoretical level. There are three syntheses, two within his social theory, one within his IR theory. For his social theory, as we will develop in some detail, he opts for an idealist approach with a 'rump materialism'. This allows for brute material forces to have some effects on the constitution of power and interest, even if always mediated by ideas (Wendt 1999: 96, 109–13). In turn, this will eventually lead him to accommodate causal and constitutive theorising within a version of 'sophisticated positivism', as he later calls it (Wendt 2000: 173). In a way, he tries to assimilate (natural) science within a qualified scientific realism as a base for a social science. For his IR theory, it is the basic dual ontology of agency and structure, irreducible to each other, which ultimately allows him to assimilate rationalism/individualism within his wider constructivism.

'Rump materialism', scientific realism and 'sophisticated positivism'

Although Wendt reserves a predominant place for philosophical idealism and culture in his theory – otherwise it would hardly qualify as constructivist – he also includes a rump materialism: it is 'not ideas all the way down', as he writes. This rump materialism is the residual category of what is 'effective' in our social world and yet not based on culture, that is, shared beliefs. It includes human nature, a weak version of technological determinism, and geography/natural resources (Wendt 1999: 130–1, 136).

From this assumption of rump materialism, Wendt sees a logic running through scientific realism, which fundamentally says that there is a world independent of our thought, to reach eventually his synthesis, namely a sophisticated positivism which, in his reading of the hard sciences, allows a juxtaposition of causal and constitutive theorising. This logical path has been at the centre of a theory-internal criticism by other scientific realists. Although the first step, a certain link between materialism and scientific realism, is usually acknowledged, the second step is not: positivism is necessary neither for scientific realism, nor for having the possibility of a social science (Patomäki and Wight 2000; Brglez 2001).

We would frame this critique in a different way. If we carefully follow Wendt on his logical path, the final destination which Wendt calls positivism has little to do with positivism as commonly understood in the discipline. For laying out this discussion, we will bracket the question of scientific realism and concentrate on the other steps in Wendt's argument, namely rump materialism, Wendt's conception of science, and finally his dual mode of theorising.

Starting from a mainly idealist ontology, Wendt's residual or rump materialism is, as Wendt (1999: 136) himself acknowledges, relatively inconsequential for the social scientist. The acceptance of rump materialism neglects the question of where the significant problematique for social scientists qua social scientists is to be found (Guzzini 2000a: 160; Kratochwil, chap. 2 this volume, pp. 41–3). If we watch a red light as a social scientist, we are not interested in the residual matter of electric circuits but, for instance, in the norms which the interpretation of this sign mobilises.

For a constructivist, it is not the existence of a world independent of our thought that is at stake, but whether we can have unmediated access to it. Wendt does not hold this position any more than do post-positivists. In his response to Doty (2000), Wendt claims the position of sophisticated positivism to be his own, where all observation is theory-laden and theories cannot be tested against the world but only against other theories, and that, as a result, knowledge can never have secure foundations (Wendt 2000: 173). This is most probably not the positivism Krasner (2000) speaks of when endorsing Wendt's move.[4] It is in fact a version of constructivism which, albeit begrudgingly, accepts the necessary epistemological component besides the basic ontological one: constructivism is most coherently about the construction of social reality *and* the social construction of knowledge (Guzzini 2000a; Adler 2002).

In other words, Wendt can make a claim for positivism only because he has voided the concept to such an extent that it becomes synonymous with a commitment to scientific work, broadly understood as making analyses to allow us a better understanding of the world. This Wendtian criterion does not distinguish positivists from non-positivists, but scholars from non-scholars. And since the scientific enterprise is defined with weak discriminatory criteria, it largely coincides with the way interpretivists have conceived of *social* science, in opposition to traditional natural science, in the first place.

This tension in Wendt's approach might best be illustrated by another claim he makes when responding to Doty's critique. He says that Doty 'proceeds more or less as any positivist would – amassing data and developing the best narrative

---

4 Also, as Kratochwil (chap. 2 this volume) notes, this last move creates a tension in his position insofar as he needs to combine *his* idea of scientific realism and the fact that one cannot test against an outside world.

she can to make sense of them' (Wendt 2000: 173). His charge is that post-positivists, far from being radical, are basically very conventional when they do empirical work.

Wendt's response creates a paradox: if post-positivist empirical analyses were so conventional, why is the discipline so adamant in refusing them a 'scientific' stamp of approval? When universities (prominently in the United States but also elsewhere) offer 'scientific method' courses, concept or discourse analysis does not exactly figure prominently in the syllabuses (see also the critique by Alker 2000). The reaction within the discipline is not to say that post-positivism is respectable and nothing new, but that it leads to bad science or no science at all. In other words, if Wendt's positivism is content with an empirical analysis done as a narrative approach which makes sense of the world as well as possible, then he joins company with post-positivists, not positivists, as usually understood in the discipline. Thus, we have travelled together with Wendt in the direction of his roadmap sign 'positivism', but we reached 'a non-positivistic social science of international relations' (Smith 2000: 152, n. 8). The real issue at stake is not positivism versus post-positivism, but what exactly this non-positivist 'social science' is all about.

Wendt's vision of a social science again displays his synthesising attitude by offering a dual mode of theorising. Wendt tries to assimilate some features of classical positivism into his wider approach (whatever the name) by insisting that, besides causal theorising, there is 'constitutive' theorising more interested in the 'what' and 'how possible' questions. By showing that there is also constitutive theory in the hard sciences, Wendt tries to get interpretivists to look at what the no-longer-so-hard sciences really are, before dismissing any attempt to integrate the scientific endeavour, here and there. Using the same argument, he tries to get 'positivists' to understand that exactly because their vision of science is outdated they need to give up the idea that only causal theorising is science.

This opens up the final question about the relationship between causal and constitutive theorising. Here, it is not entirely clear where Wendt would position himself. One possibility is a refined version of the classical division of labour between concept formation, understood as variable operationalisation, and then (causal) analysis. In this scheme, constitutive theorising would be basically no theorising on its own but the first step of more positivist research designs, as argued by King, Keohane and Verba (1994) and feared by Smith (2000): first take Wendt and then add KKV and stir.

Although Wendt chooses not to rebut this way of seeing it, it seems to contradict the thrust of his argument. He insists quite strongly that constitutive theorising is an equally important source of knowledge in its own right, not just a means to another end. When Weber (1980 [1921–2]), after decades of research, put his framework of central concepts at the beginning of his *Economy and Society*, this already included a major part of his social theory, as the often quoted definitions (understandings) of the state and power/authority bear witness. Hence, concept formation is not simply the operationalisation of variables but an important part of our knowledge in itself. For Wendt, the choice between the two fundamentally depends on the questions one chooses to ask which, in turn, are not independent of meta-theoretical commitments (Wendt and Duvall 1989).

Moreover, Wendt not only introduces constitutive theorising as equally legitimate, he also qualifies which type of causal theorising is acceptable today for a self-regarding scientific realist. It is not the covering-law model usually taught in our textbooks. The subsumption under a covering law does not explain anything, but simply states a regularity. In other words, the famous 'if . . . then' explanations, purged of spurious correlations, are just another set of data (regularities), nothing more. Causality lies in process-explanations which go beyond Humean causality. This places Wendt close to the causality concept in relationism (for IR, see Jackson and Nexon 1999), in critical realism (Patomäki 1996; Patomäki and Wight 2000; Brglez 2001), in qualitative comparative sociology, such as Charles Ragin's (1987: 88–119) multiple conjunctural causation (see also Ragin 2000: 88–115) and also in historical sociology (Tilly 1995). This part of the argument seems to exclude an unqualified division of labour between constructivists on one hand (constitutive theory) and KKV's research design on the other.

In this reading, Wendt's synthesising strategy is indeed much more harmful to established positivist research designs than to post-positivist ones. His sophisticated positivism keeps one single element of positivism, namely that there is in principle no difference between natural and social sciences, but qualifying it to such an extent that his social science looks pretty similar to the type of qualitative research advocated by those post-positivists who have asked for more methodological self-awareness (Milliken 1999; Neumann 2001).[5] Hence, the implication of his assimilating strategy, and the flip-side of his reply to Doty, is that it is not fortuitous if he finds post-positivist empirical research fairly conventional, since this, and not established positivism, would correspond closely to the convention of *his* social science.

A dualist ontology and the assimilation of individualism/rationalism

Upholding the autonomy of a holistic component in his conception of the agent-structure debate is Wendt's second basic ontological decision. Wendt strongly supports the sociological turn in the social sciences. In this move he is the most different from much of what counts as middle-ground constructivism since he refuses to have his theorising restricted to a theory of action – even a 'thick' one, such as that inspired by Habermas's communicative action (Müller 1994; Risse 2000).

The choice of a dualist ontology, respecting both agency and structure, is carried out through a threefold conceptual split (see Figure 5.1): at the level of action (between identity/interests and behaviour), at the level of structure (between a

5 For a discussion of constructivist research which looks at what they call 'positivist-leaning' and post-positivist research designs, see Klotz and Lynch (2001).

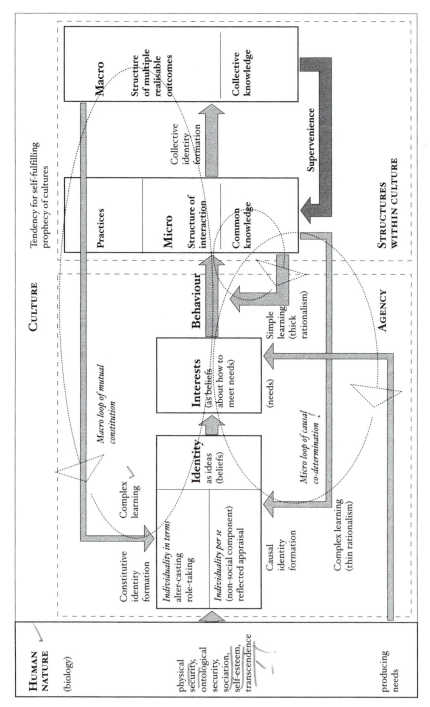

Figure 5.1 Wendt's synthesis in *Social Theory of International Politics*.

macro- and a micro-structure) and in their feedback relation (between constitutive and causal links). In turn, this conceptual apparatus then allows him to assimilate no fewer than three other social theories ranging from the most limited one, behaviouralist rational choice, to his own all-encompassing synthesis.

The origin of the threefold conceptual split is to be found in Wendt's plea for a dual ontology. In 1987, Wendt argued that discussions in IR tended to conflate research design with methodological and ontological questions, levels of analysis with the agent–structure debate.[6] There was a tendency to trivialise important questions. For it is trivial to say that there are agents who find themselves in a wider context which imposes systematic constraints and privileges on them. Any analysis worth its name will combine a micro- and a macro-level, even if only by assuming one constant.

Hence, the level of analysis gives no indication of meta-theoretical choices. Waltz's theory was called structuralist because his level of analysis was systemic; but the underlying logic of explanation was derived from the individualist level (for this argument, see Ashley 1986 [1984]). His structure is also not more than the interaction of states. In other words, Waltz's so-called structural realism focuses on the macro-level of a methodological and ontologically individualist approach.

The more important issues lie elsewhere. For one, it is consequential whether or not a scholar accepts that things we do not see, including structures, can have effects and therefore can be said to exist. Denying this follows the path of empiricism, but also of methodological individualism where all social facts are, in the long run, to be reduced to the effects, intended or not, of individual actions. Supporting the statement, as Wendt does, leads to a social theory that includes a holistic ontology.

At the same time, Wendt wants to keep certain insights from individualist approaches. He agrees with Giddens's (1984) influential analysis which tries to show that neither agency nor structure can be reduced to the other. His attraction to Giddens's structuration theory lies in its dual ontology, both individualist and holistic.

Yet, once having chosen a dual ontology, Wendt faces the problem of how to theorise the relationship between the two. That is so because the classical inclusion of the factor of time into the scheme simply 'stretches out' but does not resolve the reductionism. According to this solution, today's structures are the sedimented effect of yesterday's actions and interactions; and they constrain or make possible tomorrow's actions and interactions. But, as long as this leaves no independent status to the structure, it is ultimately individualist.

With time being no sufficient solution, since it does not guarantee dualism, i.e. the thinking of two independent yet connected dynamics, a dualist approach leads to the conceptualisation of two overlapping circles, to a 'dyadic' approach. The point of overlap could be thought of as the moment or level of interaction as proposed by, e.g., Guzzini (1993: 471–4) and Daase (1999: 259–68) in following up

6 See also the exchange between Wendt (1991; 1992b) and Hollis and Smith (1991; 1992).

the early agent–structure debate in IR (Wendt 1987; Dessler 1989; Hollis and Smith 1990; Carlsnaes 1992).

Wendt follows this idea of an in-between level by doubling his structure into a micro-structure (the interactionist level) and a macro-structure (see Figure 5.1, right half). The relationship between the two is one for which he borrows the concept of 'supervenience' from the debates on the philosophy of mind. Supervenience means 'that macro-structures are both not reducible to and yet somehow dependent for their existence on micro-structures' (Wendt 1999: 155–6).

This fundamental distinction immediately sets the stage insofar as it makes visible the difference between the structural level in individualist and holistic approaches. For the micro-structure is the only structure individualism can conceive of, the only structure 'seen' from a purely individualist standpoint. Yet for Wendt individualism cannot explain 'multiple realizability'. By this, Wendt means that certain unit- or interaction-level states of affairs are sufficient for the existence of a macro-state – but their existence is not necessary for producing that macro-state. This contradicts individualism since in individualism any structure must necessarily be derived from the lower level, that is, a certain pattern of interaction will always produce a certain macro-structure. If it is possible that a certain macro-structure can correspond to a number of interaction-level practices, each of them or their combination being sufficient for its existence, while none of those is necessarily producing it, then something escapes an explanation which goes bottom-up.

This pair of structures is further specified through the parallel distinction between common and collective knowledge (Wendt 1999: 160–5). Common knowledge stands for 'interlocking beliefs', which implies not only shared beliefs but the mutual awareness of these. Common knowledge is the background assumption in individualist intentional theories of action which make (tacit) co-ordination possible. Yet this is not enough to capture cultural structures for which Wendt refers to collective knowledge. As an illustration, Wendt refers to collective memory:

> As long as individuals see themselves as having an allegiance and commitment to the group, collective memories will be available as a resource for mobilising collective action even if they are not believed, in a phenomenological sense, by individuals, and in this way they can help to explain patterns in aggregate behaviour.
>
> (Wendt 1999: 163)

Having made out of collective and common knowledge the lynchpin of culture and of his theory, two further distinctions logically follow. First, since he conceives of idealist structures, Wendt argues that important effects of cultural structures are similar to language, i.e. not causal, but constitutive. 'Thinking depends logically on social relations, not just causally. Human beings think through culture. And since the structure of shared beliefs is ultimately a linguistic phenomenon, this means that language does not merely mediate thinking, it makes thinking possible'

(Wendt 1999: 175). In other words, it is not possible to see the relationship between agency and structure only in terms of pre-existing entities which would *co-determine* each other, as causal explanations would. Instead, they are always also 'entities in the making', in a loop of *mutual constitution* of their very properties (for the causal and constitutive loops, see respectively the lower and upper half of Figure 5.1). Based, in turn, on this distinction between causal and constitutive effects of cultural structures, Wendt's theory must eventually specify the different places of this constitution. This leads Wendt to distinguish between agent properties, namely identity and interests, and agent behaviour.

With these three distinctions – between micro- (interaction) and macro-structure, causal and constitutive effects of cultural structures, and agent properties (identity/interest) and behaviour – Wendt has his conceptual grid in place to play out his assimilating strategy. His theory will, in fact, assimilate no fewer than three other theoretical enterprises (see the three dotted loops in Figure 5.1). We will present them in terms of their comprehensiveness.

The narrowest theory to be assimilated is rational choice, or what Wendt calls thick rationalism. In this theory, the agent–structure link is understood as a very small loop between the micro-structure of interaction and the agent's behaviour, excluding identity. This approach, despite its materialist setting while expressed in utilitarian terms (value-maximisation), does include an ideational component to the extent that behaviouralist rational choice is based on the triad of desires (interests/preferences), beliefs and action. In case the micro-structure changes (via the intended or unintended effects of action), it can also affect future action through a change in the beliefs used for the calculus. Wendt calls this simple learning. Yet, this approach divorces beliefs from desires in the first place, a stance which Wendt shows to be highly contestable. And it entirely neglects identity formation. As nicely put by Ruggie (1998a: 19, emphasis in original), 'a core constructivist research concern is what happens *before* the neo-utilitarian model purportedly kicks in.'

A slightly wider agent–structure approach to be incorporated into Wendt's constructivism is, in fact, the full rationalist action theory programme, called thin rationalism for its less constraining assumptions as compared to behaviouralist rational choice. This includes the possibility to think of ways in which desires are causally affected by cultural structures. Hence, what is crucial here is Wendt's identity/interest vs. behaviour distinction (see Figure 5.1). To some extent, Wendt constructs this thin rationalism which is not yet much theorised in the literature. According to him, the causal effects of micro-structure on identity-interest formation correspond to 'reflected appraisals', that is actors learn identities and interests as a result of how significant others treat them (Wendt 1999: 171). The link between identity and common knowledge allows for the larger micro-loop of causal co-determination.

A third agent–structure approach which Wendt's constructivism can include is the classical (holistic) sociological approach. Here, Wendt can play out the other two distinctions. First, he prolongs the structural loop by including the macro-structure. Then, his approach can include complex learning through the constitutive effects of cultural structures on agent identities. Identities are seen as roles which are internally related to role-identities of other actors, in the form of role-taking and alter-casting: 'By taking a particular role identity Ego is at the same time "casting" Alter in a corresponding counter-role that makes Ego's identity meaningful' (Wendt 1999: 329). This link of identity formation at the collective and individual levels constitutes the macro-loop of mutual constitution (see Figure 5.1).

And, finally, in his own view, Wendt's constructivism goes beyond a purely cultural approach insofar as his rump materialism, more precisely human nature, has a double impact. First, the autonomy of mental states is the non-reducible biological component of individual identity formation. Second, the five basic characteristics of human nature which Wendt develops give rise to needs which are part of interest formation.

This last addition achieves an ambitious meta-theory which, after all has been said and done, is still heavily idealist. Hence, for the social scientist the important claim is 'that power and interest have the effects they do in virtue of the ideas that make them up' (Wendt 1999: 135). Indeed, Wendt repeatedly stresses the pivotal importance of shared beliefs, that is, culture. Culture influences behaviour, constitutes the meaning of behaviour and even constructs identities and interests. His conception of language (see above) does exclude any type of biological reductionism. In principle, it could be made more compatible with more language-based constructivists such as Onuf (1989) and Kratochwil (1989), but Wendt never really develops it (Zehfuß 1998; Zehfuss 2001). His conscious downgrading of epistemological issues on the meta-theoretical level and his less hermeneutic IR theory produce this curious type of constructivism where language is very much out of the picture, despite his repeated reference to its centrality.

A cultural theory of the state-system: assimilating the 'neo-neo' synthesis

Once the meta-theoretical deck is stacked this way, Wendt is free to derive a theory of IR in Part 2 of the book. Here, his general strategy of combining disciplinary-orthodoxy with meta-theoretical heterodoxy produces a theory of IR which, despite the heavy holistic-idealist component, looks quite familiar to IR scholars. As already mentioned, being an orthodox in terms of disciplinary self-understanding, Wendt came up with a theory of the state-system, adding a cultural component. But Wendt's theory looks familiar for two further reasons. First, Wendt again uses a strategy assimilating already known theories. Indeed, in his embrace, he does to institutionalism what institutionalism did to realism. Second, the three cultures he describes have a clear English School ring to them. As will be argued below, Wendt not only has an orthodox view on the discipline, he also holds an orthodox view of international society.

As in the meta-theoretical field, Wendt tries to encompass already existing approaches within a wider framework. He does this by combining two methods. The first one is an offshoot of the meta-theoretical enlargement beyond rationalism. In other words, Wendt simply translates the need for a theory of structure/culture and wider theory of action into a framework of analysis which swallows the rationalist component of the 'neo-neo' synthesis between institutionalism and realism (Wæver 1996). The other method is connected to this general idea: Wendt takes over the strategy of complementarity which was used by institutionalists in their critique of realism.

Neo-institutionalism, despite much academic politics, never claimed that all of realism was wrong. It harked back to classical critiques of realism, often realists themselves, such as Wolfers (1962) and Aron (1962). Wolfers tried hard to show that a one-sided realism, which would understand state behaviour strictly in terms of power maximisation, got it wrong. Politics was to be thought of in a continuum between the pole of power and the pole of indifference. At the latter pole, thinking in terms of power would have unintended effects. Indeed, although it might be correct to think in terms of preventing the worst case, sometimes it is the effect of this worst-case thinking which is the very worst case to be prevented. Although this might now sound 'constructivist' to some ears, it is not exclusively so. Wolfers simply drew together the different lessons from World Wars I and II.

The result of such a critique of one-sided realism was that all theories needed to accommodate cases or (scope) conditions where realist power politics could be expected to prevail, and those where they could not. In the heyday of the transnationalism/interdependence literature, the influential statement of the paradigm in Keohane and Nye's *Power and Interdependence* (1977) never said that realism was always wrong. Politics was conceived on a continuum between power politics and complex interdependence. The more we were facing the latter conditions, the less realism would apply. Therefore, there has actually never been a 'neo-neo' debate but rather an attempt of one neo to gobble up the other. The neo-institutionalist pole always embraced neo-realism as a special case of its own approach.

Using this strategy of assimilating complementarity, Wendt, in turn, embraces the neo-neo synthesis within his wider 'constructivist' framework (Wendt uses 'constructivism' for both his meta-theoretical and his theoretical level). He comes up with a matrix of 3×3 boxes (Wendt 1999: 254) with one side of the matrix defined by the degree of cultural internalisation (coerced, self-interested, norm-internalised) and the other side defined by the degree of society (which corresponds to the Hobbesian, Lockean and Kantian cultures). Having based the theory on the relentless (re)construction of collective identities, Wendt needs a process component. For this, he uses three different degrees of cultural internalisation of roles ranging from coercion via self-interested calculus to identity change. The more internalised the roles, the more the culture will have a self-fulfilling tendency. This holistic component of the third level is beyond the neo-institutionalist synthesis which can accommodate the first two levels. Having thus based the theory on an idealist structural level, Wendt proposes three different collective identities of the inter-state system – the Hobbesian, Lockean and Kantian cultures – which function as the broad scope conditions for understanding the agency role-identities (from enemy to friend), and hence the behaviour of states. Again, the third (Kantian) culture, as exemplified by security communities, tends to go beyond the neo-institutionalist synthesis of Hobbesian and Lockean cultures typical of classical writers such as Wolfers or the regime approach in IR, at least if more than opportunist calculus is assumed (see also the discussion in Hasenclever *et al.* 1997).

Besides this strategy of assimilation, his theory looks familiar since it is couched in terms reminiscent of the English School's triad of realism (Hobbes), rationalism (Grotius) and revolutionism (Kant) (see also the discussion in Suganami 2001). Indeed, given Wendt's constructivism, and hence commitment to reflexivity, this similarity is an even stronger endorsement than is usually acknowledged. For the three traditions of the English School can be understood at the level of the observer and of the actor. At the level of observation, Wendt is perfectly right to say that his theory has a richer meta-theoretical and theoretical framework. At the same time, it is perfectly possible to read the English School as an attempt to 'understand' the languages of international society at the level of the actors themselves. In other words, the fact of the three cultures is not necessarily imposed by an observer who cannot possibly think of other options. Rather, it reflects the self-understood range of political cultures within the diplomatic field of international society itself. Since his is a reflective theory, Wendt sees himself bound by what he understands to be the self-understanding of international society. Wendt is orthodox not only in the self-understanding of the discipline, but also in the self-understanding of international society.

Yet, reading Wendt's theory as having merely added some new drawers to the expanding wardrobe of IR misses perhaps the most important contribution: its crucial process character. This theory, even more than institutionalism, is out to establish the scope conditions under which we might be able not only to recognise certain agent and collective identities, but to understand when we are where, and how we move from here to there. Having insisted that his theory is basically about process, the static matrix recedes somewhat into the background and questions of change and historical dynamics come to the fore. As Ringmar (1997: 285) had noted earlier on, Wendt wants to return history to neo-realism, to put the neo-realist (static) picture into motion.

It is therefore not fortuitous that critics have concentrated on exactly this dynamic component. They focus on Wendt's theory of structural change and collective identity formation, as well as on his vision of politics and progress (respectively, Drulák 2001, Sárváry 2001; see also their chapters in this volume). In their own way, they all deal with the *politics of structural change* in Wendt's theory – and find either 'history' or 'politics/diplomacy' still wanting.

When disciplinary orthodoxy fails to meet theoretical heterodoxy?

This chapter has argued that Wendt's social theory of International Relations mixes orthodoxy in terms of the discipline's self-understanding with heterodoxy in terms of the theory itself. Wendt makes a very ambitious attempt to assimilate existing knowledge in IR and in social theory in a relentless quest for preservation, accumulation and synthesis. Indeed, by blending a theory of scientific progress with a theory of historical progress (see Sárváry 2001), his theory displays this quest in terms not only of science but indeed of nothing less than world history.

This is an enterprise of tall proportions. It explains a series of reactions towards his work. First, although widely quoted, there is a general neglect of the issues Wendt raises. Since the theory weaves all its parts together, it is not all that easy, and certainly not always correct, to 'pick and choose'. Although written in a perfectly accessible way, it builds up an argument where the pieces fall into place bit by bit. It needs the patience of a consumer used to the incremental stages of old cooking recipes, 'slow food', as it were. And it also explains the immediate suspicion of those, as perhaps best expressed by Behnke (chap. 3 this volume), who are wary about grand theoretical enterprises in general, and about the strong liberalism which comes through his vision of progress.

But perhaps another way to read Wendt is to do to him what he does to the discipline. He is self-consciously positioning himself in present debates about the self-understanding of the discipline. He sees a need to get social theory into IR without losing too much of an oversight of what IR is actually about. As a good holist, he does not want us to lose sight of the wood for the trees. He asks the discipline to think big and to think big things together. In his view, he must therefore synthesise. But such a synthesising approach only makes sense if scholars eventually depart from it. No discipline worth its name survives if made up by a community of only synthesisers. In the very self-understanding of a reflective science, any synthesis can only be temporary. It is a means, not an end in itself. In the self-consciousness of the discipline, a synthesis can only be 'assimilated' if it is explored and eventually exploded, again.

Hence, rather than dismissing Wendt for the big questions he dares to ask, and to which his answers will ultimately be judged insufficient, one might take his attempt at synthesising simply as one way, among others, for probing the many 'wires' in contemporary IR theorising. Doing so points to many instances in which the different aspects of his ambitious project might undermine each other. Since this chapter concentrated on the mix of disciplinary orthodoxy and theoretical challenge, we will highlight some tensions in this particular synthesis.

The tensions arise out of the clash of two orthodox choices, crucial perhaps for the self-understanding of much of the discipline, but which substantially restrict the impact of his theoretical challenges. The first choice is to define IR out of the self-definition of its dominant discourses, which gives primacy to tradition and, in particular, to statism. The second, related to it, is the choice to let the self-understanding of the traditional society of states define international politics. Neither of these choices is necessary for Wendt's constructivism since his, like any, meta-theory allows for a series of compatible approaches.

Our criticisms fundamentally derive from the implications of the role given to the state in Wendt's theory. By this, we refer not only to his state-centrism but also to the conscious essentialisation of the state: for Wendt, states are also people, a move which allows him to use symbolic interactionism as his theoretical backbone.[7] The two main implications are that his *Social Theory of International Politics* opens up IR for social theory, but not sufficiently, and restricts our understanding for the always contested borders of international politics.

A first criticism would start by saying that, even if we take the society of states as the given focus, there is no need to give the state such an under-sociological essence. There are at least two ways to make a thicker social theory of it. One way out would have been to herald Ashley's idea for a social theory of IR, to which Wendt explicitly refers. Ashley (1987) argued in support of looking at the community of realists to locate the inter-subjectivity of the international society. This move, which is reminiscent of the English School (see also Cronin 1999), would require a more interpretative analysis of (transnational) political elites, rather than its black-boxing under the heading of corporate or role-identity. In a processual and constructivist theory, role-identity formation has a locus in particular life-worlds, such as the diplomatic field for international society. We would think that sociological institutionalism, and in particular Bourdieu's field theory (Bourdieu 1980), would offer some avenues for a necessarily more micro-sociological underpinning of a constructivist theory (Guzzini 2000a; Leander 2000, 2001c).

In fact, even if we take the focus on states for granted, one would also need to unpack the slot Wendt left for corporate identity. Wendt openly says that he is not writing a theory about (state) identity formation in a move similar to Waltz (1979) when the latter refused to write a theory of foreign policy. But this assumes that the two can be unconnected, which has been shown as erroneous for Waltz (Guzzini 1998: 125–41) and is arguably so for Wendt (Zehfuss, chap. 6 this volume) who is asked also to endogenise corporate identity formation (Cederman and Daase, chap. 7 this volume).[8]

The second criticism involves Wendt's understanding of international 'politics'. It draws on the implications of a brief remark in the book where Wendt (1999: 194) acknowledges writing a theory of the inter-state system and not of international politics at large. Now this might open up another of Pandora's boxes, as much as his blending out of agent-identity formation. It makes the title of Wendt's book as much a misnomer as the title of Waltz's. Waltz might be excused since he might actually believe that his theory is all there is to international politics. But Wendt is aware of the wider field, and yet closes that path down.

The underlying reason for this narrow definition of politics is that Wendt, like Waltz, tends to start from agents to define their practices (Jackson and Nexon 1999). Having settled on states, and unitary ones, Wendt's theory necessarily reduces the nature of politics to what states think of it, actually something a structurationist should not do. For it is not states that define 'politics', but political processes that define their agents (and structures). Starting, like the English School

---

7 This seems to clash with his scientific realism for which states cannot have the same properties as humans (Wight 1999).
8 The original reference was to their so far unpublished manuscript.

(see the critique in Guzzini 2001), from the agent end, Wendt does not address the always contested border of the political (for this critique, see also Kratochwil, chap. 2 this volume, p. 43), of what is of a public and not simply a private concern in international relations, of what is part of international governance and what is not – perhaps the political question *par excellence*. Instead, he takes it for granted and subsumes it under the progressive domestication of violence under the different stages of collective identities.

This narrow view of politics has quite limiting consequences for the international theory Wendt can come up with. To some extent, the book is not a theory of international politics but, seen from a reflexive angle, a theory of how international politics is understood within the classical diplomatic field. Since the borders of international politics are already set there, his theory does not touch on questions of the redefinition of polities in some of the processes bundled under the label 'globalisation' (Leander 2001b, 2006). Indeed, following a disciplinary orthodoxy informed by Waltz, the borders between politics and economics, so painfully torn down by some scholars in IPE, are simply re-erected. Political economy disappears and hence even the question of whether international society is still best understood as the pure society of states and not, for instance, as a hybrid including the 'international business civilisation' with New York, Chicago and Los Angeles as its capital (Strange 1990) and Davos as its meeting point.

Tying the definition of politics to the state undermines even the understanding of the inter-state system, that is, the very core of Wendt's definition of politics. When he assumes the successful domestication and monopolisation of violence by states, he excludes from his view how this field has been reorganised, indeed 'privatised' away from the state (Leander 2004, 2005).

In other words, Wendt's orthodoxy in terms of the self-understanding of the discipline, along with his orthodoxy in defining politics in terms of the self-understanding of the international society of states alone, undermines the very processual character his theory should in fact have and limits the heterodox challenges of his theory of international *politics*. It produces a blind spot in his constructivism which one can, in turn, observe.

Conclusion

This chapter has argued that Wendt's project is best understood as a grand synthesis rather than a *via media*. This synthesis makes divergent positions in IR complementary by reconfiguring and assimilating them under a new encompassing framework. Such a synthesis is much less innocent to other theories than a *via media*. We find that, despite its references to materialism, rationalism and positivism, the overall picture is one heavily tilted towards holism, idealism and an understanding of science which has little to do with positivism as usually understood in IR. In this context, it comes as no surprise that Wendt's present project is to use the idea of complementarity in quantum theory – a post-positivist natural science, as it were – as a basis for his social theory.

Moreover, we argued that Wendt's theoretical challenge uses a strategy of sharing (or simply assuming) a very traditional self-understanding of the discipline. At a time when the languages of the practitioner and the observer are drifting apart, Wendt finds a base for his theoretical communication not in a renewed practical language, but in the conventions of disciplinary identity. Knowing that one can no longer talk the same language, he decided at least to talk about the same and hence unchanged topic. Rather than stressing tensions within his synthesis, this chapter thus emphasised the (reflexive) implications which this taking for granted of the self-understanding of both the discipline and international society has for his theoretical project: it tacitly reifies both self-understandings at a time when they are challenged.

6   Constructivism and identity

A dangerous liaison[*]

Maja Zehfuss

Introduction

Alexander Wendt's *Social Theory of International Politics* has been predicted to gain a status similar to that which Kenneth Waltz's *Theory of International Politics* is thought to have enjoyed in the 1980s.[1] This is even before it has had a chance to make an impact on the discipline. If any further proof were needed for the continuing rise to fame of constructivism in International Relations, this would be it. Constructivism has been explained, applied, positioned. It has been celebrated by some and dismissed by others. Whatever one's view on the matter, constructivism has become increasingly difficult to avoid. Meanwhile, it is important to ask what we might need constructivism for. Given the intellectual diversity of work which has been labelled constructivist, it seems impossible to address this question adequately. Nevertheless it appears that more often than not constructivism is related to an exploration or at least appreciation of the issue of identity in international politics.[2] The significance of identity for constructivist arguments may be more problematic than it seems at first. For constructivism and identity are in a dangerous liaison. In this article, I argue that Wendt's constructivism needs identity as a central concept but that this very concept threatens to undermine the possibility of his constructivism. Although I do not explore this in as much detail, I suggest that the problematic of this dangerous liaison also has some relevance to other approaches which subscribe to the project of 'seizing the middle ground' (Adler 1997).

In this article, I neither aim to propose an alternative approach to the study of identity nor do I seek to review comprehensively all aspects of Wendt's work. Rather I single out Wendt's conceptualization of identity in order to demonstrate how his

* I would like to thank James Davis, Jenny Edkins, Stuart Elden, Friedrich Kratochwil, Steve Smith, Nick Wheeler, Alexander Wendt and two anonymous reviewers for insightful comments on various versions of this piece. Special thanks are due to Roger Tooze who inspired me to write it in the first place.
1 ('Forum on *Social Theory of International Politics*' 2000: 123); Alker (2000: 141); Smith (2000: 151). Note also Friedrich Kratochwil's worry that Wendt's approach might become the new orthodoxy (chap. 2, this volume).
2 See Jepperson *et al.* (1996); Adler (1997: 344, 348); Checkel (1998: 325); Hopf (1998: 172); Katzenstein *et al.* (1998: 682); Price and Reus-Smit (1998: 259); Ruggie (1998a: 4); Guzzini (2000a: 149).

argument comes apart because of its own assumptions. On the one hand, the possibility of constructing different anarchies is fundamental to Wendt's approach as it is this which constitutes the departure from rationalist or 'mainstream' theory. Anarchy, as he put it in an early piece, is 'what states make of it'. This claim rests on the constructedness of identity as the character of anarchy depends on how identities and hence interests are defined. On the other hand, Wendt proposes a 'scientific' theory of the international system. This makes it necessary, in Wendt's view, to take states as given. I will argue that within this approach identity is, and indeed due to its logic must be, conceptualized as circumscribable state identity. In other words, Wendt needs identity to be constructed but at the same time in some ways given. The necessary givenness can only be upheld by excluding dimensions of constructedness from view.

I relate this problematic to the redefinition of the role of the Federal Republic of Germany (FRG) in international politics after the end of the Cold War to include the possibility of military involvement abroad. The upshot of this move is not to suggest better ways of analysing the case at hand or to show that Wendt's approach would work if only he had taken into account the aspects of the identity problematic explored here but to show why, in my view, Wendt's approach cannot work. As my argument involves engaging in considerable detail with both Wendt's claims and the redefinition of the FRG's role in international politics after the end of the Cold War, it may be useful to outline the key moves before embarking on the detailed analysis.

I start by showing the significance of identity to Wendt's approach. The conception of identity is crucial to both the constructivist move and the systemic character of Wendt's argument, even if it is not its declared focus. I neither doubt nor ignore Wendt's focus on the international system. The point, however, is to demonstrate that the structural move relies on identity, more specifically on a particular treatment of identity. In a second step, this problematic is related to a Wendtian reading of the redefinition of the role of the FRG in international politics after the end of the Cold War.[3] This analysis focuses on state interaction in which identities are defined and sustained or changed. While the approach clearly addresses the problematic of the situation at hand, the illustration points up limitations. Hence, having demonstrated the centrality of identity, I move on to consider the problems of Wendt's conceptualization of identity. Debates in Germany about military involvement abroad are explored to show that identities are more complex than a Wendtian account is able to acknowledge. This recontextualization of the issue of identity is important to illustrate what Wendt's approach excludes. It highlights the consequences of buying into Wendt's impossible theory, the price we pay, in other words, for his constructivism.

In the fourth section I elaborate the dilemma of identity in Wendt's constructivism. The unity of identity, which he needs for his approach, is imposed through exclusions. Wendt's exclusions are not innocent methodological choices. That

---

3 Note that I do not claim that Alexander Wendt would read the situation in this way.

which he excludes threatens the very possibility of his argument. If the self cannot be defined apart from context, if identities are inherently contradictory, if identities depend on concrete articulations for their existence, as is argued here, then Wendt's 'via media' might not be possible. If Wendt's 'via media' is in danger of coming apart because one of its key concepts is as necessary as it is impossible, then we may have worries about others attempting similar moves.

Of course, Wendt's constructivism is 'thin' (Wendt 1999: 2) and 'thicker' constructivists may wish to disassociate themselves from his formulation. I certainly do not claim that all constructivist work is just like Wendt's.[4] However, the problematic of identity in Wendt's work can be seen as illustrating a fundamental tension within the kind of constructivism which aims to capture the middle ground. Thus, I conclude by suggesting that the tension in Wendt's work does not bode well for the move whereby constructivists situate themselves *between* rationalists and 'more radical interpretivists' (Adler 1997).

The significance of identity

The identity move

Wendt set out some time ago to show that (neo-)realists are wrong – it is not an unchanging fact that the international realm is a self-help system. Rather, the international environment is created and re-created in processes of interaction. The key move in this argument, or so I claim, is that actors' identities are not given but are developed and sustained or transformed in interaction (Wendt 1996: 48; 1992a; see also Wendt 1999; Hopf 2000: 370). Briefly, a 'world in which identities and interests are learned and sustained by intersubjectively grounded practice, by what states think and do, is one in which "anarchy is what states make of it"' (Wendt 1992b: 183). Wendt has much refined his argument since he published his influential 1992 article (see Wendt 1999). Yet the claim that the way international relations are played out is not given but socially constructed remains central (ibid.: 70).

According to Wendt, it is the intersubjective rather than material aspect of structures which influences behaviour. Intersubjective structures are constituted by collective meanings. Actors acquire identities, which Wendt defines as 'relatively stable, role-specific understandings and expectations about self' (1992a: 397; see also 1999: 21), by participating in collective meanings. Identity is 'a property of international actors that generates motivational and behavioral dispositions' (ibid.: 224). Thus identities are significant because they provide the basis for interests. Interests, in turn, develop in the process of defining situations (1992a: 398; 1999: 231, 329f.).[5] Identities are the basis for interests and therefore more fundamental (ibid.: 231).

4 See Zehfuß (1998), Zehfuss (2001).
5 For more on this, see Wendt (1999: chaps 5 and 6).

Wendt discusses how different kinds of anarchy are constructed in interaction between states (see esp. 1999: chap. 6). What kind of anarchy prevails depends, according to this argument, on what kinds of conceptions of security actors have, on how they construe their identity in relation to others. Notions of security 'differ in the extent to which and the manner in which the self is identified cognitively with the other, and . . . it is upon this cognitive variation that the meaning of anarchy and the distribution of power depends' (1992a: 399f.). Accordingly, positive identification with other states will lead to perceiving security threats not as a private matter for each state but as a responsibility of all. If the collective self is well developed, security practices will be to some degree altruistic or prosocial (ibid.: 400f.). Wendt therefore discusses whether and under which conditions identities are more collective or more egoistic (1996; 1999: esp. 336–69). Depending on where states fall on the continuum from positive to negative identification with other states, they will be more or less willing to engage in collective security practices. Crucially, conceptions of self and other, and consequently security interests, develop only in interaction (1992a: 401; see also 1999: 36). Therefore identity is the key to the development of different security environments or cultures of anarchy.

This relationship between conception of self and other and the prevailing security environment puts identities at the core of the approach. The 'culture of anarchy' depends on how identity gets defined (1999: chap. 6). *Social Theory of International Politics* may not be an investigation into identity formation (1999: 11; 2000: 175) but the concept of identity is crucial to Wendt's argument. According to Wendt, the 'daily life of international politics is an on-going process of states taking identities in relation to Others, casting them into corresponding counter-identities, and playing out the result' (1999: 21). The international system would not be played out in different cultures of anarchy were it not for different conceptualizations of identity. Hence, identity matters not merely when we look at specific states. It is the key to Wendt's *systemic* argument.

What is important is that the concept of identity integrates several crucial moves. Identity relates to the intersubjective aspect of structures and, therefore, its significance establishes the move away from a materialist argument (see 1999: 23f.) and towards the claim that reality is constructed. The proposition that identities and not merely behaviour are shaped by structures or patterns of interaction is construed as setting the approach apart from rationalism (1995: 71f.; see also 1999: 27, 35, 44). According to this argument, rationalists, such as game theorists, may admit that identities change but only prior to interaction, outside the realm of that which rationalists want to analyse (1999: 315f.). Constructivists, on the other hand, are concerned to show that identities may change through interaction and that this matters. Moreover, the claim that definitions of identity, which are subject to change, influence security practices and ultimately the type of anarchy states find themselves in establishes that the self-help system, although ingrained at this time, is not a given, unchanging fact. Identity provides a category which may change but which at the same time is 'relatively stable'. As Wendt puts it, 'identities may be hard to change, but they are not carved in stone' (ibid.: 21).

Transforming definitions of self is more than altering behaviour and therefore a demanding process. It is important to explicate further how this complex issue is conceptualized.

Identity change: showing that identity matters

The key question is then how identities are constituted. After all, 'anarchy is what states make of it' because states' identities are made, not given. Wendt argues that conceptions of self and other come out of interaction between states. State actors, which always have an institutional legal order, the claim to a monopoly on the legitimate use of organized violence, sovereignty, a society and territory (1999: 202–14), exist prior to interaction. Independent of social context, states have four 'national interests' – to preserve and further their physical security, autonomy, economic well-being and collective self-esteem (ibid.: 235–7). Yet, beyond this, reality develops through social interaction in which '[c]onceptions of self and interest tend to "mirror" the practices of significant others over time' (1992a: 404; also 1999: 327, 333f.). In the article 'Anarchy is What States Make of It' this process is illustrated in a story which is worth quoting at length:

> Consider two actors – ego and alter – encountering each other for the first time. Each wants to survive and has certain material capabilities, but neither actor has biological or domestic imperatives for power, glory, or conquest . . . and there is no history of security or insecurity between the two. What should they do? . . .
>
> In the beginning is ego's gesture, which may consist, for example, of an advance, a retreat, a brandishing of arms, a laying down of arms, or an attack. For ego, this gesture represents the basis on which it is prepared to respond to alter. This basis is unknown to alter, however, and so it must make an inference or 'attribution' about ego's intentions and, in particular, given that this is anarchy, about whether ego is a threat. . . . Alter may make an attributional 'error' in its inference about ego's intent, but there is no reason for it to assume a priori – before the gesture – that ego is threatening, since it is only through a process of signaling and interpreting that the costs and probabilities of being wrong can be determined. Social threats are constructed, not natural.
>
> (1992a: 404f.; see also 1999: 328–35)

Accordingly, whether a self-help situation ensues depends on social interaction. The story illustrates how social acts are conceptualized in Wendt's work. In *Social Theory* they are systematically broken down into four 'scenes'. First, *ego*, based on its definition of the situation, engages in an act which signals to *alter* both which role *ego* is planning to take in the interaction and which corresponding role it envisages for *alter*. In the second scene, *alter* interprets the meaning of *ego*'s action in relation to its own perception of the situation. *Alter*, on the basis of its interpretation, which may have involved learning, now engages in an action of its own. This constitutes a signal to *ego* in the same way in which *ego*'s action had been one to *alter*. Finally, in the fourth scene, *ego* responds (1999: 330). Thus Wendt (ibid.: 330f.) describes social acts as processes of signalling, interpreting and responding in which shared knowledge is created and social learning may occur.[6]

Identities and interests are not only created in such interactions, they are also sustained that way (Wendt 1999: 331). Through repeated interactive processes stable identities and expectations about each other are developed. Thereby actors create and maintain social structures (1992a: 405f.), which subsequently constrain choices. Once structures of identity and interests have been created they are not easy to transform because the social system becomes an objective social fact to the actors. Actors may have a stake in maintaining stable identities (ibid.: 411), due to external factors such as the incentives induced by established institutions and internal constraints such as commitment to established identities (1999: 339f.). In *Social Theory* Wendt speaks of the logic of the self-fulfilling prophecy which sustains the identities and interests created in interaction (ibid.: 331, see also 184–9). Nevertheless, identity transformation is possible not only in first encounters, as the illustration may seem to suggest, but is, Wendt argues, also relevant when a shared culture already exists (ibid.: 328).[7]

If we use these conceptualizations to think about the issue of the FRG making military involvement abroad one of its practices after the end of the Cold War, we find that the FRG enters the stage as a unitary actor complete with intentions, beliefs and desires (1996: 59; 1999: 197). The FRG enters the interaction as an individual. It knows that it is 'the FRG', a state actor (cf. 1999: 225). Its existence as a state actor is independent of the international system and – before engaging in any interaction at all – it is equipped with the desire to survive. This is part of its 'corporate identity' which refers to the 'intrinsic qualities that constitute actor individuality' (1996: 50). In the case of state actors, this aspect of identity is based on domestic politics which Wendt considers 'ontologically prior to the states system' (ibid.), 'exogenously given' (1999: 328). As they are part of corporate identity, state actors enter the interaction having some pre-existing ideas about who they are even beyond their awareness of their individuality and their ability to act. At the time of the Gulf War the FRG represented itself as a non-military actor in the international realm. In a government statement shortly before the end of the ultimatum against Iraq, Helmut Kohl, the Chancellor of the FRG, spoke of solidarity with the Americans, the British and the French who carried the main burden in defending law and liberty in this case and of the financial burden for the FRG (Deutscher Bundestag 1991a: 22). This implies that participation in a military operation in the Gulf simply was not at issue for the FRG at this stage.[8]

6   On the limitations of this conceptualization of social acts, see also Zehfuß (1998).
7   For a critique of the notion of first encounter in Wendt (1992a), see Inayatullah and Blaney (1996). Wendt (1999: 141) now acknowledges that even actors encountering 'the Other' for the first time will already have ideas about Self and Other.
8   Witness the parliamentary debates on 14, 17 and 30 January 1991 (Deutscher Bundestag 1991a, 1991b, 1991c). There was, however, a brief debate in August 1990 about a potential contribution

Such behaviour would have interfered with the conception of self. Being non-military was part of the FRG's articulated identity. Article 87a section 2 of the Basic Law for the Federal Republic of Germany (*Basic Law for the Federal Republic of Germany* 1995) was read to rule out the external use of military force for other than defensive purposes. Government statements and international treaties affirmed that 'only peace [would] emanate' from German soil (Genscher 1990: 1201; Kohl 1990: 1227; 'Vertrag über die abschließende Regelung in bezug auf Deutschland' 1993: Article 2). In the past, the FRG had not participated in any military operations abroad and had explicitly rejected such a possibility at least in one case. In the 1980s, in the context of the Iran–Iraq War, the Americans had repeatedly demanded that the Europeans participate in interventions outside the NATO area (Philippi 1997: 60f.; *Der Spiegel*, 30 November 1987: 19–21). At the time, the FRG refused to do more·than deploy one destroyer, one frigate and one supply vessel to the Mediterranean, where they took over positions the US Navy had to abandon because of redeployments to the Gulf region (*Der Spiegel*, 20 July 1990: 121–3; *Frankfurter Allgemeiner Zeitung* (*FAZ*), 10 August 1990: 5; *Süddeutsche Zeitung* (*SZ*), 11–12 August 1990).

However, corporate identity which is exogenous to international politics represents only one aspect of a state's identity. It is the 'site' or 'platform' for other identities (Wendt 1999: 225). In *Social Theory* Wendt distinguishes three other such identities – type, role and collective (ibid.: 224–30).[9] What is important to my argument is the distinction between one pre-given corporate identity and other aspects of identity, made through the process of relating to other actors, which can take 'multiple forms simultaneously within the same actor' (ibid.: 230). Thus I recall Wendt's earlier conceptualization where he opposed 'corporate identity' to 'social identity' which develops only through social interaction, a distinction which he supported by referring to the concepts of 'I' and 'me' in George Herbert Mead's work (Mead 1934).[10] Briefly, the process whereby a state defines its interests precisely and goes about satisfying them depends partially on its notion of self in relation to others, that is, social identities or roles. These are 'sets of meanings' that an actor attributes to itself while taking the perspective of others – that is, as a social object' (1996: 51). Actors have several social identities but only one corporate identity. Social identities can exist only in relation to others and thus provide a crucial connection for the mutually constitutive relationship between agents and structures. This type of identity is continuously (re)defined in processes of interaction. In some contexts social identities are relatively stable. This, however, is

to UN forces in the Gulf region and the possibility of sending minesweepers to the Gulf. The government decided that this would be unconstitutional. See *Süddeutsche Zeitung* (*SZ*), 10 August 1990: 2; *Frankfurter Allgemeine Zeitung* (*FAZ*), 16 August 1990: 2; *SZ*, 16 August 1990: 1; *FAZ*, 18 August 1990: 4; *SZ*, 21 August 1990: 2; *FAZ*, 21 August 1990: *SZ*, 22 August 1990: 4–8.

9 Wendt claims that the last is a distinct combination of the first two (1999: 229) and is, due to their fuzziness, himself unsure how to distinguish between the different categories (ibid.: 224).

10 I do not consider here whether this is in itself a problematic move. For such a critique, see Palan (2000: 591f.).

See Haas

also a result of actors' practices, not a natural fact (ibid.). Although interaction is usually aimed at satisfying interests, actors also try to sustain their conception of themselves and others (1999: chap. 7). Sometimes identities are, however, transformed. Identity change requires social learning. Hence, the transformative potential is mediated through the interaction between *ego* and *alter* in which social learning occurs (ibid.: 326–35).[11]

One of the concrete mechanisms of identity transformation which Wendt considers is based on conscious efforts to change identity. Actors, he argues, are able to engage in critical self-reflection and they can transform or transcend roles. *Ego* may decide to engage in new practices. As the new behaviour affects the partner in interaction, this involves getting *alter* to behave in a new way as well. This process is not just about changing behaviour but about changing identity. As *alter*'s identity mirrors *ego*'s practices, changing *ego*'s practices influences *alter*'s conception of self. When one partner in interaction presents the other with a new role definition, Wendt speaks of 'altercasting', that is, 'an attempt to induce alter to take on a new identity . . . by treating alter as if it already had that identity' (1992a: 421; see also 1999: chap. 7). This only produces the desired effect if the other reciprocates, in other words, if the other takes up the new role.

As we have seen, at the time of the Gulf War the FRG displayed an identity which involved a definition of self as non-military, more precisely as a state which would use military force only for purposes of (collective) self-defence. However, this presentation of self became contested by others. As role definitions by significant others are important and because of the significance of interaction between actors developed above, contestations may influence the FRG's definition of identity. Who is a *significant* other depends on power and dependency relationships (1999: 327, also 331). Therefore, the US should have this role vis-à-vis the FRG but probably also those other entities to which German politicians refer when they speak of 'our friends and partners' – the member states of NATO, the EU, the WEU and the UN.[12] In August 1990 the US requested military support for a possible intervention in the Gulf, at least the deployment of minesweepers to the eastern Mediterranean in order to protect the Suez Canal. The FRG was also asked to participate in a potential WEU operation in the Persian Gulf (*Der Spiegel*, 20 August 1990: 121; Kaiser and Becher 1992: 14).[13] These requests implied a new representation of the FRG. They treated the FRG as if military intervention abroad was a type of behaviour which was compatible with its identity, as if the country contributed to international military operations, even though it had never

11 See also Wendt's earlier explication of 'strategic practice' (Wendt 1996: 56–8).
12 For references to Germany's 'friends and allies' or 'friends and partners' see, for example, Geiger (CDU/CSU) in Deutscher Bundestag (1990b: 18848); Helmut Kohl (Chancellor) in Deutscher Bundestag (1991c: 68, 70) and (1995b: 6632); Volker Rühe (Defence Minister) in Deutscher Bundestag (1993a: 11485); Bundesministerium der Verteidigung (1994: 43, section 312); Klaus Kinkel (Foreign Minister) in Deutscher Bundestag (1994: 21169) and (1995a: 3956). For Wendt on friendship in international politics, see Wendt (1999: 298f.).
13 *Der Spiegel* (11 February 1991: 19) lists a whole series of NATO demands.

done this before. This can be read as an attempt at 'altercasting' (see Wendt 1999: 329, 331). In other words, the US and the WEU behaved towards the FRG as if it already had a new role in the hope that the FRG would do what this new role, rather than the old, demanded of it. The FRG did not, however, respond favourably to the attempt – it turned down the requests on constitutional grounds. The FRG merely sent several ships to the Mediterranean, in order to relieve the US of NATO duties there, but these vessels had to stay within the boundaries of NATO territory.[14] They could go neither to the eastern Mediterranean to secure the Suez Canal nor to the Gulf region itself. The FRG also, reluctantly and on as low a level as possible, granted a request by NATO partner Turkey to deploy forces to its southern border in order to deter a potential Iraqi attack (*Der Spiegel*, 7 January 1991: 20; *FAZ*, 5 January 1991: 2; *FAZ*, 19 January 1991: 5).

At the same time statements of German leaders suggested that the FRG *wanted* to take on the new role but considered it impossible to do so. In particular the Chancellor and the Foreign Minister repeatedly spoke of Germany's willingness to take on more international responsibility, including the participation in international military operations, but its inability due to constitutional restraints to do so for the time being.[15] Wendt acknowledges the significance of such 'rhetorical practice' (Wendt 1996: 57) or verbal communication (1999: 346f.). However, *behaviour* is construed as the key to identity change. The interaction between *ego* and *alter* Wendt describes is all about physical gestures. An advance, a retreat, a brandishing of arms, a laying down of arms or an attack are the examples Wendt gives for a gesture (1992a: 404; see also 1999: 326–35). Two areas of political behaviour could be seen as communicating in this vein the willingness or otherwise of the FRG to take on the new role – participation in other international military operations abroad after the Gulf War and the restructuring of the armed forces to make such participation possible.[16]

The interaction between the FRG and its significant others did not end with the FRG rejecting the new role it was presented with. In 1992 the UN asked for a deployment of the German army, the *Bundeswehr*, for its large peace-keeping operation in Cambodia. The request was for paramedic personnel with military training rather than for armed forces, so as 'not to embarrass the Germans' (*Der Spiegel*, 18 May 1992: 27). The FRG agreed to contribute to this operation, which could be defined as a humanitarian mission and which therefore was not 'as

---

14 See *SZ* (11–12 August 1990: 1); *Der Spiegel* (4 February 1991: 18–22); *Der Spiegel* (21 January 1991: 20); see also *FAZ* (11 August 1990: 2) which, however, cites the German government as claiming that the vessels were 'supplements' rather than replacements for NATO units redeployed to the Gulf region. See also note 5.

15 For example, at the meeting of the Council of Ministers of the WEU on 21 August 1990, at a NATO conference on 10 September 1990 and during the visit of US Foreign Secretary James Baker in the FRG. See Kaiser and Becher (1992: 85f.).

16 One might also want to consider changing the constitution as a symbolic act signalling the willingness to take on the new role. However, it is unclear how domestic norms could figure in Wendt's approach.

military' as participating in the Gulf War would have been. In other words, the identity changes required for this operation were somewhat less ambitious. A series of requests for deployments of the *Bundeswehr* followed. By 1995 the German armed forces had participated in UN missions in Cambodia, Somalia, Iraq, Bahrain, Georgia, the Adriatic Sea, Bosnia-Herzegovina and the former Yugoslavia and contributed to airlifts to Rwanda, Sarajevo and East Bosnia (Bundesministerium der Verteidigung 1998; also Mutz 1993). Yet in many cases the FRG imposed some limitation on its involvement. In the monitoring of the embargo against the former Yugoslavia, German ships were allowed only to monitor, not to stop and search (*Der Spiegel*, 27 July 1992).[17] German surveillance aircraft carried no weapons (*Der Spiegel*, 3 August 1992: 36; *SZ*, 16–17 July 1994: 1). In the UN mission to Somalia the Germans insisted on deploying the *Bundeswehr* only to a 'secure environment'.[18] *Luftwaffe* soldiers serving as part of AWACS crews were not allowed to enter Austrian or Hungarian airspace, that is, leave NATO airspace (*FAZ*, 20 November 1992: 1–2).[19] When the multinational crews operating AWACS reconnaissance aircraft as part of Operation Deny Flight were asked to pass on information to fighter aircraft in order to enforce the flight ban over Bosnia, a fierce debate ensued between the governing parties as to whether the German soldiers had to be withdrawn.[20] There were also restrictions, if gradually fewer, on direct involvement in the former Yugoslavia.

Although the FRG never fully embraced the role offered to it by its significant others, the overall drift of its responses seemed to be that it was willing to move away gradually from its former non-military role. This message was underpinned by aspects of its behaviour which related to the FRG's capacity to engage in military operations. In the early 1990s the FRG started restructuring its armed forces. This was necessary because the soldiers of the East German army had to be integrated into the *Bundeswehr* and the overall number of troops had to be reduced in order to comply with disarmament treaties. Moreover, and crucially in this context, it was argued that the armed forces had to prepare for new tasks. In talks about the future structure of the *Bundeswehr* in early 1991, the governing parties agreed to create an intervention force and the Defence Minister demanded the acquisition of weaponry which would increase the mobility of the armed forces (*Der Spiegel*, 25 March 1991: 93; *Der Spiegel*, 4 February 1991: 22; also *Der Spiegel*, 3 June 1991: 22f.). In September 1992, the army, under Helge Hansen, was the first to restructure its forces so as to create crisis reaction forces (*Der Spiegel*, 7 September 1992: 23–4).

In November 1992 the Defence Minister finally issued new guidelines for defence policy. The armed forces now were not only to protect Germany and its citizens against external threats. They would also serve world peace and

17 This limitation was lifted in July 1994 (*SZ*, 23–4 July 1994: 1, 2).
18 See *SZ* (16 April 1993: 2); *Der Spiegel* (19 April 1993: 21f.); *Der Spiegel* (26 April 1993: 18); *FAZ* (20 April 1993: 1–2).
19 This limitation was lifted in July 1994 (*SZ*, 23–4 July 1994: 1, 2).
20 See *Der Spiegel* (18 January 1993: 18–20); *Der Spiegel* (5 April 1993: 18–22); *SZ* (3–4 April 1993: 1); *FAZ* (3 April 1993: 1–2).

international security in accordance with the UN Charter and provide aid in emergency situations and support humanitarian missions (Bundesministerium der Verteidigung 1992; Bundesminister der Verteidigung 1993). As the 1993 Plan for the *Bundeswehr* and the 1994 White Paper show, the armed forces were to be restructured so as to make them far more mobile then before (Bundesminister der Verteidigung 1993; Bundesministerium der Verteidigung 1994: esp. chap. 5). The 1994 White Paper on security mentioned three capabilities which the armed forces had to develop – the capability to defend the FRG and the Alliance; the capability to participate in multinational efforts at crisis management in the framework of NATO and the WEU; and the capability to participate in UN and CSCE operations in an appropriate way (Bundesministerium der Verteidigung 1994: 91, section 519). Accordingly, the establishment of rapid reaction forces as part of the overall structure of the *Bundeswehr* was planned (ibid.: 93, section 527). The creation of multinational forces was another aspect of planning which expressed the FRG's willingness to get more involved militarily. In October 1991 Kohl and Mitterrand proposed a European rapid reaction force. Europe was to have 50,000 troops based on the Franco-German Corps which already existed. All this was to be realized in the framework of the WEU (*Der Spiegel*, 21 October 1991: 18–20; *SZ*, 22 January 1993: 2). The initiative developed into setting up what was now called the *Eurokorps*. The tasks of the *Eurokorps* included operations for the preservation and re-establishment of peace, also outside of NATO territory (*Der Spiegel*, 18 May 1992: 30; *SZ*, 13 May 1991: 2; *SZ*, 15 May 1992: 2; *SZ*, 22 May 1992: 1).

These efforts at restructuring the armed forces make sense only if military intervention abroad was to become a practice which the FRG was willing to engage in repeatedly. At the same time there was increasing actual involvement in international operations. Both can be read as gestures signalling the FRG's willingness to reciprocate the attempts by its 'friends and partners' at 'altercasting' and gradually take on the new role. The Wendtian approach suggests that this reflects a change not merely in behaviour but in identity (see Wendt 1999: 26). An actor's social identity depends on relationships and indeed is thought to reflect the behaviour of others towards it. Thus the new way in which its significant others treated the FRG would influence its definition of self. The notion that the FRG was undergoing a transformation of identity seems reasonable as repeated military deployments abroad and acquiring an intervention capacity were bound to interfere with a conception of self which had been strongly non-military.

However, we get little sense of what exactly happens when identities, which Wendt after all considers to be 'relatively stable' (Wendt 1992a: 397; 1999: 21), change. Sujata Chakrabarti Pasic has pointed out that 'having no concrete conceptualization of identity formation that engages the actual social levels of states' sociality' (1996: 89) is a problem in Wendt's work. In my view, the centrality of physical gestures in Wendt's explication of social action renders it impossible to analyse identity transformation as a discursive process. The recognition of 'rhetorical practice' (Wendt 1996: 57) or verbal communication (Wendt 1999: 346f.) as significant is a step in the right direction but it fails to address *how* discourse should be analysed.[21] This omission is crucial because the assumption that states are pre-given, unitary actors depends on it. As will be demonstrated in the next section, the competing identity narratives highlighted by an exploration of the discursive constitution of identity endanger this assumption and hence the possibility of Wendt's systemic theory.

Moreover, there is the problem of disentangling identity and behaviour because Wendt claims that it is not just behaviour but identity that changes. Yet it is unclear, with respect to an actual case such as the one considered here, what exactly sets apart identity transformation from a mere change in behaviour. Although Wendt's claim that the way in which others treat an actor will affect its conception of self rather than just the way it behaves seems plausible, it is hard to pin down the qualitative difference between the two. After all, in his approach we are forced to infer actors' self-understandings from nothing but their behaviour. If an identity matters only in its realization in certain types of behaviour, then it is difficult to see what should justify calling it 'identity' rather than 'behaviour'. The idea that identities are relatively stable is certainly of no help as the possibility of identity transformation, of moving from one kind of anarchy to another, is crucial.

In order to detect any identity change, it must be possible to identify the identity an actor 'has' at any given point in time. *Ego* presents *alter* with a new identity which *alter* either takes up or refuses. Contestation over the identity takes place only between *alter* and *ego*. Although there may be a gradual adjustment of the ideas about self and other on both sides, it is a contestation over two alternative but clearly recognizable notions of identity. How either the actors or the ideas about self and other are constituted in the first place is not part of the account. This exclusion takes as given what are political constructions but it is necessary for Wendt's approach. Hence, identity is not only significant for Wendt's constructivism; it is also problematic.

The problem of identity

Telling identity

If we look beyond Wendt's account we find that Germans engaged in fierce arguments about the limitations which their constitution and their history imposed on them. They accused each other of changing the nature of the FRG, militarizing foreign policy and being irresponsible and short-sighted.[22] Engaging these debates about German identity in some detail provides the material with which to show, in

---

21 Kratochwil's insistence on the significance of descriptions seems to point in a similar direction (this volume, pp. 41–2).
22 See, for example, Günter Verheugen (SPD) in Deutscher Bundestag (1993a: 11480); Andrea Lederer (PDS/Linke Liste) in Deutscher Bundestag (1993b: 12942); Rudolf Scharping (SPD) in Deutscher Bundestag (1995a: 3960); Hermann-Otto Solms (FDP) in Deutscher Bundestag (1994: 21180).

the following section, that taking identity and its construction seriously has the potential to undermine Wendt's approach.

Articulations of 'German' identity often rely on contextualizing what is considered German now with respect to the historical experience of the Third Reich. In his first statement after unification, the Federal Chancellor asserted, for instance, that future policies of the FRG would be guided by an awareness of 'German history in all its parts and of the responsibility which follows from it'. He reminded people that the creators of the Basic Law had been led by a double oath – 'Never again war! Never again dictatorship!' (Deutscher Bundestag 1990a: 18019). This double commitment against war and against dictatorship was put forward as unproblematic. The two principles were presented as complementary. The 'Never again war' principle was also invested into the Two-Plus-Four Treaty which states that 'only peace will emanate from German soil' ('Vertrag über die abschließende Regelung in bezug auf Deutschland' 1993: Article 2). Accordingly, Heidemarie Wieczorek-Zeul of the Social Democrats considered the people's resistance against plans for military involvement an expression of 'that which has been collected in the tradition of military restraint in Germany in the decades after the war' (Deutscher Bundestag 1993a: 11489f.). Her fellow party member Peter Glotz argued that the 'Germans have led enough wars in this century. [They] are not available and pretty unsuited for the task of world policeman or assistant world policeman' (Deutscher Bundestag 1993b: 12968). Germans had killed millions of people in this century and millions of Germans had been killed. Glotz claimed that therefore the Germans had a right to say that they would help financially, logistically and so on but that they wanted to be left alone with respect to war (ibid.: 12969). Thus, both Wieczorek-Zeul and Glotz cited the 'Never again war' principle as the reason for their opposition to military involvement abroad.

However, the commitment to a German state which was defined as a non-military international actor became increasingly difficult. This position was confronted with a new normative contradiction between 'Never again war' and 'Never again dictatorship'. As Alice H. Cooper observes,

> Incipiently during the Gulf War and emphatically in Bosnia, parts of the left saw themselves confronted with a conflict between fundamental values that had been considered mutually reinforcing during the Cold War: between antifascism and pacifism; between internationalism and pacifism; and between collective security and antimilitarism.
>
> (Cooper 1997: 103)

The conflict between pacifism and anti-fascism was thrown into sharp relief in the summer of 1995 when Joschka Fischer, the leader of the Alliance 90/the Greens parliamentary group, wrote a letter to his party entitled 'The catastrophe in Bosnia and the consequences for our party' (Fischer 1995). A key question of the letter was: 'Can pacifists, can especially a position of non-violence just accept the victory of brute, naked violence in Bosnia?' (ibid.: 1148). Fischer argued that the line would have to be drawn somewhere because otherwise this fascism with its violent politics would not stop. The Bosnian war threw up basic questions and led to a fundamental conflict of three basic values of the Greens' political convictions: life and freedom were opposed to the principle of non-violence (ibid: 1149). Fischer pointed out that both possible options with respect to the war in Bosnia – protecting the UN safe areas or withdrawing – touched upon the conflict between those basic values. Practical answers were necessary and they had to address the question of resistance and therefore violence (ibid.: 1152). In sum, although he almost hid it between the lines, Fischer backed the idea of military intervention.

In an interview following the publication of the letter, Fischer described the contradiction he saw himself confronted with – violence, on the one hand, always leads to more violence but, on the other hand, survival sometimes depended on it. Merely watching the success of the new fascism was damaging the moral substance of the left. Fischer said that the core of his political identity was based on two 'Never again' principles, 'Never again war' and 'Never again Auschwitz'. The big contradiction, which was impossible to resolve, was that it might not be possible to prevent Auschwitz without war. He recommended that his party stand up for this contradiction rather than aim to resolve it in one way or another (*Der Spiegel*, 21 August 1995: 28f.). In 1999, now Foreign Minister of the FRG, Fischer supported and implemented *Bundeswehr* participation in Operation Allied Force in relation to Kosovo. He was convinced that only the last resort of violence had been possible in this case (*SZ*, 25 March 1999: 1).

The contradiction between the rejection of war and the opposition to oppression and barbarity was a problem not only for the left. The governing parties continuously referred to the traditionally important notion of military restraint. In the parliamentary debate about the ruling of the Federal Constitutional Court, which had removed most perceived constitutional restraints against military intervention abroad, the Foreign Minister, Klaus Kinkel, was at pains to make clear that the so-called culture of restraint would remain. There would be no militarization of German foreign policy (Deutscher Bundestag 1994; also Kinkel 1994: 4). However, he argued that the increasingly widespread UN practice of peace-keeping and especially peace-making posed a new problem. Now, Germany was not in the position of a potential aggressor; rather, it was asked to use the military instrument to end wars others had started. Thus, the 'Never again war' principle as it had traditionally been understood came under challenge. The context made it possible to rearticulate the principle and represent military involvement as not about waging war at all. On the contrary, as Wolfgang Schäuble put it, it was 'about securing the peace task of the Bundeswehr also for the future of our country, namely to avoid war at all costs' (Deutscher Bundestag 1993b: 12934). The principle that Germans must not engage in war was then not at all applicable to the problem at hand, as military involvement abroad was about preventing war rather than engaging in it.

This brief illustration of representations of the 'Never again war' principle shows that it was articulated in different ways. 'Never again war' could either mean what it had referred to traditionally, that is, that German soldiers should not engage in fighting. On the other hand, as the above shows, it could also mean that war had to be stopped, that is, that German soldiers had to fight in order to prevent war. It could also be overruled by the 'Never again dictatorship' principle. The move whereby the need to prevent dictatorship or fascism was represented as the reason why German military involvement was necessary can be seen in Kinkel's speech during the parliamentary debate about a German contribution to the protection and support of NATO's rapid reaction force in the former Yugoslavia on 30 June 1995.

The need to contribute to the military force in Bosnia was based, in Kinkel's argument, on the need to show solidarity with those countries which had been carrying the burden of the loss of lives of their citizens in an effort to help other human beings, in particular France and Great Britain, and with those 'innocent' people who were dying cruel deaths in the former Yugoslavia (Deutscher Bundestag 1995a: 3955f.). Germany needed to show solidarity with its allies because Germany had received protection and solidarity with respect to security issues from its friends and partners during the Cold War. In order to justify the deployment, Kinkel proceeded to present his version of the meaning of history for the political decision at issue. During the Cold War, he argued, Germany, in view of its history and the division of the country, focused on territorial defence. This 'culture of restraint' had been good and accepted. Yet now Germany was expected 'to actively contribute towards the protection of the international order and of human rights, especially in Europe' (ibid.: 3957). Kinkel argued, then, that Germany had 'a political and moral obligation to help, also and particularly in view of. . . history' (ibid.). He noted that it had been the Allies who, *using military force*, had freed the Germans from Nazi dictatorship and had made a new democratic beginning possible (ibid.). Thus he likened German military intervention in the former Yugoslavia to the Allied involvement in the Second World War and thereby created a new historical contextualization. The Germans are shifted, in this narrative, to the position of those who liberate, who constitute the hope for 'innocent' people living and dying in conditions of war and oppression. This move makes the *Bundeswehr* similar to the heroic liberators of the Second World War bringing peace and freedom rather than to *Wehrmacht* troops committing atrocities in the Balkans.

Those who wanted the peace-keepers to remain in Bosnia had to contribute to making this possible. According to Kinkel, this was not about lowering the threshold for German military involvement abroad. The decision under discussion was not about waging war but about preventing war. The claim that the German Tornado fighters would wage war, he argued, turned things on their head. In fact, they would act only in the event of an aggression against the troops of the rapid reaction force. Kinkel claimed not to understand the policy of the opposition who were in favour of the UN remaining in Bosnia but refused to deploy Tornado fighters. He implied that this policy amounted to supporting that UNPROFOR should remain in Bosnia to the last Frenchman or Briton (Deutscher Bundestag 1995a: 3957f.). Kinkel finished his speech by asking the members of parliament, also of the opposition, to show solidarity with 'our allies, our soldiers, but in particular with the people in a truly sorely afflicted country!' (ibid.: 3959).

In his case for deploying soldiers to the former Yugoslavia, Kinkel thus recontextualized the 'Never again war' principle in two ways. The FRG had to deploy troops in order to show solidarity with its Western partners and in order to help fellow human beings who were suffering. As Kinkel stressed, the FRG would not even exist had it not been for the intervention of the Allies in the Second World War. The creation of the FRG was made possible through a military intervention which put an end to the barbarity of the Nazi regime; therefore such intervention is at least sometimes good. Indeed, the use of force can be necessary in order to prevent war and further suffering. It does not in itself constitute war, which, of course, the government does not want to get involved in. This move entails a further recontextualization. The kind of military operation envisaged is removed from the 'war' category. As a result, the 'Never again war' principle has clearly been rearticulated. It now refers to preventing other people's wars rather than German wars. This representation of the principle is inherently contradictory, however. It relies both on the notion that the violence of military force, that is, war, will produce good results in the given circumstances and on the idea that the use of military force at issue does not constitute the violence we call war. Yet, this contradiction did not hinder this new narrative from becoming an accepted way of telling identity.

These debates could in some way be read to confirm what Wendt argues. In the contestation over German identity the boundaries of the self seemed to matter. It is possible to argue that, in order to have many of these discussions, the people on whose behalf the military was to intervene had in some way to be seen as worthy of the effort, as human, and therefore in some way as part of the self. In that sense, they were made part of a collective identity. The Western partners were also treated as part of the self when the Foreign Minister argued that the FRG could not support a policy which in effect amounted to fighting to the last Frenchman. Something similar might be said about *Bundeswehr* participation in Operation Allied Force in relation to Kosovo, which was, according to Federal Chancellor Gerhard Schröder, undertaken to protect others (Deutscher Bundestag 1999: 2571) and in which NATO was represented as the key actor.[23] Germany played a role only insofar as it was part of NATO. Yet these debates are fundamentally in tension with Wendt's conceptualization of identity. Whether the FRG should value avoiding war over fighting fascism or vice versa cannot really be explicated in terms of the boundary of the self. Both 'Never again war' and 'Never again fascism' are principles which take into account the needs of others. They do not represent a competition between a more egoistic and a more collective definition of identity. The debates were also very much about who the self *should* be, a dimension which Wendt does not mention very much. A number of different representations of identity were articulated *within* the FRG. Hence, the question of what identity is to be attached to the notion of 'German' or 'Germany' was a contested issue not only between the FRG and its significant others.

23 See Federal Chancellor Gerhard Schröder's statement on the occasion of NATO's fiftieth anniversary (Schröder 1999: 193).

Yet the important point is not that Wendt 'brackets' the domestic and excludes the normative but the significance of this move for his approach.[24] Structural change, and thus a key focus of systemic theorizing, supervenes identity change (Wendt 1999: 338). Thus identity transformation is significant, even if not a focus of the theory as such. However, the exploration of German contestations over identity provides the material with which to demonstrate that Wendt's bracketing of domestic politics and his related failure to take the discursive production of identity seriously is not an innocent methodological choice but a necessary move if identity is not immediately to threaten his constructivist project.

The identity of identity

The contestations over German identity show a complexity which is not admissible within Wendt's framework. In other words, they suggest that that which Wendt excludes threatens the very possibility of his argument. Wendt's conceptualization of identity assumes it to be a bounded category and, more importantly, needs it to be so. It is an identity without difference. This unity of identity is imposed through multiple exclusions which concern the genesis and type of actor and, most fundamentally maybe, the kind of project Wendt's approach is supposed to be. It is precisely the possibility of the latter which is, however, threatened by the dangerous liaison with identity.

Wendt asks us to assume two actors, *ego* and *alter*, who then come to interact only after we have imagined them on their own. This starting point, he tells us, is an 'interactionist convention' (Wendt 1999: 328). Analogously, in order to follow his argument we have to imagine states as prior to and independent from social context. Wendt seems to have no problem with this move, which has already been criticized by Pasic in relation to his earlier work (1996: 86–90).[25] Wendt even knows what the actors are like before they come to be part of a context. He defends an anthropomorphic conception of the state (Wendt 1992a: 397, n. 21; 1999: 10, 215). What I want to draw attention to here is that the assumption of unity which goes along with this anthropomorphic conception of the state leads to a specific understanding of identity which seems problematic in relation to the issues raised by the debates on German military involvement abroad.[26] It makes it impossible to acknowledge the complexity of identity and ultimately restricts identity to a question of boundaries.

The logic of the 'Never again war' narrative and its rearticulation relies on equating 'the FRG', 'Germany' and 'the Germans'. This betrays a specific understanding of identity. The notion that the FRG must not engage in war

---

24 Ted Hopf (2000: 372f.) makes a number of similar observations about Wendt's ambiguous attitude towards the domestic and its implications without, however, drawing my conclusions.

25 Naeem Inayatullah and David Blaney (1996: esp. 72–5) also make a number of similar observations in their critique of Wendt's 'Anarchy is What States Make of It'.

26 On the assumption of unity and the consequence of identity, see also Pasic (1996: 100).

because of historical lessons is based on the idea that the FRG is somehow the contemporary expression of that entity which was the Third Reich from 1933 until 1945. The FRG represents itself and is represented by others as the successor of the Nazi state. In a conceptualization which takes states as given it cannot be otherwise. On the other hand, the FRG is at the same time portrayed in many ways as the negation of the Nazi state. The FRG is constitutionally committed to the equality of men and women from all backgrounds, for instance. One of the defining characteristics of the FRG as *different* from the Third Reich used to be its renunciation of the use of military force other than for (collective) self-defence. Article 87a (2) of the Basic Law, which was thought to rule out military operations beyond defence, had been portrayed as the product of the lessons of the Second World War. Government statements and international treaties affirmed that 'only peace [would] emanate' from German soil (Genscher 1990: 1201; Kohl 1990: 1227; 'Vertrag über die abschließende Regelung in bezug auf Deutschland' 1993: Article 2). Hence the equation of 'Germany' and 'the FRG' is more problematic than it would at first seem. At the same time, the rejection of armed force makes sense only in the context of the history of the Third Reich and thus relies on this very equation. In the debates on military involvement abroad it was never contested that the Germans and the FRG had to define their identity in relationship to the Nazi state. However, the concrete expression of this relationship, and therefore of German identity, was very much at issue.

The issue was further complicated by the substantive disagreement over the implications of that relationship. Defining the identity of the FRG as following on from but at the same time fundamentally different from the Third Reich could mean to reject participation in war altogether. Traditionally, 'Never again war' had referred to just that. However, it could also mean opposition to fascism and the human suffering caused by it. Ideally, it would have meant both but, as the two came to be seen to contradict each other, subscribing to either principle led to differing notions of identity. One stressed the non-military character of the FRG, the other the responsibility to end oppression. These competing definitions of identity were experienced as a genuine normative contradiction which could not easily be resolved. In this situation another move of equating two entities provided the space for a new narrative. The Foreign Minister likened the *Bundeswehr* to Allied troops liberating the Germans and others from dictatorship and oppression (Deutscher Bundestag 1995a: 3957). This made possible prioritizing the 'Never again fascism' principle because, as the example of the Allied intervention in the Second World War and the subsequent foundation of the FRG showed, wars of liberation potentially had very good consequences. Moreover, the old 'Never again war' logic was not applicable to the situation at hand as German military involvement would be about avoiding or ending wars rather than waging war. UN operations were, in other words, not really war. Thus, participating in UN operations could, in the new articulation of the 'Never again war' principle, again constitute an active opposition to both war and dictatorship.

Thus, German military involvement abroad was construed as *both* problematic *and* necessary because of the history of the Third Reich. The *problematic* aspect becomes obvious in the claim that the *Bundeswehr* should not go where the *Wehrmacht* had caused havoc during the Second World War.[27] It is also implicit in the fear that any *Bundeswehr* deployment abroad would lead to a remilitarization of German foreign policy?[28] On the other hand, the idea that participation in international operations was *necessary* to live up to the historical responsibility[29] was also at least partially based on Germany's responsibility for the Second World War and the Holocaust. The difference from the Nazi past was as fundamental to this argument as the identity with the Nazi state. This representation of identity thus always already involved a 'difference *with itself*' (Derrida 1992: 9f.). If the relationship between the Nazi state and the FRG had been one of identity *only*, the idea of sending its troops abroad would certainly not have found the support of European neighbours.

The difference of the FRG with Germany's past – while at the same time representing the FRG as 'Germany' and therefore as identical with its past – was established not only through its non-military character but crucially also through the integration with the West. The acceptance of Western values through integration into Western institutions is represented as the key difference between the dark Germanies of the past and the enlightened, responsible Germany of today (Habermas 1993 [1986]: 43f.). In his speech justifying the deployment of German troops to support NATO's rapid reaction forces in the former Yugoslavia, Foreign Minister Kinkel puts this decision into the context of a series of historical decisions which, with the exception of *Ostpolitik*, were all represented as instances where the seriousness of the FRG's commitment to Western integration was seen to be at issue – rearmament, joining NATO, the renunciation of nuclear weapons and the implementation of NATO's twin-track decision (Deutscher Bundestag 1995a: 3955). Part of the problem was that the contradiction between the commitment to military abstention and the commitment to Western integration which both establish the desirable difference from that other, darker Germany are in tension. For the partners in NATO demanded a military contribution and military integration worked to involve the *Bundeswehr* in international operations more or less automatically.[30] It is important to note that, even once this tension is resolved in favour of discarding military abstention, the narrative on identity, though presented as referring to a coherent entity, still relies on both the special responsibility derived from the FRG's identity with the Nazi state and its ability to deliver a better future to the people in the former Yugoslavia through military intervention which relies on the FRG's difference from the Nazi state.

My 'Wendtian' reading excluded these intriguing aspects of identity representation. Clearly, the problem is not that Wendt's framework fails to address the

27 This has been termed the Kohl doctrine (Joffe 1994) but the point was also subscribed to by others. See, for example, Kinkel (1994: 7) and Joschka Fischer (Bündnis 90/Die Grünen) in Deutscher Bundestag (1995a: 3975).
28 For example, Peter Glotz (SPD) in Deutscher Bundestag (1993b: 12970).
29 Klaus Kinkel (Foreign Minister) in Deutscher Bundestag (1994: 21166).
30 Note specifically the controversy around the AWACS mission in 1993.

specifics of German identity construction. It is more fundamental. Wendt's anthropomorphic concept of the state cannot cope with identities which are unstable in themselves. Identity change is merely about shifting from one relatively stable identity to another. States are unitary actors with minds, desires and intentions. Wendt's recognition that domestic politics influences state behaviour and state identity fails to address the complexity of the issue at hand (Wendt 1999: 264, 364). The exclusion of the process of the construction of the state as a bearer of identity and of domestic processes of articulation of state identity are part of the problem. This reduces identity to something negotiable between states. It is not surprising, given this starting point, that Wendt is concerned mainly with the *boundaries* rather than with the content of theories about the self (1999: 229, 241f., 243, 305, 317).[31] Wendt addresses identity as the question of who is considered part of the self. If other states are considered part of the notion of self, in other words, if the boundary of the self gets pushed outwards beyond the boundary of the state, Wendt argues that there exists a collective rather than an egoistic definition of identity (1996: 52f.; 1999: 229). He informs us that the 'constructivist model is saying that the boundaries of the Self are at stake in and therefore may change in interaction, so that in cooperating states can form a collective identity' (1999: 317). The question of who is considered part of the self is certainly an important one. Yet the particular way in which it is posed excludes consideration of the significant process of constructing 'Germany' or any other state as a subject and the relevant agent in the first place.

The necessary multiplicity of origins referred to in telling identity puts into question the naturalness of the succession of German states – Third Reich, old FRG, new FRG – which is used as the basis for claiming a special responsibility. This seemingly natural narrative of identity also denies the history of the German Democratic Republic (GDR). Foreign Minister Kinkel argued that the Allies had liberated the Germans and made a democratic beginning possible (Deutscher Bundestag 1995a: 3957). Moreover, 'Germany' had been protected by the Western Allies during the Cold War and therefore they could now legitimately expect solidarity from the Germans (ibid.: 3956). This erases the existence of the other Germany which was anything but protected by those Western allies and claims the solidarity of those Germans who did not enjoy this protection but now, as citizens of the FRG, have become part of the collective telling of identity. The slippage between 'Germany', 'the FRG' and 'the Germans', sometimes even when reference is clearly made only to the old FRG, works to obscure the making of identity through discourse. The equation of the FRG with Germany and earlier German states seems to be in accordance with common sense. Recognizing that any representation of the FRG involves incorporating a number of different sources of identity, even if one is ostensibly prioritized over the other, exposes the non-natural character of the identity which provided the basis for the justification

---

31 It could be argued that the discussion of 'type' and 'role' identities addresses issues of content (Wendt 1999: 225–8).

of German military involvement abroad. Things were much less clear than some wanted to claim. The Nazi past meant both that the FRG should use the military and that it could not use it. Moreover, the FRG had to intervene militarily abroad to prove its membership of the Western community but its interventions were good only because it was already considered part of the West.

The contingency and even inherently contradictory character of these expressions of identity is, I argue, not only invisible through Wendt's framework but in tension with his conceptualization of identity. The illustration suggests that it is impossible to circumscribe 'the identity' the FRG 'has' or to list the characteristics which 'having' a certain identity entails. Identities depend on concrete articulations. Whether the FRG is thought to be different or like the Third Reich in any given situation is not clear a priori. In Wendt's framework, however, just that identity of both is assumed. When, in his theoretical argument for the constructedness of anarchy, Wendt asks us to think of two actors, *ego* and *alter*, this starting point is presented as innocent, as relatively free of prior assumptions (Wendt 1992a: 404f.; 1999: 328)[32] and indeed as necessary. Actors, according to Wendt, have to be identified '[b]efore we can be constructivist about anything' (1999: 7). For a systemic theory of international politics, more specifically, states must be treated as given (ibid.: 244). This 'essentialist' (ibid.: 198) claim seems problematic for a 'constructivist' theory (see also Doty 2000: 138; Kratochwil, this volume, pp. 23, 38). Taking state actors as given presupposes the identity between 'the FRG' and 'Germany'. It is therefore impossible for this approach to appreciate the ambiguity involved in construing the identity of 'the FRG' with 'Germany' and therefore 'the Third Reich'. This identity is taken as given, presumably on the basis of (limited) spatial continuity.

Wendt informs us that '[w]hat makes . . . Germany "Germany" is primarily the discourse and agency of those who call themselves Germans, not the agency and discourse of outsiders' (1999: 74). The identity of the state as Germany is therefore not created in social interaction. It is, as corporate identity (ibid.: 328), prior to international politics. Wendt's starting point obscures that this representation is neither necessary nor innocent. The identity between different German polities, as far as it exists, is an accomplishment of discourse. The argument that solidarity with the West is necessary as a repayment of protection during the Cold War makes sense only if 'Germany' can be construed as being identical with 'the FRG', excluding the GDR. The shift towards using the military abroad relied on this problematic equation. The exclusion of the consideration of the relevant self which is reflected in Wendt's approach to the analysis of international politics is a political move in that it establishes a non-natural relationship as given and unchangeable.

Wendt defends at length his belief that state agents have essential properties (Wendt 1999: 198–214). These are meant to set them apart from 'dogs, trees,

---

32 David Campbell also takes issue with this (1996: 12f.; 1998: 219–22). From a different perspective, Inayatullah and Blaney (1996: 73) and Pasic (1996: 87–90) raise this point as problematic as well.

football teams, universities, and so on' (ibid.: 213f.). Wendt does not consider the constitution of states as subjects in the first place.[33] Thus, viewed in the context of Wendt's framework the issue considered here must be construed around *a state with an identifiable identity*, what is denoted by 'Germany'. The insecurity of the German state's identity can thus at best be considered a curiosity. Although Wendt claims that '[h]istory matters' (ibid.: 109), multiple histories do not. 'Germany' makes an appearance only as a unified entity. Considering identity, in this setting, does not make thinking more problematic. There is no space for contemplating Jacques Derrida's claim that 'self-difference, difference to itself [*différence à soi*], that which differs and diverges from itself, of itself' is always part of cultural identity (Derrida 1992: 10). Rather, as David Campbell points out, '"identity" is rendered in essentialist ways as a variable that can be inserted into already existing theoretical commitments' (Campbell 1998: 218).

Excluding consideration of the genesis of the actor is not the only problem. Wendt argues that what he calls 'ideas' have both constitutive and causal effects (Wendt 1998; 1999: chap. 3). Although he is more concerned to make a case for the significance of constitution, based on his commitment to scientific realism he also considers identity a causal category which helps explain international politics (1998: 107; 1999: 93, 229).[34] Wendt insists that 'the basic realist idea that scientific explanation consists in the identification of underlying causal mechanisms . . . does apply to the social sciences' (1987: 355; see also 1999: 77) and explicitly 'endorses a scientific approach to social inquiry' (1999: 1).

This creates further problems. The illustration in this article shows that identities as they are defined in discourse fail to be logically bounded entities. Identities are continuously articulated, rearticulated and contested, which makes them hard to pin down as explanatory categories. The stories we tell about ourselves are, as the rearticulation of the 'Never again war' principle shows, not necessarily coherent. If identity is to 'cause' anything, however, it must be an antecedent condition for a subsequent effect and as such distinguishable from that which it is causing (Wendt 1998: 105; 1999: 25, 79, 167). At one point, Wendt tells us that, as part of his argument, he is advancing 'a simple causal theory of collective identity formation' (1999: 317). On the other hand, structure is supposed to have causal effects on identity (ibid.: 144). Here, identity is effect rather than cause, but the requirement of clear separation remains.[35] Wendt's treatment of identity as something which is attached to and negotiated between pre-existing anthropomorphic actors and which *explains* (or is explained) requires conceptualizing identity as a unitary, circumscribable concept. It makes necessary the identity of identity.

33 Campbell points this out as well. See Campbell (1998: 220f.).
34 Steve Smith (2000: 157) claims that Wendt's constitutive theory is basically a form of causal theory. On Wendt's commitment to scientific realism and its problems see also Kratochwil (chap. 2 this volume).
35 Roxanne Lynn Doty also comments on the need clearly to categorize, define and distinguish for what Wendt wants to do and the impossibility of this task (Doty 2000: 137f.).

Although Wendt argues that the world is constructed, there are certain aspects of the world which, based on a defence of scientific realism (esp. Shapiro and Wendt 1992; Wendt 1999: chap. 2), he takes as given. What is particularly surprising is that it is precisely with respect to the key move of identity (trans)formation that Wendt evades the implications of the argument that that which we call reality is constructed rather than given. Acknowledging that identities do not exist apart from articulation and contextualization, have no clear bounds and fail to be logically coherent, as the illustration suggests, would threaten the premises of the approach.

The threat is fundamental as it endangers the project. Wendt tells us that he is seeking a '"via media" through the Third Debate' (Wendt 1999: 40, 47). This 'via media' entails addressing social construction, or what Wendt calls 'an idealist and holist ontology', while 'maintaining a commitment to science' (ibid.: 47).[36] Wendt discusses the philosophical grounding which he claims for this middle way in great detail in chapter 2 of *Social Theory*. In terms of International Relations, what he is claiming is a departure from rationalism (1995: 71f.; 1999: 27, 35) which does not force him to give up science as he understands it, which does not, in other words, force him to subscribe to 'postmodernism'. The claim that 'anarchy is what states make of it' revolves around the idea that identities are socially constructed and may be changed, even if such identity transformation is not easy. This is what distinguishes Wendt's approach from rationalist thinking in International Relations. It is thus crucial to establishing constructivism as something fundamentally different from 'mainstream' theorizing. Although Wendt, in his recent work, argues that 'there is no contradiction between rationalist and constructivist models of the social process' (1999: 366f.), he does uphold a difference in analytical focus between the two. Constructivist models will be most useful, he tells us, when we have reason to think that identities and interests will change (ibid.: 367). Thus, as before, the possibility of identity change establishes the difference between rationalism and constructivism. Yet, at the same time, identity must not be as malleable, contingent and elusive as the illustration in this article suggests. For acknowledging that identity is 'never given, received or attained' (Derrida 1998: 28) would entail a move in a direction which Wendt seems to fancy even less than the rationalism of the 'mainstream'. In a collection of 'constructivist' contributions to the study of national security, the authors of the chapter explicating the analytical framework, one of whom was Wendt, felt it necessary to point out that their usage of the term 'identity' did not signal a 'commitment to some exotic (presumably Parisian) social theory' (Jepperson *et al.* 1996: 34). This may have been a flippant remark. However, if thinking through the claim that identity is constructed leads us to recognize that the subjects themselves do not exist apart from context, then Wendt, and some other constructivists, have a problem with the space which they are attempting to carve out for themselves. The 'via media' (Wendt 1999: 40–7) or 'middle ground'

---

36 On the problematic of the via media and science, see also Kratochwil (chap. 2 this volume) and Smith (2000). See also Wendt (2000).

(Adler 1997), where Wendt and some other constructivists clearly aim to locate their approaches, may just not be as stable a place as they think.

Conclusion

Wendt's departure from the traditional conceptualizations of international politics lies in his claim that the situation in which we find ourselves is not an expression of natural necessity but a construction. This claim, I argued, relies on conceiving of state identity as at the same time changeable and relatively stable. Hence, I contend that identity is a key concept in Wendt's work but at the same time in a dangerous liaison with his constructivism. Wendt insists that he is not interested in identity formation, that his analytical focus is the state system (Wendt 1999: 11; 2000: 175 but see Wendt 1999: 318–36).[37] I do not dispute either of these claims. What I argue is that his theory hinges on a conception of identity which is deeply problematic. Therefore, I first showed the significance of the concept of identity in Wendt's work. I then related it to the reconstruction of Germany's identity as an international actor after the end of the Cold War in a twofold way. On the one hand I showed where a Wendtian reading of identity in this situation might lead us. On the other hand I demonstrated how taking the construction of identity seriously destabilizes the possibility of a Wendtian analysis. The approach comes apart when we consider how identity and subjectivity come to be. In order to clarify this point I showed that Wendt's approach implied the possibility of identifying actors' identities as circumscribable entities at any given point in time and that this failed to take account of the complexity of the phenomenon of identity. The point is thus not that Wendt ought to take account of domestic discourse or normative issues. It is more fundamental. Wendt's argument cannot be saved through the introduction of a more sophisticated conceptualization of identity. It needs the very notion of identity which makes it fall apart. Wendt's constructivism does not work.

If my argument holds, this poses a serious problem for Wendt's approach. However, while this may be of interest to Wendt and those looking for a reason not to read the many pages of *Social Theory of International Politics*, it is so far merely implicit how this argument might be of wider relevance, how it is, as my title suggests, an argument about 'constructivism'. Given not only the intellectual diversity of constructivist work but also my argument about the impossibility clearly to delineate identity I will make no attempt, in explicating this relevance, to circumscribe the identity of constructivism. In other words, I do not offer a definition of constructivism. Instead I will explore what we are told we need constructivism for.

The point of constructivism is often thought to be its ability to address the social construction of the world without abandoning the idea of scientific explanation as it is commonly construed in International Relations. This is why constructivism is

---

37 Hopf also points out that, despite Wendt's claim that his main goal is not explaining identities and interests, he nevertheless 'goes on to treat the issue for the next 400 pages' (Hopf 2000: 370).

frequently portrayed as situated in the middle of a split between rationalistic and reflective international relations theories or as mediating between the two.[38] Even Nicholas Onuf's approach, which otherwise appears rather different from Wendt's work, has been described as possibly 'a third way in the third debate' (Kubálková *et al.*1998: 20). Emanuel Adler's description of the constructivist project in terms of 'seizing the middle ground' between 'rationalist and relativist interpretive approaches' (Adler 1997: 322) perhaps comes closest to Wendt's idea of a 'via media'. Adler is concerned, among other things, to demonstrate 'constructivism's scientific basis' (ibid.: 320). Constructivism explains (ibid.: 328–30). The 'constructivist dependent variable' may be, Adler argues, the transformation of identities and interests (ibid.: 344; see also Ruggie 1998a: 4). If Adler adequately represents the constructivist project, it would seem that worries similar to the ones I have established in relation to Wendt's specific formulation apply. The concern with causality and explanation can certainly be found in a variety of constructivist work.[39] I have shown, however, that the notion that identities or their transformation can be treated as variables within a causal explanation is problematic.

Yet much is being made of precisely this aspect of constructivism. Constructivists, in contrast to so-called postmodernists, respect the established procedures and methodologies of social science and engage in debate with rationalists (Katzenstein *et al.* 1998: 677; see also Copeland chap. 1 this volume, p. 3), or so the argument goes. Hence, Adler's 'primary goal' is to distinguish between 'postmodern, poststructuralist, critical theory and (postmodern) feminist' approaches on the one hand, and constructivism on the other (Adler 1997: 332; see also Hopf 1998: 171). The point is then, in Guzzini's (2000a: 148) somewhat ironic words, that constructivism 'does not succumb to the sirens of poststructuralism'. However, in conforming to such procedures and methodologies constructivism is in danger of missing something crucial, namely the politics of representing and constructing social worlds. The contingent, elusive and even contradictory character of German identity, as it was represented in the debates, must be excluded if the supposedly scientific standards are to be upheld. The fascinating, subtle creation of the subject in the process of telling history, and thus identity, is not part of an analysis which starts by postulating subjects. Hence, political questions, for instance about how subjects come to be in the first place, are ignored. Therefore, constructivism and identity may be in a dangerous liaison not only because identity is both necessary for and a danger to the approach. The liaison also endangers the possibility of considering the political implications of constructing and representing identity. As a result, constructivists may just miss the politics in international relations.

---

38 Wendt (1992a: 394); Wendt (1999: 40, 47); Adler (1997); Hopf (1998: 199); Smith (1997: 183–7). For a critical analysis of the consequences of this move for Wendt's *Social Theory*, see Kratochwil (chap. 2 this volume).

39 See, for example, Finnemore (1996: 14–28) and most of the contributors to Katzenstein (1996b); see also Jepperson *et al.* (1996: 52–65), Wæver (1997: 24) and Checkel (1998: 327).

Construed as identity + culture

7 Endogenizing corporate identities

The next step in constructivist IR theory[*]

Lars-Erik Cederman and Christopher Daase

Introduction

Now that constructivism has established itself in International Relations, a debate has emerged among constructivists about their paradigm's outer boundaries. This boundary-drawing exercise serves to demarcate constructivist research from epistemological relativism and to render constructivism more readily applicable to empirical research. Moderate constructivists have contributed greatly to opening the IR research agenda. Rather than focusing merely on behavior and interests, scholars as a result now routinely analyze identities and cultural factors. From this perspective, the attempt at 'seizing the middle ground' makes a lot of sense (Adler 1997).

Yet, in the process of rendering their version of constructivism more manageable and to distance themselves from postmodernist approaches, 'moderate' constructivists such as Wendt (1999) may have jettisoned too much ontological baggage from the theoretical agenda. Despite their efforts to endogenize the social identities of states and other actors, these scholars agree with rationalists in treating the very existence and spatio-temporal extension, i.e., the corporate identities, of the actors as fixed and pre-social entities.

We argue that this analytical position imposes restrictions on our theoretical repertoire. As a way of extending constructivist theorizing in IR, we turn to Georg

* Earlier versions of this article were delivered at Uppsala University; the Annual Meeting of the American Political Science Association, Boston, 2–6 September 1998; the Third Pan-European International-Relations Meeting of ECPR/ISA, Vienna, 16–19 September 1998; NUPI at Oslo; the Graduate Institute for International Studies at Geneva; the Summer School at the Central European University at Budapest on 'The Sociological Turn in Theories of International Relations'; and at the John M. Olin Institute for Strategic Studies at Harvard University. We thank the participants at those meetings, Ron Jepperson, Alex Wendt, an anonymous reviewer, and the editor of the EJIR for their helpful comments. Cederman wishes to acknowledge the support of the Robert Schuman Center at the European University Institute and the John M. Olin Institute for Strategic Studies.

1 For examples of empirical applications, see the essays in Katzenstein (1996b), and further references in Adler (1997), Checkel (1998) and Hopf (1998). See Guzzini (2000a), Guzzini and Leander (chap. 5 this volume), and Kratochwil (chap. 2 this volume) for more radical, epistemological critiques of mainstream constructivism.

Simmel's sociational framework.[2] While joining moderate constructivism on the epistemological middle ground, sociational constructivism avoids its ontological restrictions by problematizing the actors' corporate identities, rather than just their social roles.

Most importantly, sociational analysis offers an account of processes involving the appearance and disappearance of political actors as well as boundary transformations. But the endogenization of corporate identities also elucidates other, less profound processes. In this chapter we apply a sociational framework to the familiar problem of cooperation and conflict in the international system. Without proper endogenization of states' corporate identities, Kant's peace plan will be little more than a domestic-level effect. A sociational perspective, by contrast, accounts for the emergence and survival of democratic security communities against a backdrop of conquest and other types of geopolitical turbulence. Moreover, without a sociational perspective on nationalist conflicts, these phenomena will continue to be equated with a mere absence of trust within a world populated by fixed states. The sociational approach opens the door to a more comprehensive analysis of nationalist violence as an integrated part of more fundamental processes driven by the tension between states and nations.

International relations theory as problem-driven endogenization

Whereas conventional classifications of theoretical debates in IR pit one level of analysis against another, we view theory development as a pragmatic quest for successively increased endogenization. The more theorists problematize aspects of social reality, the more they perceive it to be constructed. Endogenization stands for problematization of theoretical entities as dependent variables, as opposed to their exogenization as assumptions, parameters or independent variables.[3]

Endogenization is not an end in itself and may sometimes even be more of an obstacle than an advantage. The process of relaxing assumptions makes it difficult to anchor research problems in a tractable framework of analysis. By definition entailing more 'moving parts', endogenization exacerbates theoretical complexity. This certainly makes the task of theory-building and theory-evaluation harder. Yet, unlike Waltz (1979), who prioritizes parsimony at any cost, we follow contemporary philosophy of science in claiming that simplicity and elegance have to be weighed against other scientific objectives. For example, it would be absurd always to seek simplicity at the expense of explanatory scope, heuristic understanding and empirical accuracy (Miller 1987).

This chapter introduces a problem-driven evaluation of the comparative advantages of sociational constructivism in relation to other types of constructivism and

---

2 'Sociation' is Wolff's (1950: lxiii) translation of the German term *Vergesellschaftung*.
3 We use the language of dependent and independent variables without implying any one-shot, unidirectional scheme of explanation that excludes causal feedback.

mainstream approaches. In order to do that, this section considers problematiz-ation of three classes of theoretical entities. First, there is interaction, which comprises patterns of conflictual and cooperative behavior between given actors. We further employ Wendt's (1994) dichotomization of social and corporate identities, to distinguish two other candidates for endogenization. Drawing on Mead's (1934) distinction between 'I' and 'me', Wendt defines corporate identities as 'the intrinsic, self-organizing qualities that constitute actor individuality' and social identities as the 'sets of meanings that an actor attributes to itself while taking the perspective of others, that is, as a social object' (Wendt 1994: 385). Applied to human beings, corporate identities define their 'body and experience of conscious-ness' and social ones their 'social role structure of shared understandings and expectations' (Wendt 1994).

With respect to collective actors, social identity captures the group's defining characteristics (type identity) or the members' collective conception of the group's mission or role within a given social setting. Corporate identity at this level constitutes a group's very existence and its extension in time and space. As pointed out by Wendt (1999: 225) a group's 'body' invariably has material manifestations, such as the individual members themselves, border posts, offices buildings, etc., but the corporate existence also hinges on intangible factors. Some notion of group consciousness would typically have to constitute the group's 'collective mind'. Complex social organizations also require codified membership criteria and organization principles, as exemplified by constitutions and legal principles such as sovereignty.[4]

In abstract terms, the difference between social and corporate identities corresponds closely to Abbott's (1988: 172) distinction between 'variable-based science' and 'the central subject/event model'. Whereas the former assumes that the 'social world consists of fixed entities (the units of analysis) that have attributes (the variables)', as for example social identities, the latter rejects the limiting assumption of fixed entities with attributes by endogenizing the corporate identities of the units (see also Abbott 1992, 1997).

Unlike social identities, then, corporate identities are configurations rather than mere properties of otherwise given actors. As such, they can undergo 'entity processes' with respect to both their existence and their extent. While existential entity processes include creation and destruction of specific historical actors, such transformations can also be analyzed with respect to the emergence or disappear-ance of actor types, as in Gilpin's notion of systems change (Gilpin 1981). Boundary-defining processes, by contrast, always refer to specific actor configur-ations, and feature both merger and division (Abbott 1988, 1995).

4 More recently, Wendt (1999: 224–33) proposed two additional conceptual categories, namely 'type' and 'collective' identities. For the purposes of this chapter, we treat both type and role identities as sub-classes of social identities. Moreover, we refrain from singling out collective identities as a separate, mutually exclusive category since both role and corporate identities can be thought of in both individual and collective terms.

A few examples may help clarify these abstractions. Whereas states' social identities include being a small or a great power, friend or foe, a Western or a non-Western state, etc., their corporate identities are constituted by their territory, legal frameworks and other institutions. Nations also have both social and corporate identities. Their social identities derive from scripts linked to their founding myths or to some other nation. For instance, the Polish nation was mythologized as Messiah. By contrast, the Canadian national identity to a large extent consists in *not* being associated with the United States. Finally, nations' and ethnic groups' corporate identities define the boundaries and membership criteria of the people belonging to them. Mergers and splits of ethnic groups, for example, do not have to alter these actors' relational conceptions, but, by definition, do change their corporate identities (Horowitz 1975).

This conceptualization featuring '*levels* of social construction' (Wendt 1999: 244) helps us describe how the quest for theoretical generalization in IR proceeds in three steps (see Figure 7.1). Neorealism and neoliberalism can be seen as attempts to problematize interstate behavior as a non-trivial systemic feature, thus endogenizing interaction (box 1). Not satisfied with this level of abstraction, social constructivists climb to the next rung of the endogenization ladder in their insistence that neither the role they play (box 3) nor interstate behavior (box 2) can be explained without problematizing social identities. Sociational constructivism, finally, goes even further by including corporate identities in the set of problematic concepts. Without this step, it is impossible to explain the emergence or change of the actors themselves (box 6). Moreover, sociational theories may also deepen explanations of social identities (box 5) and interaction (box 4).

This step-wise logic strongly resembles the taxonomic perspective adopted in Jepperson, Wendt and Katzenstein's theoretical overview:

> First, environments might affect only the *behavior* of actors. Second, they might affect the contingent *properties* of actors (identities, interests, and capabilities). Finally environments might affect the *existence* of actors altogether. For example, in the case of individual beings, the third effect concerns their bodies, the second whether these bodies become cashiers or corporate raiders, and the

Theoretical entity to be endogenized	Neorealism, neoliberalism	Social constructivism	Sociational constructivism
Corporate identities			6
Social identities		3	5
Interaction	1	2	4

Figure 7.1 Successive endogenization in IR theory.

> first whether or not the cashiers go on strike. Theories that call attention to
> lower-order construction effects may or may not stress higher ones.
>
> (Jepperson *et al.* 1996: 41)

While their own version of constructivism is limited to a problematization of
the two first aspects, the existential perspective corresponds to the sociational
approach of this chapter.

The first analytical shift can be dealt with quickly since it is by now familiar
ground. In his well-known reformulation of realist theory, Waltz (1979) took issue
with 'reductionist' thinking that explains interaction as a direct consequence of
actors' characteristics at the individual or state levels. Instead of such straightforward extrapolations, neorealists employ rationalistic models and metaphors to
illustrate the 'security dilemma', according to which anarchy alone suffices to
provoke conflict despite comparatively benign actor preferences (e.g., Jervis 1978).
Though disagreeing with neorealism's pessimistic predictions about interstate
behavior, neoliberals similarly distance themselves from second-image accounts
by making anarchy their analytical starting point (e.g., Oye 1986).

As a second step of endogenization, constructivism aims at breaking the
neorealist and neoliberal dominance in IR theory. Instead of postulating the
primacy of physical security under anarchy, constructivists typically problematize
actors' social identities and role complexes. This theoretical move enables these
scholars to cover the development of trust that transcends security dilemmas (Adler
and Barnett 1996; Adler 1997; Hopf 1998; Jepperson *et al.* 1996; Checkel 1998;
Wendt 1992a, 1994). Moreover, social constructivists argue that, despite their
willingness to rely on domestic-level explanations, neoliberals also tacitly adhere to
a reified approach to agency.

Taking issue with postmodern solipsism, however, these scholars typically
refrain from endogenizing corporate identity:

> Like rationalists, modern constructivists have been largely content to take as
> 'exogenously given' that they were dealing with *some* kind of actor, be it a state,
> transnational social movement, international organization or whatever. As
> such, the constructivist concern with identity-formation has typically focused
> on the construction of variation within a given actor class (type or role
> identities), rather than explaining how organizational actors come into being
> in the first place (corporate identities).
>
> (Fearon and Wendt 2002: 63)

Indeed, the overwhelming majority of rationalists *and* constructivists leave
corporate identities untouched. We believe that this key assumption derives
directly from an underlying tendency to anthropomorphize collective actors.
Especially explicit in rationalistic accounts, this theoretical strategy draws on social
contract theory (Lessnoff 1990) by transferring its logic from the individual level to
the interstate system (Beitz 1979):

Like seventeenth- and eighteenth-century social contract reasoning, rational action theory taken to this extreme makes the existence of social institutions problematic but leaves the existence of individuals unexamined, as though those individuals were never socially constituted. This then poses the insoluble problem of trying to explain the creation of social institutions . . . as the product of the action of individuals imagined to exist externally to those institutions.

(Calhoun 1991: 61; see also Meyer *et al.* 1987: 18)

The anarchy problematique in IR theory differs very little from the Hobbesian dilemma except that the main protagonists are states and not individuals. Though most social constructivists adopt a more sanguine view on order without a contract than do neorealists, their very framing of this question also presupposes a 'state of nature' as the analytical starting point, for states, like individuals, are assumed to exist 'prior to interaction' (Wendt 1999: 234, 244, 328; see also Mercer 1995).

To his credit, Wendt belongs among the few theorists who have rendered this analytical shift explicit. Using the metaphorical formula 'States are people too', Wendt (1999: 215–23) defends his anthropomorphic perspective against individualist objections.[5] In his view, anthropomorphization 'is not merely an analytical convenience, but essential to predicting and explaining [the state's] behavior, just as folk psychology is essential to explaining human behavior' (Wendt 1999: 21).[6]

Rejecting this position, we argue that anthropomorphic notions of agency are not always necessary or desirable and that, in their absence, the analysis does not have to degenerate to postmodernist relativism. To drive home this point, we turn to Simmel's sociational theory.

The principles of sociational constructivism

As opposed to Durkheim's structuralist invocation of 'social facts', Georg Simmel proposed a dynamic framework of sociation (*Vergesellschaftung*) that closes the loop between agency and interaction. Instead of privileging either actor or structure as the ontological starting point, his notion of sociation traces the production and reproduction of both actors and structures.[7] In Helle's words – 'In society, a formative process leads to the emergence and change of social constructs; and the

---

5 Wendt's heavy reliance on Mead's social theory also explains his tendency to exogenize corporate identities. It is well known that Meadian identity theory focuses on the 'me' while leaving the 'I' under-theorized (Charon 1998: 93–5; see also Tenbruck 1985).
6 By ceding this much ontological ground, Wendt has in effect withdrawn from his earlier position on the agent–structure problem (Wendt 1987). In his recent book, Wendt (1999: 155–6) clarifies this shift from the notion of 'mutual constitution' to 'supervenience'.
7 Since our main point is ontological, we will not let Simmel's epistemology, which foreshadows contemporary constructivism (e.g., Adler 1997; Wendt 1999) detain us here (see Simmel 1989 [1890]; but also Helle 1988; Boudon 1989).

living reality, which forms the process, is the dynamic of interaction' (1988: 106). Thus, seen from a sociational perspective, society is not a static structure, but rather an emerging entity generated and constituted by an ongoing process, which Simmel labels sociation. Sociation, then, is the result of interaction (*Wechselwirkung*), that is, the coming together, and apart, of both social and corporate identities.

In other words, Simmel's main idea is to explore both social and corporate identity-formation as an integrated part of interactive processes generating, and generated by, individual actors. If society, in its most general sense as a large group, is defined as 'the psychological interaction among individual human beings' (Simmel 1950 [1911]: 9), then the process linking individuals together both as products and as members of society is called sociation (cf. Simmel 1992 [1908]: 16).[8] This latter term should not be reserved only for large and permanent groups. In fact, sociation appears everywhere in human interaction – 'Sociation continuously emerges and ceases and emerges again. Even where its eternal flux and pulsation are not sufficiently strong to form organizations proper, they link individuals together' (Simmel 1950 [1911]: 9–10).

Interaction processes in Simmel's sociology can be of many types, including exchange, conflict and domination, all depending on the specific situation. For example, Simmel's well-known conflict hypothesis states that, far from always being exclusively disintegrating, conflictual interactions between two groups of individuals often trigger a sociational dynamic. This not only strengthens the internal cohesion of pre-existing groups or creates group consciousness where it did not exist prior to conflict. It also creates boundaries between the conflicting parties while connecting them as parts of a social configuration (Simmel 1955 [1908]).

According to Simmel, it makes little sense to postulate a 'state of nature' or an analytical phase 'prior to interaction'. Rather, the sociational approach problematizes the generation and regeneration of both individual and collective corporate identities as an ongoing process. Faced with the dynamic nature of world history, sociational theory must inquire into 'the processes – those which take place, ultimately, in the individuals themselves – that condition the existence of the individuals in society. It investigates these processes, not as antecedent causes of this result, but as part of the synthesis to which we give the inclusive name of "society" ' (Simmel 1992 [1908]: 8).

Together with his contemporaries Weber and Durkheim, Simmel aspired to analyze the modern social world, especially the momentous revolutions that the Western world underwent during the nineteenth century (Nisbet 1966). As opposed to Weber's individualism and Durkheim's structuralism, however,

8 Note that the English translation of *Gesellschaft* as 'society' often brings with it state-centric assumptions (Lapid and Kratochwil 1996). Moreover, Simmel's emphasis on society/*Gesellschaft* should not be seen as being incompatible with community/*Gemeinschaft*. In Simmel's terminology, the latter can be seen as a special case of the former. Drawing on Tönnies's (1957) distinction between society and community, Weber's (1962) dichotomization of *Vergesellschaftung* and *Vergemeinschaftung*, however, treats them as separate and dichotomous.

Simmel's relational epistemology and flexible ontology enabled him to ask three fundamental questions that eluded the other sociologists – how can macro-level groups such as states and nations exist at all despite (i) the large number of people involved, (ii) their long duration and (iii) their vast spatial extension?

(i) Cohesion through intersubjective categorization

To Simmel, intersubjective communication poses a fundamental puzzle. In his famous essay 'How is Society Possible?', Simmel (1992 [1908]) presupposes that all personal communication is subject to certain cognitive distortions. These should not be seen as mere 'misperceptions'; instead, they constitute a fundamental fact of life that prevents us from fully assuming the role of others. Consequently, all social actors are forced to rely on certain generalizations and their mutual relations are determined by varying degrees of incompleteness:

> Whatever the cause of this incompleteness, its consequence is a generalization of the psychological picture that we have of another, a generalization that results in a blurring of contours which adds a relation to other pictures to the uniqueness of this one. We conceive of each man – and this is a fact which has a specific effect upon our practical behavior toward him – as being the human type which is suggested by his individuality. We think of him in terms not only of his singularity but also in terms of a *general category*.
>
> (Simmel 1992 [1908]: 10, emphasis added)

Because of the inherent cognitive limitations of the human mind and the logistical constraints implied by personal communications, categorical classification takes on more importance the larger the group becomes. But there is always a personal residual that escapes categorization even in large, impersonal groups:

> Every member of a group which is held together by some common occupation or interest sees every other member not just empirically, but on the basis of an aprioric principle which the group imposes on everyone of its participants. Among officers, church members, employees, scholars, or members of a family, every member regards the other with the unquestioned assumption that he is a member of 'my group'.
>
> (Simmel 1992 [1908]: 11)

The introduction of a qualitatively distinct, abstract way to conceptualize actors makes it possible to study the balance between the individuality and collective conformity without prejudging the 'groupness' of social entities (Brubaker 1998). Modern social theory has revived this theme through the concept 'catnet' (White 1992; Emirbayer and Goodwin 1994). Bringing together the principles of category and network into one concept, this notion follows Simmel in emphasizing that social cohesion depends not only on direct relations in networks, but also on culture represented as categories. Differently put, all organizations can be classified as to how much 'catness' and how much 'netness' they feature. Whereas an informal friendship network scores high in terms of netness its catness is rather low. The reverse holds for a national community, since the categorical similarity of national belonging holds people together without there being any direct personal network links (Tilly 1978: 63).

Categorical action at the collective level differs fundamentally from personal interaction because, when applied to groups, it features individuals 'acting on the basis of a categorization of self and others at a social, more "inclusive" or "higher order" level of abstraction than that involved in the categorization of people as distinct, individual persons' (Turner 1987: 2). It is impossible to say whether categorization leads to more or less cooperative interactions in general. In some cases, abstractly role-playing individuals are prone to behave in a more conflictual manner since the constraints on interpersonal behavior usually dampen aggression (e.g., Milgram 1974). In other cases, categorical representation of agency opens up new opportunities for cooperation. For example, collective action problems trapping individuals may find their solution in culturally defined coalitions (Calhoun 1991).

Although the exact effect of categorization cannot be predicted in the abstract, it can be suggested that symbolic framing of actions and actors is capable of altering strategic settings abruptly. This is particularly true for transformations of previously interpersonal interaction contexts into categorical exchanges. New actors can thus be born or disappear 'overnight' without accompanying change in the cultural 'raw material', which is typically quite stable. What matters, rather, are 'imagined communities' (Anderson 1991) based on politically relevant categories rather than all cultural traits – 'The features that are taken into account are not the sum of "objective" differences, but only those which the actors themselves regard as significant' (Barth 1969: 14). This enables political entrepreneurs to manipulate the cultural details required by political identification. By endogenizing categorical corporate identities, sociational theory allows the analyst to investigate how much room there is for collective individuality, which in turn is likely to have considerable repercussions for the modes of interaction.

(ii) Duration through intergenerational transmission mechanisms

If mass-based intersubjective communication appears puzzling, then the interlinking of successive generations within large-scale organizations seems at least as problematic. To illustrate, it is truly astonishing that the Catholic Church has survived a couple of millennia and that the corporate identities of the old West European nations can be traced back several centuries.

In everyday situations, humans routinely reify groups and therefore take their persistence for granted. Yet, like individuals, these macro-entities also undergo intergenerational entity processes (Abbott 1992). The reason why individual members fail to perceive these processes has to do with their groups' involving too many people, their (usually) evolving too slowly and, most importantly, their taking on a timeless, law-like, reified flavor (Simmel 1992 [1908]: 556). Thus, the cognitive difficulty of grasping the logic of these macro-processes stems from the relatively fast turnover of individual members compared to the duration of the collective.

Once having endogenized the temporal persistence of collective corporate identities, Simmel asks: 'What particular types . . . of indirect or direct interactions are at play when one talks of the self-preservation of a social group?' (Simmel 1992 [1908]: 559). In response, he proposes a series of general mechanisms that serve the essential function of group maintenance. First, many sociational forms simply depend on their spatial delimitation. Serving as a paradigmatic example, the state typically uses its territorial boundaries to define group membership. The problem of duration is thus solved by spatialization of succession, in that every newly born individual within certain boundaries belongs to the group in question. In world politics, it is of course primarily the territorial state that relies on these principles through the citizenship criterion of *jus solis* (Brubaker 1992).

Second, other groups hold together based on the biological or social transmission from one generation to another. Here the non-simultaneous overlapping of the generations guarantees continuity despite high rates of turnover. Nevertheless, the assimilation rate limits the speed of change that can be tolerated without loss of corporate identity. Primary socialization through kinship offers an obvious illustration of this second type of mechanism (see Calhoun 1997).

Third, there are purely cognitively defined notions of group consciousness without any direct anchoring in the physical world. Ethnic communities based on putative descent illustrate this possibility (Weber 1962). Submission to an abstract ideological principle, such as socialism or nationalism, is another case in point. Instead of reifying the concept of social contract, Simmel analyzes the severe logistical difficulties confronting democratically and otherwise voluntarily organized groups. Again categorization plays a crucial role in providing bonds among people most of whom have never met and will never be able to meet, in this case because of long distances (Gilbert 1989).

In very general terms, Simmel's three sets of mechanisms account for the maintenance of large-scale groups over time. How do they affect the chances of cooperation and conflict in International Relations? Whereas much has been written about the evolution of strategies and norms over time, especially in iterated games that generate cooperative outcomes, few IR theorists have been able to trace the evolution of actors with any precision. Mostly, evolutionary arguments have been invoked to justify the rationality assumption, with cursory references to 'stabilizing' selection mechanisms (e.g., Waltz 1979; though see Kahler 1999).[9]

By contrast, a sociational perspective can show exactly how turnover affects behavioral patterns. Although it can be safely assumed that Darwinian selection in highly competitive environments weeds out unconditionally cooperative members, this is not the only possible outcome in less competitive settings (Spruyt

---

9 Wendt (1999) expands on Waltz's dichotomy of socialization and evolution by distinguishing between social and natural evolution. Yet, because of its adherence to the 'essentialist state', the Wendtian framework is as unable to theorize changing corporate identities as Waltz's.

1994). Alternative organizational forms have existed side by side for long periods. Indeed, rationalistic *post hoc* justifications fail to trace the actual unfolding of such processes in the presence of massive path-dependence (Arthur 1994; March and Olsen 1998). The main problem with conventional evolutionary arguments in IR is that they usually adopt too short a time perspective, thus losing sight of the evolutionary dynamic. As Elias (1978: 20) suggests, 'certain social transformations can only be achieved, if at all, by long and sustained development spanning several generations.' But such a broad analytical sweep requires that corporate identities be endogenized because, with few exceptions, political units do not remain constant over long periods of world-historical time, and it cannot be excluded that such changes influence the patterns of cooperation and conflict.

Apart from the direct influence of transmission mechanisms on interaction, some interaction patterns originate as side-effects from the desire to create, uphold, destroy and transform corporate identities as history unfolds. In these cases, self-reproduction typically deflects behavior in directions that deviates from what would otherwise be expected from entirely secure actors. Meyer, Boli and Thomas (1987: 23) remind us that 'the common notion that the actor performs the action is only a half-truth – at the institutional level, action also creates the actor.'

There can hardly be any doubt that these temporal mechanisms are crucial for interaction processes, seen from a macro-historical vantage point. But the picture would remain hopelessly incomplete without the spatial dimension.

(iii) Embodiment through boundary formation

In the spatial realm, sociational theory also helps to overcome formidable cognitive obstacles. In the modern world, territories with their sharply marked borders seem fixed. As opposed to this reifying tendency, Simmel (1992 [1908]: 688) considers spatial mappings to be socially constructed – 'It is not space, but the mental linking and summarizing of its parts that is of social consequence.' Sociation, therefore, may or may not be spatially represented. Whereas the territorially defined state corresponds to the former case, the global market exemplifies the latter possibility. Moreover, it follows that territorial exclusivity, such as that imposed by sovereignty, also often needs to be treated as an emergent feature. This also means that sociational theory must endogenize the boundaries themselves, because 'the boundary is not a spatial fact with social implications, but rather a sociological fact that forms spatially' (ibid.: 697).

Given the social aspect of space, the question, then, is how large groups succeed in holding together over vast territories. As in his analysis of temporal transmission processes, Simmel uncovers generic connecting mechanisms. Depending on whether they operate internally or externally, these can be divided into two large categories of space-transcending processes. Inside their boundaries, highly developed groups promote unity over large distances through an objectified and standardized culture, as represented by language, law and lifestyles. According to Simmel (1992 [1908]: 756), three mechanisms help produce such unity, namely institutions, written communication and internal migration. The external dimension comprises both the movement of people across boundaries, for example, confronting sedentary groups with immigrants and foreigners, and intergroup conflict featuring at least two groups as wholes.

The latter case evokes the aforementioned conflict hypothesis. The sociational logic becomes clear once one realizes the sociological significance not only for 'the reciprocal relations of the parties to it, but for the inner structure of each party itself' (Simmel 1955 [1908]: 87). It would be a mistake to follow Coser (1964) in viewing Simmel's conflict theory as a mere behavioral hypothesis involving exogenous actors (for a cogent critique, see Sylvan and Glassner 1985). As we have seen, the whole point of Simmel's project is to problematize corporate identities as emergent features of human interaction processes, rather than focusing on interaction among fixed actors.

Further underlining the centrality of endogenization, Simmel distinguishes between cases in which the cohesion of an already existing group increases as it enters into an antagonistic relationship with another group, and those cases where there was no pre-existing group consciousness before conflictual interaction – 'Conflict may not only heighten the concentration of an existing unit, radically eliminating all elements which might blur the distinctness of its boundaries against the enemy; it may also bring persons and groups together which have otherwise nothing to do with each other' (Simmel 1955 [1908]: 98–9).

Once formed through conflict, groups sometimes dissipate as soon as the external threat disappears. In keeping with his anti-individualist philosophy, however, Simmel rejects a mechanical interpretation of groups as aggregates always serving purely instrumental purposes, such as is the case with the neorealist view of international institutions (e.g., Mearsheimer 1994–5). Simmel notes that, in many cases of state-formation, 'it is characteristic that the unity, while it originates in conflict and for purposes of conflict, maintains itself beyond the period of struggle. It comes to have additional interests and associative forces which no longer have any relation to the initial militant purpose' (Simmel 1955 [1908]: 101). In many ways anticipating the unification of the West during the Cold War, Simmel suggests that:

> the synthetic strength of a common opposition may be determined, not by the number of shared points of interest, but by the duration and intensity of the unification. In this case, it is especially favorable to the unification if instead of an actual fight with the enemy, there is a permanent *threat* by him. . . . This is a case of a peculiar type: a certain distance between the elements to be united, on the one hand, and the point and interest uniting them, on the other, is a particularly favorable constellation for unification, notably in large groups.
>
> (ibid.: 104, 105)

These observations about the spatial mapping of sociational processes show that these processes do not have to respect the state's territorial anchoring, or its mutual exclusivity.

Although territorial considerations have remained curiously absent in mainstream IR theory, some theorists have revived the interest in spatial analysis. Abbott, for one, has attempted to resuscitate the interest in Simmel's intellectual heirs in the Chicago School of sociology, according to which 'one cannot understand social life without understanding the arrangements of particular social actors in particular social time and places' (Abbott 1997: 1152). Contemporary social theory, anthropology and geography have also contributed to bringing the focus on socially constructed boundaries back in to the social sciences (e.g., Giddens 1979; Sahlins 1989; Paasi 1996; Agnew 1998).

More concretely, spatial representation has important implications for the way that international interactions develop. First of all, space seldom enters the analysis in systems constituted by a small number of actors – in a strictly bipolar system local and global interaction amounts to the same thing. The situation in complex systems that are populated by a large number of actors is quite different, however. There the interaction topology becomes crucial (Cohen *et al.* 2001). In particular, complexity theory indicates that the chances of cooperation may be greatly enhanced by local clustering. The basic idea is that if cooperating actors are allowed to cluster together their chances of mustering collective defense are accordingly enhanced (Axelrod 1984: chap. 8). But spatial interdependencies also account for the diffusion of conflict through contagion, so, as in the discussion of temporal mechanisms, all we can say in general is that, in many cases, the inherently territorial layout makes a difference for cooperation in world politics.[10]

This implies that ignoring space in complex interaction systems is neither a neutral nor a realistic assumption.[11] Ultimately, the actual territorial mapping of corporate identities influences the patterns of cooperation and conflict. This becomes especially noticeable if actor types are associated with incompatible spatial representations – 'The danger posed by the hereditary organization to the state lies precisely in the indifference of its logic to spatial relations' (Simmel 1992 [1908]: 771, authors' trans.)

But space is not merely a passive arena in which interactions take place. Simmel's conflict hypothesis shows that actors often try to improve their position by devising strategies that completely reconfigure the interaction topology, including reconstructing boundaries and the set of legitimate actors. These options remain outside the scope of rationalist analysis, which focuses on self-strengthening through internal and external balancing, and conventional constructivism, which considers the transformation of roles and attitudes, but not of boundaries.

---

10 Of course, diffusion is not unique to sociational theory. Yet, most conventional treatments of diffusion attempt to study spatial auto-correlation locally within very strict bounds (e.g., Siverson and Starr 1990).

11 The absence of a territorial dimension could bias outcomes toward conflict because, if all actors are able to interact with each other regardless of distance, the clustering mechanism cannot operate. Despite the arguably space-transcending effects of nuclear weapons and globalization, distance-related constraints retain a crucial influence on interaction in world politics (Collins 1986: chap. 7).

Illustrating the sociational aspects of interaction in world politics

In this section, we demonstrate the advantages of applying the concept of sociation as a way to explain cooperative and conflictual interaction processes. Obviously, endogenization of corporate identities may serve the direct purpose of explaining these directly. Explanations of why international actors emerge and vanish is a legitimate aim in its own right. By reframing what has usually been conceived of primarily as behavioral phenomena as processes involving changes in corporate identities, however, we select two cases to illustrate how to surpass conventional rationalistic and constructivist approaches on their own 'home turf'. Before turning to nationalist conflict, we sketch how sociational theory can be applied to the pattern of cooperation among democracies.

'The democratic peace is what states make of it'

A majority of IR scholars accept the claim that democratic states hardly ever fight each other. Yet, although this stylized fact has attracted much attention, it remains 'an empirical regularity in search of a theory' (Hopf 1998: 191). Hoping to solve the puzzle, social constructivists have recently proposed a reconceptualization of the democratic peace as a Deutschian security community (Adler and Barnett 1996). This conceptual shift traces the role of democracy in the reconfiguration of states' social identities while keeping the states' corporate identities constant. By relaxing this assumption, a sociational approach to the democratic peace offers an even more versatile interpretation of the phenomenon.

Based on the same logic as Figure 7.1, Figure 7.2 compares different levels of endogenization in the democratic-peace literature. The evolution of contemporary liberal thought in IR starts with the attempt to improve on classical liberalism. Whereas the latter theories typically assume that there is something about the internal structure of liberal democracies that makes them more peaceful than other states, 'dyadic liberalism' rejects a reductionist explanatory scope by locating the causal nexus at the interaction level (box 1). Going beyond this conceptualization, social constructivists typically introduce the notion of a democratic security

Theoretical entity to be endogenized	Dyadic liberalism	Social constructivism	Sociational constructivism
State and community boundaries			6
Democratic trust		3	5
Democratic cooperation	1	2	4

Figure 7.2 Comparing liberal theories of peace and cooperation.

community generating inter-democratic trust (box 3) to account for the emergence of cooperation among democracies (box 2). Finally, in order to explain such cooperative patterns (box 4), sociational theorists insist on problematizing the boundaries of both states and security communities (box 6) as a complement to treating the latter as attitudinal properties of otherwise given actors (box 5).

In the following we will briefly survey the three main theoretical shifts, starting with the interaction-based liberalism. Following Doyle's (1983a) 'rediscovery' of Kant's peace conjecture, quantitative scholars have been able to establish the democratic peace as an 'empirical law' (Levy 1988). As opposed to the monadic argument that democracies are inherently more peaceful, the dyadic hypothesis asserts that democratic states do not fight each other, but remains agnostic regarding these states' general conflict propensity (see review in Chan 1997).

Although there is strong evidence for the existence of a separate democratic peace, the precise causal mechanisms continue to elude researchers. One problem afflicting most quantitative studies is that conventional dyadic theory exogenizes perceptions of democracy by skipping over the crucial link of mutual recognition. This is a serious oversight because, in the absence of intersubjective trust and understanding, the democratic peace fails to operate, as illustrated by Anglo-American relations in the early nineteenth century (Owen 1994).

This is where social constructivism enters the picture. While keeping the state system fixed, these theorists reinterpret the democratic peace as a stable and mutually reinforcing constellation of pacific social identities that Wendt (1999: chap. 6) refers to as a 'Kantian culture'. Similarly, Risse-Kappen argues that the neoliberals' normative argument should be put on a constructivist footing. In his view, 'enmity as well as friendship in the international system neither results from some inherent features of the international distribution of power, as realists would assume, nor from the domestic structure of states as such, as . . . liberals argue. Rather it is socially constructed' (1995a: 503).

The notion of pluralist security community of Deutsch *et al.* (1957) constitutes an important stepping stone in constructivist theory-building. Although Deutsch did not limit his concept to democratic regimes, a good case can be made for democracy playing a crucial role in the development of peaceful norms (Eberwein 1995; Risse-Kappen 1996). Conceptually, security communities have the advantage of incorporating the normative aspect of the democratic peace (Figure 7.2, box 3), as opposed to treating it merely as a behavioral absence of violence (Adler and Barnett 1996; Adler 1997; Wendt 1999: chap. 6).

Despite the relative scarcity of work along these lines, it is already clear that social-constructivist explanations provide a deeper understanding of the causes generating the democratic peace. Most obviously, purely instrumental renderings of the phenomenon fail to convince since war has become unthinkable among modern democracies. After all, the reasons preventing the US from invading Canada have nothing to do with cost-benefit analysis.

Given the promise of social constructivist explanations, it may seem premature to reach for the next step of the endogenization ladder. Nevertheless, we contend that explicit problematization of the corporate identities of states and democratic security communities will prove necessary for gaining a complete understanding of the democratic peace as a slowly developing spatio-temporal process.

In its original Kantian formulation (Kant 1970a, 1970c), the democratic peace should not be seen as a constant law but as a macro-historical process unfolding since the late eighteenth century (Huntley 1996; Cederman 2001a). As such, it cannot easily be disentangled from the process of state-formation. But if that is true, social constructivism based on the 'essential actors' fails to represent, let alone explain, changes of state boundaries generated by integration and disintegration processes. Such constructivism can explain socialization processes within a given state framework, such as Germany's and Japan's democratization *after* World War II, but more fundamental transformations, including cases of conquest and the world wars themselves, remain outside the purvey of the theory. Moreover, because conventional constructivist analysis reduces security communities to abstract properties, such as friendship and trust, their very spatio-temporal extension remains out of grasp. Ultimately the success of the democratic peace hinges on the operation of existential and boundary-related entity processes that determine the growth (and possible disappearance) of democratic states and their security communities.

It is true that conventional social constructivist theory captures the effect of category-dependent strategies quite well. For example, Wendt (1992a: 397) observes that 'states act differently toward enemies than they do toward friends because enemies are threatening and friends are not.' Once the attention turns to the actual spatio-temporal mechanisms that implement categorical categorization, however, sociational theory becomes indispensable. Kant's (1970c) own peace plan outlines the contours of such a macro-historical process theory. Kant conjectured explicitly the ecological conditions under which a successful spread of democracy would occur. Among the central propositions, we find the idea that the democratic security community might crystallize and grow around a strong democratic state (or a republic, to use Kant's own terminology):

> For if fortune directs that a powerful and enlightened people can make itself a republic, which by its nature must be inclined to perpetual peace, this gives a fulcrum to the federation with other states so that they may adhere to it and thus secure freedom under the idea of the law of nations. By more and more such associations, the federation may be gradually extended.
>
> (Kant 1970c: 103)

In addition, such an internally peaceful (con)federation would not survive if it were to adopt a pacifist stance in its external interactions. Rather, Kant expected that these states 'will protect one another against external aggression while refraining from interference in one another's internal disagreements' (Kant 1970b: 165).

About two centuries later, Deutsch and his collaborators similarly observed that security communities often owe their existence to the early emergence of a democratic regional hegemon – 'Contrary to the "balance of power" theory, security-communities seem to develop most frequently around cores of strength' (Deutsch *et al.* 1957: 28). Thus, the Deutschian concept of security community is more than a dimension-less variable measuring trust and friendship. Its spatio-temporal extension, including its territorial boundaries, plays a key role in determining its success. It would be hard to account for the long-term survival of the democratic peace without the sociational emphasis on geographic and tag-based clustering (Cederman 2001b). Indeed, empirical evidence confirms that democracies have a tendency to cluster together (Gleditsch and Ward 2000).

At the same time, a macro-historical perspective forces the analyst to factor in the evolution of states. Assuming that democratic states could not be absorbed and conquered, as they were by Hitler's Germany, biases the analysis unduly in a liberal direction. To the extent that democracies are more efficient war-fighters, however, the possibility of conquest may actually work in their favor in the longer run. According to Kant's (1970a) famous dialectical hypothesis, democracies are more effective war-fighters than authoritarian regimes. This implies that an increase in warfare will help democratic states increase their share of the international system, which in turn undermines war as an institution.

In sum, while social constructivism helps to shift the interpretation of the democratic peace as a purely behavioral phenomenon, it fails to lay the foundation of a comprehensive process explanation. Wendtian constructivism makes it both too easy and too hard to analyze the potential for liberal cooperation in the international system: too easy because essentialized cooperators are not exposed to the challenges of conquest; and too hard because they obscure potential cooperation-enhancing mechanisms by ontological fiat rather than based on theoretical or empirical arguments.

'Nations and states made war; war made nations and states'

Our second illustration features a comparison of approaches to nationalist conflict. Nationalist strife, or what is usually referred to as 'ethnic conflict', has assumed a central role as arguably one of the most serious threats to post-Cold War security.[12] It is thus not surprising that IR scholars have attempted to make sense of what appears to be a litany of unfathomable irrationality and cruelty. Paralleling the graphical display of the previous debate, Figure 7.3 compares the levels of endogenization in explanations of nationalist conflict (the lowest row). The middle row corresponds to role complexes characterized by mistrust. Finally, the very boundaries and existence of states and nations tap the sociational dimension.

Again we trace the development of theorizing as a succession of endogenization efforts. Whereas rationalistic theorists have striven to overcome 'primordialist' concepts of ethnic violence (box 1), social constructivists argue that conflict (box 2)

---

12 Despite its general theoretical importance (see Cederman 2002b), the difference between ethnic groups and nations is not crucial here and so we will refer to nationalist and ethnic conflict synonymously.

Theoretical entity to be endogenized	Ethnic security-dilemma	Social constructivism	Sociational constructivism
Boundaries of states and nations			6
Intergroup mistrust		3	5
Intergroup conflict	1	2	4

Figure 7.3 Comparing theories of nationalist conflict.

cannot be understood without an account of how security communities break down (box 3). Finally, in their explanations of nationalist conflict (box 4), sociational analysts assert that both states and national communities should be theorized in their entirety (box 6) rather than as a mere bundle of norms associated with fixed actors (box 5).

Journalistic analyses of nationalist conflict often interpret violence as an expression of 'ancient hatred'. Such accounts suggest that hostility suddenly flares up because of long suppressed hatreds. In the former Yugoslavia and Soviet Union, 'ancient-hatred' theory claims that the collapse of the communist systems' unfettered age-old animosity between well-defined, pre-existing ethnic groups. With few exceptions, academic specialists believe that this approach to nationalism is fundamentally misleading (see, e.g., Hardin 1995: 9, 147–50).

Neorealist scholars have leveled powerful critique against the 'ancient-hatred' conception of ethnic conflict (see especially Posen 1993). Rejecting group-based hatred as a necessary condition for violence, they endogenize conflictual inter-actions by transplanting the logic of the interstate version of the security dilemma to an ethnic setting (Figure 7.3, box 1). Rational-choice theorists have further elaborated this scenario by interpreting ethnic conflict as a Pareto-inferior out-come of an ethnic collective-choice dilemma (Hardin 1995; Fearon 1998). Whether explicitly rationalist or not, these studies rely on an underlying philo-sophical outlook derived from Hobbesian social contract theory that rules out trust in the absence of state enforcement. Inter-ethnic fear, rather than genuine hatred, drives the conflictual spiral, with war as a tragic but logical endpoint. Moreover, the ethnic groups themselves are treated as undifferentiated, given units. Except for the tacit role change, plugging in ethnic groups in lieu of states, this scenario fits comfortably into a purely neorealist framework.

Unsatisfied with such accounts, Lapid and Kratochwil (1996: 115) claim that Posen's explanation 'brings to the fore "primordial" (that is, original and unchangeable) loyalties, blithely neglecting both the role of the Yugoslav state in constructing these identities and the cynical rewriting of history that is taking place to fit present political purposes.' Does contemporary IR constructivism rectify this shortcoming? It is not easy to answer this question, because, so far, very few social constructivists have accepted the challenge.

Far from the main focus of his analysis, Wendt's approach to nationalism fails to account for ethnic and nationalist groups as corporate identities. In Wendt's words, 'nationalism may be in part "primordial" and thus inherent in societies' self-conception as distinct groups' (1994: 387). In the light of these limitations, one is inclined to agree with Pasic's critique – 'Even though an abundance of theorizing on nationalism and other societal factors has taken place, Wendt's justifications for their general dismissal propagates the mainstream understanding that these levels of analysis are systematically exogenous, empirical/historical, or simply unnecessary for theory' (1996: 89). The freezing of corporate identities and the lack of differentiation of actor types together block progress in analyzing nationalism. The hesitation to engage in sociational analysis 'induces the imagination of static actors and the stubborn maintenance of tenuous boundaries (state/society, domestic/international) set by the field of international relations' (ibid).

A sociational approach to nationalist conflict promises to circumvent these conceptual hurdles. To see this, it is useful to return again to the conceptual dimensions covered in the previous section. Categorical identities play a central role in nationalism. In close agreement with Simmel's emphasis on such identities, Ernest Gellner asserts that, in contrast to pre-modern society which was based on direct interpersonal relationships, the large scale of the nation requires abstract categorization – 'In modern societies, culture does not so much underline structure: rather it replaces it' (Gellner 1964: 155; see also Gellner 1983; Anderson 1991; Calhoun 1991). As opposed to illiterate peasants, modern citizens need to possess a modular communicative capacity that can be acquired only through formal education in a high language.

Thus, modern national identities should not be confused with pre-modern, ethnic cores – 'Nationalism is not the awakening of nations to self-consciousness: it invents nations where they do not exist – but it does need some pre-existing differentiating marks to work on, even if . . . these are purely negative' (Gellner 1964: 168). This fundamental constructivist point shows that there is no simple one-to-one correspondence between ancient, cultural groups and modern political identities (Calhoun 1997: 48).

To some extent, conventional constructivist analysis helps to account for this shift of framings. What is less clear, however, is how to explain the spatio-temporal mechanisms responsible for the creation, maintenance and dissipation of national identities and state organizations. In many particularly turbulent cases, mere endogenization of nations within an exogenous state framework does not suffice because nation-building co-evolves with state formation (Hintze 1975). In fact, most constructivist theories of nationalism analyze the emergence of national consciousness and its political repercussions within a given state framework (Cederman 2002b).

In situations characterized by drastic boundary transformations, in contrast, it makes little sense to talk about the 'domestic' and 'international' realms. Under such conditions, what was literary 'inside' yesterday becomes 'outside' tomorrow and vice versa (Walker 1993). It has even been suggested that Yugoslavia in the 1980s should be theorized as a system of 'international relations' (Ramet 1992). Theoretical schemata and disciplinary categorizations that 'hard-wire' the internal–external distinction into units of analysis and causal explanations rule out change of territorial and national boundaries by assumption.

In fact, ethnic conflicts typically feature both national communities and states as the main protagonists, and it is the interaction between these actor types that drives the conflictual dynamics (see Daase 1999). To illustrate the highly problematic nature of the domestic–foreign boundary, we turn to Brubaker (1995), who combines insights from social theory with careful empirical work in his recent studies of East European nationalism (see also Weiner 1971). Instead of placing immutable ethnic groups in a rigid state framework, he singles out a trio made up of 'national minorities, nationalizing states, and external national homelands'. On this view, conflict is triggered by nationalizing states' attempts to impose their own narrow definition of cultural identity on reluctant minorities, which are supported by their kin's homeland state. As an illustration of this irredentist constellation, Brubaker contends that, 'while the Slovenian issue was indeed dyadic, the Croatian conflict was, from the beginning, fundamentally triadic, involving a tension-fraught dynamic interplay between an incipient national minority (Serbs in Croatia), an incipient nationalizing state (Croatia), and an incipient external national homeland (Serbia)' (1995: 120).

Efforts to recast this triangular interaction as a bilateral conflict inevitably lead to serious distortions – 'Construing [the Croat drive for autonomy and independence] as a *secessionist* movement, the dyadic view obscures the extent to which it was also, and inseparably, a *nationalizing* movement' (Brubaker 1995: 121). Such cases of 'competing nationalization' are hard to square with the security-dilemma logic of Posen and Fearon, not merely because of its dyadic actor typology, but also on account of the conflict-seeking preferences on both sides. In the Yugoslav case, both Serb and Croatian elites preferred conflict as a way to reconfigure the ethno-political map.

Most dramatically, 'ethnocidal gerrymandering' features authoritarian power-holders threatened by sudden democratization, and unsurprisingly represented some of the worst human-rights abuses since World War II. In Rwanda, the Kigali government's meticulously planned genocide served to reshape the nation by simply murdering the Tutsi ethnic group and the entire political opposition whether Tutsi or Hutu (Prunier 1995). Indeed, even in the most extreme cases, there is a perversely 'constructive' aspect of violence that can be exploited by ruthless leaders – 'Genocide, after all, is an exercise in community building. . . . Killing Tutsis was a political tradition in postcolonial Rwanda. It brought people together' (Gourevitch 1998: 95–6).

Likewise, Milosevic's notorious decision in 1990–1 to combine nationalization of his own federation with its territorial 'amputation' in order to vindicate the principle of ethnic nationalism, thus securing his grasp of power (Gagnon 1998). Despite the ensuing warfare, these priorities suited the late Croatian president Tudjman as well. Thus, explanations that reify state and national boundaries cannot provide an accurate description of these strategies. More ominously, treating groups' corporate identities as if they were unproblematic even risks playing into the hands of the perpetrators of genocide by retroactively legitimizing their preferred group boundaries (Lapid and Kratochwil 1996; Gagnon 1998).

In general, a sociational perspective that refrains from freezing corporate identities allows the analyst to capture real actors' efforts to create and reshape political space, most notably states and nations' boundaries. To uncover systematically the specific mechanisms responsible for such processes lies beyond the scope of this chapter. Suffice it to say that mass media, education, language policy and deliberate campaigns of violence are often used by state actors to alter and move national boundaries, and in some cases even to create new national communities. Common to these processes is that identities do not change merely in terms of their cultural content but also with respect to membership.

Conclusion

In this chapter, we have argued that sociational theory usefully widens the constructivist research agenda. To illustrate its promise, we have highlighted the 'value added' of this approach compared to rationalist and conventional constructivist perspectives in two specific research problems centering on interaction. Nevertheless, our advocacy of the neo-Simmelian approach should not be interpreted as a wholesale endorsement. Though in many senses the most general of all IR perspectives, sociational constructivism does not 'subsume' other paradigms across the board.

It is thus appropriate to close this chapter by saying a few words about the general conditions under which sociational theory is likely to bear fruit. In our two illustrations we have concentrated exclusively on cases where explanation of interaction patterns requires sociational contextualization. In addition, the endogenization of social identities may have to be seen as a side-effect of sociational processes. Finally, if change of corporate identities is at stake, there is no substitute for sociational theory. As a rule, the more profound and turbulent the change, the more useful the Simmelian approach becomes. We expect it to be indispensable in accounting for 'systems change', since macro-historical processes entail the change and maintenance of not only specific corporate identities, but also generic actor types (Gilpin 1981).

Indeed, the analyst should think twice before resorting to all-out endogenization. Where corporate identities can safely be assumed to remain constant, sociational constructivism could lead to analytical 'overstretch'. Because of its high explanatory ambitions, the Simmelian approach necessarily involves more 'moving parts', thus necessitating more extensive empirical coverage than do less general perspectives. Still, it would be a mistake to avoid such research questions because of their difficulty. To do so implies succumbing to 'method-driven' research (Abbott 1988; Shapiro and Wendt 1992).

Yet, avoiding method-driven thinking does not mean that anything goes. Rather, it entails tailoring and adapting one's research methods to the substantive problem at hand. A complete discussion on methods suitable for sociational theorizing would require another article. However, it is clear that our illustrations underscore the need to complement the conventional methodological toolbox with more context-sensitive methods, whether drawn from historical sociology (e.g., Skocpol 1984; Griffin and Van der Linden 1999), 'narrative positivism' (e.g., Abbott 1992) or computational modeling (e.g., Axelrod 1997; Cederman 2002a).

Finally, it should be emphasized that the sociational theory-building venture does not end with Simmel. On the contrary, it is alive and well in sociology and social theory. A new wave of work combining historical sociology with IR theory provides powerful concepts for sociational theorizing in world politics (Hobden and Hobson 2002). In addition, sociational constructivism in IR has much to learn from more recent work in the Simmelian process tradition, including the Chicago School of sociology (Abbott 1997), Elias's (1982 [1939]) process theory, Giddens's (1979) structuration theory and the relational approach of Emirbayer (1997), to name a few prominent sources of inspiration. In view of the relevance of these scholars' ideas and the ubiquity of corporate identity change in the international system, it is hard to see how IR constructivists could avoid taking the sociational plunge.

8 Reflexivity and structural change*

Petr Drulák

International change is one of the key issues in constructivist reflection on international politics, and Alexander Wendt, a leading constructivist, has shown a consistent interest in its theorizing. He dedicated the final chapter of his *opus magnum* (Wendt 1999, hereafter *Wendt I*) to structural change, and he also addresses the topic again in a recent article in the *European Journal of International Relations* (Wendt 2003, hereafter *Wendt II*).

Comparing the two texts, one can see that his first conceptualization of structural change differs significantly from the second. The most visible differences are already signalled in the title of the article: 'Why a world state is inevitable'. *Wendt I* views structural change as ideational change in cultures of anarchy in the world of states; *Wendt II* adds to this an institutional super-change, in the shape of a transition from the world of states to a world state. Both approaches argue for a progressive view of history, from war to peace. However, *Wendt I* uses a soft teleology, seeing progress as a matter of a historical contingency, making cautious arguments for the possible irreversibility of what has been achieved so far (Wendt 1999: 311–12), while *Wendt II* argues that progress is a result of historical necessity based on a deterministic teleology of mankind.

A less visible, but perhaps more fundamental, difference concerns the role of reflexivity on which this chapter focuses. Guzzini (2000a: 150) observes that, although reflexivity is one of the central concerns of constructivism, it is strangely neglected in most constructivist theories. Wendt exemplifies this paradox. Reflexivity plays a decisive role in the substantive theorizing of structural change in *Wendt I* but it is missing from its scientific realist meta-theory. It is one of the major, albeit somewhat hidden, forces in *Wendt I*. As such, it is awarded the role of the *deus ex machina* which suddenly appears when naturalist explanations are exhausted. *Wendt II* seems to resolve this inconsistency by getting rid of reflexivity completely.

This chapter outlines a series of amendments to *Wendt I* and *II* which will allow reflexivity to be brought back in. Firstly, I show how reflexivity can be approached

* I am grateful to Pavel Barša, Stefano Guzzini, Friedrich Kratochwil, Lucie Königová, and Anna Leander for their thought-provoking comments on earlier drafts. I would also like to thank to Nicola Owtram and Alexander Maxwell for language correction.

and why it is important in *Wendt I*, but also why it cannot be fully included there. Secondly, I redefine the meta-theory of *Wendt I*, to do justice to the role that reflexivity plays at the level of substantive theorizing. Thirdly, I show that the absence of reflexivity in *Wendt II* leads to an extremely mechanistic view of human evolution, which is narrower than that in *Wendt I*, but I also show that reflexivity can be brought back in if the original framework of the historical process is loosened a bit.

No change without reflexivity

I argue that reflexivity plays a decisive role in the explanation of structural change in *Wendt I*. According to Wendt, reflexivity explains why 'the Gorbachev regime virtually single-handedly ended the Cold War' (1999: 76). Thus, reflexivity is one of the most significant sources of the structural change that will allow for a shift from the contemporary international system to a future system of world peace (ibid.: 375). Wendt explains the shift with reference to symbolic interactions and causal master variables. I will show that neither interactions nor master variables can be effective without reflexivity. But to do this, a discussion of the concept of reflexivity is in order.

What is reflexivity?

Despite its importance in *Wendt I*, the concept of reflexivity it is neither introduced nor developed there. Below, I suggest a possible understanding of reflexivity which, I believe, would be consistent with Wendt's use of the term. I have drawn on two bodies of literature which are close to *Wendt I*, namely the literature on learning in IR which Wendt himself absorbed into his theorizing and the literature on reflexive modernity, which provides a possible context for constructivist theorizing (Guzzini 2000a: 152–3). The result of this is that I treat reflexivity in terms of 'internal learning' (Haas 1990) and 'rule-altering politics' (Beck 1994).

The framework that *Wendt I* outlines for understanding structural change implies that reflexivity is covered by the concept of social learning as introduced by Nye (1987: 380). At the first glance, it seems to work. *Wendt I* distinguishes between two 'levels of learning' (Levy 1994: 286). While rationalist 'simple learning' refers to changes in behaviour, the constructivist 'complex learning' addresses changes in identities. *Wendt I* covers both levels and gives enough prominence to the constructivist complex learning.

However, a second glance reveals some problems. Nye treats the learning of actors as induced from the outside, whereby all the examples of learning are attributed to objective events in the world out there (Nye 1987: 384). In a similar vein, Levy (1994: 286) speaks about 'experiential' learning, distinguishing it from, for example, deductive learning. The focus on experiential learning is not totally innocent as it leads Levy to exclude from his perspective changes in 'principled beliefs' (Goldstein and Keohane 1993: 9) and other normative changes, comparing them to 'a religious revelation' (Levy 1994: 286). However, complex learning can be understood as experiential learning in the sense that changes in the environment are reflected by actors and lead to changes in their identities, and not just to behavioural adaptation. In this sense, subjects are shaped by the dynamics of their objective environment.

The way in which *Wendt I* addresses reflexivity does not fit with this learning approach. Even though it is not properly introduced as a fully fledged concept in *Wendt I*, reflexivity is referred to as a subjective force which brings about social innovations. It is to a large extent independent of prevailing social and material conditions, creating 'trust before the conditions that it is normally thought to require exist' (Wendt 1999: 363). Hence, Wendt refers to the kinds of moves that are made when actors transcend their experience, e.g., treating the Other as a friend despite previous experience of mutual rivalry, or constructing experience in a particular way, e.g., persuading the Other that they share a common fate. In these cases, actors are creative against the backdrop of their previous experience, thus changes in their subjectivity cannot be attributed directly to the changes in the environment. Moreover, their creativity can lead to changes in their identities, which can result in changes in the environment: if a state treats another state as a friend, despite their rivalry, they may become friends. In this perspective, the objective environment is changed as a result of changes in the subject. I will reserve the term reflexivity for these processes.

The learning perspective can, however, be useful when addressing the concept of reflexivity, although it has to be refocused. *Wendt I* distinguishes between complex and simple learning, but not between learning incentives, even though this is a well-established distinction in the learning literature (Rosenau 1986; Haas 1990).[1] For example, Ernst Haas (1990: 7) builds his argument that international organizations are important innovators on the assumption that learning also comes from the inside and is not induced only from the outside. Haas's discussion shows why the distinction is important. It concerns the 'locus of change' and innovation. Only if actors are able to 'learn' without obvious external stimuli can they be agents of change rather than its mere followers, and only then can they be seen as innovators capable of making creative moves.

Unlike learning (Levy 1994: 283), reflexivity, as used by Wendt, always involves policy change, at least at the actor level. The specificity of reflexivity as political practice can be captured through the notion of 'rule-altering' politics, distinguishing it from unreflexive 'rule-directed' politics (Beck 1994: 35–6).[2] While rule-directed politics operate within the given rules, rule-altering ones aim at 'the switching of the rule system' (ibid.: 35) and at replacing it with a new system.

---

1 Rosenau (1986: 864–5) considers there to be two ways of learning: '(a) when external stimuli are so persistently and startlingly different as to jolt habitual modes and foster new patterns more appropriate to the evolving circumstances; or (b) when new skills, capabilities, and/or responsibilities develop within the actor, forcing the old, habitual ways to yield to new ones.'

2 Beck (1994: 38) understands rule-altering politics as 'creative and self-creative politics which does not cultivate and renew old hostilities, nor draw and intensify the means of its power from them; instead it designs and forges new content, forms and coalition.'

Hence, reflexivity refers to both internal learning and rule-altering politics; this implies that it can be a powerful engine of change, but also makes it difficult to theorize. It is creative in that it brings about new realities which cannot be causally connected to external circumstances. While it is not totally independent of them, it is not bound by them as tightly as complex learning. This implies two things: firstly, reflexivity contains an enormous transformative potential, as recognized by Wendt (1999: 363), since it is not straitjacketed by objective preconditions. Secondly, its quasi-independence of external conditions makes its theorization difficult.

This difficulty concerns primarily explaining-based theories, and by necessity such theories as that in *Wendt I*, which strive for a single perspective marrying causal explanation with interpretative understanding (Hollis and Smith 1990). Explaining-based theories focus on causal relations in objective reality. They can thus deal with reflexivity only with difficulty, since it is not determined by this causality. Reflexivity brings about creative acts. As Salthe and Matsuno (1995: 332) observe, 'capricious choice from random distribution is the only possible model of creative action . . . in such scientific discourse'. Thus, from an explaining-based perspective, reflexivity can be considered as a matter of historical contingency or even chaos, something which simply emerges from a black box from time to time and which cannot be properly explained.

On the other hand, reflexivity is amenable to interpretative perspectives which focus on subjectivity in social life. Salthe speaks about 'the position of an internal actor' which makes creativity 'a perfectly natural explanation' (Salthe and Matsumo 1995). However, not only does reflexivity exist at the subjective, individual level, implied by the internal actor position, it can also emerge at the intersubjective, social level. It will be argued that Wendt's distinction between micro-structure and macro-structure can be used to distinguish between individual and social reflexivity. Still, acts of both kinds of reflexivity gain their meaning only against the backdrop of social rules and institutions. Therefore, if we want to understand reflexivity as a meaningful action rather than abstracting from it or treating it as random, we need an interpretative perspective which addresses subjective and intersubjective dimensions of social life.

All the same, an explaining-based perspective can be a fair choice for the subject matter, including reflexivity, if it provides new insights into other features of social life and if it opens space for reflexivity as a contingency. I claim that in this perspective *Wendt II* fares worse than *Wendt I*.

The link between reflexivity and contingency reminds us that reflexivity, which is often viewed as a positive move that improves the human condition, does not have to be treated in this way. Contingency works either way and social innovations can be both good and bad. More importantly, such a normative judgment would imply that reflexivity is bound by a particular philosophy of history transcending all reflection. This, however, would be a self-destructive view of reflexivity, as it would lead to the conclusion that reflexivity ends at the moment when the 'right' theory or philosophy is discovered. I claim that the shift from a cautious progressivism in *Wendt I* to the fully fledged teleology in *Wendt II* epitomizes the shift to a theory beyond reflection, from which genuine reflexivity has been banned.

Wendt on structural change

Having introduced reflexivity, I will now examine its role in the mechanisms of change in *Wendt I*. Firstly, I briefly describe Wendt's concepts of structure and mechanism of change. Secondly, I show that the symbolic interactionist account of production and the reproduction of international structure can work only under reflexivity. Thirdly, I show that reflexivity is also essential to the working of master variables.

Wendt I defines structural change as a transition from one culture of anarchy to the other. Wendt addresses the international structure as a culture, arguing that 'the deep structure of an international system is formed by the shared understandings governing organized violence' (1999: 313). He distinguishes three cultures of anarchy: Hobbesian, Lockean and Kantian. Each of these is associated with a particular role which prescribes the way in which states see themselves and treat one another; these roles are those of enemy, rival and friend.[3]

Wendt's account of structural change is open to historical contingency. Even though he offers a general symbolic interactionist framework which shows how a transition between two cultures of anarchy can occur, each instance of transition is treated as a case per se. In this respect, he focuses on the possibility of transition from Lockean culture, which serves as a model for the current Westphalian system, to Kantian culture. This openness to history is important since reflexivity is a historical contingency in theoretical frameworks such as Wendt's.

The general symbolic interactionist framework is based on a dyadic model according to which identities are learned and reproduced in the interaction between two actors, the Self and the Other. This interaction is shaped mainly by the individual representations about each other's role in the relationship. The interaction reflects these representations and generates reactions to them, as well as reactions to these reactions in which the reflexive Self adjusts its behaviour according to its understanding of the Other's behaviour. This process of mutual learning leads to the establishment of identities, each identity referring to both the role of the Self and the role of the Other. The repetition of interaction without new learning contributes to an internalization of identities. In contrast, for Kantian identities to emerge, the Self must start treating the Other *as if* they were friends; if this persists and the Other starts treating the Self in the same way, they may over time develop Kantian identities (Wendt 1999: 342).

If this mechanism is to work, both complex learning and reflexivity are needed. Let us look at both in more detail, starting with complex learning. Complex learning refers to a mere reaction to the move of the Other. It thus contributes to an internalization of identities, but has no transformative potential beyond that of misreading the moves of the Other. Changes can come only from the world out

---

3 While Hobbesian enemies do not recognize the right to exist in relation to one another, Lockean rivals do, though it does not prevent them from pursuing their interests in wars. Kantian friends may have mutual differences, but they never use violence to resolve these.

there. All the same, accounts based on complex learning differ from rationalist accounts of simple learning. The latter address only objective conditions, without looking into the ways in which these objective conditions are translated into the minds of the actors, while the former argue that to be significant the objective conditions have to be reflected and translated into the subjective realities of the actors. In this perspective, complex learning seems to embody Wendt's *via media* between rationalism and reflectivism.

Reflexivity instead leads to new moves in the game. When Self starts treating the Other *as if they were friends*, even if they are in fact rivals or enemies, individual reflexivity is at work. If Self succeeds at convincing the Other that they are friends, social reflexivity emerges. Reflexivity thus cannot be directly associated with specific objective conditions or existing rules. If we evaluate the reflexive moves according to these external yardsticks, they are mistaken as they do not correspond to reality. Treating a rival as a friend may prove to be a costly mistake, and the same goes for making the first co-operative move in a tit-for-tat strategy under Hobbesian conditions. Rule-altering moves cannot be made if actors simply follow the rules. The role of reflexivity is to break the extant rules and to replace them with new ones. It is this relative independence of reality which gives to reflexivity its transformative potential. *Wendt I* wants to tap this potential whenever Wendt speaks about reflexivity. Gorbachev's New Thinking (individual reflexivity) and its contribution to the end of the Cold War (social reflexivity) is its most obvious example (Wendt 1999: 76, 363, 375).

The symbolic interactionist framework shows how a transition to Kantian culture is possible in general. However, *Wendt I* also comes up with four groups of causal forces, 'master variables', presenting the specific mechanism through which states may start to treat each other as if they were friends. All the master variables need both complex learning and reflexivity in order to be effective.

The most prominent variable is self-restraint – a necessary though not a sufficient condition for transition to a Kantian system. It refers to acts of the Self which signal to the Other that the Self respects its difference and will be self-limiting towards it, thus creating the basis for mutual trust. Wendt (1999: 360) outlines several ways based on simple or complex learning which may lead to self-restraint, including coercion by a third party, repeated interactions or shared democratic norms. However, it can also be achieved by a unilateral self-binding 'with no expectation of specific reciprocity' (ibid.: 362). Self-binding 'has fewer preconditions than the others' and 'it may be able to create trust before the conditions that it is normally thought to require exist' (ibid.: 363). As such, it is conditioned by individual reflexivity on the part of the state, which is expected to recognize its own contribution to the self-fulfilling prophecy of the security dilemma and to make a risky gesture of good will towards the rival. Wendt mentions Gorbachev's New Thinking policies and his peace initiatives as examples of self-binding.

Self-restraint needs to be allied with another master variable (interdependence, common fate and homogeneity) to make the transition to Kantian culture possible.

Even though these master variables refer to inherently pre-social conditions (a high density of interactions, a common threat and an identical feature in corporate identity),[4] Wendt argues that a key step in their becoming master variables is the reflexive appraisal of the pre-social conditions. This makes them dependent on a successful complex learning. Moreover, Wendt also points to the role of reflexivity as referring to creative acts without which the master variables would not work. In the case of interdependence, he refers to someone 'who ha[s] the bright idea of portraying the situation as interdependent in the first place, for which there is no guarantee' (1999: 347). In brief, the efficiency of the master variables is to a large extent conditioned by someone's making a new move and starting to treat an Other *as if* they were interdependent, homogeneous or sharing a common fate. Without this reflexive move, the Kantian culture can never be achieved.

No reflexivity within scientific realism

Despite the importance of reflexivity for conceptualizing the structural change in *Wendt I*, the epistemological position Wendt develops does not allow for reflexivity to be theorized. Thus, he removes what seems to be the most important source of change from his meta-theoretical framework. I develop three claims in this connection. Firstly, Wendt struggles with the meta-theoretical legacy of neo-realism, or, more broadly, of positivist structuralism, which significantly constrains his possibilities of theorizing change in general and reflexive change in particular. Secondly, his theoretical framework accommodates causality, which he considers as vital for theorizing the change. Thirdly, the accommodation of causality prevents the accommodation of reflexivity, which I call the paradox of change.

Old debts

Neo-realism is a springboard from which *Wendt I* develops his own theory in both positive and negative terms. This is a tricky starting point for the theorization of structural change since, as this section will develop, neo-realism has often been criticized for its ahistoricity and its overly narrow view of international change. In the neo-realist perspective, the most important change is a change in the distribution of power (Waltz 1979: 100–1), such as that from multipolarity to bipolarity, and even this change is left unexplained and treated as exogenous to structure. Criticisms of neo-realism are aimed at both its meta-theory and its substantive theorizing.

Meta-theoretical criticism (Cox 1986 [1981]; Ashley 1986 [1984]; Walker 1993) targets structuralism, positivism, state-centrism and utilitarianism in particular as the main obstacles to a proper understanding of change. It reminds us of the

4 They are either material phenomena or phenomena which are not socially constructed on the international level. As such, they can be accommodated within neo-liberal accounts. In this volume, Hidemi Suganami (chap. 4) points to the close affinity between Wendt and the neo-liberal evolution of co-operation.

tension inherent in the concept of structural change as such, since it draws on the theory of structure as well as a theory of change, even though each of the theories tends towards its own, contrasting ontological and epistemological commitments. The former tends towards positivism, while the latter tends towards historicist or hermeneutical arguments.[5] Therefore, any attempt at providing a meta-theoretical framework for the theory of structural change, and especially an attempt inspired by neo-realism, has to compromise between positivist and non-positivist ontologies and epistemologies.

Wendt I is aware of this tension and strives for a compromise, maintaining a positivist epistemology, but a post-positivist ontology. Wendt argues that his ontology is idealist and holistic,[6] and not materialist and individualist like Waltz's. This idealist and holistic ontology should make it possible to consider the international structure as a distribution of ideas, and to conceptualize structural change as the change in ideas shared by international actors.

Wendt I also reacts to the most common criticism of neo-realism at the substantive level, which says that it could be made more dynamic by including interactions in the international structure (Ruggie 1986 [1983]; Axelrod 1984; Oye 1986; Buzan *et al.* 1993: 70; Buzan and Little 1996). Interactions are addressed primarily in the symbolic interactionist framework. They are described as part of the structure, called the micro-structure, and as causal master variables. Hence, both the micro-structure and master variables provide the dynamism of the theory.

Wendt I seems able to combine all the strengths of both the constructivist and the rationalist approaches to change. Compared with neo-realism, both idealist ontology and interactions would contribute to a richer account of structural change: the former brings in alternative anarchies, the latter provides for a mechanism of transition between the alternatives. A constructivist ontology allows Wendt to see the identities of international actors as 'always in process', dependent on minds and practices which open a variety of alternative international systems. Yet, as a scientific realist, he can suggest a causal mechanism of transition between alternatives, which is where constructivism usually fails.[7] Unfortunately, the story does not go as smoothly as Wendt would have us believe, as it ends up in what I call the paradox of change.

---

5 Walker (1993: 113), for example, speaks about two philosophical traditions ('between eternity and history, between identity and difference in time') whose clash is translated into an opposition between structuralism and historicism. While structuralism claims 'transtemporal, transspatial abstract universalism', historicism stresses temporal flow and shows how seemingly atemporal structures are historically constituted and reified.

6 Wendt's holism postulates a dialectical relationship between structure and agency and argues that agents are to some extent ontologically independent of structures (but not the other way round!). It is in fact an agent-oriented holism.

7 For the problems that constructivism has in explaining transitions between alternatives which it is so good at sketching, see Finnemore and Sikkink (1998), Hopf (1998:180) and Ruggie (1998b).

The paradox of change

The paradox of change shows the implications of the meta-theoretical framework of scientific realism for theorizing change as Wendt understands it.[8] It refers to the situation in which the meta-theoretical framework of *Wendt I* provides the causal explanations necessary for dealing with the mechanism of transition between alternative cultures of anarchy, but the framework actually excludes reflexivity, although it is thanks to this that the alternatives can be developed in the first place. I will focus on three issues which are crucial to understanding this paradox. The starting point is that Wendt considers causal explanations as essential to his account of change. Following this, scientific realism is extremely useful, as it provides the framework for causal theorizing in a way that alternative meta-theories do not. However, Wendt's scientific realism cannot provide a framework for understanding reflexivity.

Wendt (1999: 86) expects that the incorporation of causal theorizing will make the theory dynamic in accounting for 'transitions from one state to another'. In this connection, causality is supposed to give added value to constructivism, as it reveals the mechanism of transition between the alternative structures. This is usually missing in constructivist analysis, which is constitutive rather than causal and thus 'inherently static' (ibid.: 185–6).

Now it can be argued that, thanks to its inclusion of the causal theory of reference (Wendt 1999: 57–60) and to its postulates of the existence of unobservables, scientific realism provides better grounds for theorizing causality than other meta-theories (ibid.: 82).[9] However, the scientific realist framework works best when dealing with natural kinds in the shape of material objects. To make it relevant for social science, Wendt has to blur the distinction between social kinds, such as states, and natural kinds, such as atoms. At the same time, he remains aware that the distinction exists. In this way, he comes close to the position of naturalist monism, which argues for the same framework for both social and natural sciences.

This naturalist framework results in the reification of social kinds. When dealing with the 'objectivity' of social kinds, Wendt (1999: 69–71) tries to answer several objections against treating social and natural kinds in the same way. The most

8   A more complex criticism of Wendt's epistemological position has been provided by Smith (2000). For a different version of scientific realism used in IR theory, see Patomäki and Wight (2000) and Brglez (2001).

9   For the failure of empiricist positivist and post-positivist frameworks to provide for causality, see Patomäki and Wight (2000: 229–30). The most widespread positivist conception of causality, based on Hempel's D-N model, cannot account for causality between unique events, since it presupposes the working of general laws and, more importantly, it fails to distinguish correlation from causation unambiguously (Suganami 1996: 116–28; Patomäki and Wight 2000: 229–30). Hempel's deductive-nomological model assumes that a causal relationship between a particular event and its causes is based on the logical deductibility of the relationship from an empirically confirmed general law connecting this kind of cause with this kind of event (Hempel 1965; Suganami 1996). Post-positivists, on the other hand, either do not strive for causal explanations at all or redefine causality to make it fit into their meta-theory (Suganami 1996: 134–8).

important objections address the existential dependence of social kinds on one another, and on human beliefs and practices. Wendt suggests three possible solutions. Firstly, he claims that social kinds have a material base and, as such, are ontologically dependent on natural kinds. Secondly, social kinds are to some extent self-organized rather than completely dependent on one another. Thirdly, he sees social kinds as independent of the minds of the individuals who want to explain them. However, these claims reify social kinds either by 'push[ing] us towards materialism' (ibid.: 73) or by establishing a firm distinction between subject and object. This makes the theory inappropriate for moments of reflexivity when actors 'transcend the subject–object distinction and create new social kinds' (ibid.: 76).

As Wendt admits, a well-grounded scientific realism is not able to account for reflexivity.[10] Moreover, this kind of scientific realism clashes with symbolic inter-actionism. He clearly shows that identity is dependent on the representations that actors make to one another: 'who Ego is, in the interaction, is not independent of who Ego thinks Alter thinks Ego is' (Wendt 1999: 335), which makes epistemology co-determine ontology.[11] Nevertheless, Wendt inconsistently concludes that 'the ontology of social life is consistent with scientific realism' (ibid.: 76). However, as Kratochwil (chap. 2 this volume) observes, this conclusion 'does not follow'. To sum up, complex learning in which subjects are shaped by objects does fit in the framework; the reflexivity which refers to subjects bringing about new social realities, such as Kantian norms, does not.

Despite its lack of logical force, this conclusion could be accepted if reflexivity merely played a negligible role in Wendt's theorizing. But, as has been shown above, the opposite is true. Reflexivity plays a decisive role in his explanation of structural change.

Keeping reflexivity

Reflexivity can be dealt with in an alternative, hermeneutic framework.[12] Alas, the consistent use of hermeneutics prevents us from understanding causality,[13] and an unqualified embrace of hermeneutics would make us repeat the paradox of change in a reversed configuration. My thought was spurred by a somewhat unexpected hint at the end of *Wendt I* (1999: 367), where he suggests a temporal division of labour between different forms of rationalism and constructivism. In line with this

---

10 He admits that reification is a precondition of 'a clear distinction between subject and object', that transformations in which social theories become part of the social world 'violate the assumptions of the causal theory of reference' and that 'if societies were constantly doing this . . . we could not be realists about society' (Wendt 1999: 76).

11 Wendt (1999: 335) rightly argues that the 'joint constitution of identity is ultimately difficult to reconcile with the methodological individualism . . . which holds that thought, and thus identity, is ontologically prior to society', while failing to mention that, for the same reasons, it is difficult to reconcile with his kind of scientific realism.

12 This section draws on my previous discussion of reflexivity (Drulák 2001).

13 Skinner (2000 [1985]: 7) characterizes Gadamerian hermeneutics as 'a model in which we are not in the least concerned with the search of causes or the framing of laws.'

suggestion, I argue that the paradox of change can be addressed by a combination of two epistemologies, scientific realism for stable times and hermeneutics for times of change. Firstly, I claim that Wendt's distinction of micro-structure and macro-structure implies a distinction of two different temporal layers – *l'événement* and *la longue durée*. Secondly, I briefly introduce a hermeneutical framework within which the distinction between micro-structure and macro-structure is used to distinguish between individual and social reflexivity. Thirdly, I argue that the dynamics of each of the two temporal layers can be accommodated with a different epistemological framework.

Micro, macro and time

Wendt comes up with a broad concept of structure that is analytically divided into a micro-structure and macro-structure. Firstly, I briefly introduce the two concepts showing their different temporal qualities. Secondly, I associate these concepts with the concepts of *événement* and *longue durée* developed by the French historiographical school of *Les Annales*.

The micro-structure refers to the interaction of the units, while the macro-structure is said to supervene over it. While the micro-structure is constantly moving, the macro-structure is more stable. According to the principle of supervenience, there are 'many combinations of . . . interactions that will realize the same macro-level state' (Wendt 1999: 152). Change in the macro-structure implies a change in the micro-structure, but not the other way round. This is because there are macro-level phenomena and systemic tendencies which can only be recognized on the macro-level.

The micro–macro distinction is then applied to the analysis of culture as socially shared knowledge, distinguishing between common knowledge on the micro-level and collective knowledge on the macro-level. Collective knowledge supervenes on common knowledge. Common knowledge is '*nothing but* beliefs in the heads' of agents; with each change in belief 'the cultural forms constituted by common knowledge become literally different' (Wendt 1999: 161). Collective knowledge is a group-level phenomenon which may include beliefs to which each member of a group does not have to subscribe individually but which he respects on account of his 'allegiance and commitment to the group' (ibid.: 163). Again, several states of common knowledge are multiply realizable in one state of collective knowledge.

Wendt's discussion of micro–macro phenomena has important implications for change. Even though he says that 'we should not treat structure and process as different levels of analysis' and that micro- and macro-levels 'are [both] structured and *both* instantiated by process' (1999: 186), the former refers to realities which change all the time – hence, it gravitates to process and agency – while the latter refers to extremely stable reality, close to what is usually understood as structure.[14]

14 The different roles played by micro- and macro-structures with respect to change become obvious when we consider that Wendt implies that the international system has experienced only

It is the principle of supervenience which makes the macro-level more structural and the micro-level more processual. Wendt later introduces the concept of a 'tipping point' (ibid.: 264), that is, the threshold beyond which changes in the micro-structure turn into structural change.[15]

It can be argued that this difference between micro and macro is not specific to *Wendt I* but that it epitomizes a more general rule. This more general perspective can be found in the concept of scalar hierarchy developed in the literature on self-organization (Salthe 1985; Salthe and Matsuno 1995). The scalar hierarchy refers to two levels of observation: the focal level where the entities under consideration are situated (in our case the level of states) and the higher embedding level which sets the framework, or boundary conditions, for activities at the focal level (in our case the international system or the culture of anarchy). As Salthe and Matsuno argue, the two levels have 'different relaxation times, the lower the level, the faster entities located there will change' (1995: 330). In this connection, the higher level sets boundary conditions which are seen as fixed from the lower level.

This observation can be applied to the Wendtian distinction between micro-structure and macro-structure, as well as to analogous distinctions in other fields. On this basis, a common denominator exists between the macro–micro distinction of Wendt and the *longue durée* and *événement* introduced by the French historical school of *Les Annales*. Both deal with the same problem of relating two layers of social reality which are temporally distinct, and both address the tension between structure and history.

In the case of *Les Annales*, the tension shows when dealing with the relationship of different time layers, namely, between the centuries-long perspective of the *longue durée*, the decades-long perspective of *conjonctures* and the immediate perspective of *événement* (Clark 2000 [1985]: 182). Unusually for a historian, Braudel (1969) concentrates on the macro-level of the *longue durée*, writing 'structural history', while paying less attention to historical events. He is also criticized for failing to bring the accounts on different layers into a coherent whole rather than offering three unconnected stories. Followers of Braudel further developed the concept of the *longue durée*, liberating it from its materialist focus and investigating, among others, the evolution of culture and mentality (Vovelle 1982; 1988: 85–6). Nevertheless, the problem of connecting the *longue durée* and events remains open, as proved by discussions of the different options of their relations.[16]

one change in macro-structure so far, from Hobbesian to Lockean culture, and that it may be going through another one right now, from Lockean to Kantian culture.

15 A useful conceptualization of the tipping point can be found in Finnemore and Sikkink (1998: 901), where the authors argue firstly that 'norm tipping rarely occurs before one-third of the total states in the system adopt the norm' and secondly that 'critical states' join 'without which the achievement of the substantive norm goal is compromised'.

16 As Vovelle (1988: 97) puts it: either 'de la structure à l'événement, en passant par la longue durée' or 'de l'événement à la longue durée'.

Hermeneutics and reflexivity

The distinction between micro-structure and macro-structure also makes it possible to elaborate on a previous distinction between individual and social reflexivity. However, as argued, reflexivity does not fit into the meta-theoretical framework of *Wendt I*. Therefore, I start with the introduction of a meta-theoretical alternative.

Hermeneutics provides a possible meta-theoretical framework in which reflexivity becomes something more than a mere contingency. The hermeneutical framework actually seems to underlie some important parts of the substantive theorizing in *Wendt I*, since it provides grounds for symbolic interactionism (Outhwaite 2000 [1985]: 33). When addressing reflexivity, Wendt refers to Giddens's notion of 'double hermeneutics' (Giddens 1990), which can be seen as a defining feature of the constructivism in IR (Guzzini 2000a).[17]

Giddens (together with Habermas and others) belongs to the group of social theorists who have developed the concept of reflexive modernity by drawing on the philosophical hermeneutics of Gadamer (Outhwaite 2000 [1985]: 28). Gadamer's elaboration of the Heideggerian concept of the hermeneutic circle makes the notion of reflexivity more tangible. It is a circle in which we move when trying to gain knowledge, 'seeking to understand the whole in terms of its parts, and its parts in terms of the contribution they make to the meaning of the whole' (Skinner 2000 [1985]: 7). Gadamer (1990 [1960]: 270–305) argues that understanding is dependent on pre-existing structures (*Vorstrukturen*) which are themselves historical and subject to change. He thus rehabilitates tradition, authority and prejudice as preconditions of our knowledge (*Vorurteile als Bedingungen des Verstehens*), as its *horizon*. Reflexivity can thus be understood as perpetual movement in the hermeneutic circle in which we try to understand things at the same time in which the very conditions of this understanding change (the horizon of things).

Now, drawing on the distinction between micro-structure and macro-structure, reflexivity can be conceptualized at two levels: individual and social. In this connection, social reflexivity, resulting from moves in a hermeneutic circle of macro-structural collective knowledge, supervenes on individual reflexivity which is brought about by movement in hermeneutic circles of micro-structural common knowledge.

The mechanism connecting the two kinds of reflexivity looks as follows: agents observe the world against the horizon of the particular culture of anarchy. Consequently, either they keep this horizon, thus reproducing the collective horizon in their individual horizons of common knowledge, or they are reflexive about the

---

17 Giddens's (1990) application of hermeneutics to social science results in the concepts of reflexive modernity and double hermeneutics. He defines modernity as a reflexive system which continually evaluates and remakes social practices. A decisive role within the ongoing reflection is played by social science, which provides the concepts and guidance for social action. Unlike natural science, social science thus re-creates the object of its enquiry. Giddens uses the notion of double hermeneutics, where social knowledge reflects and remakes the social conditions on which it existentially depends, to argue that modernity is deeply and inherently sociological.

horizon. Such individual reflexivity results in a deviation of common knowledge from collective knowledge. However, reflexivity gains its social significance only once it also takes place at the level of collective knowledge (after reaching the tipping point). At this point, we speak about structural change as a change in the macro-structure.

Temporal division of labour

To do justice to both causal theorizing and reflexivity, I suggest combining scientific realism and hermeneutics using the two temporal layers or two faces of the structure. On the one hand, hermeneutics should provide us with a meta-theoretical framework for understanding both the daily (re)production of identities, including individual reflexivity, and structural change in the *longue durée* resulting from social reflexivity. On the other hand, scientific realism should give us a framework to account for causal relations between events. Hence, events would be subject to two readings: a hermeneutic reading to look into the production and reproduction of identities through events, and a scientific realist reading to analyse their interactions, while assuming stable identities. This solution is quite close to the metaphor of particles/waves dualism used in the physics of light (Guzzini and Leander, chap. 5 this volume). Whereas scientific realism considers identity to be stable and particle-like, hermeneutics sees it as changing and wave-like, yet both refer to the same phenomenon.

Moreover, this solution is to some extent implied by two suggestions in *Wendt I*. Firstly, Wendt (1999: 148) argues that the micro-structure can be understood with the individualist methodology of rational choice, e.g., using game theory, while the working of the macro-structure can be grasped only with a holistic approach. Secondly, he suggests a 'temporal division of labor: rationalism for today and tomorrow, constructivism for the *longue durée*' (ibid.: 367), even though he acknowledges that such a merger of rationalism and constructivism is possible only if we treat rationalism 'as a methodological convenience' (ibid.) while the ontology remains constructivist.

The idea of the temporal division of labour has been criticized by Friedrich Kratochwil, but his criticism is only partly justified. Kratochwil considers the *longue durée* only in the context of Braudel's work, where 'identities . . . "wash out" over long periods' (Kratochwil, chap. 2 this volume). Thus he neglects, for example, analyses of culture and mentalities in the *longue durée* (Vovelle 1982, 1988). Neither is it correct to interpret the *longue durée* simply as the long run or a long period (Kratochwil, chap. 2 this volume), since the term usually refers to social time. As Ruggie (1998b: 875) observes, the distinction between the *longue durée* and *l'histoire événementielle* is not only about duration but also about the different framing of causal factors. It is in the dimension of the *longue durée* that Ruggie sees structure being 'brought to life'.

To sum up, hermeneutics is indispensable both when dealing with *événement* (micro-structure) and when addressing the *longue durée* (macro-structure). But when dealing with events, the macro-structure is more or less static and social kinds are reified, and so reflexivity, which takes place at the individual level only, is hidden under the social surface. This makes them amenable to scientific realist, causal accounts. On the other hand, when social reflexivity redefines the macro-structure, it makes the structure move, breaking the distinction between object and subject, and excluding scientific realist causal accounts. Obviously, the tension between epistemology and ontology is still present as it concentrates in the micro-structure. However it is less of a burden than the Wendtian scientific realist solution whereby reflexivity is either ignored or identified with contingency at best. Moreover, as argued, any theory of structural change may expect a similar kind of tension.

Goodbye reflexivity

Wendt I struggles with reflexivity; *Wendt II* does not seem to care about it any more. Whereas reflexivity plays an important role, despite the meta-theoretical difficulties, in the substantive theorizing in *Wendt I*, it disappears totally from *Wendt II*. This section develops two claims. Firstly, *Wendt II* can be understood as a rather rationalist elaboration on *Wendt I*, answering several questions about change that were left open in *Wendt I*. Secondly, the answers lead to a mechanistic account of change which provides space neither for reflexivity, nor for contingency as its positivist proxy.

Teleological struggle for recognition / power / stability

The discussion of structural change in *Wendt I* generates several questions which are acknowledged but not really answered. Without wishing to address all of them, I focus on those two which are answered in *Wendt II*: why is historical progress irreversible, and how can a well-internalized culture of anarchy change without experiencing exogenous shocks? I claim that the answers imply an almost realist understanding of international relations in terms of hierarchy, stability and power.

Wendt I cautiously argues that, despite historical contingencies, the Lockean culture of anarchy we achieved is unlikely to be reversed and, moreover, is likely to be replaced by Kantian culture. This soft teleology of *Wendt I* is replaced by a deterministic teleology of *Wendt II*. Not only is the transition to Kantian culture inevitable, but the Kantian culture of anarchy itself is not a terminus and will of necessity result in a world state.

This full embrace of the teleological argument answers the first question, but it also forces *Wendt II* to conceptualize world politics in terms of stability and hierarchy. To avoid the metaphysical reflections about the purpose of the historical process which is implied by teleological thinking, *Wendt II* uses the concept of stability. The inspiration comes from Byerly, who notes with respect to teleological explanations that 'one way the implicit reference to conscious purposes might be bypassed is to appeal to configurations that have greater stability' (Byerly 1979: 172). The idea that more stable states of the system are more likely to occur than unstable ones can indeed provide a possible answer to the question for the purpose of history. However, the system theories on which Wendt draws condition stability by hierarchy: really stable complex systems are assumed to be hierarchical. Anarchical systems are seen as immature and unstable predecessors of hierarchical systems. This is the path taken by *Wendt II.*

The resurrection of the logic of anarchy is a necessary corollary. While *Wendt I* is loath to attribute any explanatory power to anarchy as such, claiming it is an 'empty vessel', *Wendt II* fills the vessel with new contents in seeing it as both a realist struggle for security and a struggle for recognition (Wendt 2003: 507–10). Even the most cultivated kind of Kantian culture is still subject to the logic of anarchy and generates too much uncertainty. Therefore, it cannot provide ultimate stability, which is achievable only in the hierarchical setting of the world state – something with which Morgenthau or Carr would happily agree. The fact that everyone treats the other as friend is insufficient unless such a treatment is enforceable. This move also implies a revision of the understanding of internalization introduced in *Wendt I*. *Wendt I* argues that well internalized norms do not have to be enforced externally, as they constitute the identities of the actors. On the other hand, arguments in *Wendt II* imply that Kantian culture cannot be internalized unless the institutional checks of the world state are in place.

The stability itself is conditioned by the mutual recognition of all humans as equal subjects. Wendt argues that such recognition is not possible in the anarchical world of states, as the very idea of sovereignty implies the unequal treatment of citizens and non-citizens. Drawing on *Wendt I*, he outlines four anarchical stages of the process towards the world state – the Hobbesian culture of system of states, the Lockean culture of society of states, the Kantian culture of world society and the Kantian culture of collective security – to show that none of them guarantees equal recognition, and therefore none is stable in the long run. However, each constitutes a temporary equilibrium, a 'local attractor', which may last for centuries before it is finally superseded by a more stable stage.

Unlike *Wendt I*, *Wendt II* provides a general theory of the internal dynamics of the international system, explaining why even well-internalized cultures of anarchy can change. The engine of change consists of a struggle for recognition. Wendt takes over the Hegelian model of the master/slave relationship to show how these asymmetrical identities generate a drive for change. As long as some subjects are given inferior status with regard to other actors, they will resist this status and struggle for equality. Moreover, even superior actors cannot be happy with their status unless it is recognized by subjects equal to themselves.[18]

This important innovation introduces the question of power and its unequal distribution into the theory. The power dimension was already mentioned in *Wendt I*. Here, it is argued that 'having more power means Ego can induce Alter to change its definition of the situation more in light of Ego's than vice-versa' (1999: 331). However, *Wendt I* fails to develop the full potential of this factor with respect

---

18   This argument makes sense in a dyadic relationship where the slave is his master's only other. But it is not very convincing in a world of several actors who are both masters and slaves. This situation can lead to a Kautskyan world where masters recognize one another as equal while happily exploiting their respective slaves.

to the asymmetrical roles, implicitly assuming in his discussion of the development of identities that the interaction takes place in an equal relationship. The status derived from this recognition, i.e., master/slave or, more generally, superior/ inferior, refers to what used to be called prestige. Prestige was an important feature of power in the classical realist literature, the policy of prestige being one of the three 'basic manifestations of the struggle for power' (Morgenthau 1985: 86). Realists see prestige as instrumental to the more material ends of the policy, but the concept of recognition turns this hierarchy upside down, subordinating other goals to the supreme goal of equal recognition. This move makes sense if power is understood as a social construction (Wendt 1999: 371), since then the web of (un)recognitions between actors constitutes the power distribution among them. From this perspective, the struggle for recognition can be read as a struggle for power, a common engine of change in most realist theories.

The struggle for recognition in *Wendt II* is subject to the same equilibrium law as the realist struggle for power. Whereas subjects resist the asymmetrical distribution of identities in *Wendt II*, realist states resist the asymmetrical distribution of power. Both the balance of power and equal recognition guarantee an equality and reciprocity among the subjects. Moreover, both *Wendt II* and Morgenthau agree that the stability of equilibrium is only temporary under anarchy and that a lasting equilibrium can be achieved only under hierarchy. Morgenthau's conclusion (1985: 559) that durable peace can be achieved by 'the creation of an international community as foundation for a world state' is quite similar to Wendt's idea that the Kantian culture of world society and collective security will lead to a world state, the only difference being Wendt's conviction of the necessity of the transition deriving from his teleology.

Yes to change, no to reflexivity

Wendt II both specifies and reshapes his original theory of structural change by introducing teleology and the struggle for recognition. However, these innovations make the resulting theory more mechanistic and incapable of addressing reflexivity. Still, both teleology and the struggle for recognition could include it. I will hint at directions in which they can be redefined in a more inclusive way.

The direction of change is set by a metaphysical assumption that the international system tends towards stability. Each of the four states of the international system is defined by 'boundary conditions', which place macro-structural rules over the behaviour of units such as cultures of anarchy. But Wendt's account also implies the existence of 'super-boundary conditions', or a 'super-macro-structure', which sets stability as the ultimate goal of the system as such, selecting more stable states over less stable states. As argued, Wendt has good reasons for assuming stability. But in doing so he virtually bars reflexivity and even contingency from his framework.

The idea of a well-defined, inevitable end-state is at odds with the possibility of social reflexivity and innovation in macro-structure. A new move can be made only as a result of individual reflexivity, with no way of being translated into social reflexivity, or as a result of complex learning consisting of recognition of the teleological inevitability of the world state.[19] Acknowledgement of social reflexivity would require a framework which is at least open to contingency, therefore cannot be made part within Wendtian teleology.

Two amendments are possible which allow us to keep teleology and to accommodate reflexivity. Firstly, redefining the concept of an attractor provides a more open perspective on structural change. Wendt defines four 'local attractors', four states of temporary stability, and one global attractor, the end-state of an ultimate stability. However, complexity theory, from which the concept of an attractor is taken, understands attractors as both stabilizing and destabilizing forces, since attractors 'act to pull a complex dynamic system out of instability or chaos into order or vice versa' (Albrecht 2000: 413). Chaos must not be understood only negatively. On the contrary, complex systems are conceptualized as being 'on the edge of chaos', which provides for innovation and creation (ibid.). Drawing on our previously established identity of reflexivity and chance, social reflexivity could be conceptualized as the second global attractor which pulls the system into creative, and sometimes indeed destructive, instability.

Secondly, 'emergent' teleology would much better reflect reflexivity than Wendt's immanent teleology. By this view, the path of the international system would not be defined a priori by stages and a well-known end-state. There would be finality in the system, but this finality would emerge from the tension between stability and social reflexivity. Thus the end-state itself would be subject to reflexivity and change. This perspective of emergent teleology suggests (Albrecht 2000: 417) that 'the direction of increasing complexity and diversity in life is the outcome of necessity (order) and chance (chaos).' This brings us back to the movement in the hermeneutical circle where the reflexive subject is conditioned by the necessity of pre-existing structures within which it can exercise individual reflexivity. If the conditions are right, this may lead to social reflexivity (seen as contingent or chaotic from outside). This kind of teleology cannot boast bold predictions about the inevitability of anything, but it does not force us to ignore historical contingency.

Indeed, *Wendt II* could be read using this perspective if 'inevitable' is replaced with 'likely'. Wendt claims that the world state would not mean the end of history but that it 'would be the end of just one kind of history', arguing that, when 'one telos is over, another [is] just beginning' (2003: 528). Hence, the world state could be seen as the telos which emerged at a particular historical juncture and towards which the current international system seems to be heading, providing no other historical juncture occurs whereby a new telos would emerge.

The struggle for recognition plays an important role in Wendt's teleology, inspired by what Ringmar called 'the recognition game' (Ringmar 2002). Ringmar's account works well as a thin constructivist alternative to rationalist approaches, especially when applied to the analysis of the Cold War, the focus of

19 In this respect, complex learning is highly welcome as it can speed up the inevitable. As Wendt says, 'better to "get with the program" than wait till it gets to you' (Wendt 2003: 530).

his article. However, it is not easily reconcilable with the theory outlined in *Wendt I*. Firstly, it offers a more narrow view of subjectivity. Secondly, it takes into account only complex learning and not reflexivity. Both features are also part of *Wendt II*.

Ringmar and Wendt argue that states have no subjectivity (Ringmar 2002: 118–19; Wendt 2003) in Hobbesian conditions as they do not recognize one another as subjects worthy of existence in the destructive war of all against all. In accepting this, *Wendt II* does away with a rather convincing part of *Wendt I*, in which it is argued that states can develop quite a robust Hobbesian culture of anarchy in which war has a value per se (1999: 274). In such conditions, states recognize one another as mortal enemies to be destroyed in a 'good fight'. This narrower understanding of subjectivity unnecessarily constrains our view of the variety of ways through which subjectivity can be constituted. Given that it ignores the more violent ways of constituting subjectivity, its picture of recognition and ensuing subjectivity is too rosy.

Ringmar's historical analysis is telling. Whereas *Wendt I* pictures the end of the Cold War as an example of reflexivity, Ringmar relies only on learning. This is not just a coincidence. An account which would rely on reflexivity, such as *Wendt I*, does not fit into the framework of *Wendt II*. Games and struggles for recognition apparently follow the same logic as the realist theories of the balance of power to which they were supposed to provide an alternative. The two stories of Soviet policy at the end of the Cold War show how the theoretical and meta-theoretical differences between complex learning and reflexivity can translate into empirical accounts.

Ringmar's interpretation can be summed up fairly briefly: 'Russians wanted the respect of the world, and when the West started to change, the Russians had to follow' (Ringmar 2002: 130). He criticizes the widespread interpretation which claims that the poor state of the Soviet economy, which threatened the Soviet Union's strategic positioning towards the West, made Gorbachev embrace reform, which then led to the demise of the system. However, his own explanation follows the same structural logic according to which the Soviets were forced to change by blind forces. Unlike the rationalists, he is not thinking of the forces of economy or raw material power, but those governing the social structures of recognition. Still, blind forces they are that destroy actors who do not respect them. *Wendt I* criticizes this position (Wendt 1999: 129): 'Structural conditions did not force self-awareness on the Soviets. Soviet behavior changed because they redefined their interests as a result of having looked at their existing desires and beliefs self-critically.'

Such a conclusion would be difficult to sustain in *Wendt II* unless the self-critical gaze or reflexive intentionality were interpreted only in terms of complex learning, as recognizing the inevitability of the world state. However, that would still mean that self-awareness was enforced by the structural conditions: the looming world state.

Yet the struggle for recognition does not have to imply the Hegelian finality of the world state and the absence of social reflexivity. As Brewer (1991) showed, people are quite creative in making groups with which they identify and whose recognition they seek. If these groups are to fulfil their purpose by satisfying the basic human need for identification, they cannot be too heterogeneous or too open. Therefore, a strong argument can be made that the struggle for recognition is open-ended and that mankind is likely to remain divided in exclusive groups which will be open to outsiders only to some extent, as are states today.[20]

Conclusion

Referring to the works which preceded *Wendt I* and *Wendt II* (Wendt 1987, 1992a), Ringmar (1997) has characterized the Wendtian project as a struggle between science and history. He has argued that these two modes of thought, which Wendt tries to bring together by making neo-realism more historical, are incompatible. If we consider history and positivist science as two extremes between which a middle ground is sought, then *Wendt I* moves closer to positivism and farther from history, while the teleology of *Wendt II* drives us away from both. Despite this, I am convinced, unlike some more radical critics (e.g., Behnke, chap. 3 this volume), that Wendt has made a serious contribution to our thinking about IR, on which it is worth elaborating.

This chapter has offered an attempt at such an elaboration. Its starting point was the strange contrast between the prominent place awarded to the fundamental international change in *Wendt I* and *Wendt II*, and the rather inadequate treatment of the issue in both works. I attributed these difficulties to Wendt's meta-theory and I tried to amend them in a way which would bring the theory closer to history. The amendments drew on the suggestions that Wendt makes on the margins of his two works. I picked up three such suggestions: repeated references to reflexivity, the suggestion of a temporal division of labour between rationalism and constructivism, and the idea that the telos of the system can be subject to historical change. All the three suggestions go against the thrust of the theorizing of the texts which include them, and all offer new perspectives from which the texts can be re-read and amended.

The chapter has offered such amendments. It has elaborated on the temporal division of labour between hermeneutics for the *longue durée* and scientific realism for events. It has also suggested a different understanding of teleology which respects historical contingency. Both amendments bring in reflexivity as an essential part of the theory, which is very much in the spirit, though it does not always keep to the letter, of Wendt's theorizing. The amendments make the theory more historical, but with costs. The costs consist in a loss of parsimony and in the introduction of hermeneutics. This makes the theory less 'scientific', in the sense of being less capable of providing simple, atemporal laws of politics which would prepare us for the future. These costs should be accepted, however. They can be understood as an investment in the never-ending struggle between science and history.

20 It does not make too much sense to predict the structure and the kinds of these groups as they will be constituted not only by objective factors, e.g., connected with the working of the global economy, but also by a fundamentally unpredictable reflexivity.

9 No place for politics?

Truth, progress and the neglected role of diplomacy in Wendt's theory of history[*]

Katalin Sárváry

This chapter investigates how Alexander Wendt's idea of the inevitability of a world state (Wendt 2003) affects his theory of International Relations (IR) as compared to his *Social Theory of International Politics* (Wendt 1999). It focuses on two questions: whether the theory is plausible, and, whether or not the theory works, i.e., what it contributes to practice. Indeed, the chapter makes a dual claim: Wendt's recent work about the inevitability of a world state continues to propose an implausible account of progress, but paradoxically enables a better understanding of the role of agency and politics.

For Wendt, his theory's determinism is a reflection of, and follows from, the deep structure of the world. Wendt's scientific realism is, in turn, inseparable from his view of historical progress. What makes scientific progress inevitable, i.e., a rump material reality science is trying to describe, is the same reality that moves history towards progress. This substantially reduces the scope for agency, and consequently diplomacy, in a double sense: it limits the very stakes of diplomacy and also the actual choices diplomats have.

Despite his adding teleology to *Social Theory*, I will argue that the other modifications of Wendt's theory (his assumption of progress on Hegelian rather than Kantian lines, and the related revaluation of the meaning of human violence) paradoxically create a new scope for agency at the micro-structural level. These two opposite tendencies towards determinism and voluntarism were already inherent in *Social Theory*, but have become accentuated in Wendt's rearticulation of his theory. In my reading, they follow from the uneasy compromise between Wendt's scientific realism and constructivism.

This chapter examines these two opposite tendencies at work in Wendt's theory. The first part deals with Wendt's dual conception of scientific and historical

[*] This chapter reflects on my earlier critique of Wendt's theory of change and diplomacy (Sárváry 2001) in the light of Wendt's subsequent writing on the teleology of a world state. I still feel indebted to the earlier discussions during the workshops held at the Central European University, Budapest, and at the late Copenhagen Peace Research Institute (COPRI). I wish to thank first of all Stefano Guzzini and Anna Leander, as well as the other participants, in particular Andreas Behnke, Milan Brglez, Petr Drulák, Alexander Astrov and Corneliu Bjola. Alexander Maxwell provided helpful language-editing.

progress in *Social Theory* and its amendment in the light of teleology. The second part focuses on the new scope for agency at the micro-structural level. This reconstruction will question Wendt's structural bias and the solution he offers to the above tension. Both theories, so my main critique, are prisoners of our contemporary thought about politics and legitimacy that confer plausibility to Wendt's descriptions, but for the same reason make them vulnerable. Thus, despite an important opening to politics at the micro-structural level in his recent turn, his view of politics remains too determinist and underestimates the stakes of diplomacy.

From hidden progress to teleology: a reconstruction of the 'progress' of Wendt's argument

The dual conception of scientific and historical progress in Social Theory (1999)

Wendt privileges a scientific realist epistemology over a constructivist one. He maintains that the outside world imposes serious limits on our representations of it. Scientific representation tries to uncover the deep structure of the world, compared to other representations. This explains the success of science: as Wendt says, 'science is successful, because it gradually brings our theoretical understanding of the world into conformity with the deep structure of the world out there' (1999: 65). This reflects a progressive view of science.

Similarly, Wendt privileges a scientific realist ontology over a constructivist one. He maintains the existence of a rump material world of natural kinds with causal powers. Wendt denies that his position would be identical with epistemological foundationalism. Yet he implies something very similar when he maintains that 'the meaning' of this rump material reality, which constrains social reality through its causal powers, is independent of cultures and interpretation. Our knowledge about natural kinds (by which he means humans, cats and dogs) is trans-historically valid, universal knowledge.

The gradual progress of science means that our present knowledge is closer to 'the truth' than was our knowledge in the past. Our present knowledge is, therefore, universally valid knowledge. Behind this perspective is not only a progressive view of science, but also a view of progress with a direction that ultimately leads to an understanding of the more complex social reality, to the image of the accumulation of knowledge in the natural sciences. Wendt projects this universally valid and superior knowledge of the present onto his interpretation of the past, including his interpretation of different cultures.

Wendt's conception of historical progress cannot be treated in isolation of his progressive view of science (Sárváry 2001). Through the mediation of a rump reality, political actors arrive at interpreting reality around them in a similarly progressive way, just like Wendt himself. Contemplating the same reality makes the diplomat, who is both an observer and an actor on the international scene, read history in a similar way to the scientific observer and construct historical reality accordingly. Wendt's dual conception of progress explains why he decides not to theorize disruptive change. Wendt assumes a unidirectional structural logic of historical progress, which can only temporarily be disturbed by what he calls 'external shocks'. Compared to the logic of progress, disruptive change seems 'abnormal', not something to be systematically guarded against. It is for this reason that Wendt devalues diplomacy.

Thus for the most part, according to Wendt, actors are forced to follow the logic of progress and gradually internalize new norms. 'Reality' forces actors to recognize those causal mechanisms (homogeneity, common fate, interdependence) that 'push' them towards higher cultural forms by inducing them to practise self-restraint in their relations (1999: 355). Actors may disturb this endogenous and unidirectional structural logic when they fail to recognize or decide to act against these causal mechanisms. But because of the high costs involved, the impossibility of acting against 'reality' in the long run and the 'conservative' nature of a given culture, these exogenous shocks are rare compared to the endogenous and unidirectional progressive logic that structural change takes (ibid.: 312). This ultimately allows Wendt to downgrade the consideration of a possible structural regress.

Since Wendt assumes the three active (or efficient) causes of structural change (i.e., interdependence, homogeneity and common fate) to increase over historical time, he assumes that actors have to recognize this, which, in turn, will 'induce' them 'to engage in pro-social behavior' through practising self-restraint, the enabling or permissive cause of structural change (1999: 343, 357). Subjectively, the practice of self-restraint can also be imposed on states (the realist explanation) or be the result of a spillover of their domestic identities (the liberal explanation). Yet, coercion and self-interest can only lead to first- or second-degree internalization of the norms of a given culture of anarchy. They cannot affect state identities (ibid.: 310).

Wendt, therefore, denies any relationship between culture (shared knowledge about states' posture towards each other as 'enemies', 'rivals' or 'friends') and cooperation within one cultural form (1999: 253, 259). This is because, ultimately, 'roles are structural positions not actor beliefs' (ibid.: 258). Cooperation is therefore dependent on third-degree internalization of roles (i.e., on legitimacy), when states subjectively identify with the role-structure of a given culture of anarchy. Wendt's notion of progress between different cultures of anarchy elaborates the observation that some societies are more integrated than others. More integrated societies not only share the knowledge that the Other is an enemy, a rival or a friend, but in the latter Kantian culture the gap between states' domestic and international identities is substantially reduced. In other words, states share a 'we' identity in a Kantian culture. As states progress in their relations towards a higher culture of anarchy, the possibilities of non-violent conflict resolution increase.

While the realist and the liberal explanations of self-restraint can also lead to structural change in the long run through the emergence of legitimacy and collective identities, the third pathway to cooperation could be seen as an explanation of 'sudden' structural change where the actors' role is upgraded. This happens when a major actor unilaterally redefines his identity as a 'we' identity through self-binding. Self-binding requires self-reflection by an actor about its own contribution to a security dilemma and a credible redefinition of its own role in the reproduction of a non-cooperative role-structure through visible self-sacrifices (Wendt 1999: 360–2). Self-restraint is a causal variable, while self-reflection is constitutive of actors' identity and interests. Thus, ultimately, the role of actors in structural change is their ability to reflect on their own ideas concerning the outside world and their place in it (these ideas, however, remain restricted to the question whether enmity, rivalry or friendship dominates this world). Only then can actors emancipate themselves from reified social kinds (ibid.: 76) and escape the structural logic in which they are temporarily locked. According to Wendt, 'structural change occurs when actors redefine who they are and what they want' (ibid.: 336–7). Wendt provides Soviet New Thinking as an example of sudden structural change through the self-binding and redefinition of Soviet identity (ibid.: 76, 129, 363, 375). The consequence for his substantive theory is a strange combination of structuralist and voluntarist theory. On the one hand, there is a structural reality beyond human control that moves history towards peace through certain causal mechanisms (the four master variables). On the other hand, there are actors whose ideas can dramatically change this 'endogenous' and 'unidirectional' historical development.

After he has eliminated a serious theoretical consideration of structural regress as contradictory to the progressive structural logic of anarchy, Wendt's view of *contingent* historical change is limited to a question of time: how long does it take for cultural time to move forward from Hobbesian to Kantian anarchy? Wendt's answer rests on his insight concerning the conservative nature of different cultures of anarchy. Since each culture is sustained by inter-subjectively shared practices and understandings which are resistant to change (1999: 311), its underlying 'conservative' nature represents an obstacle to progress once a certain level of development has been reached. Only reflexivity can transcend this conservative nature of structure and speed up progressive change. As will be argued below, it is through stimulating actors' reflectivity that the amendments introduced by Wendt create an opening to politics. This opening is, however, coupled with a view of progress that is explicitly deterministic, since it posits the inevitability of a world state as the ultimate structural logic of anarchy. It is to this latter innovation that we now turn.

Progress through teleology (2003)

In *Social Theory*, Wendt fails to consider seriously the possibility that progress would be non-linear or that structural change would be regressive. For his dual conception of progress produces a theoretical blinder. The idea of progress in *Social Theory*, therefore, rests on rather weak foundations. It is based on an intuition that thinks of political rights as properties that individuals and states are unwilling to surrender once they have internalized them (1999: 311–12). The unfolding of progress in history is justified in these terms. Moving from a lower to a higher cultural form is described as a cultural evolution through a cumulative acquisition of rights by states and a parallel elimination of violence in their relations. Thus states acquired the right to sovereignty in the Lockean and 'the right to freedom from violence and security assistance' in the Kantian culture of anarchy (ibid: 312). But this process is contingent on the avoidance of external shocks or disruptive change, i.e., external to the otherwise progressive historical logic identified by Wendt. On the basis of this intuition, Wendt can only say that the history of international politics has an endogenous, unidirectional dynamic towards progress. But Wendt adds that '[t]his process may not survive exogenous shocks, like invasion (the barbarian invasion of Rome) or a revolution in the domestic constitution of member states (the American and French Revolutions) (ibid.: 312).[1]

Wendt's (2003) 'teleological theory of the logic of anarchy' is meant to remedy the weakness of the progressive assumption in his *Social Theory*. Wendt advances the strongest possible argument for progress when he says that a world state is both inevitable and represents the last stage of progress in the history of mankind (Wendt 2003: 491). In his approach to teleology, Wendt identifies with Hegel, who 'took the stronger, ontological view that nature itself was teleological'. This is a move away from *Social Theory* and also from Kant, who 'believed that purposiveness was not an objective feature of nature and thus teleological explanations were of heuristic value only' (ibid.: 531). More clearly than in *Social Theory*, this new turn allows micro-processes to be non-deterministic, non-linear, often blocked or historically contingent; yet all pathways still lead to one telos: a world state. 'In that respect the theory is progressivist, although in an explanatory rather than normative sense' (ibid.: 492).

Wendt updates his ideas about the logics of identity formation with new insights from self-organization theory and causality. In *Social Theory*, identity formation emerged as an evolutionary process through natural and cultural selection (the latter implying imitation and social learning). In contrast, self-organization theory helps imagine 'order' where the corresponding identities emerge spontaneously from the interaction of individual and system dynamics.

Three causal mechanisms are at work. Natural selection is replaced by the 'bottom-up process' of individual self-organization towards increasingly more stable end-states (upward causation), where the process is driven towards fixed-point attractors (such as the state or the macro-level tendency of balancing). Structural constitution is responsible for downward or formal causation on the basis of information coded at the system's level (e.g., the Waltzian argument that the structure of anarchy selects for balancing). But, in order to do justice to self-organization theory, Wendt has to admit that it identifies a variety of end-states other than fixed-point attractors, the equivalent of equilibria in economics. These include periodic, quasi-periodic and even chaotic attractors (2003: 501). Moreover, he has to admit that much work on self-organization theory rejects teleology.

1 Note that what Wendt calls external shocks are outstanding episodes of history. But if we consider them to be external to whatever endogenous historical process, we have to wonder what remains of history in that process. These are also episodes where actors fail to cope peacefully with demands for change, which therefore shed some light on the stakes of action on the historical stage.

In fact it seems that Wendt turns to what he calls 'causal pluralism' to find a justification for teleological explanations, which he does by introducing final causation. Final causality is able to support the stronger, 'developmental' approach to a teleology directed towards the future, as opposed to the weaker evolutionary approach adopted in *Social Theory* that refers more to questions of origin (2003: 497–8). Teleology also solves the problem of change, which poses a problem for constructivist theories in general.

> Downward causation is biased toward homeostasis and so does not explain change, and self-organization theory's upward causal focus on non-linear dynamics does not explain their direction. What is missing is an explanation of the tendency of systems to progress toward a state of 'completed development'. For this we need to add final causation to the picture, which refers to the role of end-states in channeling system dynamics toward certain outcomes.
>
> (2003: 501)

Wendt insists that his teleological theory also stands if we do not attribute intentionality to the structural level, implying that the end-state towards which the system develops is a non-intentional end-state. System change towards progress is now explained through the instability of earlier forms of political organization. The interaction between processes of self-organization and the process of structural constitution directs structural change towards collective identities through the instability of earlier forms. After four intermediary stages, this will ultimately make a world state inevitable. Wendt would not need to stretch his teleological explanation so far as to reach a world state that transcends anarchy towards hierarchy (both Kant and Hegel reject this possibility). Wendt does so because he identifies anarchy with instability, which is a new causal mechanism at work towards higher (more stable) forms of organization, and because he assumes, on the basis of his domestic experience, that a world state is a stable end-state.

This is a significant departure from *Social Theory*, where the assumption of structural progress towards peace rested on the assumption that 'anarchy' is not necessarily unstable. Wendt now returns to a Waltzian conceptualization of structure in his reliance on a structural explanation of war in the absence of centralized authority or the monopoly of legitimate use of violence, although for Wendt the logic of anarchy ultimately transcends the current structure of the international system. Technological development and the consequent destructiveness of wars, as well as the instability of any 'attractor' other than a centralized legitimate authority, are the underlying causal mechanisms that spur world-state formation.

The introduction of new and less 'harmonious' causal mechanisms that drive historical progress leads to a less smooth picture of the transition from one to a higher culture of anarchy. In *Social Theory*, this progressive picture is only victim of the possibility of stagnation, where, depending on the degree of internalization of its norms, the temporary stability of one culture of anarchy represents an obstacle to forward movement. The new theory also holds out for the possibility that progress might be disturbed by violent intervals and setbacks. The parallel causal mechanism is also less harmonious at the micro-structural or interaction level, where structural change is driven by a struggle for recognition.

These additions seem able to handle the possibility of conflicts emanating from the coexistence of different cultures of anarchy, which the old theory failed to take into account. This coexistence implies an asymmetric relationship between members of different cultures of anarchy with the result that 'some are more recognized than others'. Similarly, it seems able to account for potential conflicts emanating from the lack of legitimacy of an international order, when actors are forced into roles and yet identification with these roles is weak, because neither self-interest nor legitimacy but force alone is the underlying reason (first-degree internalization of cultures of anarchy). Finally, the emphasis on recognition is able to accommodate group fights for popular sovereignty. As such, it is able to explain war other than wars between already established states, which is also a move away from *Social Theory*. The coexistence of different cultures of anarchy, the potential instability of anarchies with weak norms, and lack of recognition of some groups together make the world of 'anarchies' unstable when compared to the hierarchic organization of a world state. Since the ultimate source of conflict is the denial of recognition of the subjectivity of *individual* human beings, the world of anarchies populated by states, which limits recognition to states, seems less stable compared to a world state. Progress between different stages of development now implies not only an expansion of rights of states, but also the gradual recognition of individuals' subjectivities, which invites examination as to what happens at the interaction or micro-structural level. The second part of the chapter is devoted to this question.

Expanding space for diplomacy on the micro-structural level

Wendt's assumption of progress, now buttressed by a telos, is not without consequences at the level of politics. In this respect, the difference compared to *Social Theory* is even more marked than the difference between implicit progress and teleology. Peace is disturbed by individuals' and groups' struggles for the recognition of their identities. An evolutionary view of progress and emphasis on physical security left diplomacy largely under-theorized in *Social Theory*, there understood as mere adaptation to the immanent logic of progress. Now, the possibility of violent setbacks and the stakes of recognition in the new theory upgrade the roles and responsibilities of actors in shaping their own and their common destinies. First, an element of 'choice' for individuals is admitted, a choice between physical security vs. struggle for recognition or between refusing or granting recognition. This implies, moreover, that actors need more interpretive work to decipher the 'direction' of progress. They finally need reflexivity to be able to break cycles of violence and turn back/reorient the course of history towards more peaceful solutions.

Although teleology is a significant departure compared to *Social Theory* that works against reflexivity (Wendt 1999: 17), in what follows I will not attempt to reconcile teleology with reflexivity on the historical plane (see also Drulák, chap. 8 this volume). Instead, I take the different route of turning to the interaction level, where reflexivity has become upgraded in the new theory. This approach seems to follow more readily from, yet remain consistent with, the other innovation of Wendt's theory: the interpretation of history as a struggle for recognition. Indeed, should we accept the claim that history is a struggle for recognition, it would certainly not follow that this struggle will, of necessity, find a 'harmonious' and 'stable' 'resolution' in 'a' 'world state'. Although Wendt's claims acquire plausibility on the basis of a conventional experience of living in a contemporary Kantian culture of anarchy, his 'solution' begs many questions.

I claim that, because Wendt offers a structural resolution of the tension between teleology and his acknowledgement of a more conflictual reality, he underestimates the scale that conflicts between states can potentially take. The significant differences between the two theories, however, provide enough reasons to doubt Wendt's assumption of progress and his claim to 'know' the logic and direction of anarchy towards the inevitability of a world state. It can be seen to support the alternative view, namely that theory offers but an explanation of history *ex post* that evolves in response to historical changes, rather than embodies the revelation of the teleological logic of anarchy. This second part examines some of the problems with Wendt's answer, demonstrating at the same time that, as a result of the reorientation of theory, the scope for politics/diplomacy has increased.

The limited space for diplomacy in Social Theory *(1999)*

Wendt's assumption of progress in *Social Theory* did not leave much room for actors, since it specified both the direction that change will necessarily take, and its immanent logic – even identifying the stages of development. What the theory left largely unexplained is the interpretative work, with its many potential failures and harsh consequences, that actors must perform to arrive at a developmental model similar to Wendt's. Taking progress for granted, the theory also remained blind to the possibility that even identifying change as progress might depend on an interpretation from the actors' point of view.

This deficiency was countered by the plausibility of Wendt's account. Plausibility was achieved by the theory's reliance on a familiar but optimistic view of international politics, a dominant (modern) conception of legitimate international politics and the case or contingency that Wendt was contemplating reality from this perspective. These three elements in *Social Theory* can be summarized as follows: states have progressed in their relations compared to those pertaining in Hobbesian anarchy; democratic states do not fight wars; and, linked to this, progress in international relations is identical with progress towards peace. The remaining sections will show how these three assumptions downgrade diplomacy in *Social Theory* (1999). The last section shows what difficulties Wendt's theory meets when these assumptions do not hold: i.e., in First Encounters.

Progress from the Hobbesian state of nature? Responsible diplomacy and the risk of cultural regress

Wendt's 1999 model relies on certain 'common-sense' understandings that are taken for granted only as long as they appear legitimate. Two common-sense understandings in particular bind our interpretation and imagination of change: the sovereign state as the only legitimate and imaginable political unit and an interpretation of history as progress in states' relations.

Given the present structure of international politics, it is understandable why we tend to project our view of the sovereign state as the central constituting unit of the international system onto the past. The English School argued a long time ago that the 'bias' of the assumption of the sovereign state (Wight 1966) is at the same time the precondition of international relations in that 'one cannot talk properly of international relations before the advent of the sovereign state' (Wight 1991: 1). Yet it is all the more important to emphasize that our inclination to take the sovereign state as the only possible constituent unit of politics is not supported by historical record.

In this respect the Hobbesian state of nature can in no sense help us understand the origins of the states system (Wight 1977). As we have seen, Wendt reconstructs international history as progress from Hobbesian anarchy. In doing so, he projects our modern, Eurocentric view of the 'universe' to the past. Within Western culture, however, the idea of the state patterned on the image of Leviathan only became prevalent in the sixteenth century. Projecting the state, as we know it today, back to the beginning of history risks reifying the state. It tends to support the belief that the sovereign state, as if given by nature, requires no political effort to bring about and to perpetuate its existence. Similarly, the pre-given categories of change and the theoretical view of 'historical' progress from the 'lower-level' Hobbesian to the 'higher-level' Kantian culture deludes us into believing that 'progress there has been', and that in this evolution we have less and less reason to fear about the future.

Potentially, however, the historical record offers the possibility of an interpretation of structural regress instead of progress in state relations. Martin Wight has long made the claim that, even though we tend to think of the three traditions in the succession given by Wendt, the historical record in Europe suggests that the modern states system did not emerge from a Hobbesian culture:

> In the historical development which led to the state of affairs which is the subject-matter of international relations, first, there was an effective society of sates, the *Respublica Christiana* with a degree of constitutional unity, ecclesiastical and political, which fluctuated from time to time, but which for about five hundred years (AD 700–1200) was out of any comparison greater than the constitutional unity of the society of states since then. . . . Only lastly and latest did the bonds between them [i.e., between the various members of the *Respublica Christiana*] become so slight that they accepted warfare as ultimately regulative of their relationship, and repudiated any allegiance to a political superior.
>
> (Wight 1991: 9)

Traditional IR theory, while recognizing in the political organization of mankind into sovereign states one of the causes of wars, sees from there (or from the recurrent experience of war) no historical necessity which would lead to a world state. In the Classical view, transcending the current political organization towards a world state would require the prior construction of a world community (Morgenthau 1948). In the absence of a world community, a world state only elapses into civil war or disintegration (Bull 1966b). Wendt does not address these counter-arguments, as his theory of progress ignores the historical interpretation of cultural regress that speaks of the disintegration of a world state (of the *Respublica Christiana*) and, lately, of the weakening of international society (Morgenthau 1948; Wight 1977; Bull and Watson 1984).

While Wendt is in principle aware of the possibility of disruptive change, e.g., in the form of an external invasion or domestic contestations (Wendt 1999: 188), it does not ultimately affect the progressive logic of anarchy. It is as if communities were at the mercy of blind forces external and internal, as if the normative goal of practitioners of politics were not continuously directed towards averting disruptive change. The relatively rare exceptions of disruptive change can therefore be seen as a consequence of these human efforts of responsible and creative politics. Conversely the possibility of disruptive change comes to embody the stakes of diplomacy. Recognition of the ever-present possibility of exogenous shocks could refute our expectation that once the internalization of a 'higher'-level culture occurs 'there is little chance of it degenerating into a Hobbesian one'.

Wendt's *Social Theory of International Politics* is devoid of politics precisely because its structural bias fails to address what actors do when they do not passively adapt to the structural logic of change, but instead confront the dilemmas of change through doing politics. Even progress, since it is an interpretation from the actors' point of view, requires creativity to translate it as legitimate change for a given community. Often this implies a re-reading of the past in the attempt to tell a progressive story. These human efforts, directed towards ensuring the stability of a given order or towards legitimizing change, become visible only in failure. Once the reasons of disruptive change are believed to be outside human control, human responsibility escapes us.

It is understandable why a legitimate order does not consider the possibility of disruptive change: this is exactly how legitimacy works. The underlying norms of legitimacy objectify and naturalize the constructed nature of a given order, often preventing the possibility of imagining an alternative. By acting against self-reflexivity, norms not only induce communities to 'forget' about the contingent origins of a given order, but they easily induce them to 'forget' the stakes of politics. In particular, during a period of legitimacy and peace, the human effort that brought such a world into existence is forgotten and change is viewed with optimism (Kissinger 1957). Wendt seems to fall into this very trap when he emphasizes the endogenous structural logic that leads to progress. The political challenge for actors to ensure peaceful change thus gives way to a gradual change of the 'structure' towards peace.

Creative diplomacy and peaceful change: a critique of Wendt's assumption of progress towards peace

Wendt's theory can be read as an expression and an explanation of the prevalent liberal creed which sees democracy as the Hegelian end of history (Fukuyama 1992), resulting in a Kantian peace between liberal democratic states (Doyle 1983a, 1983b; see also R. Cohen 1994; MacMillan 1995; Risse-Kappen 1995a). However, this progressive story, as well as international peace and the continuing existence of security communities, depend on political legitimacy, and are thus the result and the normative goal of diplomatic action that is able to ensure the legitimacy of the current arrangement in the future.

Once we grant that the stability/instability of any culture of anarchy depends on legitimacy, the identification of progress with peace, conceived negatively as the absence of war, appears misleading. First, the absence of war in itself might be no more than the illusion of peace. This is particularly so when legitimacy is weak and peace is precarious. Second, peace is the central challenge of diplomacy under any cultural form, and, therefore, it cannot be a general law of international politics under the Kantian culture of anarchy, simply through deciding that this culture equals peace by definition. Finally, it is an open question whether 'peace' should be given priority over other values such as freedom of action (including freedom from interference) or justice (Bull 1984). Kissinger argues that stability (peace) 'depends on the degree to which [an international order can] reconcile what makes the constituent societies feel secure with what they consider just' (Kissinger 1994: 27).

Given the nature of legitimacy and its intrinsic link to stability and peace, the question arises whether it makes sense to speak of an evolution of structure at all. To the extent that we want to compare two cultures of anarchy, we have to find a common denominator, yet made impossible by the competing values of the Lockean and Kantian cultures – sovereignty/freedom of action vs. peace. Fighting minor wars is legitimate in a Lockean culture, but not in a Kantian culture of democratic peace. Through the Kantian lenses of the ideal of peace, the Lockean culture might, therefore, seem inferior. But it is ultimately not possible to reduce the problem of order to the problem of peace, for the central question in a Lockean culture is not peace in itself, as the absence of war, but the quality of peace. Peace means the impossibility of great power war only if based on a generally accepted legitimacy (Kissinger 1957: 1–2). If political legitimacy is the ultimate question/ challenge or ideal of political action, whether we are in a Lockean or a Kantian culture of anarchy, then can we say that the Kantian culture is superior? What we can say is that the concept of political legitimacy has changed. Nor can we pass judgement on the concept of political legitimacy in the past with today's concept based on our relatively short experience of living in a Kantian culture of anarchy after the Second World War.

If, however, we take legitimacy to be a recurrent problem of politics, all the three cultures of anarchy become potentially relevant. This implies that political legitimacy, once created, requires not merely reproduction but sometimes change. For there is no guarantee that the temporarily fixed meaning of legitimacy will not erode. In a context where legitimacy is temporary, context-dependent and contingent, progress means peaceful change only if it implies the preservation of political legitimacy despite change or the peaceful redefinition of political legitimacy both require creative diplomacy. But when diplomacy fails, change is often not peaceful precisely because it implies a potential for conflict/violence in the name of competing concepts of legitimacy. We are then forced to recognize that there are periods in history when political actors arrive at the conclusion that peace can be secured only through war (Kissinger 1957: 1).

Cultural incomprehension in the language of scientific explanation

Comparison between cultures is so difficult that speaking of progress becomes difficult. This can be shown not only by a comparison of the change of political legitimacy over time, but also by the obstacles to communication and understanding between different cultures. Wendt's explanation of the Aztec–Spanish encounter is an example of this incomprehension. It similarly offers an illustration of the limited scope for diplomacy in *Social Theory*. Illustrating this argument requires a closer examination of Wendt's description of the way identities emerge in social interaction (for a critique similar to the following, see also Inayatullah and Blaney 1996).

Wendt draws on symbolic interactionism as the model of all interactions. He emphasizes the volitional character of actors' choices in symbolic interaction in the form of role-taking. Their freedom of choice, however, is constrained by power, pre-existing understandings and the role taken by the Other. Ideas are dependent on the 'representations' available to actors, but they transcend these representations in interaction to the extent that ideas about Alter will be constitutive of its role *vis-à-vis* Ego (Wendt 1999: 328–31). '[W]ho Alter is, in this interaction, depends on who Ego *thinks* Alter is' (1999: 335, emphasis in original).

Emphasizing the relational aspect of roles, Wendt recognizes the joint constitution of both identities and their corresponding social realities. At the same time, he repeatedly reminds us that the 'accuracy' of our representations matters when it comes to an evaluation of the outcome of interaction: 'On the basis of their representations of Self and Other, Alter and Ego each construct a "definition of the situation". The accuracy of these definitions is not important in explaining action (though it is in explaining outcomes)' (1999: 329).

Wendt's reconstruction of the Aztec–Spanish encounter offers a returning illustration:

> In 1519 Montezuma faced the same kind of epistemological problem facing social scientists today: how to refer to people who, in this case, called themselves Spaniards. Many representations were conceivable, and no doubt the one he chose – that they were gods – drew on the discursive materials available to him. So why was he killed and his empire destroyed by an army hundreds of times smaller than his own? The [scientific] realist answer is that Montezuma was simply wrong: the Spaniards were not gods, and had come instead to conquer his empire. Had Montezuma adopted this alternative representation

of what the Spaniards were, he might have prevented this outcome because that representation would have corresponded more to reality. ... The external world to which we ostensibly lack access, in other words, often frustrates or penalizes representations. Postmodernism gives us no insight into why this is so, and indeed, rejects the question altogether.

(1999: 56–7)

Since states try to influence the outcome of an interaction through power, not only the representations available to actors but also power relations determine the outcome of the interaction. It is in this sense that the outcome of the Aztec–Spanish encounter is puzzling for Wendt and in need of explanation. The ultimate peril of the Aztecs and the scale of violence (massacre) committed on them, despite their overwhelmingly superior (man)power compared to the Spaniards, is perplexing.

According to Wendt, the Aztec representation of reality was wrong in more than one respect: in mistaking humans for gods, but also in mistaking a relationship of 'enmity' for an encounter with gods. It is worth noting the extent to which Wendt relies again on our common-sensical and contemporary attitude when he takes the description of 'humans' and of 'power' in purely a material sense and rejects the existence of gods as unreal a priori. The outcome of the encounter appears puzzling only from the viewpoint of this material perspective. This perspective, moreover, provides the standards against which Wendt evaluates the rightness or wrongness of representations. This standard derives from our present knowledge, based on a scientific representation of reality, which we assume represents progress over the Aztec truth, owing to the progress of science.

Imagining the encounter from the viewpoint of the Aztecs, however, the puzzle disappears. It can be shown, moreover, that not only their collective representation but their experiences from interaction, including the Spanish representation of reality, were responsible for the Aztec belief that the Spaniards were gods. The very scale of violence committed without social meaning, coupled with disinterest in the victims, contrasted sharply with the Aztecs' public and symbolically charged sacrifice of highly praised victims (Todorov 1984: 144). This reinforced the Aztec suspicion that they were dealing not with human beings but with angry, even vengeful, gods.

If Wendt's meta-theory cannot account for the Aztec representation of reality, it is also unable to do justice to the contemporary representation by the Spanish side. For the latter, the stakes of interaction implied not merely survival but the conversion of the Indian population to Christianity (Todorov 1984). This was complemented by the judgement that Aztec culture was barbarian. Viewing the scale of massacre, however, the question that increasingly concerned contemporaries was what Christians were allowed to do with barbarians.

We lose completely sight of this ethical dimension of contemporary debates in Wendt's reconstruction, which relieves the Spanish side from responsibility by reducing questions of politics to questions of knowledge. On this basis, the peril of the Aztecs is explained by their mistaken representation of reality, emphasizing reality's ability to frustrate, even punish, wrong representations. The only responsibility for the massacre lies with the mistaken collective representations of the Aztecs. Such an interpretation denies a moral aspect to politics even in the limited sense it preoccupied contemporaries. If we are not ready to accept this conclusion, we have to ask whether it makes sense to describe the dilemma Montezuma faced as an epistemological problem, instead of a political and ethical dilemma confronting the two parties to the interaction.

The struggle for recognition: a new scope for agency / diplomacy in 2003

In 2003, Wendt moved to a theory of history based not only on teleology, but also on a struggle for recognition. Sub-state actors are now participating in international relations, sometimes fighting violently for the recognition of their subjectivity, sacrificing their lives in protest against a denial of recognition or as a form of expressing identity needs. This testifies to an important shift of emphasis. In *Social Theory*, a human 'need for recognition' was listed as a fundamental biological and therefore material (!) need in Wendt's theory of human nature, following physical security 'in order of importance' (Wendt 1999: 131–2). In the new theory, this order has been reversed in favour of identity needs:

> At the micro-level, recognition is not the only desire at work in the system: physical security is another, which may induce actors to put their lives before recognition. It might be thought that security is more fundamental, on the grounds that one cannot enjoy recognition if one is dead. But the desire for recognition doesn't work that way. As a precondition for genuine subjectivity recognition is part of what makes security worth having in the first place, and people will often sacrifice their lives for it.
>
> (Wendt 2003: 514)

The resulting vision of history is obviously more violent and disruptive. How can this be reconciled with a teleology of peace? What ensures progress in the end? I would argue that Wendt offers an unconvincing structural resolution of this tension, because it reduces politics to rationality imposed on actors by a structural logic. Doing so, the theory fails to appreciate the stakes of conflicts, including the potential for mass destruction over the realization of the world state, which Wendt in his preoccupation with the survival of the world state, does not notice.

Responsible diplomacy (2003) amid risks of cultural regress, or: the world state as an emerging actor?

Wendt continues to avoid the question of how to conceptualize the violent intervals separating different stages of development, as well as the potential obstacles to the realization of the world state. While *Social Theory* left the violent intervals between the Hobbesian and Lockean and again the Lockean and Kantian cultures largely unacknowledged, they have now become more visible. This acknowledgement of a less smooth development is a significant departure from *Social Theory*, and leaves some room for considering the possibility of cultural regress and the role of actors.

Violence plays an important role in world state formation. On the macro-level, the causal mechanism behind the progressive development is the instability of local attractors (e.g., the state) as a result of technological development, which allows for new forms of violence and resistance. Instability manifests itself, however, not in the potential for war but the experience of war. Thus, on the micro-level, it is the experience of violence and peace-creating counter-moves that apparently cause the moments of structural change (2003: 523). Wendt expects that rationality will ultimately overcome violence in favor of more peaceful/progressive solutions, 'forcing' states 'to see the light':

> It may take some time for Great Powers – and perhaps especially 'hyper-powers' like the United States – to see the light. But if the choice is between a world of growing threats as a result of refusing to fully recognize Others versus a world in which their desires for recognition are satisfied, it seems clear which decision rational Great Powers should make.
>
> (2003: 524–5)

This seems to be a normative statement. Yet Wendt claims that he speaks of progress in an explanatory rather than a normative sense. For this, we must try to imagine how violence ultimately forces major actors to understand the inevitability of world-state formation. Structural change is partly structure-driven. This might explain Wendt's comment that the state, as a local attractor, has also been an inevitable answer to the instability of earlier structural forms:

> What precisely is it that causes systems to develop toward their end-states? The general answer is instability. As we saw above, the boundary conditions of self-organizing systems select among their elements for behaviors and properties that are consistent with system maintenance, but this process is not deterministic, since there are usually many ways to maintain a system. This means that a lot may happen at the micro-level that is not controlled by the macro. These happenings will periodically generate dynamics that threaten the system's viability. A developing system will respond to such threats by elaborating its structure – encoding new information in its boundary conditions – so as to further constrain its elements. Insofar as that stabilizes the system temporarily it will constitute a 'local' attractor.
>
> (2003: 502, one reference omitted)

We have, in other words, self-organization not only at the level of states, but also at the systemic level, which selects behaviour in a similar way as Waltz's anarchic structure rewards balancing and punishes non-balancers by eliminating them (2003: 500–1; as a result Ashley's 1986 [1984] critique of Waltz's structuralism reapplies to Wendt).

States that 'fail to see the light' are still states that fail to interpret and respond to violence in the right, enlightened way. Even if not eliminated, their misrepresentation of violence will presumably result in an upsurge of violence. Given the technological potential at the disposal of states, the upsurge of violence can lead to total war and even to the destruction of mankind.

Wendt considers the eventuality that a world state will fail to materialize because of an external shock, such as an asteroid impact or ecological collapse. Organisms and all open systems may die, as he observes, but one should not confuse death with a 'stable' end-state: in the absence of these shocks, 'a normal teleological system will indeed inevitably finish its development' (2003: 532, n. 34).

What is striking here is that Wendt does not see this external shock coming from human agency, as in *Social Theory*. As Wendt himself notes, he offers a stronger claim for teleology than a liberal idea of universal peace contingent on human agency (2003: 492). That the potential for the destruction of humanity is not theorized is not a mistake. Rather, it is the clue to what Wendt's structural point of view ('the macro-structure of all pathways') means: structural constitution means world-state formation. This is not contingent on human agency, because human agency is not the question, for Wendt is looking at reality from the viewpoint of an emergent actor, i.e., the world state in the making. Within a world state, states lose their individuality and intentionality. If the survival of states becomes to some extent meaningless, it is because of the structural context of a world-state point of view. In this context, there will be no more states: the state disappears as an entity and is replaced by a new unit of analysis. This new unit of analysis is humanity at large, but only if organized into one society and one state. Systemic rationality and intentionality overtakes human agency. Even the question of survival emerges, not in relation to the survival of mankind or the society of states, but as the question of the survival of the world state.

The structural bias of Wendt's theory should not prevent us from seeing what it requires from actors. In *Social Theory*, the conceptualization of progress as a gradual evolution from Hobbesian anarchy towards peace limits reflexivity to actors' choices in First Encounters and explains the rare cases of sudden structural progress. Despite emphasizing actors' roles in the joint constitution of identities and the corresponding norms of interaction in First Encounters, Wendt assumes the actors' ability to escape Hobbesian anarchy to be minimal. It is possible in principle that states will think about each other as rivals or even as friends, which prompts Wendt's statement that ideas are self-fulfilling prophecies. However, the absence of shared knowledge about each other and the world, as well as disparities in power, 'normally' work against a peaceful outcome. It is for this reason that Wendt speaks of Hobbesian First Encounters as 'the archetype' of relations of enmity, which initially describes a social relationship devoid of culture (shared knowledge) (2003: 267). The low probability of peaceful solutions in First Encounters justifies the description of history as progressive. Starting from the baseline of conflictual First Encounters, *Social Theory*'s progressive story works 'perfectly well' without reflexivity, relying on causal mechanisms only, since the actors' unacknowledged choices practically deny them freedom of action.

By contrast, the new theory, by abandoning the story of a smooth and gradual evolution towards peace, confronts actors with choices beyond First Encounters. Acknowledging violent setbacks between progressive episodes in states' relations amounts to relying more on actors' reflexive abilities to interpret violence in the 'right' way such as to transcend instability towards new and increasingly progressive forms of social relations, including cooperation with respect to the control of violence. It follows not only that actor responsibilities are significantly upgraded. The new theory relies to a greater extent on creativity, all the more so since now reflexivity is also required of major actors such as the United States, for non-violent solutions to result.

A critique of Wendt's assumption of progress towards peace

Wendt continues to link his concept of progress and peace, with the amendment that peace is now possible only within a state. Instability pushes states to make a world state out of anarchy where world-state formation means progress, since it leads to the domestication of conflicts through 'thin recognition'. 'Thin recognition' implies the recognition of the difference of the Other 'as an independent subject within a community of law', so that conflicts between individuals, groups or states are settled without resort to violence (2003: 511).

The idea that only a world state can offer a stable solution to peace follows logically from liberal thought. This is a powerful assumption, one which even determines the division of labour between social science disciplines (Onuf 1989; Kratochwil 1989), including political theory and international relations (Wight 1966). In Wendt's historical reconstruction the conventional description of the international realm as anarchic is taken for granted. Against the acceptance of the eternal verity of Hobbesian anarchy and conflict, Wendt explains progress historicizing the neoliberal insistence of the possibility of cooperation under anarchy (Oye 1986). Progress is described not in economic terms, but in terms of increased cooperation with respect to the legitimate use of violence in the relations between states: a conceptualization very similar to the definition of peace within domestic societies. Within the liberal scheme, the 'discovery' of the world state as the ultimate direction of historical progress is indeed the logical final addition.

The difference between Wendt's definition of a world state as a legitimate monopoly over the use of violence and his claim that 'we will get a Weberian world state by creating a Hegelian one' (Wendt 2003: 504) lies in the legitimacy conferred on the state by individual subjects. Taking the legitimacy of the world state for granted, Wendt does not address the potential conflict emanating from competing identity claims between communities over the realization of a world state. He also fails to explain whether/how different communities will live together in what world state or whether/how individuals will exchange loyalty from contemporary states to solidarity towards each other. Finally, the danger of having so much power concentrated in one centre escapes attention (Bull 1966b). Wendt's structural point of view, in other words, means that his theory still evades the *political* questions of world-state formation and the role of diplomacy in the reconciliation of competing ideas about political organization.

Obstacles to communication between cultures (2003)

The shift of emphasis from physical/material survival as a powerful force driving humans' actions to the demand for the recognition of subjectivity (identity) has far-reaching consequences for diplomacy. Wendt finds the source of conflict in human nature, which continues to explain the anarchic nature of the international system, despite progress towards cooperation in the legitimate use of violence. However, Wendt also recognizes the nature and the power of legitimacy, which explains why local attractors such as the state or different cultures of anarchy can be stable, if only temporarily, as well as the difficulty of change between attractors or moving to a new principle of legitimacy.

As 'legitimacy' in general, the Kantian logic underlying Kantian culture is not easily comparable with teleology, and even works against it. Not only is it a problem for the Kantian culture of security communities to admit sub-state actors as legitimate actors on the scene of world politics, but the identification of peace with progress easily implies a corresponding identification of violence with the unprogressive ('unsociable'). This is reinforced by the Kantian culture's preference for a peaceful mode of persuasion through words to persuasion through force, a preference which limits the problem of cross-cultural 'communication' to the verbal aspect of conversation. While the difficulty of global conversation is acknowledged, the need for it is increasingly recognized as the only means to avoid violence (see also the exchange between Dallmayr 2001; Connolly 2001; Rengger 2001).

Against the horizon of a Kantian logic, which tends to limit our understanding of violence, Wendt advances his own interpretation of the meaning and potential communicative message of violence from a teleological point of view. He rejects the conventional view that 'fear, insecurity, or aggression' are 'essential parts of human nature'. Nor is human nature inherently selfish or power seeking (Wendt 1999: 131–3). What motivates conflict is not a struggle for power (which, following Kant, Wendt calls 'unsociable sociability') but struggles for the recognition of subjectivities, i.e., identity (Hegel) (2003: 493). Fear, insecurity and aggression 'are effects of unmet needs and therefore [are] contingent' and 'socially constructed' (1999: 132). The logic of anarchy is, therefore, not driven by the universal logic of power, or by the universal struggle for security/survival, as in Waltz's theory (Wendt 2003: 510). Rather it is driven by the universal logic of identity and a universal desire for recognition (ibid.: 511). Like the struggle for power (and the urge to exert influence on others), the struggle for recognition can animate human encounters at all levels: between individuals, groups or states.

Wendt's unconventional explanation of violence invites reflection and understanding from those subject to violence. Since progress is identified with peace, and Kantian culture is defined as the stage of progress where states acquire freedom from violence and security assistance by right, the Kantian culture of anarchy is vulnerable both to condemnation and to the refusal to reflect on any causes of violence other than irrationality or immorality. This has implications for responding to demands for recognition, which can also appear illegitimate because they are advanced by groups or individuals. That Wendt rejects the dominant view, and offers an unconventional explanation of violence, can be read as an acknowledgement of the difficulty of communication between Kantian and other cultures.

His redefinition of human nature also draws attention to the communicative aspect of violence. This seems important especially in a Kantian culture where attention to communication seems to be limited to verbal conversation. Against this prevalent view, Wendt's conceptualization emphasizes that violence is the result of *interaction* and is meant to convey meaning. It is not merely the fear, aggression or desire for power of selfish actors, but is a demand for recognition as an equal from the Other. This redefinition both contributes to and calls for our understanding of violence.

While Wendt admits that dominance or recognition can be established through an asymmetric relationship (e.g. the coercive relationship between master and slave), this possibility he interprets as being less stable compared to recognition of the other party as an equal. Most effective norms derive from collective or 'we' identities. On this basis, Wendt argues that struggles for recognition presuppose symmetric recognition in the long run. Although asymmetric recognition can last over long periods of time, 'desires for recognition' ultimately 'undermine systems that do not satisfy them' (2003: 514).

These innovations imply not merely the acknowledgement of a more complex reality ('people want to live, yet they sometimes choose to die'), but also the recognition that this reality is not so easily identifiable. This is important for the link between the epistemological and ontological component in Wendt's theory, since he maintains that reality determines outcomes and punishes mistaken representations.

Advancing an alternative interpretation, one could argue that Wendt also acknowledges that no obvious interpretation and answer to the problem of violence is readily available. Positing a choice for individuals between survival as a non-subject or the risk of self-sacrifice for recognition – and for states between granting/refusing recognition – posits the necessity of judgement. Naming these alternatives and simultaneously offering an explanation of the logic of resisting progress is a significant departure compared to the alternatives available to actors in *Social Theory*, i.e., to follow or not the structural logic of anarchy. In 1999, there was no motive behind resisting progressive change, which could thus be explained only by a mistaken representation of reality.

It is as if Wendt's alternative explanation *was meant to persuade us* what counts as the right interpretation according to the structural logic of anarchy. This shift in the conceptualization of violence works towards encouraging conciliatory moves, which would enable the realization of peace in a stable end-state. Conciliatory moves can be justified by acknowledgement of both parties' responsibility for violence. Granting that violence is the result of asymmetric recognition and the absence of shared knowledge about the Other means that the source of external threats lies partly in us. This position could allow us to respond to violence not in kind, but by working out the legal guarantees of the recognition of Others. In this sense, conciliatory moves and structural progress require reflective actors. Wendt's shift of position to a 'global' perspective is itself a self-reflective move compared to *Social Theory*.

Conclusion

This chapter has compared Wendt's recent theory about the inevitability of a world state to the ideas expressed in *Social Theory* with regard to the possibilities the theory creates for diplomacy/politics. The first part argued that Wendt's historical progress follows from his scientific realism and reflects a progressive view of science. Teleology is but a stronger version and justification of the assumption of progress, which leads to an even more deterministic view of history and, thus, further reduces the scope for human agency. I claim that assuming progress underestimates the stakes of change and, therefore, the responsibilities actors face and the imagination they need in their attempts to cope with change.

In particular, both theories underestimate the stakes of change. *Social Theory* could interpret history as progressive because history ends in democratic peace through a gradual elimination of violence and the parallel emergence of collective ('we') identities. From the viewpoint of diplomacy, *Social Theory* underestimated the role of diplomacy in maintaining peace and also the potential for violence in the case of future conflicts. Now that violence becomes substantially upgraded compared to *Social Theory*, the stakes of world-state formation (e.g., the possibility of mass destruction) escape attention, because a new level of structure is added, that of the world state, and Wendt contemplates the survival not of humanity, but of the world state. Looking for an argument supporting the inevitability of a world state, Wendt mentions collective memories of violence, but fails to consider the danger that human beings may not survive these experiences to remember. Or, if they do, the scale of destruction could set back human civilization to such an extent as to prevent organization into a world state.

But the stakes of world state formation have also been underestimated, even if we assumed that it could happen. The problem is the positive presumption associated with a world state, which reflects the not too recent expectation that order within a world state is inevitable. This is clearly a form of presentism, which, moreover, restricts our imagination of potential future political organization into units other than the state. Only if we posit violence as the major problem of the international as opposed to the domestic realm, and only if we imagine 'the domestic' on the lines of Western democracy, will we tend to find a solution to violence in a world state. If, on the other hand, the sovereign freedom of states as it developed within Western Europe is believed to be a surer guarantee against violence, both domestic (in the limited state tradition) and international (Wight 1966: 23; Bull 1966b: 50), the possibility of a world state appears as a frightening prospect. It is not only not associated with progress, but is seen as the potential for totalitarian violence, especially within the technological development of our century.

The second part argued that, despite teleology, Wendt introduces new opportunities for agency at the micro-structural level. Wendt's progressive account is weakened by the acknowledgement of violent intervals before stability is reached in a new attractor, as well as by the important role and the nature of legitimacy. While the assumption of progress within the same culture of anarchy seems justifiable, to interpret as progressive the move from one to another culture of anarchy can be questioned. The potential for violence and competing legitimacies, acknowledged by Wendt as existing realities, can offer competing interpretations. These question both a universal progressive logic and the easy, non-contradictory identification of that logic. They also reveal a difficulty of communication across cultures and between different 'legitimacies'.

Wendt's innovations on the macro- and micro-structural levels, thus, act in opposite directions, with opposing consequences for diplomacy. While Wendt offers a structural resolution of this tension (and of the agent–structure debate), the same innovations can be employed to question whether the theory is able to support its claim that teleology or progress is a property of the world. While there is no point in denying that the state has come to occupy our horizon of the imaginable and the conceivable, as Wendt's theory amply demonstrates, whether it is inevitable is a question to be answered in an unknown future.

10 *Social Theory* as Cartesian science

An auto-critique from a quantum perspective[*]

Alexander Wendt

Social Theory of International Politics (*Social Theory*) has two parts, one substantive and one philosophical. The former develops a theory of the international system as an emergent phenomenon. The elements of the system are assumed to be states, which are treated as intentional actors or 'people' (also see Wendt 2004). The system itself is seen as an anarchy, the structure of which is defined in cultural rather than material terms. The culture of the international system can take at least three different forms – Hobbesian, Lockean, and Kantian – depending on whether states constitute each other as enemies, rivals, or friends. Progress from a Hobbesian to a Kantian culture is not inevitable, but can result from historically contingent processes of collective identity formation among states. Anarchy is what states make of it.

Various parts of this argument have since been taken up by others. The claim that states are people too led to a lively symposium in *Review of International Studies* (2004); the three cultures of anarchy figure centrally in Barry Buzan's (2004) majesterial reworking of the English School, Dustin Howes's (2003) discussion of state survival, and Scott Bennett and Allan Stam's (2004) behavioral test of various international theories; Hidemi Suganami (chap. 4 this volume) sees collective identity formation as an idea particularly worth following up; and so on. But in light of IR scholars' strong interest these days in non-state actors, domestic politics, and globalization, *Social Theory*'s concern with states and anarchy looks admittedly a bit old-fashioned. Perhaps partly for this reason, even though the book challenges realist and rationalist models of international politics in important ways, its substantive part has provoked relatively little criticism (though see Dale Copeland's review, reprinted here as chap. 1), unless to question the whole idea of states systemic theory.

[*] For very helpful conversations and comments on this chapter I am grateful to Dimitris Akrivoulis, Badredine Arfi, David Art, Amar Athwal, Boaz Atzili, Andreas Behnke, Stefano Guzzini, Anna Leander, Oded Lowenheim, Patchen Markell, Jennifer Mitzen, Vincent Pouliot, Chris Wendt, Colin Wight, and Rafi Youatt.

The same cannot be said of the book's philosophical part. There I tried to do something that, in a justly classic paper, Friedrich Kratochwil and John Ruggie (1986) in effect said could not be done: find a *via media* between positivism and interpretivism by combining the epistemology of the one with the ontology of the other. This idea is not new, going back to Durkheim if not to Kant, and continues in different forms today in Roy Bhaskar's (1979) *The Possibility of Naturalism,* John Searle's (1995) *The Construction of Social Reality,* and others. But after their 'Third Debate' most IR scholars today seem to think the idea of such a *via media* is incoherent; one must be either a positivist or an interpretivist. Although greeted skeptically by many positivists, it seems especially to exercise interpretivists, who see it as not only philosophically but politically problematic, threatening, in their view, to foreclose important questions about world politics.

In one way or another such philosophical concerns inform most of the critiques collected in this volume.[1] Lacking space to do more, I shall consider just eight, in four groups. The first group deals with state agency: 1) that treating states as 'agents' at all is intrinsically problematic (Cederman and Daase; Suganami; Zehfuss); and 2) that *Social Theory* under-theorizes the role of reflexivity in structural change (Drulák; Sárváry). The second focuses on the agent–structure problem: 3) that states are not ontologically prior to the states system (Behnke; Cederman and Daase; Kratochwil); 4) that the claimed mutual constitution of agent and structure is nothing more than two descriptions of the same thing (Suganami); and 5) that uncertainty about intentions is so profound that anarchy constrains states regardless of system culture (Copeland). The third addresses the relationship between ideas and material conditions: 6) that the distinction is 'phony' because it presupposes a basis for making it in the first place (Behnke); and 7) that ideas only matter when deeply internalized, and so power and interest do most of the work in world politics (Copeland). And, finally, a fourth group 8) makes various epistemological arguments specifically against the *via media* (Behnke; Kratochwil; perhaps Suganami).

In reflecting on these criticisms one could hardly ask for a better starting point than Stefano Guzzini and Anna Leander's outstanding précis of *Social Theory*. More than a précis, however, their essay suggests that the book is less a *via media* than an attempted synthesis of previously opposed positions – positivism and interpretivism, rationalism and constructivism, realism and idealism – which now appear as aspects or moments of a larger whole. Among other things this calls attention to the importance of having metaphysical foundations that can ground such a synthesis. In *Social Theory* this was at least implicitly supplied by Cartesian dualism, according to which mind ('ideas') and matter ('rump materialism') are distinct, irreducible substances. If that dualist premise be taken as given, then I think the philosophical argument of *Social Theory* is still basically correct.

That said, I didn't spend much time in the book talking about its implicit dualist standpoint, which I only really became conscious of as a result of its critics. The

---

1 Also see the Forum on *Social Theory* in *Review of International Studies* (2000).

virtue of dualism is that it accommodates what I take to be two fundamental truths: that ideas cannot be reduced to material conditions (the 'interpretivist moment'), and that we can nevertheless achieve increasingly adequate knowledge of the world through the scientific method (the 'positivist moment'). The problem with dualism is that very few scientists and philosophers take it seriously. Contemporary thinking about the mind is dominated by the materialist worldview of classical physics, according to which ultimately reality is purely material. On that view, the mind is nothing but the brain, and *Social Theory*'s claim that ideas are ontologically autonomous must therefore ultimately be mistaken.

Social science today shares this classical worldview. This is clearest in modern positivism, which is the direct heir to systematic efforts in the eighteenth and nineteenth centuries to model the social sciences on classical physics (see Mirowski 1988; B. Cohen 1994). For positivists, nothing in social life precludes the kind of objective analysis characteristic of classical physicists' observations of matter. A classical worldview is less apparent in interpretivism, with its explicit rejection of 'social physics'. But interpretivists have never doubted the classical assumption that ultimately reality is purely material, only that an analysis from such a point of view could capture what really matters in social life, namely meaning. As such, interpretivist work too has at least implicitly been structured by the mind–body problem as conventionally (i.e., classically) posed, which asks how the mind relates to a material base. It could hardly have been otherwise, since there has been no quantum revolution in social science, and these are the only two worldviews we have. Most social scientists would probably agree that physics should have the last word on reality, in the sense that, if something seems incompatible with it, such as fairies, ghosts or reincarnation, then it cannot be said to exist. To that extent physics is a reality constraint on our work, and the only alternative to quantum physics is classical.[2]

The track record of classical social science is mixed, at best. Although social scientists have made important strides in explaining social life, metaphysical disputes plague our work, and even our best theories face significant anomalies. But the track record of philosophy of mind is even worse, where the mind–body problem remains as much a 'problem' as ever despite centuries of hard work. Thus, granting that dualism is an inadequate basis for social science, there is little reason to think that materialism is much better. This prompts a heretical thought: what if the limitations of contemporary social science and philosophy of mind alike lie in their common assumption that the relationship of mind (ideas) to body (the material world) must be compatible with classical physics?

This is the starting point for a radical proposal in the philosophy of mind, that consciousness is a macroscopic quantum mechanical phenomenon. Human beings are in effect 'walking wave particle dualities', not classical material objects. This possibility has been mooted by prominent philosophers and physicists since

---

2 Which is not to deny that there is considerable variation within each, but these variations are structured by agreement on certain first principles.

the quantum revolution in the 1920s, but it was only in the early 1990s – with ground-breaking work by Stuart Hameroff, Roger Penrose, Giuseppe Vitiello, and others – that serious scientific inquiry began. Even so, at this stage the 'quantum consciousness hypothesis' remains highly speculative, and most philosophers and scientists would probably reject it out of hand. But it has some very attractive features, and given the failure to solve the mind–body problem by classical means it is being taken increasingly seriously.

In my current research, then, I am 'betting' that the quantum consciousness hypothesis is true and exploring what its implications for social science might be.[3] That there are such implications is not guaranteed, since even if the hypothesis is true it might not scale up to the social level; at most psychology might be affected, not social science. So there are really two bets here, not just one. However, in my view if the first bet is justified then the second probably is as well, since consciousness is the basis of social life.[4] The implications for social science could be profound. A quantum social science would not wholly invalidate classical social theories, any more than quantum physics did classical. But it would call into question many of our deepest assumptions about human beings and how we study them. In my own case, it would emphasize much more than *Social Theory* did the becoming ('wave') as opposed to the being ('particle') aspect of social life, and the inherently participatory character of social science in this process. These claims will not be news to post-modernists, who have been saying such things for some time – but without a basis in natural science. A 'quantum post-modernism' would be thoroughly naturalistic, challenging today's moderns and post-moderns alike.[5]

All this puts me in a rather awkward position in responding to *Social Theory*'s critics, since I am already reconsidering its argument from the ground up. In some cases I now agree with them, and in others I still disagree but not for the old reasons. So to accommodate this awkward position this chapter will take the form of an 'auto-critique' of *Social Theory* from a quantum perspective. This self-criticism will take up much of my time, leaving less to engage the critics directly – although I hope to show they are equally caught up in classical assumptions. But it should be more interesting for you, the reader, than a point-by-point defense of *Social Theory*, and with the quantum approach in hand I should be able at least to gesture toward a proper response.

In what follows I first define the mind–body problem and indicate its relevance to social science. I then offer a diagnosis of what is causing the problem and show how the quantum consciousness hypothesis solves it. In the third section I explore

---

3 See Wendt (n.d.).

4 The idea of a quantum social science was first proposed by William Munro in his presidential address to the American Political Science Association in 1928 (Munro 1928). It has since been taken up by Matson (1964) and Becker (1991), although mostly at the level of metaphor. Zohar and Marshall's (1994) more popularly oriented text is an important exception.

5 The affinities between quantum theory and post-modernism have been noted before by Major-Poetzl (1983), Plotnitsky (1994), and Akrivoulis (2002), among others.

some general implications for social science, and then in the fourth turn to *Social Theory*'s critics.

The mind–body problem and social science

In this chapter I am suggesting that the mind–body problem is a fundamental problem of *social science*, not just neuroscience, and that consideration of it therefore might shed light on important controversies in the study of world politics. This might seem a quixotic claim. Social scientists are not schooled in the mind–body problem as part of their training, and I have seen very few attempts to make a connection in print.[6] After all, doesn't each science have its own domain, with society the preserve of social scientists, and the mind of neuroscientists (e.g., Fodor 1974)? What could one possibly have to do with the other?

On one level not much, since as I argued in *Social Theory*, macro-level phenomena usually cannot be reduced to micro. To that extent, if we want to explain what is unique to social life we need to treat it as having its own structure and dynamics, far removed from neurons firing in the brain.

However, on a deeper level the answer is quite a lot. In order to do their work social scientists first have to make ontological and epistemological assumptions, even if only pragmatically, about the nature of social reality and their relationship to it. Crucial among these are what to do with two features of the human condition that differentiate us from ordinary physical objects, namely consciousness and meaning. Unfortunately, the nature of consciousness and meaning forms the heart of the mind–body problem, and as such until it is solved we will not know for sure whether they matter, how they matter, or how we should study them. So, since social science can't begin without at least provisional answers to these questions, we in effect have to place bets on what are deeply contested philosophical issues. Predictably, this generates corresponding debates within social science over questions that implicate the mind–body problem, including the relationship between objective science and human self-understandings (positivism vs. interpretivism), ideas and the material world (idealism vs. materialism), and agency and social structure (individualism vs. holism).

My larger argument in this chapter is that these debates are rooted in a problematic assumption, shared by all parties, that the mind is somehow a classical mechanical phenomenon. To set that argument up, however, I first need to say a few words about what the mind–body problem is, its traditional solutions, and how these solutions map onto different approaches to social science.[7]

In a nutshell, the mind–body problem is about how to explain the existence and workings of the mind in a way that is consistent with the modern scientific worldview, which assumes that ultimately reality is purely material ('all body' as it were). 'Mind' here has two dimensions that bear on how the problem is understood:

6 Though see Viale (2000), Sawyer (2001), and Smith (2003).
7 For an overview of contemporary scholarship on the mind–body problem, see Block *et al.* (1997).

cognition, or how we know things about the world; and *experience* or *consciousness*,[8] the feeling of 'what it is like' to have a mind (Nagel 1974). Scientists have made substantial progress on explaining cognition, which David Chalmers (1996) therefore calls the 'easy problem.' But on explaining experience they have made none. We know we have experience from, well, experience itself, but there is no apparent way to reconcile this fact with modern science. By rights it seems consciousness should not exist, and as such neither should meaning, which presupposes consciousness. Chalmers calls this the 'hard' problem. Difficult as the easy problems may be, the hard problem of consciousness is much deeper, and my sole concern below.

To be sure, philosophers have no shortage of ideas about how to solve it. There are three broad strategies: materialism (today usually called physicalism), the linguistic turn, and dualism – all of which, as we shall see, presuppose a classical ontology.

Most contemporary neuroscientists and philosophers of mind are materialists, who assume that consciousness can be explained in physical terms, where 'physical' is understood to mean the hard, material objects of classical physics. Modern materialism is a big tent, ranging from hard-core 'eliminativists' at one end, who think the very idea of consciousness is pre-modern and should be eliminated from our discourse, to soft-core 'emergentists' at the other, who think consciousness is an emergent phenomenon at high levels of material complexity. What all materialists share, however, is a belief that in the end it's 'matter all the way down.'

Consider now what kind of social science will ensue from such an assumption. If consciousness can be explained in material terms, then it is hard to see what difference it could make in the world. Even emergentists, who think consciousness is not reducible to matter, have difficulty with the idea of 'mental causation' that consciousness could somehow make things happen in ways over and above its physical basis in the brain. From a materialist perspective, in short, consciousness does not seem to 'matter.'

This I take to be the essence of positivism in the social sciences, which observes a 'taboo of subjectivity' (Wallace 2000). Its most extreme form is behaviorism, which eschews any reference to what goes on inside people's heads, but even positivisms that grant an explanatory role to the mind (understood as 'cognition) do not take consciousness (experience) seriously. Consider rational choice theory, which explains behavior by reference to desires and beliefs. How are these understood? As properties of the brain, no different in kind than other material objects.[9] The result is a 'computational' model of man – human beings are nothing but sophisticated information-processing machines, the subjective experiences of

---

8 The term 'consciousness' is sometimes used in the literature to cover both cognition and experience, but this can be confusing, and as such I shall use it to designate only experience, reserving the term 'mind' for both.

9 See especially Davidson (1963), although he believes this ontological position is compatible with the epistemological autonomy of the social sciences.

which make no difference and can therefore be ignored. Such a purging of subjectivity from social science has an important epistemological implication, in turn, which is that human behavior can be fully accounted for, at least in principle, by the objective, third-person methods of natural science. 'Understanding' can be reduced to 'Explanation' (cf. von Wright 1971; Hollis and Smith 1990).

Of course, probably few rationalists would deny that human beings are conscious,[10] and as such may see computationalism as more a heuristic device than fully fledged metaphysical commitment. But the result is nevertheless to leave out of their theories an aspect of the human experience – experience itself – that seems fundamental to our existence. Charles Siewert (1998) argues that, if given the choice between being conscious or being a zombie (someone just like ourselves but without consciousness), most of us would choose consciousness. So having consciousness somehow matters to us, a lot, yet it appears nowhere in the rationalist model; as far as the latter is concerned, we may as well be machines or zombies. This strange neglect stems, I suggest, from an implicit materialism telling us that consciousness is epiphenomenal.

Curiously, however, despite today's widespread consensus on a materialist approach to consciousness, there is little evidence it is true. As Jerry Fodor, a prominent philosopher of mind, describes the state of his art,

> [n]obody has the slightest idea how anything material could be conscious. Nobody even knows what it would be like to have the slightest idea about how anything material could be conscious. So much for the philosophy of consciousness.
>
> (Quoted in Kirk 1997: 249)

Perhaps neuroscience will one day vindicate materialism, but increasingly skeptics doubt it. There seems to be an ineradicable 'explanatory gap' between first- and third-person epistemologies (Levine 2001), which suggests a corresponding ontological gap between consciousness and matter. To social scientists some form of emergentism might seem to offer the best hope to bridge these gaps, but most philosophers think that at the crucial step in the argument it in effect says 'and then a miracle happens . . . ,' which is no bridge at all. This is why there is still a mind–body 'problem,' and as long as there is, a taboo of subjectivity in social science will have no metaphysical basis.

Interpretivists think that consciousness and meaning matter in social life, so much so that ignoring them would be to strip social life of precisely what constitutes its specificity. From this perspective turning social science into social physics makes little sense. Instead of Explanation we need Understanding, the recovery of the socially shared understandings that make actions meaningful. Social inquiry is more like reading a text than observing physical objects. Consciousness is the

---

10 Although the view that consciousness is an 'illusion' is growing in popularity; see the special issue of *Journal of Consciousness Studies* (2002) devoted to this topic.

starting point of such readings, and since we know we have it, it does not really matter where it comes from; we can take it as given and proceed from there.

From this perspective the traditional mind–body problem is fundamentally misposed (see Bennett and Hacker 2003). Consciousness and meaning are constituted intersubjectively, in language, and as such the mind is *social* all the way down. Importantly, the linguistic turn does not challenge the assumption that the mind is dependent on the brain and thus at some level material. Rather, it changes the question: from how the mind, as some kind of interior, private phenomenon, hooks onto the body, to how a public, shared language enables us to talk about the 'mind' at all. Since shared language is an emergent, macro-level phenomenon, for purposes of social science Understanding can play an irreducible role, even if materialism is true.

Pragmatically there is much to be said for changing the question in this way, and in *Social Theory* I also argued for the social character of the mind. But side-stepping the traditional mind–body problem still leaves us with the question of how consciousness and meaning are possible in the first place, given the materialist view that they are nothing but the motions of matter in the brain. The reason rocks don't have consciousness is not because they don't have language, but because they don't have brains. Language may be a necessary condition for human subjectivity, but it is not sufficient.

Given the failure of materialism and the linguistic turn, Cartesian dualism has been the traditional default approach to the mind–body problem. Taking as its starting point Descartes' *cogito* – 'I think, therefore I am' – the Cartesian worldview makes at least four assumptions.[11] First, reality out there is not part of you or me in here, which means we must distinguish subject and object. Second, we can acquire knowledge of external reality through the scientific method. Success in science depends, third, on maintaining a distinction between fact and value. And, finally, dualism itself: mind and matter are distinct, irreducible substances, '*res cogitans*' and '*res extensa*,' each with its own laws of motion. Importantly, dualists share with materialists the view that matter is purely physical, and that minds are located within material bodies. This disposes both toward methodological individualism, or the belief that social facts must be reducible to facts about individuals. But against materialism dualists think that the mind is not itself a material phenomenon, and therefore has its own conditions of existence.

Social Theory is a 'Cartesian science' in 'three and a half' of these four respects (cf. Bramhall 1986). It makes a subject–object distinction, is committed to the scientific method, distinguishes facts and values, and at least implicitly assumes a dualism of mind and matter. On the other hand, I embraced the interpretivist view that social facts help constitute the mind and so cannot be reduced to facts about individuals (methodological holism), in which 'half' respect the book is decidedly anti-Cartesian. Thus, even though I have been criticized for not taking seriously the

---

11 I use the term 'Cartesian' here in the broad sense customary today, which includes ideas from other early modern thinkers such as Bacon and Newton.

specifically linguistic aspect of social life, as Guzzini and Leander (chap. 5 this volume) point out I end up in much the same place, emphasizing the irreducible role of shared meanings in social life.[12] This difference notwithstanding, however, by virtue of its dualist ontology in particular *Social Theory* is fundamentally Cartesian in its worldview.

Regrettably, this ontology is probably false. There is no evidence that the mind is a substance distinct from matter. As far as mainstream neuroscience is concerned we are nothing but brains, and as such materialism must somehow be true. But as we have seen there is no evidence that it is, either. Given the manifest importance of consciousness to human beings this result is a serious embarrassment for modern science, and raises deep questions about its underlying ontology.

i.e. mind & body exists.

The road to quantum consciousness

Faced with such an intractable problem, it makes sense to step back and ask why explaining consciousness in scientific terms is so 'hard?' From a quantum perspective it may be the materialist assumption, shared by all sides of the debate, that matter is purely material. 'Purely material' here means that the elementary foundations of subjective experience have no phenomenological or subjective aspect of their own. Consciousness does not go all the way down, but is either reducible to, identical with or emergent at high levels of material complexity. This is unlike reduction, identity, or emergence anywhere else in Nature, however, since it requires squeezing a qualitatively novel form of being – subjectivity – out of purely material objects. It is this qualitative novelty that makes the hard problem so hard.

The proposition that matter is purely material is a metaphysical assumption, not a scientific one, but is so taken for granted by the modern mind as to seem almost trivially true. To deny it seems absurd, reason enough to reject whatever might follow. And yet, the materialist view of matter might not be true. It is rooted in classical physics, which does indeed describe matter in materialist terms. But in the early twentieth century classical physics encountered significant anomalies at the sub-atomic level that led to the quantum revolution. Quantum mechanics enables us to manipulate sub-atomic reality with an extraordinary degree of precision, and is arguably the most well-confirmed scientific theory in history. What it shows is that the classical description of matter clearly breaks down at the micro-level; in effect, classical matter *itself* does not go all the way down. At bottom it is replaced by the quantum.

However, what the quantum is, nobody knows. Which is to say, even though physicists know how to use quantum theory, they do not understand it, what it is telling us about the nature of reality. Quantum metaphysics is 'under-determined' by its physics (French 1998), and as such requires an 'interpretation' of the theory.

---

12 E.g. Fierke (2002) and Kratochwil (chap. 2 this volume).

Philosophers have been intensely debating which interpretation is correct since the 1930s, and show no signs of stopping soon. Over a dozen interpretations now exist, with metaphysics that are not only wildly different, but simply wild. Quantum theory is so counter-intuitive that even mainstream interpretations are quite bizarre, such as the 'Many Worlds' interpretation that every quantum event splits the universe into countless other unobservable universes. Yet, because the various interpretations are empirically equivalent,[13] even though the debate has clarified their implications and swings of fashion have occurred, none has been ruled out. (This uncertainty poses a second-order problem for social scientists, in turn, since some interpretations may have many social implications, and others none.)[14] In short, the nature of the quantum is no less a mystery than consciousness. All we know for sure is that, as the great physicist John Bell once said, whatever picture of reality eventually emerges from quantum theory will surely 'astonish' us.

The quantum consciousness hypothesis suggests that the two mysteries have a common solution, namely that the quantum in effect *is* consciousness, which in some form goes all the way down in matter. Against the materialist view of matter shared by all traditional approaches to the mind–body problem, this implies a 'panpsychist' ontology, according to which matter has an intrinsically subjective aspect at the sub-atomic level. Consciousness neither reduces to matter nor emerges from it, but is present in matter all along. In the rest of this section I sketch this proposal, starting with a back-of-the-envelope introduction to quantum theory and then turning to the quantum consciousness hypothesis itself.

Quantum theory[15]

Quantum theory is perhaps best introduced by the classical worldview that it overthrew. Like quantum metaphysics, the classical worldview is an interpretation of physical theory, in this case classical physics, and as such essentially metaphysical. It makes five basic assumptions: 1) that the elementary units of reality are physical objects (materialism); 2) that larger objects can be reduced to smaller ones (reductionism); 3) that objects behave in law-like ways (determinism); 4) that causation is mechanical and local (mechanism); and 5) that objects exist independent of the subjects who observe them (objectivism?).[16] In philosophy of mind these assumptions are shared by materialists, dualists, and proponents of the linguistic turn alike, and thus by extension by most positivists and interpretivists in social science.[17]

---

13 More or less. One of the issues in the debate is whether it is legitimate to modify quantum theory to accommodate certain interpretive desiderata.

14 Complicating matters further is the danger of bogus interpretations of quantum theory being perpetrated on naïve social scientists, as we saw in the Sokal Hoax.

15 For a fuller treatment see Wendt (n.d.: chap. 3).

16 A sixth assumption, that space and time are absolute, is challenged more by relativity theory than quantum mechanics.

17 Radical interpretivists have doubts about (5), which as we shall see are best justified in quantum terms.

Quantum theory challenges all five. At the sub-atomic level physical objects dissolve into ghost-like processes; wholes cannot be reduced to parts; the world does not behave deterministically; causation is non-local; and objects do not exist independent of the subjects who observe them. Importantly, these findings do not necessarily invalidate the classical worldview at the *macro*-level, since quantum states normally 'decohere' into classical ones above the molecular level, which is why the everyday world appears to us as classical. Decoherence has been a barrier to developing a unified quantum theory encompassing both micro- and macro-levels,[18] and is a fundamental obstacle to the quantum consciousness hypothesis in particular (see below). But at least at the micro-level the quantum revolution has decisively overturned the claim of the classical worldview to provide a complete description of reality.

Although the formal structure of quantum theory is highly esoteric, its basic experimental findings are relatively straightforward, if counter-intuitive, and clearly described in a number of good, popular books.[19] The philosophical literature is also accessible, being concerned with the theory's interpretation, not its formalism (see, for example, Home 1997; Laloe 2001; Ruetsche 2002). While I can claim no understanding of quantum *physics*, with some hard work I think I have gained some of its *meta*physics, which is what matters here. Since understanding the quantum consciousness hypothesis requires some physics, however, let me start with four findings from quantum theory: wave–particle duality, wave function collapse, the measurement problem, and non-locality.

1   Wave–particle duality refers to the fact that sub-atomic phenomena have two irreducible and non-equivalent descriptions. Under some experimental conditions they are best described as waves, in others as particles. Importantly, these descriptions are not just different but mutually exclusive. This leads to Heisenberg's famous Uncertainty Principle, according to which we cannot know both the position and the momentum of a particle at the same time. A complete description of quantum systems must therefore include both descriptions, standing in a relation of what Niels Bohr called 'complementarity', where each is inherently partial.[20]

Wave–particle duality challenges two assumptions of the classical worldview. One is that science can achieve an integrated, unitary Truth about the world. Quantum theory seems to be true, but its truth requires contradictory narratives – much like the situation with Explanation and Understanding in social science, as I suggest below.

The other challenge is to the materialist view of matter. To see this it is necessary to understand the peculiar nature of waves in quantum theory. Classical waves, like

---

18 Although physicists are hard at work on this problem, trying to integrate quantum theory with relativity, which describes matter at the ultra-macro-level.

19 The best is probably still Zukav (1979).

20 On the nature of complementarity, see Held (1994). Bohr's Copenhagen Interpretation interprets the principle in epistemological terms only, which would not pose an ontological challenge to the classical worldview.

ripples on a pond, are caused by the interaction of physical objects (water molecules), and as such pose no problem for materialism. Quantum waves, in contrast, refer to the *probability* of finding physical objects (particles) at various locations. These probabilities are not determined by an underlying distribution of particles,[21] since the Uncertainty Principle tells us that as long as an electron propagates as a wave we have no basis for saying it remains a particle at all. Unlike classical waves, then, waves in quantum theory do not refer to actualities but potentialities – events that could happen, which is a much broader class than those that actually do happen.

2   Wave function collapse refers to the fact that the transition from wave to particle is instantaneous in time and has no apparent physical cause. Such 'quantum leaps' challenge the determinism of the classical worldview, and as such have caused much angst among physicists, with Einstein famously complaining that 'God does not play dice'.[22] But their anomalous character also points toward a possible solution, since wave function collapse is strongly analogous to our experience of consciousness, which involves free will and also does not seem to have a physical cause – an analogy that the quantum consciousness hypothesis will exploit.

3   The measurement problem refers to the fact that it is impossible to measure quantum phenomena without disturbing them: the process of measurement inevitably leads to a change in the appropriate description of sub-atomic particles. As long as we don't measure them, they appear as waves, and as soon as we do, as particles. This challenges another basic assumption of the classical worldview, the subject–object distinction, and with it the possibility, even in principle, of true objectivity. In quantum measurement observer and observed initially constitute a single system, rather than two, as they are classically. Far from being just a given, the subject–object distinction is now emergent from the process of measurement itself, which makes a 'cut' in a previously undivided whole. Within social science post-modernists, feminists, and others have made similar critiques of the subject–object distinction at the macro-level, but generally without a quantum basis. A quantum connection would give these critiques additional force, and point toward the necessity of a participatory epistemology in social inquiry.

4   Finally, non-locality refers to the fact that when wave functions are 'entangled' they have effects on each other in the absence of any apparent causal connection, in what Einstein called 'spooky action at a distance' (on non-locality, see Nadeau and Kafatos 1999). When one wave function changes as a result of measurement, the appropriate description of the other instantaneously changes as well. This challenges the classical worldview's mechanical theory of causation, but more

21 At least on most interpretations of quantum theory.
22 Although the evolution of the wave function is deterministic as long as it remains a wave.

fundamentally its atomism. Entangled particles do not behave as if they were distinct objects, but rather as parts of a 'superposition' of particles that absorbs their individual identities into a larger whole. This makes quantum theory radically holistic (see, for example, Bohm 1980; Teller 1986; Esfeld 2001), and again intriguingly similar to social life, at least on the argument of *Social Theory*.

Findings like these overthrew the classical worldview at the micro-level, but not at the macro, where classical thinking still dominates. The reason is decoherence. As we have seen, measuring sub-atomic systems interferes with them, collapsing quantum waves into classical particles. Importantly, this applies not just to measurements in physicists' laboratories, but in Nature everywhere. Whenever particles interact they are in effect 'measuring' each other, inducing decoherence. That's why in everyday life we see only material objects, not wave functions; quantum effects quickly wash out beyond the molecular level, leaving classical mechanics as the appropriate description at the macro.

Decoherence seems to constitute a decisive objection to the quantum consciousness hypothesis, and by extension to a quantum social science. The human brain contains over 100 billion neurons, and zillions of sub-atomic particles. In this unimaginably complex environment particles are performing countless measurements on each other, seeming to rule out any possibility of sustaining a coherent wave function in the whole brain.[23] Unless this problem can be overcome, philosophers and social scientists are right to continue treating human beings in classical terms.

The quantum consciousness hypothesis

The quantum consciousness hypothesis purports to solve the problem of decoherence, enabling a quantum explanation for human consciousness. The hypothesis has two parts: quantum brain theory and a panpsychist metaphysics.

Quantum brain theorists are trying to bridge the yawning gap between sub-atomic particles and the whole brain in such a way that quantum coherence might be transferred from the former to the latter. The key problem is identifying physical structures in the brain whose properties will insulate particles from measuring (and thus collapsing) each other, while simultaneously enabling them to be entangled (and thus having coherence). Such a balancing act is extraordinarily difficult to accomplish. Human beings are now attempting to do it artificially in the race to build a 'quantum computer', but to date we have managed to handle only a very few particles at a time (<100), whereas the brain must do it with zillions. Undaunted, quantum brain theorists have developed a variety of preliminary models of how it might do so. While not all compatible, in general they approach the problem from two directions (for overviews, see Atmanspacher 2004; Davies 2004).

Mari Jibu and Kunio Yasue (1995), Giuseppe Vitiello (2001), and others are

---

23 The warmth and wetness of the brain are also problems for quantum consciousness.

working from the top down, trying to identify the existence and physical under-pinnings of quantum behavior at the level of the whole brain. For this purpose they are using quantum field theory – a generalization of quantum theory that deals with macroscopic phenomena – to model brain activity. Working from the bottom up, in turn, Stuart Hameroff and his colleagues are trying to understand the micro-foundations of this activity.[24] Neuroscience today is based on the 'neuron doctrine,' which assumes that neurons are the smallest parts of the brain relevant to explain-ing consciousness. Yet neurons themselves are fantastically complex, each made of thousands of 'microtubules', which in turn consist of ten *million* 'dimers.' By focusing on the meso-level between sub-atomic particles and neurons the Hameroff approach seeks to show how quantum coherence in particles might 'percolate upward to,' or 'amplify,' first neurons and then the whole brain (cf. Glymour *et al.* 2001; Gabora 2002).

Experimental evidence for these models is slender and hard to come by with current technology, but the first barrier to their acceptance is theoretical: overcoming objections in principle to the idea that a structure as profoundly complex as the brain could prevent decoherence among its parts. In virtue of this problem most scientists and philosophers today reject quantum brain theory *a priori*, on the grounds that 'it can't be true therefore it isn't'. On the other hand, it has become increasingly recognized in the literature at least as a serious conjecture, even if the general view remains that it 'consists of merest possibility piled upon merest possibility teetering upon a tippy foundation of "might-be-for-all-we-know's",' and is 'no better supported than any one of a gazillion caterpillar-with-hookah hypotheses' (Grush and Churchland 1995: at 12 and 28 respectively).

In a further sign of 'acceptance,' skeptics are now beginning to take the idea seriously enough to bother criticizing it in detail, although to my mind the rebuttals have been decisive.[25] Apart from the pioneering work of its advocates, however, an important reason for the growing interest in the quantum hypothesis is that its skeptics face a fundamental problem of their own, namely the lack of a plausible alternative basis for consciousness. As we have seen, after three centuries of hard work their classical approach has failed to produce any progress whatsoever on the hard problem of consciousness. In light of this – really quite remarkable – fact, a growing number of scholars seem willing to bet on a quantum approach.

Quantum brain theory suggests that the mind is a quantum computer, rather than the classical machine assumed by most social scientists today. However, it does not yet explain *consciousness*, 'what it is like' to be a quantum computer, since there is nothing in the theory which requires that quantum brains have subjective experiences.

---

24 See Hameroff and Penrose (1996), Hameroff (2001), and Hagan *et al.* (2002). Satinover (2001) is a good overview of quantum brain theory, though skeptical of the latter's ability to explain consciousness. Still other approaches to quantum consciousness include Lockwood (1989) and Stapp (1996).

25 The most widely cited critique is Tegmark (2000), which was responded to by Hagan *et al.* (2002).

For that we need to replace the materialist view of matter that underlies classical approaches to the mind–body problem with a panpsychist ontology, which is the view that something like human consciousness goes all the way down to the sub-atomic level. This should not be confused with the idea that reality is reducible to consciousness (idealism), or that mind and matter are distinct substances (dualism). The claim of panpsychism is rather that the elementary constituents of matter have an intrinsically subjective *aspect*, and thus two irreducible manifestations – material and phenomenal, outside and inside (see Chalmers 1996; Velmans 2002; Gabora 2002). As Goethe put it, 'no matter without mind, no mind without matter' (quoted in Skrbina 2003: 25). Matter, in short, is an active, 'minded' phenomenon, not the inert, mindless substance of materialism. The question of how consciousness emerges from matter is therefore spurious, since in some sense it is there all along. What is emergent is rather the *distinction* between consciousness and purely physical matter from an underlying reality that is neither.[26] David Bohm (1980) calls this underlying reality the 'implicate order,' as distinct from the 'explicate' order of physical matter and consciousness.[27] As such, panpsychism might also be described as a 'dual aspect' or 'neutral' monism.

Panpsychism is a venerable thesis in Western philosophy – counting Spinoza, Leibniz, and Whitehead among its adherents – but to the modern mind, steeped in materialism, it may seem absurd (on the history of panpsychism, see De Quincey 2002; Skrbina 2003). Are we to believe that rocks have consciousness? However, in my view, panpsychism merits serious consideration for at least two reasons.

The first is the existence of gradations of consciousness in Nature. Panpsychism hypothesizes that 'something like' human consciousness goes all the way down, not that electrons have the same quality of consciousness that people do; what they share is only some level of subjective experience or interiority.[28] By this minimal standard, most of us would agree that dogs have consciousness, and probably mice. Intuitions will diverge the farther down the evolutionary ladder we go (do amoebas feel pain?), but even many non-panpsychists believe that all organisms have some kind of inner experience.[29] This gets consciousness down to the organic/inorganic boundary, but of course still leaves the hard part, of getting it all the way down, to lifeless matter itself.

This brings us to the second reason to take panpsychism seriously, which is that it is consistent with quantum theory, and several interpretations of quantum theory explicitly embrace it as their metaphysical framework. When asked what causes wave functions to collapse, for example, Paul Dirac, one of the founders of

26 There are various accounts in the literature of how this distinction emerges, but a particularly attractive one is that the process involves a 'temporal symmetry breaking' in the collapse of the wave function (see Atmanspacher 2003; Primas 2003), which helps make sense of the teleological, backward-referring character of human action.
27 The underlying reality might also be identified with the 'vacuum' or 'zero-point field'; see McTaggart (2002).
28 As such, panpsychism might better be described as 'pan-experientialism' (Griffin 1998).
29 See Margulis (2001), and also the literature on 'biosemiotics' (Hoffmeyer 1996).

quantum theory, answered, 'Nature makes a choice,' a suggestion he seems to have taken literally (Malin, 2001: 127). Freeman Dyson is even more explicit:

> mind is already inherent in every electron, and the processes of human consciousness differ only in degree but not kind from the processes of choice between quantum states which we call 'chance' when they are made by electrons.
>
> (Quoted in Miller 1992: 362)

Bohm's interpretation of quantum theory is also panpsychist, and so on.[30] The reason that otherwise sober physicists have turned to panpsychism is that it makes compelling sense of the otherwise inexplicable behavior of matter at the quantum level.

But are we then to believe that rocks have consciousness? No, because of decoherence. From a quantum perspective, part of what constitutes life may be the ability to maintain coherence in a multi-particle system. This can only be done by physical structures that enable quantum entanglement among their elements while insulating it from the environment through a protective boundary or skin (see Ho 1998; Seager 1995; Davies 2004). Rocks and other inanimate objects lack such structures, and so their elements quickly decohere. Organisms (by hypothesis) do have them, and thus are able to sustain quantum states at the macro-level. Arguments such as these, along with the continuing failure to solve the mind–body problem in materialist terms, have increasingly led scholars in a variety of disciplines to give panpsychism a serious look.[31]

In sum, the quantum consciousness hypothesis is a kind of 'double movement.' Quantum brain theory takes a phenomenon known to exist at the sub-atomic level, the quantum state, and projects it upward to the whole brain. Panpsychism, in turn, takes a phenomenon known to exist at the macroscopic level, consciousness, and projects it downward to sub-atomic particles. In this way two of the great mysteries of modern science – the nature of the quantum and of consciousness – solve each other, and raise the possibility of a quantum social science.

Toward a quantum social science

If the quantum consciousness hypothesis is true then the elementary units of social life, human subjects, are quantum systems – not just metaphorically or by analogy, but really.[32] This is a strong claim, and it might be asked why it is necessary. Why

---

30 See Bohm (1980, 1990), and Hiley and Pylkkänen (2001).

31 See, for example, Nagel (1979), Seager (1995), Chalmers (1996), Griffin (1998), Malin (2001), De Quincey (2002), Velmans (2002), Mathews (2003), and Skrbina (2003); cf. Litfin (2003) and Bennett (2004).

32 That said, quantum mechanics was developed to describe the behavior of sub-atomic particles, and as such strictly speaking does not apply to human beings. What we are really talking about here, therefore, is a generalized, 'weak' version of quantum theory, structurally isomorphic with

not take the weaker but perhaps more plausible metaphorical view instead, which opens up the same interpretive possibilities? In IR this has been done by Dimitris Akrivoulis (2002), who uses a sophisticated understanding of metaphor to develop an innovative, quantum post-modern reading of world politics.[33] I admire this work, but believe it would be more compelling still with a naturalistic foundation. Metaphors are optional and may be contested, whereas if the quantum consciousness hypothesis is true then we really have no choice but to go quantum if we want fully to explain human behavior. Of course, at this point we don't know if the quantum hypothesis is true, and so in one sense a realist interpretation is not yet warranted – at most we can say that human beings are 'as if' quantum systems. But we have more reason to follow up this conjecture if the suspicion is that we 'really are' quantum.

I now want to explore what this might mean for social science in general, focusing on ramifications first for our model of man and then for our model of society. I will limit myself here to ontological implications, deferring epistemological ones until the next section, where I turn to *Social Theory* and its critics.

Toward a quantum model of man[34]

The majority having gotten over physics envy decades ago, few social scientists today would emphasize how their models of man are rooted in classical metaphysics. But it follows from the above discussion that all such models – whether '*homo economicus*' or '*homo sociologicus*' – must somehow be informed by the classical worldview, since what else could their basis be? Metaphysically we have only the two choices, and an explicitly quantum social science does not exist. Thus, despite their many important differences, contemporary models of man in social science must at least implicitly share certain basic classical assumptions: that human beings are ultimately material objects, that we have determinate properties, that our behavior is caused by processes in the brain, and that we do not have free will. A quantum approach calls all four into question.

First, it suggests that consciousness plays an essential and irreducible role in human behavior. The 'difference that consciousness makes,' in other words, is that we are quantum rather than classical systems. Although there is disagreement among quantum consciousness theorists about where precisely consciousness is 'located' in human beings, in my view the most plausible answer is in the collapse of our wave functions. This process happens continually as we interact with the environment, providing a basis for our experience of a stream of consciousness.

the original but modified to take into account the properties of macroscopic systems; see Atmanspacher *et al.* (2002).

33 Other good analogical accounts include Matson (1964), Becker (1991), and Rosenblum and Kuttner (1999).

34 Feminists have convincingly criticized classical models of man for being literally about men, so I use 'man' here as a friendly provocation to consider whether the same holds for the quantum model. My suggestion is that it would not.

luftmensch

Our wave functions themselves, then, would correspond to our *unconscious*, understood not in the narrow, Freudian sense of something repressed, but in the more general sense of all the background knowledge we have about ourselves and our environment of which we are not aware when we are conscious (on various models of the unconscious, see Ekstrom 2004). According to the computational model of man that dominates contemporary cognitive and social science, it is on this level that human beings do most of their thinking. However, in contrast to the usual assumption that the unconscious engages only in classical computation, here it would engage in quantum, with its exponentially more powerful capabilities (see Penrose 1994; Latsch 2003; cf. Smith 2003).

Second, as an important part of our wave function, our knowledge of ourselves – our identity or sense of Self – does not have determinate properties at any given moment, but becomes determinate only when we act into the world (collapse). In other words, the desires and beliefs which the rationalist model of man sees as causing behavior actually do not exist *until* behavior takes place – before that point the Self is a superposition of multiple and mutually incompatible desires and beliefs. This does not mean identities are completely open-ended (in which case they wouldn't be 'identities'). Wave functions are highly structured sets of possible and probable states, making some behaviors and thus identities more likely than others. But these identities only become actualized in wave function collapse, which itself is undetermined by a physical process. This perhaps counter-intuitive idea is supported by both everyday experience and academic research. In speech, for example, we cannot be absolutely certain what we are going to say, and thus who we are going to be, until we say it. And recent experimental work on 'preference reversals' and public opinion has shown that individuals' desires and beliefs are highly sensitive to context and framing effects, which is what we would expect if they are quantum rather than classical beings (see, respectively, Slovic 1995; and Zaller 1992).

This argument points toward a post-modern, performative model of subjectivity (Butler 1997). Against the traditional view of subjectivity as a material or ideational substance, performativity treats it as a process all the way down (cf. Jackson and Nexon 1999). There simply is no agent before agency; we only become agents in and through performances. Since quantum theory is often seen as implying a process as opposed to substance ontology, it provides a natural basis for such a view. Of course, it might be doubted whether performativity theory needs a quantum basis, having been developed without it. However, recalling my naturalist assumption that social theories should be constrained by what physics tells us about the world, it is unclear how else performativity theory could be justified. If consciousness is not a quantum phenomenon, then agents are nothing but classical brains, and brains have determinate properties first, before they cause behavior.[35] Ultimately, classical agents must preexist agency. In part for this reason some

---

35 Though see Hosek and Freeman (2001), who attempt to ground performativity in a non-linear classical theory of the mind.

advocates of performativity theory have questions about how it relates to (classical) material reality (see Barad 2003; cf. Bennett 2004). The dual-aspect quantum ontology answers these questions in a way that gives performativity theory a coherent metaphysical foundation, without sacrificing its essentially non-foundational character.

Third, reasons are constitutive of action, not causes. This follows from desires and beliefs only becoming well defined in consciousness or wave function collapse. Since collapse is spontaneous and instantaneous, it cannot 'cause' behavior. Instead, collapse realizes a continuous stream of two *non*-causal, constitutive effects: phenomenal effects of determinate desires and beliefs (reasons) and physical effects of bodily states (behavior).[36] These two effects are irreducible but correlated aspects of one underlying reality. Mere behavior is thereby made intrinsically meaningful action, or behavior-for-someone.

The quantum model suggests further that reasons are not only constitutive but teleological as well (cf. Schueler 2003). In a teleological process the end-state of a system helps explain how it gets there (for further discussion, see Wendt 2003). While anathema to the classical worldview, 'final causation' makes sense if the emergence of a distinction between physical and phenomenal states involves temporal symmetry breaking, with the former moving forward in time and the latter backward (see note 26 above). On this view, human action is fundamentally anticipatory, not in the conventional sense that we act on expectations about the future, but in the radical sense that in intentional action we literally 'feel' the future through a kind of 'temporal non-locality.'[37]

Finally, quantum man should have free will. The experience of free will has always been a problem for the classical worldview, which assumes that the entire world is deterministic. This problem is mirrored in social science, where the goal is to explain human behavior as deterministically as possible, and unexplained variance in behavior is chalked up to random error rather than free will. As such, various thinkers have looked to the inherently non-deterministic character of quantum mechanics to ground our sense of free will. Yet, as critics of this move have pointed out, indeterminism is not enough, since seemingly random behavior could indeed just be random, rather than purposive or 'willed'. So at most quantum indeterminacy is necessary for free will, not sufficient. On the other hand, however, with a panpsychist interpretation quantum theory might enable us to go farther. Indeterminacy describes the situation facing an objective observer: we on the outside of a wave function cannot predict its collapse. What about someone on the 'inside'? If the quantum consciousness hypothesis is true, then action could appear non-deterministic from the outside and yet be freely willed from the inside (cf. Hodgson 2002). Novelty would then be an essential feature of human action, and perhaps so of society.

---

36 On the distinction between causal and constitutive effects, see Wendt (1998).
37 On anticipatory consciousness, see Jordan (1998) and Wolf (1998), and on temporal non-locality, Nadeau and Kafatos (1999) and Malin (2001).

Toward a quantum model of society

The quantum consciousness hypothesis suggests that individual psychology should incorporate quantum thinking, but what about the *social* sciences? We know that without a suitable physical infrastructure – in the human case a brain – quantum states immediately decohere into classical ones. Since societies don't have brains it would seem they can't be quantum systems, and so social science should remain classical. In short, by tying quantum effects to individual consciousness I seem to be engaging in a kind of reductionism that I eschewed in *Social Theory*, and foreclosing the possibility of a quantum social science.

In what follows I challenge this skeptical conclusion, arguing that quantum consciousness not only supports but deepens *Social Theory*'s holism about society. This is not to deny the specificity of the social level. Social systems do not have brains in the same sense that people do. However, I argue that, if we really are quantum beings, then our interactions will necessarily have quantum aspects that cannot be reduced to classical considerations. I offer three conjectures along these lines: 1) social systems have wave functions that constitute a collective unconscious; 2) these wave functions collapse by a process of 'intra-action' described by quantum game theory; and, most speculatively, 3) social systems are super-organisms with collective consciousness.

The collective unconscious

Earlier I defined the unconscious broadly, as all the background knowledge about self and other possessed by an individual of which she is unaware when conscious. In that case, if social systems could be said to possess shared knowledge, then it seems reasonable to think they have a kind of unconscious as well, a collective one. The collective unconscious would perform similar functions in social life that the individual unconscious does, including structuring action, providing memory, and engaging in computation. My argument suggests that these processes might be quantum in character, making social systems in effect quantum computers.[38]

The importance of shared knowledge or meaning to human interaction is at least implicitly recognized by all social theories, since without it society would be impossible. However, there are different ways to conceive the nature of this sharing. In much of contemporary social science the sharing is individualistic or 'internalist', in the sense that thoughts are assumed first to reside inside in the individual's head and only then become common knowledge. In a metaphysical sense, therefore, thought precedes language. In *Social Theory* I defended the rival holist or 'externalist' view, which is currently the mainstream in philosophy of meaning and used also in the linguistic turn. Against internalism, externalists argue that the meaning of our thoughts is intrinsically social, constituted literally by thoughts in *other* people's heads. In a metaphysical sense, therefore, language precedes thought.

---

38 The idea that social systems engage in *classical* computation is relatively well established; see Mirowski and Somefun (1998) and Clark (2003).

Quantum theory strongly supports externalism (see especially Esfeld 2001). The theory tells us that, at the moment of measurement, observer and observed are entangled non-locally and as such participate in a single wave function. It is only in making a 'cut' between them, with the act of measurement itself, that subject and object acquire completely distinct identities. If such entanglement exists even in our measurements of sub-atomic particles in the lab, then it should be present all the more so in our measurements (perceptions) of other people, who are themselves quantum systems. This is at least highly reminiscent of externalism, and as such suggests that shared meanings are the primary form that quantum entanglement takes at the human level. Social systems, in short, have[39] 'collective wave functions' – superpositions of information states held jointly by individuals (see Arfi 2005). As in individuals, collective wave functions are not conscious, since it is only in collapse that consciousness emerges. But they do structure action, provide collective memory, and engage in computation.[40]

This suggests a 'holographic' model of the relationship between the individual and society. In a hologram each part mirrors the whole, such that one could reconstruct the whole from any of the parts (see Bohm 1980). This implies a fundamentally participatory ontology radically at odds with both 'flat' ontologies that try to reduce society to individuals, such as rationalism, and 'hierarchical' ontologies that treat social structures as emergent and even constitutive of agents, such as *Social Theory*. From a quantum perspective neither looks right, since both at least implicitly assume, classically, that individual minds are at some level ontologically distinct. Given quantum entanglement at the unconscious level, the mind relates to society not through reduction, emergence, or even mutual constitution, but by in a sense *being* society, all the way down. Instead of being distinct entities, minds participate in each other's reality. In effect, they stand in a relationship of identity.[41] At the same time, however, this identity is 'incomplete' by virtue of having two different and irreducible aspects – individual and collective, subjective and objective, inside and out.[42] Like 'monads' in Leibniz's metaphysics, individuals in a hologram retain their own points of view on the collective, even while they mirror its properties (on 'quantum monadology', see Nakagomi 2003).

Intra-action and quantum game theory

Individuals and collectives are alike, then, in both having wave functions, and thus an unconscious. But in collapse they are essentially different. In contrast to the collapse of individual wave functions in a unitary consciousness, social ones

---

39 I say 'have' rather than 'are' wave functions because social systems are also patterns of actual behavior, which only take place in collapse.

40 'Mirror neurons' in the brain may provide the physical basis for this entanglement of shared meaning; see Gallese (2001).

41 See Humphreys (1997); on the problem of identity in the quantum context, see Castellani, ed. (1998).

42 This should allay any concerns that a holographic society would be like the 'Borg' on *Star Trek*, the individual members of which had no experience or will of their own.

collapse in a dispersed or 'distributed' fashion into physically separate conscious-nesses. The specificity of the social is rooted in this essential physical difference, and as such quantum theory will have to play a correspondingly different role. Instead of producing a unity of consciousness, it must produce difference.

To see what this might mean, consider first the traditional game theoretic analysis of interaction. Game theory assumes a classical, individualist ontology in which actors have determinate properties by virtue of their bodies, which are physically exogenous to interaction. Thus, before interaction begins identities are given as already different, as a brute fact of Nature. As interaction gets under way, then, it is indeed 'inter'-action, or action between different minds. From this perspective the quantum idea that difference in any deep sense could be produced in interaction seems clearly wrongheaded. All that can change in interaction are the attributes of a previously given identity.[43] This leads to a bottom-up approach to social science, which attempts to reduce social systems to their micro-foundations in the interaction of ontologically primitive elements.

In a quantum approach actors lack determinate identities before they are measured. Identity emerges from interaction itself, not before. What is onto-logically primitive is not a substance (the brain) but the process of wave function collapse in measurement, which fixes determinate identity.[44] In the case of collective wave functions this process of collapse has two aspects, collective and individual. On the one hand, since what is collapsing is a shared wave function, it seems the collective itself must be helping to choose outcomes through a kind of 'internal measurement' (Matsuno 2003) or 'downward causation' (cf. Wendt 2003). This reinforces and deepens an argument made by some classical social theorists that groups can have 'collective intentionality' irreducible to their members (Searle 1995). On the other hand, since collective wave functions are instantiated in separate brains, their collapse is mediated by individuals, who remain a locus of control in the process. Although the way in which collective intentions unfold therefore depends on how individuals express them, our consciousness of those intentions only emerges with our action (collapse). It is always in relation to the whole, in short, that consciousness of 'difference' is produced.

The classical concept of 'inter'-action, presupposing as it does physical separ-ability, seems inadequate to describe such a holistic view of social life. Thus, a plausible quantum replacement might be what Karen Barad (2003) calls 'intra'-action, which she uses to solve some problems in how performativity theory relates to material reality.[45] Intra-action describes two features of collective wave function

43 Despite challenging methodological individualism in other respects, *Social Theory* reflects this view insofar as it treats the essential state as constitutionally prior to international life, as Suganami (chap. 4 this volume) points out.

44 This might provide a quantum basis for Foucault's disciplinary view of power, of which indi-viduality is a primary effect.

45 Also see Rouse (2002). There are also parallels here to Dewey's 'transactional' approach to action; see Khalil (2003).

collapse. First, in relating to each other through shared meanings human beings are relating to something internal ('intra') to themselves of which they are only a part, which captures the sense in which at the unconscious level individuals are entangled. Second, at the conscious level they only become individuated through their actions, which captures the sense in which collective collapse is mediated by distinct bodies. The two together make it possible to see constitutional difference as emerging from an underlying unity.

This idea might help unlock the potential for social applications of quantum game theory, which has recently been developed by physicists but, with the exception of Badredine Arfi (2005) in IR and a few others, so far ignored by social scientists.[46] Quantum game theory is just like classical game theory, except that its players are 'quantum decision-makers' (Zak 2000), with indeterminate and entangled properties and strategies before action. It turns out that the effect of these changes on the outcomes of strategic interaction is significant: when non-cooperative games such as Prisoner's Dilemma or Chicken are played under quantum rules, cooperation is much easier to achieve than in the classical case. This could help explain the finding that in real life people (and states) cooperate much more than they 'should' according to classical game theory (see Ostrom 1998). Quantum game theory was not developed with such social scientific applications in mind, however, and we currently lack concepts to translate much of its formalism into social analysis. The idea of intra-action might be one place to start.

Super-organisms and collective consciousness?

Up to this point I have argued only that collectives have an unconscious, not consciousness. This conforms to our common-sense, Cartesian intuition that only brains can be conscious, which underpins social scientists' disdain for the concept of collective consciousness, eventually abandoned even by Durkheim himself (Nemedi 1995; cf. Burns and Engdahl 1998).

Nevertheless, I wonder whether the quantum argument should not be pushed further, to the conclusion that collectives do have a kind of consciousness. One reason to explore this possibility is that we talk this way all the time, most notably in IR in how we routinely attribute emotions – which in people involves consciousness – to states and other groups. Our discourse about world politics is replete with 'angry' and 'fearful' states, 'traumatized' and 'resentful' societies, and so on. How can we make sense of such emotions talk? Conventional wisdom treats it only 'as if', as merely a useful fiction for something else – aggregate emotions of individuals.[47] Yet, these 'fictions' seem to do important explanatory and interpretive work in our

---

46 Note that Arfi does not use the wave function formalism, preferring instead a more general, non-Boolean quantum logic. For an introduction to quantum game theory see Piotrowski and Sladkowski (2003).

47 Perhaps as a result IR scholarship on collective emotions is almost completely lacking, though see Hall (2003).

lives, and are hard to do without. Understanding this work would be easier if we could take collective emotions literally.

By way of concluding this section, therefore, let me briefly revisit from a quantum perspective the concept of collective consciousness. I first conceptualize collectives as super-organisms, which gives them a kind of material body, and then explore what kind of consciousness such a body could support.

Super-organisms are systems that have the functional integration and purposiveness of organisms, but whose elements are biological individuals. Insect colonies are the textbook example, but human societies have been suggested as well (for discussion and references see Wendt 2004). The concept of super-organism has long been eschewed because of its association with group selection, which evolutionary theory was thought to preclude. But in recent years it and group selection have made a big comeback (see Sober and Wilson 1998), and, importantly, from a classical evolutionary perspective. Super-organisms display a degree of common fate and collective purpose that are hard to explain in reductionist terms, and thus are increasingly seen as biological realities in their own right.

Since the problem with collective consciousness is that collectives don't seem to have the physical infrastructure for consciousness (a material body), the concept of super-organism is an important first step in the argument. The body of an insect colony is not as unitary or coherent as that of a regular organism, but it is a single material system nonetheless. Moreover, we already know from recent classical scholarship that these bodies engage in collective cognition and decision-making, making them 'forms of life' in almost every sense. A quantum view would support this argument and take it further. Quantum theory's radical holism could help dispel any classical unease about the reality of super-organisms, and allow for non-local communication among their members.

But are super-organisms *conscious*? Even granting the materiality of super-organisms, attributing consciousness to them still seems a stretch. On the other hand, I have argued that something like consciousness goes all the way down in Nature. If something as simple as an electron has a kind of consciousness, then why can't much more complex beehives? Panpsychism suggests that consciousness already comes in at least three distinct degrees or forms – that of sub-atomic particles, plants, and organisms. From this perspective the notion that super-organisms might have another, fourth type of consciousness looks less crazy.

Indeed, we have more evidence for collective consciousness than we do for electron or plant consciousness, since we participate in it every day. We identify with each other, understand each other's meaning, and feel each other's pain. We have 'We-*feeling*.' Is this not precisely what collective consciousness would be like, if it existed? Moreover, many social scientists are already willing to grant the reality of collective intentions, and, although it is contested, some philosophers think that intentionality implies consciousness (see Siewert 2002). On this view, then, collective intentions might instantiate a collective consciousness. Again, this would be distributed across individual consciousnesses, making it essentially different from the latter. But if we are monads in a social hologram then this is what we should expect: the experience of each mirrors the experience of the whole.

Much more would need to be said to make a persuasive case for such a counter-intuitive proposal, so I am merely gesturing here in the direction of an argument. My point is only that from a quantum standpoint such an argument is at least conceivable, while it is not from a classical one, suggesting that the *a priori* rejection of collective consciousness is a classical prejudice. Perhaps the prejudice is justified, but until we understand even individual consciousness the jury on collective consciousness should remain out.

My discussion in this section obviously raises more questions than it answers, and there are certain issues – such as the teleological implications of quantum consciousness, and participatory epistemology – that I have barely touched on at all. But it should be clear even at this stage that a 'Heisenberg cut' would lead to a very different picture of social life than a Cartesian one (Atmanspacher 1997). With this new standpoint in hand I now turn to my critics.

A response to the critics

In light of the foregoing discussion it is striking that none of *Social Theory*'s critics questions its implicit assumption that social life must somehow be consistent with the reality constraints of the classical worldview, suggesting they too accept this premise. As long as we continue to do so, I believe the resources for deflecting or accommodating most of their concerns can be found within the book itself. The reality constraints of the quantum worldview are quite different, however, and from this perspective some of the criticisms have more force, though not necessarily for the reasons given. With this in mind, in responding I shall first do so from a classical standpoint, and then in each case reflect on the exchange from a quantum one. As noted in the introduction, I shall address eight issues in four groups, relating to state agency, the agent–structure problem, the relationship of ideas to material conditions, and the epistemology of the *via media*.

State agency

Are states people too?

Social Theory's claim that states are actors to which we can attribute human qualities is criticized by Cederman and Daase, Suganami, and especially Zehfuss, but their skepticism is probably widely shared among IR scholars. Although the discourse of state personhood pervades IR scholarship, few of us seem willing to say that states *really are* persons. We treat state personhood as a useful fiction, a convenient metaphor for the actions of individuals, not a description of how the world really is. The ultimate basis for this skepticism lies, I think, in a tacit commitment to a physicalist view of the mind as something that can reside only in brains.

Even if we accept physicalism, such a conclusion is unwarranted for at least one aspect of state persons – their intentions. As I suggested in *Social Theory* and have argued at more length elsewhere (Wendt 2004), states are structured, self-organizing systems whose intentions are every bit as real as those of individuals.

Importantly, this does not preclude conflict within states about what their intentions should be, since macro- (state) level outcomes are multiply realizable at the micro- (individual) level. Thus, as Zehfuss shows in the German case, states may exhibit significant internal contestation over their identities, a proper understanding of which requires a close study of domestic politics. However, *Social Theory* is a book not about state identity but about the states *system*, which is irreducible to individual states. All that is necessary for the assumption of state personhood to be justified at the system level is that domestic contestation be sufficiently structured that it produces unitary collective intentions toward other states at any given moment. To be sure, were those intentions wildly chaotic over time it would be difficult to say much of interest about the international system. To that extent Zehfuss is right that systemic IR theories depend on relatively stable state identities. But in the real world we do not usually observe such chaos, even in the German case. If Germany's identity were truly chaotic it would be impossible for Germany to act coherently on the international stage, and for others to inter-act with it. This may describe 'failed states', but not most states in the system.

That said, Zehfuss makes an important point, which is that even if collective intentions are relatively coherent their identities might never be *complete*, or 'identical with themselves' (Bartelson 1998). However, does this vitiate a realist view of state agency? Perhaps a classical one, since it assumes that the properties of entities must be well defined, but from a quantum perspective such a criticism is moot. Even though quantum systems do not have determinate properties, they still have an identity in the sense that their wave functions are structured such that some outcomes are more probable than others. It is this structure that enables us to distinguish 'this' quantum system from 'that' one, and to make (probabilistic) predictions about their behavior, which is all that we minimally need for an identity statement. Thus, the fact that quantum states are not 'identical with themselves' does not preclude their having intentionality, any more than the fact that individuals' identity is never complete precludes their being intentional.

Reflexivity

Drulák and Sárváry criticize *Social Theory*'s treatment of state agency on different grounds, that it inadequately theorizes the role of reflexivity in international politics, such as Soviet 'New Thinking,' and thus the possibilities for structural change. States seem reduced to automatons or cultural dopes, condemned to repeating the structural logics to which they have been socialized. Drulák links this failure to the book's over-reliance on the epistemology of Explanation, which he argues is incapable of theorizing reflexivity. Only a turn toward Understanding – and thus implicitly consciousness – can grasp the importance of reflexivity in international life.

In one sense this objection seems misplaced, since systemic theories are intrinsically ill-equipped to explain agency, and as such it misunderstands what *Social Theory* is about. Theories of international politics should not be confused with theories of foreign policy (Waltz 1979). Each has its respective domain, and accounts developed to understand one may tell us little about the other.

However, unlike Waltz (and following Buzan *et al.* 1993), in *Social Theory* I added the interaction level of analysis to the purview of systemic theorizing, as 'micro'-structural theory. This still excludes the truly unit- or domestic level, and with it a full theorization of state reflexivity. But given the addition of the interaction level, and its use in chapter 7 to think about structural change, it seems reasonable to expect my approach at least to permit reflexivity, and even to speak to its conditions of possibility. In this *Social Theory* is only partly successful. On the one hand, its distinction between role identities and roles – the I and the Me – creates distance between the subjective and objective aspects of identity, enabling states in principle to reflect on and change their behavior. But the subjective aspect of this picture is inadequately theorized – in part because Understanding has an ambiguous status within *Social Theory*, and in part because dualism is not an adequate metaphysical foundation for consciousness.

A quantum approach could help here in three ways, and in the process take Drulák and Sárváry's criticisms further. First, as I argued above, a quantum social science might justify attributing consciousness to collectives, and specifically *self*-consciousness, which is essential if we are to think of reflexivity at the social rather than just the individual level. Second, it would justify Drulák's emphasis on Understanding as an irreducible epistemological stance (see below). Finally, the quantum approach to the Self is also promising. Rather than a well-defined classical reality that behaves deterministically, the Self as quantum wave function is a structure only of possibilities, the realization of which is non-deterministic. From this standpoint we might think of reflexivity as the conscious measurement of the state's unconscious wave function, or 'measurement of itself', which induces a collapse toward novel outcomes. The potential for such self-measurement is always there, even if not actualized in a given case.

In sum, by highlighting the role of classical assumptions about the mind in the critics' case, a quantum perspective supports *Social Theory*'s assumption that states are people too, while potentially deepening it with greater reflexivity. If we are to treat state personhood as nothing more than a 'useful fiction', we at least need to work harder to do so.

Agency and structure

This discussion has implications for how we might also respond to criticisms of *Social Theory*'s treatment of the relationship between state agents and system structure – the agent–structure problem. I take up three specific criticisms in this context: the contention of Behnke, Cederman and Daase, and Kratochwil that states are not ontologically prior to the states system; Suganami's belief that my claim that states and system cultures are mutually constitutive amounts to two descriptions of the same thing; and Copeland's claim that uncertainty about intentions is so profound that anarchy will constrain state action regardless of its cultural content.

On the essential state

The criticism that state identity is 'social all the way down' points toward an even more holistic ontology than *Social Theory*'s, and since that is very much in the book's spirit I welcome the opportunity to consider it. Although the critics make the point in different idioms, their argument comes down to the idea that to be a state presupposes a boundary between itself and the environment, and as such even its corporate identity is constitutionally dependent on other states or 'difference'. I agree that this important fact is neglected in *Social Theory*, and so the ontological priority given there to the state is too strong. Even the 'essential state' exists only in virtue of ongoing processes of differentiation from its environment.

On the other hand, none of my critics comes to grips with the main reason I stopped short of a fully socialized state, namely, that states are self-organizing systems. Like the human body, states are internally structured processes that can persist even if they are not recognized by their fellows (think of Taiwan). In short, state identity is about the production not only of difference from without, but of sameness within. The latter cannot be reduced to the former, and indeed can be expected to resist outside efforts to destroy the boundary (by attempted conquest, for example). To that extent, even as it is constitutionally dependent on difference, state agency is also exogenous to it. This is clear even in Cederman and Daase's effort to endogenize corporate identities within systemic theory. While their framework offers insight into how the specifically spatial aspects of state identities are constructed at the system level, it does not show how states acquire the internal structures that give them spatial identities in the first place. Of course, this is not to say that we cannot study how these internal structures reproduce themselves, just as we can study how the body sustains itself. But *Social Theory* is a theory of the states system, not the state. Reality is organized hierarchically, and states are simply lower in the hierarchy than the states system. Relative to the latter, therefore, their identity must at some level be taken as given, precluding a more radical holism.

Importantly, however, the idea that reality is hierarchical is a classical assumption. In the classical worldview parts necessarily have priority over wholes, since ultimately the latter consist of tiny physical objects whose identity does not depend on other objects. As we saw above, this hierarchical model of part–whole relationships is called into question by quantum theory, in two ways. First, the identity of the elementary units of reality is no longer constituted only physically but also by their wave functions, and as such they are no longer 'identical with themselves.' And second, wave functions are constantly becoming entangled with other wave functions. This means that at the sub-atomic level the parts of reality are no longer fully separable, which undermines their privileged ontological status in part–whole relationships. This not to say they lose their individuality completely, since entanglement does not pertain to the physical aspect of quantum systems: if we measure them they will still appear as separate particles. But in their wave aspect the elementary units of reality are no longer 'elementary'.

The decoherence of wave functions that accompanies the transition from the quantum to the classical world might be thought to make such a radical holism moot for IR. However, if consciousness is quantum mechanical, and individual consciousnesses are entangled through shared meanings, then the argument would extend to world politics. In their subjective or wave aspect states are not prior to the relationships in which they are embedded, and as such state identity is indeed social all the way down, as my critics have argued. At the same time, however, in its objective or particle aspect the ontological priority of the state remains, as I argued in *Social Theory*. As happens so often in quantum thinking, in short, both descriptions are necessary to capture the whole truth.

On mutual constitution

Turning now from states' essential, corporate identity to their contingent role identities, Suganami argues that my description of state agents as, for example, enemies is equivalent to describing a structure as a Hobbesian culture, and as such they cannot be mutually constitutive. If this were true it would be a significant problem for *Social Theory*'s argument. I agree with Suganami that in an important sense role identities and system structure presuppose each other, and, indeed, that is the whole point of mutual constitution. But does this mean they are *equivalent?* I don't see how it could, for precisely the reason that Suganami himself identifies, namely that one is about units and the other about the system. The example he uses to make his point, a wedding, is instructive in this respect. A wedding is not a macro-level structure like a Hobbesian culture, but a micro-level one and thus more akin to 'enmity'. Even enmity is not strictly equivalent to *being* an enemy, since it describes a relationship between two actors rather than a property of just one (role vs. role identity), but given that both are micro-level phenomena the connection is tighter. The connection becomes much looser, however, if we take a more appropriate analogue to a Hobbesian culture, namely marriage. Marriage and weddings are mutually constitutive, but they are not equivalent. Like a Hobbesian culture, marriage describes an institution, the existence of which does not depend on whether any particular individuals engage in it. By the same token, as long as states collectively see the international system in Hobbesian terms, it will have a Hobbesian logic even if a given bilateral relationship is friendly. What Suganami is missing here is the supervenient relationship between the micro- and macro-levels, which enables them to be mutually constitutive without being identical. Thus, at least from *Social Theory*'s classical standpoint, Suganami's concern seems unwarranted.

From a quantum perspective, however, the picture looks different, since my response to Suganami presupposed a hierarchical ontology of micro- and macro-levels. In quantum theory parts and whole are related by entanglement, not supervenience,[48] which calls into question the possibility of 'mutual' constitution. 'Mutuality' suggests an underlying separateness of identity, with separable parts interacting to constitute an emergent whole. In entanglement, in contrast, there is

48 See Teller (1986), Humphreys (1997), and Belousek (2003).

an important sense in which the parts do not retain a separate existence at all. This does not mean there is *no* sense in which they are separate, since if we measure them they will appear as separate particles. But as long as their entanglement is preserved they will form a single system, and to that extent a discourse of 'mutual' constitution will be inapt.

This suggests that in one sense Suganami is right, that being enemies and being in a Hobbesian culture are indeed two descriptions of the same thing. The idea of society as a hologram is relevant here, where parts instantiate and mirror the whole. However, this does not mean the relationship between the two levels is one of causal interaction, or that there are even two 'levels' at all. Insofar as enmity is entangled with a larger Hobbesian culture, then at the level of the collective unconscious they form a single undifferentiated system. What to do then with the fact that states experience themselves as differentiated agents that 'inter'-act? That happens at the level of consciousness, which I have argued is distributed. Squaring this circle is what the concept of 'intra'-action can capture – that the differential experiences of parts emerge only from cuts in a preexisting whole.

The Problem of Other Minds

Copeland's concern about my treatment of agency and structure is rather different. In his view, present and future uncertainty about others' intentions – the Problem of Other Minds – is deep and ineradicable. Given the dangers in anarchy of misplaced trust, states are forced to assume the worst about each other even if they would prefer to cooperate. In this way structure (anarchy) might constrain state action regardless of history or culture. Copeland claims that I provide no mechanism by which states can overcome this problem, and as such I 'cannot argue' that they might escape the world of *realpolitik*.

The Problem of Other Minds is an important philosophical problem even when violence is not an issue, and it is exacerbated by anarchy. So Copeland is right to raise the question, which I did not address in *Social Theory*. However, on both empirical and theoretical grounds his discussion is fatally flawed. The fact is that states do know each other's intentions most of the time, and there are good reasons – contained in the book – for why this should be so. Were Copeland correct international life as we know it would be impossible.

Let us begin on classical grounds with uncertainty in the present. How often are states uncertain about each other's intentions? Rarely. Consider other states' uncertainty about US intentions today, which given its overwhelming material capabilities should, on Copeland's view, be a source of great anxiety. States in the 'axis of evil' – North Korea, Iran, Iraq before the recent war, perhaps Cuba and Syria – are indeed worried about US intentions. Yet they have every reason to be, not because they are uncertain about US intentions, but just the reverse: because of America's demonstrated hostility. What about the other 190-odd states in the system? I see no evidence that they are worried about an impending US attack, and a similar trust pervades the vast majority of bilateral relationships in the states system today. In short, empirically, far from facing profound uncertainty, states are confident about each other's intentions almost all of the time.

How is so much epistemic security possible? Are states irrational? Most IR scholars would probably say no – that the trust states have in each other's intentions is perfectly rational, and indeed that to assume otherwise would itself be irrational. Past experience has shown that they can usually afford to reason probabilistically about each other's intentions, rather than adopting worst-case, possibilistic thinking. This points to one classical mechanism, discussed at length in *Social Theory*, by which states can solve the Problem of Other Minds: learning through reflected appraisals. By adjusting their expectations to the responses their actions elicit from Others, over time states have developed a deep reservoir of common knowledge about who they are and what they want. Had this not occurred the international system today would be far more chaotic and conflictual than it is – indeed, there would not be an 'international system' at all.

This learning process has taken place against the background of the norms and institutions of international society. These not only help states draw correct inferences about each other's intentions, but help constitute their own intentions. In this light we can see that Copeland's underlying picture of the international system is atomistic and physicalist. Like atoms in the classical worldview, in Copeland's view states exist and have intentions on their own, constitutionally independent of shared meanings at the system level. This ignores the fundamental point of chapter 4, namely that the mind is fundamentally social, and as such one cannot know even one's *own* mind if the Problem of Other Minds is not solved. In short, states need a high degree of certainty about each other's intentions to be 'states' at all.[49] This is true even in the Hobbesian culture, where states know who they are (enemies) by virtue of the shared understandings that constitute that identity. Although Hobbesian states assume the worst about each other, they do so not because they are uncertain but precisely because they know that others are out to get them (cf. Mitzen 2004). Thus, even in this hard case, structure (anarchy) does not constrain state action independent of culture.

The problem of future uncertainty does not change this conclusion significantly. True, even if they can plausibly trust the Other today, states must now also be concerned that the Other might change its mind in the future, or that a revolution will change it for them. But how often does this happen? Are state intentions highly unstable over time? Not as far as I can tell. Despite changes in administration national interests seem quite stable, in some cases over centuries. How those interests are pursued varies more, but normally within predictable constraints. Revolutions can produce dramatic changes in intentions, but they are uncommon, and revolutionary states are subject to socializing pressures that usually bring their intentions quickly into line with established norms. Copeland is right that states must be more concerned about the future than the past, since agency is always into

---

49 For an extension of this idea using the concept of ontological security, see Mitzen (2004).

the future, but in moving forward they are always looking back, using what they have learned about each other to guide their actions (cf. Wendt 2001). Not to do so would be irrational.

On the other hand, although he does not invoke quantum theory, Copeland's argument actually looks more promising from such a perspective, for two reasons. First, in quantum theory uncertainty is not merely epistemic but ontic (cf. Hardin 2003). One irony of Copeland's analysis is that in his classical worldview there is no *ontological* uncertainty, in the sense of intentions being actually uncertain. The uncertainty states face is a limit only to their knowledge about others, not whether their intentions really are indeterminate.[50] In contrast, if states are wave functions then they do not even have definite intentions until they collapse. Second, quantum actors have free will, and as such there is always a chance they will act in unexpected ways. This means uncertainty cannot be reduced beyond a certain point, no matter how much learning states do. Both the present and the future are radically open.

While this confirms Copeland's view that uncertainty about others' intentions is ineradicable, it does not warrant his repeated assertion that states *must* worry about potential material threats, because cultures of anarchy impose considerable structure on states' thinking. Even as wave functions, cultures make some outcomes more likely than others. Knowing you are in a Hobbesian culture leads to one set of plausible inferences about others' intentions, in a Kantian culture to quite another – and, indeed, it is only by participating in such cultures that states could know their own intentions, which only become determinate through ongoing cuts in their web of entanglement. As such, even the radical indeterminacy of a quantum world does not change the fundamental point that anarchy is what states make of it.

Ideas and material structure

A focus on the power of ideas is perhaps the most distinguishing feature of all constructivist IR scholarship. Yet many rationalists also think that ideas matter, and so in *Social Theory* I worked at length to clarify the relationship between the two approaches, highlighting several ways in which rationalism could be subsumed within a broader constructivist approach to world politics (cf. Fearon and Wendt 2002).

I still think that is broadly right, but I now see an important difference in how ideas can be conceptualized which requires some rethinking. The difference is between treating ideas as informational states of a machine or zombie vs. as meaningful states of consciousness. Rationalism defines ideas as information, which means they are objective phenomena knowable through a positivist epistemology. In *Social Theory* I embraced the alternative definition of ideas-as-meanings, but failed to clearly distinguish it from ideas-as-information, or to take seriously the fact that meanings presuppose consciousness, which poses problems

---

50 On the relevance of this distinction in social science, see Khalil (1997); cf. Hardin (2003).

for a positivist epistemology. In approaching anew how ideas relate to the material world, therefore, I want to frame the question more explicitly as how that world relates not to information but to 'meaningful states of consciousness.'

A phony distinction?

It is from this new starting point that I take up Behnke's claim that the question of what relationship obtains between ideas and material conditions is 'phony' because it neglects the conditions of possibility for distinguishing them in the first place, the notion of a distinction being itself an idea. Of course, in one sense this is trivially true, since only an intelligent species could formulate the 'idea' of a distinction. Thus, unless Behnke means to endorse philosophical idealism, in which it is ideas and nothing but ideas all the way down, the fact that the distinction between ideas and material conditions is itself an 'idea' is beside the point. However, his question of how we can justify the distinction is still important, since if by ideas we mean conscious ideas, then there simply is no basis for it in the classical, physicalist worldview. On that view, ideas can be nothing more than informational states of the human machine, which eliminates any fundamental distinction between them and the material world.

So how can we know there is one? The answer is first-person experience. There is 'something it is like' to have my ideas, which is essentially different from my experience of material objects. As a warrant for knowledge first-person experience has no standing in a positivist epistemology, according to which I should be a zombie. But I see no reason to believe that. Perhaps my positivist colleagues are zombies, but I have access to my own experience that they don't, which tells me that my ideas are qualitatively different from the material objects around me. It would be ironic if Behnke, a post-modernist, did not accept the evidence of his own experience and reach the same conclusion; but perhaps he is a zombie too.

This epistemic warrant for a distinction between ideas and material conditions still leaves us, however, with the question of how such a distinction is possible in the first place. In *Social Theory* I thought dualism was the answer, but a quantum approach offers a better solution, treating them as two aspects of one underlying reality. This ontology is compatible with both the third-person epistemology of positivism and the first-person epistemology of subjective experience, while avoiding the reduction of either. Instead, ideas and materiality stand in a relation of complementarity: individually incomplete, mutually exclusive descriptions of the same phenomenon.

Power and interest vs. ideas

This speaks to Copeland's realist argument that ultimately it is material factors – power and interest – that determine world politics, not ideas. Importantly, this assumes their relative weights can be meaningfully compared in the first place, as if variables in a regression equation, which in *Social Theory* I argued makes little sense. Material power is only 'power' insofar as it is meaningful, as shown by the relative threat to the US posed by five North Korean nuclear weapons versus 500 British ones. And interest is only 'interest' insofar as it is given content by ideas, as shown by the US failure to conquer the Bahamas. In each case, realism's ostensibly material factors turn out to be constituted largely by ideas; at best we are talking here about how one set of ideas ('realist' ones, perhaps) relates to another ('idealist'). As I argued in chapter 3, the only fair way to compare the relative importance of ideas and material conditions would be first to strip power and interest of their constituting ideas, isolating their brute or rump materiality (technology, geography, and human nature), and then seeing to what extent the latter constrains or causes the former. Were we to do this in IR, however, with its non-material corporate actors interacting in a space of shared meaning, it seems clear that ideas would be more important.

Nevertheless, there is a residual sense in *Social Theory* that, at least in principle, the relative importance of ideas and (rump) material conditions *could* be compared. This residual stems from the book's dualist ontology. From a quantum perspective this looks problematic. Instead of distinct substances that somehow interact, mind and matter are now complementary aspects of an underlying reality that is neither. When thinking about world politics from the standpoint of ideas we are in the realm of wave descriptions, and from a material standpoint in the realm of particle descriptions. Each is essential to IR scholarship, since human beings live in both worlds simultaneously. The relationship between the two is therefore not one of interaction (dualism) or reduction (materialism), but one of correlation. From this perspective it makes no more sense to compare the relative importance of ideas and material conditions than to compare that of waves and particles.

Problems of epistemology

Social Theory attempts to combine a positivist epistemology with an interpretivist ontology. In this last section I consider whether such a position is coherent in light of a quantum approach to social life, but first let me reiterate in what sense precisely *Social Theory* is 'positivist', since the term has two distinct meanings. It can refer broadly to a commitment to *science*, understood as a method for gaining knowledge about the world out there; or it can refer narrowly to a particular *philosophy* of science that privileges Humean causation, law-like generalizations, deductive theory, and so on. *Social Theory* is positivist only in the first, 'small-p' sense. Regarding the second it advocates an anti-positivist, realist philosophy of science, which privileges causal mechanisms, inference to the best explanation, and methodological pluralism. Although in *Social Theory* I thought I had kept these two meanings separate, the question of whether it is possible to combine 'positivism' and scientific realism continues to dog the book (e.g., Wight 2002; Brglez 2001). In the broad, small-p sense of the term the answer is clearly yes.

The most sustained and systematic critique of *Social Theory*'s epistemology is mounted by Kratochwil, who argues that I overlook the decisive role that sociology of knowledge considerations play in determining scientific truth – considerations stressed even by other scientific realists such as Bhaskar. Thus, he suggests that, rather than a neutral procedure for revealing an objective truth about Nature, science should instead be likened to a court, where socially determined burdens of proof are what count and truth is a function of consensus.

Kratochwil is certainly correct that accepting an important role for social factors in science is compatible with scientific realism. This is because, even though it implies a correspondence theory of truth and as such is foundationalist, its foundationalism is relatively weak. A strong foundationalism would be that scientists simply 'read off' the truth from reality, their discourse playing no role in producing the truth. Scientific realism rejects this naive position in favor of the view that all observation is theory-laden, which concedes an important role to discourse.

On the other hand, Kratochwil neglects the fact that it is also a fundamental assumption of scientific realism that reality constrains or regulates truth. Indeed, this is the case even in judicial proceedings. The notion that courts should try to ascertain and be governed by 'the facts' is a crucial assumption in modern judicial practice, and can lead to earlier court decisions being overturned if new facts come in; a court that refused to be constrained in this way would be a 'kangaroo' court, not a real one. To be sure, the facts may be hard to see through the fog of existing theory, and Kratochwil is correct that theories can be successful even if they do not refer correctly to reality (also see Wendt 1999: 65–7). But it is also the case that reality sometimes resists theories, and by probing this resistance scientists can bring the deep structure of reality more clearly into view. It would be hard otherwise to explain the quantum revolution; ultimately sub-atomic reality simply would not permit a classical description. In this light it is strange that Kratochwil sees my epistemology as 'monological' and his as 'dialogical'. I would say just the opposite. His view may be dialogical *among scientists*, but with respect to reality it is monological, since truth seems to be a matter for scientists alone to decide. Scientific realists would argue that just because something counts as true for us does not make it true: Nature too has a say.

For scientific realists the holy grail of this dialogue is a perfect third-person representation of Nature. Although it is perhaps never achievable in practice, we can approximate it through the discipline of objectivity, of making our measurements of Nature as passive and value free as possible. That there is at least the possibility of such an approximation is guaranteed by the classical assumption that subjects and objects are categorically distinct. If so, then we can expect that, when we ask a question of Nature in the proper way, we will get a true answer.

All of this assumes, however, that Nature has only one answer to give, that in the end there is a unitary truth because Nature can only 'be' one way. In the quantum world this is not the case. Quantum systems can 'be' two ways, particle and wave, which are irreducible, mutually exclusive, and individually incomplete. Quantum reality, it seems, always has 'two stories to tell' (cf. Hollis and Smith 1990), and so does not constitute the unitary reality constraint presupposed by even weak foundationalism. Instead, what we have is a kind of 'non-foundational foundationalism'.[51]

51 I thank Andreas Behnke for this suggestion.

When applied to social science the 'non-foundational' aspect of quantum theory points in two directions. First, we need to take more seriously the complementarity of Explanation and Understanding.[52] On the one hand, this means that the *Methodenstreit* between positivists and interpretivists is based on a false, classical premise. In quantum theory it would be absurd for the 'particle guys' to fight with the 'wave guys' about who has the truth, since the knowledge each offers is understood to be inherently partial, and so must be complemented with the other for a complete description. The 'Hobbesian' epistemological mentality one often sees in the social sciences today assumes that either Explanation or Understanding must constitute The One True Description, which from a quantum perspective is simply not the case. Instead, what we need is an 'epistemological Westphalia,' in which positivists and interpretivists recognize the other's contribution to their shared goal of comprehending social life.

More specifically, given that social science today is dominated by the positivist concern with the particle aspect of social life, what this means is taking the wave aspect – consciousness and meaning – seriously as well. In retrospect I do not feel I did that in *Social Theory*, where, despite my concern with the role of ideas in international life, I never mentioned consciousness and treated meaning as an object. To take consciousness and meaning seriously would require answering some hard methodological questions, given that consciousness is unavailable to objective, third-person inquiry. In particular, it would require coming to grips with the epistemological specificity of second- and perhaps even first-person[53] knowledge as ways of apprehending the social – in short, with the distinct requirements of a 'science of the subjective' (Jahn and Dunne 1997).[54] Of course, this has long been the argument of interpretivists, so in one sense I am saying nothing new here. But in my view most contemporary interpretivists do not take consciousness seriously either; since the post-modern 'death of the subject' many have observed the 'taboo of subjectivity' just as faithfully as positivists (cf. Freundlieb 2000). Were we to break it with the help of quantum theory, it would lead in the direction of a truly phenomenological sociology, along the lines of a Schutz, a Merleau-Ponty, or even a Collingwood, which at least in IR is not the dominant métier of interpretivists today.

The second direction in which quantum theory's non-foundationalism points is to take seriously the inherently participatory relationship of social science to its objects of inquiry. In quantum theory measurement is always productive: when we measure a quantum system we necessarily alter it.[55] This is because before the act of measurement the observer and observed are non-locally entangled – in the social context, by shared meanings – and as such parts of a larger whole. The 'cut' of measurement destroys this whole, and in so doing creates the distinction between

---

52 On quantum complementarity in the social sciences, see Apel (1984) and Rasmussen (1987).
53 For some suggestive thoughts on this case, see Rudolph and Rudolph (2003) and Petranker (2003).
54 On the role of these different kinds of knowledge in quantum theory, see Matsuno (2003).
55 Although there is debate between instrumentalists and realists about what precisely this entails.

subject and object, in what Erwin Schrödinger (1959) called the process of 'objectivation'. When the discipline of IR observes world politics, therefore, it is in effect also observing itself (cf. Albert 1999). This vitiates the positivist goal of perfect objectivity, but, importantly, it does not vitiate objectivity altogether. Rather, what it does, as feminist epistemologists have argued, is make objectivity inherently situated, or relative to a standpoint.[56]

I have only just begun to think about what such a participatory epistemology might entail for my own work, but it is clear that among other things it raises important normative questions. If IR scholars are irreducibly participants in the super-organism that is world politics, 'performing' (Weber 1998) or instantiating it holographically in our work, then we have ethical responsibilities to the other subjects of those politics in measuring them, responsibilities which we do not necessarily have if facts and values can be clearly separated as in the classical worldview. But with those responsibilities comes a capacity for collective self-consciousness that is otherwise largely missing in day-to-day international life, and as such is a basis for reflexivity and progressive change.

None of this will be news to post-modernists, and indeed the non-foundational aspect of quantum epistemology points strongly in their direction – although I'm not sure that quantum game theory is what they had in mind. But that quip also highlights the sense in which a quantum social science would still be foundation-alist. For, despite all the philosophical controversy that has surrounded quantum theory, there has never been any question that quantum physicists were doing *science*, understood as a method for gaining knowledge of the world out there. All physicists agree upon certain practices of scientific inquiry, and upon the principle that reality is a constraint on truth. It turns out that in the quantum context the reality constraint – the foundation – is not unitary, that there are always 'two stories to tell'. But this does not change the fact that, in doing physics, physicists are engaged not only in a monologue among themselves, but also in a dialogue with Nature, by which they feel constrained. In the social sciences matters are more complicated because our participation in 'Nature' is more immediate, but there too society constitutes an external reality to which proper scientific practice can provide epistemic access. Perhaps post-modernists would not reject foundational-ism in this non-unitary sense, but it does imply positivist forms of 'rigor' that some have been unwilling to embrace in the past.

Conclusion

It is common in social science today to disparage 'social physics' as a naïve way of approaching social life, one that has not proven fruitful for the development of theory and even been positively misleading. Besides, from a systems-theoretic standpoint such as *Social Theory*'s there seems little reason to think physics should be

---

56 See Haraway (1988) and, for a recent generalization beyond feminist theory, Heikes (2004). Cf. Rouse (2002).

relevant to social science anyway, since reality is stratified into multiple levels, each with its own laws of motion. Much better, then, to abandon physics envy and its implicit reductionism, and get on with theorizing about social life on its own terms. Or, if we must look to another science for foundations, let it be biology, which at least is concerned with *life*, not physics (Bernstein *et al.* 2000).

In dismissing social physics, however, what usually goes unremarked is that the models in question – corporate actors as billiard balls, utility as energy, rational actors as computational machines, and so on – are all taken from classical physics, not quantum. Thus, their perceived failure in social science could be one merely of the wrong kind of physics, not of physics *per se*. Indeed, if the argument of this chapter is right, then we should expect classical models to fail, since social life is not a classical phenomenon in the first place. Whether quantum models might do better therefore remains an open question.

Perhaps, but why do today's sophisticated social scientists need to bother with any physics, whether classical or quantum? What about the stratification of reality into multiple levels? The answer is that social life takes place in the physical world. Our bodies are physical and so is our material environment, which constrains and enables human behavior in important ways. Physics is our best description of that world, and one to which I suspect almost all social scientists, even post-modernists, would defer in thinking about what is possible in social life (no ghosts, no reincarnation, no telepathy, and so on). In this sense we are all philosophical naturalists. To be sure, this does not mean we can 'read off' social theories from physical ones, since society is an emergent phenomenon with its own specificity; and it may be that the methods of social science must differ in important ways from those of natural science. The relationship of physics to social science is one of *under*-determination, not determination. But as a metaphysical constraint it nevertheless plays a fundamental role in our work.

The question, then, is how to assert the autonomy of social science while giving physics its due. That is what this chapter, and indeed *Social Theory*, was about. Like most other social scientists, in my book I took for granted the classical description of reality as defining the metaphysical framework within which I had to work. The problem for me was that classical physics implies a materialist ontology, which does not – indeed cannot – take seriously that which is most uniquely social, namely consciousness and meaning. *Social Theory*'s solution was a Cartesian dualism, but dualism is probably wrong, and the going alternatives – also at least implicitly classical – not much better. Hence the attraction of a quantum approach, with its fundamentally different reality constraint. The quantum turn here, then, is ultimately problem-driven, rooted in an inability otherwise to reconcile consciousness and meaning with the material world.

That said, the quantum consciousness hypothesis is a radical, even desperate conjecture, for which there is only the most slender evidence so far. Despite its elegance as a solution to both the hard problem of consciousness and the problem of interpreting quantum theory, it will be years before we know whether it is true, or whether it scales up to the social level. This is a bet with long odds, in short, and so I am not advocating that quantum theory now be required reading in our graduate programs. However, given the track record of social science to date it is not clear the classical bet is any safer. Thus, until the natural sciences solve the mind–body problem the social sciences should keep their options open, and develop a quantum approach alongside its existing classical ones.

As can be seen from this chapter, a quantum social science would sometimes simply recapitulate or support existing social theories, perhaps especially post-modern ones such as performativity theory. Indeed, such redundancy is to be hoped for – if quantum ideas did not map at all onto existing social science, which is the best description we have of social life, then that would suggest that social life is not quantum mechanical. But skeptics might nevertheless see it as a problem, that quantum social science is just 'old wine in new bottles.' This value added question is an important one, and we will not be able to answer it until after a quantum social science has been developed. Nevertheless, there are several reasons to think that the transformative implications of such thinking could be profound. Long-standing metaphysical and methodological disputes might be resolved; substantive theorizing might benefit from new formalisms such as quantum game theory; empirical anomalies might be explained; and, as a bonus, if a quantum social science proved to be a success, it would be evidence that its foundation, the quantum consciousness hypothesis, is true.

However, the most basic contribution of a quantum perspective would be to enable social scientists to take consciousness and meaning seriously within a naturalistic worldview. At the moment social scientists are faced with a Hobson's choice between a positivism in which consciousness makes no difference and an interpretivism in which it has no naturalistic basis. Both approaches at least implicitly assume that human beings are classical systems. My argument in this chapter has ultimately been very simple: the difference that consciousness makes is quantum. In a sense this quantum naturalism reaffirms the goal of the *via media* between Explanation and Understanding, but in so doing jettisons the need for a 'path between' altogether, replacing it with a relationship of complementarity.

Let me close on a personal note by saying that, although hard work and at times disorienting, whether right or wrong I have very much enjoyed thinking about the possibilities raised in this chapter. For that I want to thank *Social Theory*'s critics, whose pointed questions forced me to reexamine its foundational assumptions, and Anna Leander and Stefano Guzzini, who gave me the opportunity to do so in a systematic, written form.

References

Abbott, Andrew (1988) 'Transcending general linear reality', *Sociological Theory* 6: 169–89.
—— (1992) 'From causes to events: notes on narrative positivism', *Sociological Methods and Research* 20: 428–55.
—— (1995) 'Things of boundaries', *Social Research* 62: 857–82.
—— (1997) 'Of time and space: the contemporary relevance of the Chicago School', *Social Forces* 75: 1149–82.
Adler, Emanuel (1997) 'Seizing the middle ground: constructivism in world politics', *European Journal of International Relations* 3(3): 319–63.
—— (2002) 'Constructivism and International Relations', in Walter Carlsnaes, Thomas Risse and Beth A. Simmons, eds, *Handbook of International Relations*, London: Sage, pp. 95–118.
Adler, Emanuel, and Michael Barnett (1996) 'Governing anarchy: a research agenda for the study of security communities', *Ethics and International Affairs* 10: 63–98.
——, eds (1998) *Security Communities*, Cambridge: Cambridge University Press.
Agassi, Joseph (1975) *Science in Flux*, Dordrecht: Reidel.
Agnew, John (1998) *Geopolitics: Re-visioning World Politics*, London and New York: Routledge.
Akrivoulis, Dimitrios (2002) 'The quantum metaphor in International Relations', PhD dissertation, University of Kent.
Albert, Mathias (1999) 'Observing world politics: Luhmann's systems theory of society and international relations', *Millennium: Journal of International Studies* 28(2): 239–65.
Albert, Mathias, David Jacobson and Yosef Lapid, eds (2001) *Identities, Borders, Orders: Rethinking International Relations Theory*, Minneapolis, MN: University of Minnesota Press.
Albrecht, Glenn (2000) 'Directionality theory: neo-organicism and dialectical complexity', *Democracy and Nature* 6(3): 401–19.
Alker, Hayward R. (2000) 'On learning from Wendt', *Review of International Studies* 26(1): 141–50.
Anderson, Benedikt (1991) *Imagined Communities: Reflections on the Origins and Spread of Nationalism*, London: Verso.
Apel, Karl-Otto (1984) *Understanding and Explanation: a Transcendental-Pragmatic Perspective*, trans. Georgia Warnke, Cambridge, MA: MIT Press.
Arfi, Badredine (2005) 'Resolving the trust predicament: a quantum game-theoretic approach', *Theory and Decision* 58(1): 1–48.
Aron, Raymond (1962) *Paix et guerre entre les nations*, 8th edn, Paris: Calmann-Lévy.
Arthur, W. Brian (1994) *Increasing Returns and Path Dependence in the Economy*, Ann Arbor, MI: University of Michigan Press.

Ashley, Richard K. (1986 [1984]) 'The poverty of neorealism', in Robert O. Keohane, ed., *Neorealism and its Critics*, New York: Columbia University Press, pp. 255–300.

—— (1987) 'The geopolitics of geopolitical space: toward a critical social theory of international politics', *Alternatives* XII(4): 403–34.

Atmanspacher, Harald (1997) 'Cartesian cut, Heisenberg cut, and the concept of complexity', *World Futures* 49: 333–55.

—— (2003) 'Mind and matter as asymptotically disjoint, inequivalent representations with broken time-reversal symmetry', *Biosystems* 68(1): 19–30.

—— (2004) 'Quantum theory and consciousness: an overview with selected examples', *Discrete Dynamics in Nature and Society* 1: 51–73.

Atmanspacher, Harald, Hartmann Romer and Harald Walach (2002) 'Weak quantum theory: complementarity and entanglement in physics and beyond', *Foundations of Physics* 32(2): 379–406.

Axelrod, Robert (1984) *The Evolution of Cooperation*, New York: Basic Books.

—— (1997) *The Complexity of Cooperation: Agent-Based Models of Competitions and Collaboration*, Princeton, NJ: Princeton University Press.

Barad, Karen (2003) 'Posthumanist performativity: toward an understanding of how matter comes to matter', *Signs* 28(3): 801–31.

Bartelson, Jens (1998) 'Second natures: is the state identical with itself?', *European Journal of International Relations* 4(3): 295–326.

Barth, Fredrik (1969) 'Introduction', in Fredrik Barth, ed., *Ethnic Groups and Boundaries: The Social Organization of Culture Difference*, Boston, MA: Little, Brown, pp. 9–38.

Basic Law for the Federal Republic of Germany (1995) Promulgated by the Parliamentary Council on 23 May 1949 (version in effect since 15 November 1994), official translation, Bonn: Press and Information Office of the Federal Government.

Baylis, John, and Steve Smith, eds (1998) *The Globalization of World Politics: An Introduction to International Relations*, Oxford: Oxford University Press.

Beck, Ulrich (1994) 'The reinvention of politics: towards a theory of reflexive modernization', in Ulrich Beck, Anthony Giddens and Scott Lash, eds, *Reflexive Modernization: Politics, Tradition and Aesthetics in the Modern Social Order*, Cambridge: Polity, pp. 1–55.

Becker, Theodore L., ed. (1991) *Quantum Politics: Applying Quantum Theory to Political Phenomena*, New York: Praeger.

Beitz, Charles (1979) *Political Theory and International Relations*, Princeton, NJ: Princeton University Press.

Belousek, Darrin (2003) 'Non-separability, non-supervenience, and quantum ontology', *Philosophy of Science* 70: 791–811.

Bennett, D. Scott, and Allan C. Stam (2004) *The Behavioral Origins of War*, Ann Arbor, MI: University of Michigan Press.

Bennett, Jane (2004) 'The force of things: steps toward an ecology of matter', *Political Theory* 32(3): 347–72.

Bennett, M. R., and P. M. S. Hacker (2003) *Philosophical Foundations of Neuroscience*, Oxford: Blackwell.

Berger, Peter, and Thomas Luckmann (1991 [1966]) *The Social Construction of Reality: A Treatise in the Sociology of Knowledge*, London: Penguin.

Bernstein, Steven, Richard Ned Lebow, Janice Gross Stein and Steven Weber (2000) 'God gave physics the easy problems', *European Journal of International Relations* 6(1): 43–76.

Bhaskar, Roy (1975) *A Realist Theory of Science*, Leeds: Leeds Books.

—— (1979) *The Possibility of Naturalism: A Philosophical Critique of the Contemporary Human Sciences*, Brighton: Harvester Press.

Bleiker, Roland (1997) 'Forget IR theory', *Alternatives* 22(1): 57–85.

Block, Ned, Owen J. Flanagan and Güven Güzeldere, eds (1997) *The Nature of Consciousness: Philosophical Debates*, Cambridge, MA: MIT Press.

Bohm, David (1980) *Wholeness and the Implicate Order*, London: Routledge.

—— (1990) 'A new theory of the relationship of mind and matter', *Philosophical Psychology* 3(2): 271–86.

BonJour, Laurence (1985) *The Structure of Empirical Knowledge*, Cambridge, MA: Harvard University Press.

Boudon, Raymond (1989) 'Die Erkenntnistheorie in Simmels "Philosophie des Geldes"', *Zeitschrift für Soziologie* 18: 413–25.

Bourdieu, Pierre (1980) *Le sens pratique*, Paris: Éditions de Minuit.

Bramhall, David (1986) 'Economics and Cartesian science', in Suzanne Helbrun and David Bramhall, eds, *Marx, Schumpeter, and Keynes: A Centenary Celebration of Dissent*, Armonk, NY: M. E. Sharpe, pp. 45–64.

Braudel, Fernand (1969) *Écrits sur l'histoire*, Paris: Flammarion.

Brewer, Marilynn (1991) 'The social self: on being the same and different at the same time', *Personality and Social Psychology Bulletin* 17(5): 475–82.

Brglez, Milan (2001) 'Reconsidering Wendt's meta-theory: blending scientific realism with social constructivism', *Journal of International Relations and Development* 4(4): 339–62.

Brooks, Stephen G. (1997) 'Dueling realisms', *International Organization* 51(3): 445–77.

Brubaker, Rogers (1992) *Citizenship and Nationhood in France and Germany*, Cambridge, MA: Harvard University Press.

—— (1995) 'National minorities, nationalizing states, and external national homelands in the new Europe', *Dædalus* 124: 107–32.

—— (1998) 'Myths and misconceptions in the study of nationalism', in John A. Hall, ed., *The State of the Nation: Ernest Gellner and the Theory of Nationalism*, Cambridge: Cambridge University Press, pp. 272–305.

Bukovansky, Mlada (1997) 'American identity and neutral rights from independence to the War of 1812', *International Organization* 51(2): 209–43.

Bull, Hedley (1966a) 'International theory: the case for a classical approach', *World Politics* XVIII(3): 361–77.

—— (1966b) 'Society and anarchy in international relations', in Herbert Butterfield and Martin Wight, eds, *Diplomatic Investigations: Essays in the Theory of International Relations*, Cambridge: Cambridge University Press, pp. 35–50.

—— (1984) *Justice in International Relations: The Hagey Lectures*, Waterloo, Ontario: University of Waterloo Press.

Bull, Hedley, and Adam Watson, eds (1984) *The Expansion of International Society*, Oxford: Clarendon Press.

Bundesminister der Verteidigung (1993) *Die Bundeswehr der Zukunft – Bundeswehrplan '94*, Bonn.

Bundesministerium der Verteidigung (1992) 'Militärpolitische und militärstrategische Grundlagen und konzeptionelle Grundrichtung der Neugestaltung der Bundeswehr', *Frankfurter Rundschau*, 20 February: 21.

—— (1994) *Weißbuch 1994: Weißbuch zur Sicherheit der Bundesrepublik Deutschland und zur Lage und Zukunft der Bundeswehr*, Bonn.

—— (1998) http://www.bundeswehr.de/sicherheitspolitik/unomissionen/einsaetze.htm (official website of the Federal Ministry of Defence, last updated 14 September 1998).

Burns, Tom, and Erik Engdahl (1998) 'The social construction of consciousness, part 1: collective consciousness and its socio-cultural foundations', *Journal of Consciousness Studies* 5(1): 67–85.

Butler, Judith (1997) *The Psychic Life of Power: Theories in Subjection*, Stanford, CA: Stanford University Press.

Buzan, Barry (2004) *From International to World Society? English School Theory and the Social Structure of Globalisation*, Cambridge: Cambridge University Press.

Buzan, Barry, and Richard Little (1996) 'Reconceptualizing anarchy: structural realism meets world history', *European Journal of International Relations* 2(4): 403–38.

Buzan, Barry, Charles Jones and Richard Little (1993) *The Logic of Anarchy: Neorealism to Structural Realism*, New York: Columbia University Press.

Byerly, Henry (1979) 'Teleology and evolutionary theory: mechanisms and meanings', *Nature and System* 1: 157–76.

Calhoun, Craig (1991) 'Indirect relationships and imagined communities: large-scale social integration and the transformation of everyday life', in Pierre Bourdieu and James S. Coleman, eds, *Social Theory for a Changing Society*, Boulder, CO: Westview Press, pp. 95–120.

—— (1997) *Nationalism*, Minneapolis: Minnesota University Press.

Campbell, David (1996) 'Political prosaics, transversal politics, and the anarchical world', in Michael J. Shapiro and Hayward R. Alker, eds, *Challenging Boundaries*, Minneapolis, MN: University of Minnesota Press, pp. 7–31.

—— (1998) *Writing Security: United States Foreign Policy and the Politics of Identity*, rev. edn, Manchester: Manchester University Press.

—— (2001) 'International engagements: the politics of North American International Relations theory', *Political Theory* 29: 432–49.

Carlsnaes, Walter (1992) 'The agency–structure problem in foreign policy analysis', *International Studies Quarterly* 36(3): 245–70.

Castellani, Elena, ed. (1998) *Interpreting Bodies: Classical and Quantum Objects in Modern Physics*, Princeton, NJ: Princeton University Press.

Cederman, Lars-Erik (2001a) 'Back to Kant: reinterpreting the democratic peace as a macrohistorical learning process', *American Political Science Review* 95: 15–31.

—— (2001b) 'Modelling the democratic peace as a Kantian selection process', *Journal of Conflict Resolution* 45: 470–502.

—— (2002a) 'Endogenizing geopolitical boundaries with agent-based modelling', *Proceedings of the National Academy* 99, suppl. 3: 7796–803.

—— (2002b) 'Nationalism and ethnicity', in Walter Carlsnaes, Thomas Risse and Beth Simmons, eds, *Handbook of International Relations*, London: Sage, pp. 409–28.

Cerny, Philip (1995) 'Globalization and collective action', *International Organization* 49(4): 595–626.

Chalmers, David J. (1996) *The Conscious Mind: In Search of a Fundamental Theory*, Oxford: Oxford University Press.

Chan, Steve (1997) 'In search of democratic peace: problems and promise', *Mershon International Studies Review* 41: 59–91.

Charon, Joel M. (1998) *Symbolic Interactionism: An Introduction, an Interpretation, an Integration*, Upper Saddle River, NJ: Prentice Hall.

Checkel, Jeffrey T. (1998) 'The constructivist turn in International Relations theory', *World Politics* 50(2): 324–48.

Clark, Andy (2003) *Natural Born Cyborgs: Minds, Technologies, and the Future of Human Intelligence*, Oxford: Oxford University Press.

Clark, Stuart (2000 [1985]) 'The *Annales* historians', in Quentin Skinner, ed., *The Return of Grand Theory in the Human Sciences*, Cambridge: Cambridge University Press, pp. 177–98.

Cohen, I. Bernhard (1994) 'Newton and the social sciences, with special reference to economics, or: the case of the missing paradigm', in Philip Mirowski, ed., *Natural Images in Economic Thought: Markets Read in Tooth and Claw*, Cambridge: Cambridge University Press, pp. 55–90.

Cohen, Michael D., Rick L. Riolo and Robert Axelrod (2001) 'The role of social structure in the maintenance of cooperative regimes', *Rationality and Society* 13: 5–32.

Cohen, Raymond (1994) 'Pacific unions: a reappraisal of the theory that "democracies" do not go to war with each other', *Review of International Studies* 20(3): 207–23.

Collins, Randall (1986) *Weberian Sociological Theory*, Cambridge: Cambridge University Press.

Connolly, William E. (2001) 'Cross-state citizen networks: a response to Dallmayr', *Millennium: Journal of International Studies* 30(2): 349–55.

Cooper, Alice H. (1997) 'When just causes conflict with acceptable means: the German peace movement and military intervention in Bosnia', *German Politics and Society* 15(3): 99–118.

Copeland, Dale C. (1999–2000) 'Trade expectations and the outbreak of peace: détente 1970–74 and the end of the Cold War 1985–91', *Security Studies* 9(1–2): 15–58.

—— (2000) *The Origins of Major War*, Ithaca, NY: Cornell University Press.

Coser, Lewis A. (1964) *The Functions of Social Conflict*, New York: Free Press.

Cox, Robert W. (1986 [1981]) 'Social forces, states and world orders: beyond International Relations theory (+ Postscript 1985)', in Robert O. Keohane, ed., *Neorealism and its Critiques*, New York: Columbia University Press, pp. 204–54.

Cronin, Bruce (1999) *Community Under Anarchy: Transnational Identity and the Evolution of Cooperation*, New York: Columbia University Press.

Daase, Christopher (1999) *Kleine Kriege – Große Wirkung: Wie unkonventionelle Kriegsführung die internationale Politik verändert*, Baden-Baden: Nomos.

Dallmayr, Fred (2001) 'Conversation across boundaries', *Millennium: Journal of International Studies* 30(2): 331–47.

Davidson, Donald (1963) 'Action, reasons, causes', *Journal of Philosophy* 60: 685–700.

Davies, Paul (2004) 'Does quantum mechanics play a non-trivial role in life?', *Biosystems* 78(1): 69–79.

De Quincey, Christian (2002) *Radical Nature: Rediscovering the Soul of Matter*, Montpelier, VT: Invisible Cities Press.

Der Derian, James (1995) 'Introduction: critical investigations', in James Der Derian, ed., *International Theory*, New York: New York University Press, pp. 4–9.

Derrida, Jacques (1992) *The Other Heading: Reflections on Today's Europe*, trans. Pascale-Anne Brault and Michael B. Naas, Bloomington and Indianapolis, IN: Indiana University Press.

—— (1998) *Monolingualism of the Other, or: the Prothesis of Origin*, trans. Patrick Mensah, Stanford, CA: Stanford University Press.

Dessler, David (1989) 'What is at stake in the agent–structure debate?', *International Organization* 43: 441–73.

Deutsch, Karl W. *et al.* (1957) *Political Community in the North Atlantic Area: International Organization in the Light of Historical Experience*, Princeton, NJ: Princeton University Press.

Deutscher Bundestag (1990a) *Plenarprotokoll*, Stenographischer Bericht, 11. Wahlperiode, 228. Sitzung, Berlin, 4 October: 18015–83.

—— (1990b) *Plenarprotokoll*, Stenographischer Bericht, 11. Wahlperiode, 235. Sitzung, Bonn, 15 November: 18819–59.

—— (1991a) *Plenarprotokoll*, Stenographischer Bericht, 12. Wahlperiode, 2. Sitzung, Bonn, 14 January: 21–43.

—— (1991b) *Plenarprotokoll*, Stenographischer Bericht, 12. Wahlperiode, 3. Sitzung, Bonn, 17 January: 45–55.

—— (1991c) *Plenarprotokoll*, Stenographischer Bericht, 12. Wahlperiode, 5. Sitzung, Bonn, 30 January: 67–93.

—— (1993a) *Plenarprotokoll*, Stenographischer Bericht, 12. Wahlperiode, 132. Sitzung, Bonn, 15 January: 11463–559.

—— (1993b) *Plenarprotokoll*, Stenographischer Bericht, 12. Wahlperiode, 151. Sitzung, Bonn, 21 April: 12925–3002.

—— (1994) *Plenarprotokoll*, Stenographischer Bericht, 12. Wahlperiode, 240. Sitzung, Bonn, 22 July: 21165–218.

—— (1995a) *Plenarprotokoll*, Stenographischer Bericht, 13. Wahlperiode, 48. Sitzung, Bonn, 30 June: 3953–4044.

—— (1995b) *Plenarprotokoll*, Stenographischer Bericht, 13. Wahlperiode, 76. Sitzung, Bonn, 6 December: 6631–708.

—— (1999) *Plenarprotokoll*, Stenographischer Bericht, 14. Wahlperiode, 31. Sitzung, Bonn, 26 March: 2561–618.

Diesing, Paul (1991) *How Social Science Works*, Pittsburgh, PA: University of Pittsburgh Press.

Doty, Roxanne Lynn (2000) 'Desire all the way down', *Review of International Studies* 26(1): 137–9.

Doyle, Michael (1983a) 'Kant, liberal legacies, and foreign affairs: part 1', *Philosophy and Public Affairs* 12(3): 205–35.

—— (1983b) 'Kant, liberal legacies, and foreign affairs: part 2', *Philosophy and Public Affairs* 12(4): 323–53.

Drulák, Petr (2001) 'The problem of structural change in Alexander Wendt's *Social Theory of International Politics*', *Journal of International Relations and Development* 4(4): 363–79.

Eberwein, Wolf-Dieter (1995) 'The future of international warfare: toward a global security community?', *International Political Science Review* 16(4): 341–60.

Ekstrom, Soren (2004) 'The mind beyond our immediate awareness: Freudian, Jungian, and cognitive models of the unconscious', *Journal of Analytical Psychology* 49: 657–82.

Elias, Norbert (1978) *What is Sociology?*, London: Hutchinson.

—— (1982 [1939]) *The Civilizing Process: State Formation and Civilization*, Oxford: Blackwell.

Elster, Jon (1989) *Nuts and Bolts for the Social Sciences*, Cambridge: Cambridge University Press.

Emirbayer, Mustafa (1997) 'Manifesto for a relational sociology', *American Journal of Sociology* 103: 281–317.

Emirbayer, Mustafa, and Jeff Goodwin (1994) 'Network analysis, culture, and the problem of agency', *American Journal of Sociology* 99: 1411–54.

Esfeld, Michael (2001) *Holism in Philosophy of Mind and Philosophy of Physics*, Dordrecht: Kluwer.

Fearon, James D. (1995) 'Rationalist explanations for war', *International Organization* 49(3): 379–414.

—— (1997) 'What is identity (as we now use the word)?', unpublished manuscript, University of Chicago, IL.

—— (1998) 'Commitment problems and the spread of ethnic conflict', in David A. Lake and Donald Rothchild, eds, *The International Spread of Ethnic Conflict*, Princeton, NJ: Princeton University Press, pp. 107–26.

Fearon, James D., and Alexander Wendt (2002) 'Rationalism *v*. constructivism: a skeptical view', in Walter Carlsnaes, Thomas Risse and Beth Simmons, eds, *Handbook of International Relations*, London: Sage, pp. 52–72.

Fierke, Karin M. (2002) 'Links across the abyss: language and logic in international relations', *International Studies Quarterly* 46(3): 331–54.

Finnemore, Martha (1996) *National Interests in International Society*, Ithaca, NY: Cornell University Press.

Finnemore, Martha, and Kathryn Sikkink (1998) 'International norm dynamics and political change', *International Organization* 52(4): 887–917.

Fischer, Joschka (1995) 'Die Katastrophe in Bosnien und die Konsequenzen für unsere Partei', *Blätter für deutsche und internationale Politik* 40(9): 1141–52.

Fodor, J. A. (1974) 'Special sciences (or: the disunity of science as a working hypothesis)', *Synthese* 28: 97–115.

'Forum on *Social Theory of International Politics*' (2000) *Review of International Studies* 26(1): 23–80.

Frankel, Benjamin (1996) 'Restating the realist case: an introduction', *Security Studies* 5(3): xiv–xx.

French, Steven (1998) 'On the withering away of physical objects', in Elena Castellani, ed., *Interpreting Bodies: Classical and Quantum Objects in Modern Physics*, Princeton, NJ: Princeton University Press, pp. 93–113.

Freundlieb, Dieter (2000) 'Why subjectivity matters: critical theory and the philosophy of the subject', *Critical Horizons* 1(2): 229–45.

Fukuyama, Francis (1992) *The End of History and the Last Man*, New York: Avon Books.

Gabora, Liane (2002) 'Amplifying phenomenal information: toward a fundamental theory of consciousness', *Journal of Consciousness Studies* 9(8): 3–29.

Gadamer, Hans-Georg (1990 [1960]) *Wahrheit und Methode: Grundzüge einer philosophischen Hermeneutik*, Tübingen: J. C. B. Mohr.

Gagnon, V. P. Jr (1998) '"Bosnian federation" and the institutionalizaton of ethnic division', paper presented at the workshop 'Nationalism, Federalism, and Secession', Cornell University.

Gallese, Vittorio (2001) 'The "shared manifold" hypothesis: from mirror neurons to empathy', *Journal of Consciousness Studies* 8(5–7): 33–50.

Gaskins, Richard (1992) *Burdens of Proof in Modern Discourse*, New Haven, CT: Yale University Press.

Gellner, Ernest (1964) *Thought and Change*, London: Weidenfeld & Nicolson.

—— (1983) *Nations and Nationalism*, Ithaca, NY: Cornell University Press.

Genscher, Hans-Dietrich (1990) 'Address of the foreign minister at the 45th General Assembly of the United Nations on 26 September 1990 in New York, Presse und Informationsamt der Bundesregierung', *Bulletin* 115 (27 September): 1201–6.

Giddens, Anthony (1979) *Central Problems in Social Theory: Action, Structure, and Contradiction in Social Analysis*, Berkeley, CA: University of California Press.

—— (1984) *The Constitution of Society: Outline of a Theory of Structuration*, Berkeley, CA: University of California Press.

—— (1990) *The Consequences of Modernity*, Cambridge: Polity.

Gilbert, Margaret (1989) *On Social Facts*, Princeton, NJ: Princeton University Press.

Gilpin, Robert (1981) *War and Change in World Politics*, New York: Cambridge University Press.

Glaser, Charles L. (1992) 'Political consequences of military strategy: expanding and refining the spiral and deterrence models', *World Politics* 44(2): 497–538.

—— (1994–5) 'Realists as optimists: cooperation as self-help', *International Security* 19(3): 50–90.

—— (1997) 'The security dilemma revisited', *World Politics* 50(1): 171–201.

Gleditsch, Kristian S., and Michael D. Ward (2000) 'War and peace in space and time: the role of democratization', *International Studies Quarterly* 44(1): 1–29.

Glymour, Bruce, Marcelo Sabatés and Andrew Wayne (2001) 'Quantum java: the upwards percolation of quantum indeterminacy', *Philosophical Studies* 103(3): 271–83.

Goffman, Erving (1959) *The Presentation of Self in Everyday Life*, Garden City, NY: Doubleday.

Goldstein, Judith, and Robert O. Keohane (1993) 'Ideas and foreign policy: an analytical framework', in Judith Goldstein and Robert O. Keohane, eds, *Ideas and Foreign Policy: Beliefs, Institutions, and Political Change*, Ithaca, NY: Cornell University Press, pp. 3–30.

Gourevitch, Philip (1998) *We Wish to Inform You that Tomorrow We Will be Killed with our Families: Stories from Rwanda*, New York: Farrar, Straus & Giroux.

Griffin, David Ray (1998) *Unsnarling the World-Knot: Consciousness, Freedom, and the Mind–Body Problem*, Berkeley, CA: University of California Press.

Griffin, Larry J., and Marcel Van der Linden, eds (1999) *New Methods for Social History*, *International Review of Social History*, supplement 6.

Grush, Rick, and Patricia Churchland (1995) 'Gaps in Penrose's toilings', *Journal of Consciousness Studies* 2(1): 10–29.

Guzzini, Stefano (1993) 'Structural power: the limits of neorealist power analysis', *International Organization* 47(3): 443–78.

—— (1998) *Realism in International Relations and International Political Economy: The Continuing Story of a Death Foretold*, London and New York: Routledge.

—— (2000a) 'A reconstruction of constructivism in International Relations', *European Journal of International Relations* 6(2): 147–82.

—— (2000b) 'Strange's oscillating realism: opposing the ideal – and the apparent', in Thomas C. Lawton, James N. Rosenau and Amy C. Verdun, eds, *Strange Power: Shaping the Parameters of International Relations and International Political Economy*, Aldershot: Ashgate, pp. 215–28.

—— (2001) 'Calling for a less "brandish" and less "grand" reconvention', *Review of International Studies* 27(3): 495–501.

Guzzini, Stefano, and Anna Leander (2001) 'A social theory for International Relations: an appraisal of Alexander Wendt's disciplinary and theoretical synthesis', *Journal of International Relations and Development* 4(4): 316–38.

Guzzini, Stefano, Heikki Patomäki and R. B. J. Walker (1995) 'Possibilities and limits of republican world politics: a concluding trialogue', in Heikki Patomäki, ed., *Peaceful Changes in World Politics*, Tampere: Tampere Peace Research Institute, pp. 404–30.

Haack, Susan (1993) *Evidence and Inquiry: Towards Reconstruction in Epistemology*, Oxford: Blackwell.

Haas, Ernst B. (1990) *When Knowledge is Power: Three Models of Change in International Organizations*, Berkeley, CA: University of California Press.

Habermas, Jürgen (1993 [1986]) 'A kind of settlement of damages: the apologetic tendencies in German history writing', in *Forever under the Shadow of Hitler? Original Documents of the Historikerstreit, the Controversy Concerning the Singularity of the Holocaust*, trans. James Knowlton and Truett Cates, Atlantic Highlands, NJ: Humanities Press, pp. 34–44 [reprinted from *Die Zeit*, 11 July 1986].

Hagan, Scott, Stuart Hameroff and Jack Tuszynski (2002) 'Quantum computation in brain microtubules: decoherence and biological feasibility', *Physical Review E* 65(061901): 1–10.

Hall, Rodney Bruce (1997) 'Moral authority as a power resource', *International Organization* 51(4): 591–622.

—— (1999) *National Collective Identity: Social Constructs and International Systems*, New York: Columbia University Press.

Hall, Todd (2003) 'Getting emotional: toward a theory of emotions for International Relations', master's thesis, University of Chicago, IL.

Hameroff, Stuart (2001) 'Biological feasibility of quantum approaches to consciousness', in Philip van Loocke, ed., *The Physical Nature of Consciousness*, Philadelphia, PA: John Benjamins, pp. 1–61.

Hameroff, Stuart, and Roger Penrose (1996) 'Conscious events as orchestrated space–time selections', *Journal of Consciousness Studies* 3(1): 36–53.

Haraway, Donna (1988) 'Situated knowledges: the science question in feminism and the privilege of partial perspective', *Feminist Studies* 14(3): 575–99.

Hardin, Russell (1995) *One for All: The Logic of Group Conflict*, Princeton, NJ: Princeton University Press.

—— (2003) *Indeterminacy and Society*, Princeton, NJ: Princeton University Press.

Harré, Rom (1985) *The Philosophies of Science: An Introductory Survey*, new edn, Oxford: Oxford University Press.

—— (1986) *Varieties of Realism: A Rationale for the Natural Sciences*, Oxford: Blackwell.

Hasenclever, Andreas, Peter Mayer and Volker Rittberger (1997) *Theories of International Regimes*, Cambridge: Cambridge University Press.

Hedström, Peter, and Richard Swedberg, eds (1998) *Social Mechanisms: An Analytical Approach to Social Theory*, Cambridge: Cambridge University Press.

Heikes, Deborah (2004) 'The bias paradox: why it's not just for feminists anymore', *Synthese* 138(3): 315–35.

Held, Carsten (1994) 'The meaning of complementarity', *Studies in the History and Philosophy of Science* 25(6): 871–93.

Helle, Horst Jürgen (1988) *Soziologie und Erkenntnistheorie bei Georg Simmel*, Darmstadt: Wissenschaftliche Buchgesellschaft.

Hempel, Carl G. (1965) *Aspects of Scientific Explanation and other Essays in the Philosophy of Science*, London: Free Press.

Hiley, Basil J., and Paavo Pylkkänen (2001) 'Naturalizing the mind in a quantum framework', in Paavo Pylkkänen and Tere Vaden, eds, *Dimensions of Conscious Experience*, Amsterdam: John Benjamins, pp. 119–44.

Hintze, Otto (1975) 'The formation of states and constitutional development: a study in history and politics', in *The Historical Essays of Otto Hintze*, ed. Felix Gilbert, New York: Oxford University Press, pp. 157–77.

Ho, Mae-Wan (1998) *The Rainbow and the Worm: The Physics of Organisms*, 2nd edn, Singapore: World Scientific.

Hobbes, Thomas (1968 [1651]) *Leviathan*, Harmondsworth: Penguin.

Hobden, Stephen, and John M. Hobson, eds (2002) *Historical Sociology of International Relations*, Cambridge: Cambridge University Press.

Hodgson, David (2002) 'Quantum physics, consciousness, and free will', in Robert Kane, ed., *The Oxford Handbook of Free Will*, Oxford: Oxford University Press, pp. 85–110.

Hoffmeyer, Jesper (1996) *Signs of Meaning in the Universe*, trans. Barbara J. Haveland, Bloomington, IN: Indiana University Press.

Hollis, Martin, and Steve Smith (1990) *Explaining and Understanding International Relations*, Oxford: Clarendon Press.

—— (1991) 'Beware of gurus: structure and action in international relations', *Review of International Studies* 17(4): 393–410.

—— (1992) 'Structure and action: further comment', *Review of International Studies* 18(2): 187–88.

Holsti, K. J. (1985) *The Dividing Discipline: Hegemony and Diversity in International Theory*, Boston, MA: Allen & Unwin.

Home, Dipankar (1997) *Conceptual Foundations of Quantum Physics*, New York: Plenum.

Hont, Istvan (1994) 'The permanent crisis of a divided mankind: "contemporary crisis of the nation state" in historical perspective', *Political Studies* XLII: 166–231.

Hopf, Ted (1998) 'The promise of constructivism in International Relations theory', *International Security* 23(1): 171–200.

—— (2000) 'Constructivism all the way down', *International Politics* 37(3): 369–78.

Horowitz, Donald L. (1975) 'Ethnic identity', in N. Glazer and D. P. Moynihan, eds, *Ethnicity: Theory and Experience*, Cambridge, MA: Harvard University Press, pp. 111–40.

Hosek, Jennifer, and Walter Freeman (2001) 'Osmetic ontogenesis, or olfaction becomes you: the neurodynamic, intentional self and its affinities with the Foucaultian/ Butlerian subject', *Configurations* 9(3): 509–42.

Howes, Dustin (2003) 'When states choose to die', *International Studies Quarterly* 47(4): 669–92.

Humphreys, Paul (1997) 'How properties emerge', *Philosophy of Science* 64(1): 1–17.

Huntley, Wade (1996) 'Kant's third image: systemic sources of the liberal peace', *International Studies Quarterly* 40: 45–76.

Inayatullah, Naeem, and David L. Blaney (1996) 'Knowing encounters: beyond parochialism in International Relations theory', in Yosef Lapid and Friedrich Kratochwil, eds, *The Return of Culture and Identity in IR Theory*, Boulder, CO, and London: Lynne Rienner, pp. 65–84.

Jackson, Patrick Thaddeus (2001) 'Constructing thinking space: Alexander Wendt and the virtues of engagement', *Cooperation and Conflict* 36(1): 109–20.

Jackson, Patrick Thaddeus, and Daniel H. Nexon (1999) 'Relations before states: substance, process and the study of world politics', *European Journal of International Relations* 5(3): 291–332.

Jaeger, Hans-Martin (1996) 'Konstruktionsfehler des Konstruktivismus in den Internationalen Beziehungen', *Zeitschrift für Internationale Beziehungen* 3(2): 313–40.

Jahn, Robert, and Brenda Dunne (1997) 'Science of the subjective', *Journal of Scientific Exploration* 11(2): 201–24.

Jepperson, Ronald L., Alexander Wendt and Peter J. Katzenstein (1996) 'Norms, identity and culture in national security', in Peter J. Katzenstein, ed., *The Culture of National Security*, New York: Columbia University Press, pp. 33–75.

Jervis, Robert (1976) *Perception and Misperception in International Politics*, Princeton, NJ: Princeton University Press.

—— (1978) 'Cooperation under the security dilemma', *World Politics* 30(2): 167–214.

—— (1998) 'Realism and the study of world politics', *International Organization* 52(4): 971–91.

—— (1999) 'Realism, neoliberalism, and cooperation: understanding the debate', *International Security* 24(1): 42–63.

Jervis, Robert, and Robert J. Art (1985) 'The meaning of anarchy', in Robert Jervis and Robert J. Art, eds, *International Politics: Enduring Concepts and Contemporary Issues*, Boston, MA: Little, Brown.

Jibu, Mari, and Kunio Yasue (1995) *Quantum Brain Dynamics and Consciousness: An Introduction*, Amsterdam: John Benjamins.

Joffe, Josef (1994) 'Abschied von der "Kohl-Doktrin"', *Süddeutsche Zeitung*, 16 December: 4.

Jordan, J. Scott (1998) 'Recasting Dewey's critique of the reflex-arc concept via a theory of anticipatory consciousness', *New Ideas in Psychology* 16(3): 165–87.

Kahler, Miles (1999) 'Evolution, choice, and international change', in David A. Lake and Robert Powell, eds, *Strategic Change and International Relations*, Princeton, NJ: Princeton University Press, pp. 165–96.

230   *References*

Kaiser, Karl, and Klaus Becher (1992) *Deutschland und der Irak-Konflikt: Internationale Sicherheitsverantwortung Deutschlands und Europas nach der deutschen Vereinigung*, Bonn: Europa Union Verlag.

Kaldor, Mary (1999) *New and Old Wars: Organized Violence in a Global Era*, Cambridge: Polity.

Kant, Immanuel (1970a) 'Idea for a universal history with a cosmopolitan purpose', in *Kant's Political Writings*, ed. Hans Reiss, Cambridge: Cambridge University Press, pp. 41–53.

—— (1970b) 'The metaphysics of morals', in *Kant's Political Writings*, ed. Hans Reiss, Cambridge: Cambridge University Press, pp. 131–75.

—— (1970c) 'Perpetual peace: a philosophical sketch', in *Kant's Political Writings*, ed. Hans Reiss, Cambridge: Cambridge University Press, pp. 116–30.

Kantorowitz, Arthur (1975) 'Controlling technology democratically', *American Scientist* 63(5): 505–9.

Kaplan, Morton A. (1957) *System and Process in International Politics*, New York: John Wiley.

Katzenstein, Peter J. (1996a) 'Introduction: alternative perspectives on national security', in Peter J. Katzenstein, ed., *The Culture of National Security: Norms and Identity in World Politics*, New York: Columbia University Press, pp. 1–32.

——, ed. (1996b) *The Culture of National Security: Norms and Identity in World Politics*, New York: Columbia University Press.

Katzenstein, Peter, Robert O. Keohane and Stephen D. Krasner (1998) '*International Organization* and the study of world politics', *International Organization* 52(4): 645–85.

——, eds (1999) *Exploration and Contestation in the Study of World Politics*, Cambridge, MA: MIT Press.

Keck, Otto (1995) 'Rationales kommunikatives Handeln in den internationalen Beziehungen: ist eine Verbindung von rational choice und Habermas' Theorie des kommunikativen Handelns möglich?', *Zeitschrift für Internationale Beziehungen* 2(1): 5–48.

Keohane, Robert O. (1984) *After Hegemony: Cooperation and Discord in the World Political Economy*, Princeton, NJ: Princeton University Press.

—— (1989 [1988]) 'International institutions: two approaches', in Robert O. Keohane, ed., *International Institutions and State Power: Essays in International Relations Theory*, Boulder, CO: Westview Press, pp. 158–79.

—— (2000) 'Ideas part way down', *Review of International Studies* 26(1): 125–30.

Keohane, Robert O., and Joseph S. Nye, Jr. (1977) *Power and Interdependence: World Politics in Transition*, Boston, MA: Little, Brown.

Khalil, Elias (1997) 'Chaos theory versus Heisenberg's uncertainty: risk, uncertainty and economic theory', *American Economist* 41(2): 27–40.

—— (2003) 'The context problematic, behavioral economics and the transactional view', *Journal of Economic Methodology* 10(2): 107–30.

King, Gary, Robert O. Keohane and Sidney Verba (1994) *Designing Social Inquiry: Scientific Inference in Qualitative Research*, Princeton, NJ: Princeton University Press.

Kinkel, Klaus (1994) 'Peacekeeping missions: Germany can now play its part', *NATO Review* 42(5): 3–7.

Kirk, Robert (1997) 'Consciousness, information, and external relations', *Communication and Cognition* 30(3–4): 249–72.

Kissinger, Henry A. (1957) *A World Restored: The Politics of Conservatism in a Revolutionary Era*, London: Victor Gollancz.

—— (1994) *Diplomacy*, New York: Simon & Schuster.

Klein, Bradley S. (1994) *Strategic Studies and World Order: The Global Politics of Deterrence*, Cambridge: Cambridge University Press.

Klotz, Audie (1995) 'Norms reconstituting interests: global racial equality and US sanctions against South Africa', *International Organization* 49(3): 451–78.

Klotz, Audie, and Cecilia Lynch (1998) 'Conflicted constructivism? Positivist leanings vs. interpretivist meanings', paper presented at the annual meeting of the International Studies Association, Minneapolis, MN, March 1998.

—— (2001) 'Constructing world politics: strategies for research', unpublished book manuscript.

Kohl, Helmut (1990) 'Message on the day of German unification on 3 October 1990 to all governments of the world, Presse und Informationsamt der Bundesregierung', *Bulletin* 118 (5 October): 1227–8.

Koslowski, Roy and Friedrich Kratochwil (1994) 'Understanding change in international politics: the Soviet Empire's demise and the international system', *International Organization* 48(2): 215–47.

Kowert, Paul, and Jeffrey W. Legro (1996) 'Norms, identity and their limits: a theoretical reprise', in Peter J. Katzenstein, ed., *The Culture of National Security: Norms and Identity in World Politics*, New York: Columbia University Press, pp. 451–97.

Krasner, Stephen D., ed. (1983) *International Regimes*, Ithaca, NY: Cornell University Press.

—— (1985) 'Toward understanding in International Relations', *International Studies Quarterly* 29(1): 137–44.

—— (2000) 'Wars, hotel fires, and plane crashes', *Review of International Studies* 26(1): 131–6.

Kratochwil, Friedrich (1989) *Rules, Norms and Decisions: On the Conditions of Practical and Legal Reasoning in International Relations and Domestic Affairs*, Cambridge: Cambridge University Press.

Kratochwil, Friedrich, and John Gerard Ruggie (1986) 'International organization: a state of the art on an art of the state', *International Organization* 40(4): 753–75.

Kubálková, Vendulka, Nicholas Greenwood Onuf and Paul Kowert (1998) 'Constructing constructivism', in Vendulka Kubálková, Nicholas Greenwood Onuf and Paul Kowert, eds, *International Relations in a Constructed World*, Armonk, NY, and London: M. E. Sharpe, pp. 3–21.

Kydd, Andrew (1997a) 'Game theory and the spiral model', *World Politics* 49(3): 371–400.

—— (1997b) 'Sheep in sheep's clothing: why security-seekers do not fight each other', *Security Studies* 7(1).

Labs, Eric (1997) 'Beyond victory: offensive realism and the expansion of war aims', *Security Studies* 6(4): 1–49.

Lakatos, Imre (1970) 'Falsification and the methodology of scientific research programmes', in Imre Lakatos and Alan Musgrave, eds, *Criticism and the Growth of Knowledge*, Cambridge: Cambridge University Press, pp. 91–196.

Laloe, Franck (2001) 'Do we really understand quantum mechanics?', *American Journal of Physics* 69(9): 655–701.

Lapid, Yosef (1989) 'The third debate: on the prospects of international theory in a post-positivist era', *International Studies Quarterly* 33(3): 235–54.

Lapid, Yosef, and Friedrich Kratochwil (1996) 'Revisiting the "national": toward an identity agenda in neorealism?', in Yosef Lapid and Friedrich Kratochwil, eds, *The Return of Culture and Identity in IR Theory*, Boulder, CO: Lynne Rienner, pp. 105–26.

Latsch, Wolfram (2003) 'Androids and agents: do we need a non-computational economics?', *Journal of Economic Methodology* 10(3): 375–96.

Layder, Derek (1985) 'Beyond empiricism? The promise of realism', *Philosophy of the Social Sciences* 15(3).

Leander, Anna (2000) 'A "nebbish presence": the neglect of sociological institutionalism in international political economy', in Ronen Palan, ed., *Global Political Economy: Contemporary Theories*, London and New York: Routledge, pp. 184–96.

—— (2001a) 'Dependency today: finance, firms, mafias and the state', *Third World Quarterly* 22(1): 115–28.

—— (2001b) 'The globalisation debate: dead-ends and tensions to explore', *Journal of International Relations and Development* 4(3): 274–85.

—— (2001c) 'Pierre Bourdieu on economics', *Review of International Political Economy* 8(2): 344–53.

—— (2004) 'Globalisation and the state monopoly on the legitimate use of force', *Politologiske Skrifter* (7) (www.sam.sdu.dk/politics/publikationer/skriftserier.htm).

—— (2005) 'The market for force and public security: the destabilizing consequences of private military companies', *Journal of Peace Research* 42(5): 605–22.

—— (2006) 'Shifting political identities and global governance of the justified use of force', in Markus Lederer and Phillip S. Müller, eds, *Criticizing Global Governance*, London and New York: Palgrave Macmillan, pp. 125–43.

Legro, Jeffrey W. (2000) 'The transformation of policy ideas', *American Journal of Political Science* 44(3): 419–32.

Lessnoff, Michael (1990) 'Introduction: social contract', in Michael Lessnoff, ed., *Social Contract Theory*, New York: New York University Press, pp. 1–9.

Levine, Joseph (2001) *Purple Haze: The Puzzle of Consciousness*, Oxford: Oxford University Press.

Levy, Jack S. (1987) 'Declining power and the preventive motive for war', *World Politics* 40(1): 82–107.

—— (1988) 'Domestic politics and war', *Journal of Interdisciplinary History* XVIII(4): 653–73.

—— (1994) 'Learning and foreign policy: sweeping a conceptual minefield', *International Organization* 48(2): 279–312.

Lewis, David (1987) *On the Plurality of Worlds*, Oxford: Blackwell.

Linklater, Andrew (1996) 'The achievements of critical theory', in Steve Smith, Ken Booth and Marysia Zalewski, eds, *International Theory: Positivism and Beyond*, Cambridge: Cambridge University Press, pp. 279–98.

Litfin, Karen (2003) 'Towards an integral perspective on world politics', *Millennium: Journal of International Studies* 32(1): 29–56.

Lockwood, Michael (1989) *Mind, Brain and the Quantum: The Compound 'I'*, Oxford: Blackwell.

Luhmann, Niklas (1984) *Soziale Systeme*, Frankfurt am Main: Suhrkamp.

—— (1997) *Die Gesellschaft der Gesellschaft*, Frankfurt am Main: Suhrkamp.

Lynn-Jones, Sean M. (1998) 'Realism and America's rise: a review essay', *International Security* 23(2): 157–82.

Lynn-Jones, Sean M., and Steven E. Miller (1995) 'Preface', in Michael E. Brown, Sean M. Lynn-Jones and Steven E. Miller, eds, *Perils of Anarchy: Contemporary Realism and International Security*, Cambridge, MA: MIT Press, pp. ix–xiii.

Mackie, John J. (1974) *The Cement of the Universe: A Study of Causation*, Oxford: Clarendon Press.

MacMillan, John (1995) 'A Kantian protest against the peculiar discourse of inter-liberal state peace', *Millennium: Journal of International Studies* 24(3): 549–62.

McTaggart, Lynne (2002) *The Field: The Quest for the Secret Force of the Universe*, New York: HarperCollins.

Major-Poetzl, Pamela (1983) *Michel Foucault's Archaeology of Western Culture: Toward a New Science of History*, Chapel Hill, NC: University of North Carolina Press.

Malin, Shimon (2001) *Nature Loves to Hide*, Oxford: Oxford University Press.

March, James G., and Johan P. Olsen (1998) 'The institutional dynamics of international political orders', *International Organization* 52(4): 943–69.

Margulis, Lynn (2001) 'The conscious cell', *Annals of the New York Academy of Sciences* 929: 55–70.

Matheny, Albert R., and Bruce A. Williams (1981) 'Scientific disputes and advisory procedures in policy making: an evaluation of the Science Court', *Law and Policy Quarterly* 3: 341–64.

Mathews, Freya (2003) *For Love of Matter: A Contemporary Panpsychism*, Albany, NY: SUNY Press.

Matson, Floyd (1964) *The Broken Image: Man, Science, and Society*, New York: George Brazilier.

Matsuno, Koichiro (2003) 'Quantum mechanics in first, second and third person descriptions', *Biosystems* 68(2–3): 107–18.

Maturana, Humberto R., and Francisco J. Varela (1992) *The Tree of Knowledge: The Biological Roots of Human Understanding*, London: Shambhala Publications.

Mead, George H. (1934) *Mind, Self and Society: From the Standpoint of a Social Behaviorist*, Chicago, IL: University of Chicago Press.

Mearsheimer, John J. (1994–5) 'The false promise of international institutions', *International Security* 19(1): 5–49.

Mercer, Jonathan (1995) 'Anarchy and identity', *International Organization* 49(2): 229–52.

Meyer, John W., John Boli and George M. Thomas (1987) 'Ontology and rationalization in the Western cultural account', in George M. Thomas, John W. Meyer, Francisco O. Ramirez and John Boli, eds, *Institutional Structure: Constituting State, Society and the Individual*, Newbury Park, CA: Sage, pp. 2–37.

Milgram, Stanley (1974) *Obedience and Authority*, New York: Harper & Row.

Mill, John Stuart (1975 [1859]) *On Liberty*, ed. David Spitz, New York: Norton.

Miller, Dale (1992) 'Agency as a quantum-theoretic parameter', *Nanobiology* 1: 361–71.

Miller, Richard W. (1987) *Fact and Method: Explanation, Confirmation and Reality in the Natural and the Social Sciences*, Princeton, NJ: Princeton University Press.

Milliken, Jennifer (1999) 'The study of discourse in international relations: a critique of research and methods', *European Journal of International Relations* 5(2): 225–54.

Mirowski, Philip (1988) *Against Mechanism*, Totowa, NJ: Rowman & Littlefield.

Mirowski, Philip, and Koye Somefun (1998) 'Markets as evolving computational entities', *Journal of Evolutionary Economics* 8(4): 329–56.

Mitzen, Jennifer (2004) 'Ontological security in world politics', manuscript, Ohio State University, OH.

Moravcsik, Andrew (1997) 'Taking preferences seriously: a liberal theory of international politics', *International Organization* 51(4): 513–55.

Morgenthau, Hans J. (1936) 'Positivisme mal compris et théorie réaliste du droit international', in *Tirade aparte de la 'Colección de Estudios históricos, jurídicos, pedagógicos y literarios': homenaje a D. Rafael Altamira*, Madrid, 20 pp.

—— (1948) *Politics Among Nations: The Struggle for Power and Peace*, New York: Knopf.

—— (1985) *Politics Among Nations: The Struggle for Power and Peace*, 6th edn, New York: Knopf.

Müller, Harald (1994) 'Internationale Beziehungen als kommunikatives Handeln: Zur Kritik der utilitaristischen Handlungstheorien', *Zeitschrift für Internationale Beziehungen* 1(1): 15–44.

—— (1995) 'Spielen hilft nicht immer: Die Grenzen des Rational-Choice-Ansatzes und der Platz der Theorie kommunikativen Handelns in der Analyse internationaler Beziehungen', *Zeitschrift für Internationale Beziehungen* 2(2): 379–99.

Munro, William (1928) 'Physics and politics – an old analogy revised', *American Political Science Review* 22(1): 1–11.

Mutz, Reinhard (1993) 'Die Bundeswehr steht am Ende ihrer Geschichte als Friedensarmee', *Frankfurter Rundschau*, 16 July: 10.

Nadeau, Robert, and Menas Kafatos (1999) *The Non-Local Universe: The New Physics and Matters of the Mind*, Oxford: Oxford University Press.

Nagel, Thomas (1974) 'What is it like to be a bat?', *Philosophical Review* 83(4): 435–50.

—— (1979) 'Panpsychism', in *Mortal Questions*, Cambridge: Cambridge University Press, pp. 181–95.

—— (1986) *The View from Nowhere*, Oxford: Oxford University Press.

Nakagomi, Teruaki (2003) 'Quantum monadology: a consistent world model for consciousness and physics', *Biosystems* 69(1): 27–38.

Nemedi, Denes (1995) 'Collective consciousness, morphology, and collective representations: Durkheim's sociology of knowledge, 1894–1900', *Sociological Perspectives* 38(1): 41–56.

Neumann, Iver B. (2001) *Mening, materialitet, makt: en innføring i diskursanalyse*, Bergen: Fakbogforlaget.

Newton-Smith, William H. (1990) *The Rationality of Science*, London: Routledge.

Nisbet, Robert A. (1966) *The Sociological Tradition*, New York: Basic Books.

Nye, Joseph S., Jr. (1987) 'Nuclear learning and US–Soviet security regimes', *International Organization* 41(3): 371–402.

Onuf, Nicholas Greenwood (1989) *World of our Making: Rules and Rule in Social Theory and International Relations*, Columbia, SC: University of South Carolina Press.

Ostrom, Elinor (1998) 'A behavioral approach to the rational choice theory of collective action', *American Political Science Review* 92(1): 1–22.

Outhwaite, William (2000 [1985]) 'Hans-Georg Gadamer', in Quentin Skinner, ed., *The Return of Grand Theory in the Human Sciences*, Cambridge: Cambridge University Press, pp. 21–40.

Owen, John M. (1994) 'How liberalism produces democratic peace', *International Security* 19(1): 87–125.

Oye, Kenneth, ed. (1986) *Cooperation under Anarchy*, Princeton, NJ: Princeton University Press.

Paasi, Anssi (1996) *Territories, Boundaries and Consciousness: The Changing Geographies of the Finnish–Russian Border*, New York: Wiley.

Palan, Ronen (2000) 'A world of their making: an evaluation of the constructivist critique in International Relations', *Review of International Studies* 26(4): 575–98.

Pasic, Sujata Chakrabarti (1996) 'Culturing international relations theory: a call for extension', in Yosef Lapid and Friedrich Kratochwil, eds, *The Return of Culture and Identity in IR Theory*, Boulder, CO: Lynne Rienner, pp. 85–104.

Patomäki, Heikki (1996) 'How to tell better stories about world politics', *European Journal of International Relations* 2(1): 105–33.

Patomäki, Heikki, and Colin Wight (2000) 'After postpositivism? The promises of critical realism', *International Studies Quarterly* 44(2): 213–37.

Penrose, Roger (1994) *Shadows of the Mind: A Search for the Missing Science of Consciousness*, Oxford: Oxford University Press.

Petranker, Jack (2003) 'Inhabiting conscious experience: engaged objectivity in the first-person study of consciousness', *Journal of Consciousness Studies* 10(12): 3–23.

Philippi, Nina (1997) *Bundeswehr-Auslandseinsätze als außen- und sicherheitspolitisches Problem des geeinten Deutschlands*, Frankfurt am Main: Peter Lang.

Piotrowski, Edward W., and Jan Sladkowski (2003) 'An invitation to quantum game theory', *International Journal of Theoretical Physics* 42(5): 1089–99.

Plotnitsky, Arkady (1994) *Complementarity: Anti-Epistemology after Bohr and Derrida*, Durham, NC: Duke University Press.

Popper, Karl (1994) *The Myth of the Framework: In Defence of Science and Rationality*, ed. Mark A. Notturno, London and New York: Routledge.

Posen, Barry R. (1993) 'The security dilemma and ethnic conflict', in Michael E. Brown, ed., *Ethnic Conflict and International Security*, Princeton, NJ: Princeton University Press, pp. 103–24.

Price, Richard, and Christian Reus-Smit (1998) 'Dangerous liaisons? Critical international theory and constructivism', *European Journal of International Relations* 4(3): 259–94.

Primack, Joel, and Frank von Hippel (1974) *Advice and Dissent: Scientists in the Political Arena*, New York: Basic Books.

Primas, Hans (2003) 'Time entanglement between mind and matter', *Mind and Matter* 1(1): 81–119.

Prunier, Gérard (1995) *The Rwanda Crisis: History of a Genocide*, New York: Columbia University Press.

Ragin, Charles C. (1987) *The Comparative Method: Moving Beyond Qualitative and Quantitative Strategies*, Berkeley, CA: University of California Press.

—— (2000) *Fuzzy-Set Social Science*, Chicago, IL: University of Chicago Press.

Ramet, Sabrina P. (1992) *Nationalism and Federalism in Yugoslavia, 1962–1991*, Bloomington, IN: University of Indiana Press.

Rasmussen, Erik (1987) *Complementarity and Political Science: An Essay on Fundamentals of Political Science Theory and Research Strategy*, Odense: University of Southern Denmark Press.

Rengger, Nicholas (2001) 'The boundaries of conversation: a response to Dallmayr', *Millennium: Journal of International Studies* 30(2): 357–64.

Reus-Smit, Christian (1997) 'The constitutional structure of international society and the nature of fundamental institutions', *International Organization* 51(4): 555–89.

Ringmar, Erik (1996) 'On the ontological status of the state', *European Journal of International Relations* 2(4): 439–66.

—— (1997) 'Alexander Wendt: a social scientist struggling with history', in Iver B. Neumann and Ole Wæver, eds, *The Future of International Relations: Masters in the Making?*, London and New York: Routledge, pp. 269–89.

—— (2002) 'The recognition game: Soviet Russia against the West', *Cooperation and Conflict* 37(2): 115–36.

Risse, Thomas (2000) '"Let's argue!": communicative action in world politics', *International Organization* 54(1): 1–39.

Risse-Kappen, Thomas (1995a) 'Democratic peace – warlike democracies? A social constructivist interpretation of the liberal argument', *European Journal of International Relations* 1(4): 491–517.

—— (1995b) 'Reden ist nicht billig: Zur Debatte um Kommunikation und Rationalität', *Zeitschrift für Internationale Beziehungen* 2(1): 171–84.

—— (1996) 'Collective identity in a democratic community: the case of NATO', in Peter J. Katzenstein, ed., *The Culture of National Security: Norms and Identity in World Politics*, New York: Columbia University Press, pp. 357–99.

Rittberger, Volker, ed. (1993) *Regime Theory and International Relations*, Oxford: Oxford University Press.

Rorty, Richard (1991) *Objectivity, Relativism, and Truth*, Cambridge: Cambridge University Press.

Rosenau, James N. (1986) 'Before cooperation: hegemons, regimes, and habit-driven actors in world politics', *International Organization* 40(4): 849–94.

Rosenblum, Bruce, and Fred Kuttner (1999) 'Consciousness and quantum mechanics: the connection and analogies', *Journal of Mind and Behavior* 20(3): 229–56.

Rouse, Joseph (2002) *How Scientific Practices Matter: Reclaiming Philosophical Naturalism*, Chicago, IL: University of Chicago Press.

Rudolph, Lloyd, and Susanne Rudolph (2003) 'Engaging subjective knowledge', *Perspectives on Politics* 1(4): 681–94.

Ruetsche, Laura (2002) 'Interpreting quantum theories', in Peter Machamer and Michael Silberstein, eds, *The Blackwell Guide to the Philosophy of Science*, Oxford: Blackwell, pp. 199–226.

Ruggie, John Gerard (1986 [1983]) 'Continuity and transformation in the world polity: toward a neorealist synthesis', in Robert O. Keohane, ed., *Neorealism and its Critics*, New York: Columbia University Press, pp. 131–57.

—— (1998a) *Constructing the World Polity: Essays on International Institutionalization*, London and New York: Routledge.

—— (1998b) 'What makes the world hang together? Neo-utilitarianism and the social constructivist challenge', *International Organization* 52(4): 855–85.

Sahlins, Peter (1989) *Boundaries: The Making of France and Spain in the Pyrenees*, Berkeley, CA: University of California Press.

Salthe, Stanley (1985) *Evolving Hierarchical Systems: Their Structure and Representation*, New York: Columbia University Press.

Salthe, Stanley, and Koichiro Matsuno (1995) 'Self-organization in hierarchical systems', *Journal of Social and Evolutionary Systems* 18(4): 327–38.

Sárváry, Katalin (2001) 'Devaluing diplomacy? A critique of Alexander Wendt's conception of progress and politics', *Journal of International Relations and Development* 4(4): 380–402.

Satinover, Jeffrey (2001) *The Quantum Brain: The Search for Freedom and the Next Generation of Man*, New York: John Wiley.

Sawyer, Keith (2001) 'Emergence in sociology: contemporary philosophy of mind and some implications for sociological theory', *American Journal of Sociology* 107(3): 551–85.

Sayer, Andrew (1997) 'Essentialism, social constructionism and beyond', *Sociological Review* 45(3): 453–87.

Schmalz-Bruns, Rainer (1995) 'Die Theorie des kommunikative Handelns – eine Flaschenpost? Anmerkungen zur jüngsten Theoriedebatte in den Internationalen Beziehungen', *Zeitschrift für Internationale Beziehungen* 2(2): 347–70.

Schmidt, Siegfried J., ed. (1987) *Der Diskurs des radikalen Konstruktivismus*, Frankfurt am Main: Suhrkamp.

Schneider, Gerald (1994) 'Rational choice und kommunikatives Handeln: Eine Replik auf Harald Müller', *Zeitschrift für Internationale Beziehungen* 1(2): 357–66.

Schröder, Gerhard (1999) 'Statement of the Federal Government on the occasion of the 50th anniversary of the North Atlantic Treaty Organization on 22 April 1999, in Presse und Informationsamt der Bundesregierung', *Bulletin* 19 (23 April): 193–5.

Schrödinger, Erwin (1959) 'The principle of objectivation', in *Mind and Matter*, Cambridge: Cambridge University Press, pp. 36–51.

Schueler, G. F. (2003) *Reasons and Purposes*, Oxford: Oxford University Press.

Schweller, Randall L. (1996) 'Neorealism's status quo bias: what security dilemma?', *Security Studies* 5(3): 90–121.

Seager, William (1995) 'Consciousness, information, and panpsychism', *Journal of Consciousness Studies* 2(3): 272–88.

Searle, John R. (1995) *The Construction of Social Reality*, New York: Free Press.

Shapiro, Ian, and Alexander Wendt (1992) 'The difference that realism makes: social science and the politics of consent', *Politics and Society* 20(2): 197–223.

Siewert, Charles (1998) *The Significance of Consciousness*, Princeton, NJ: Princeton University Press.

—— (2002) 'Consciousness and intentionality', in *The Stanford Encyclopedia of Philosophy*, Stanford, CA: Stanford University Press; http//plato.stanford.edu/entries/consciousness-intentionality/.

Simmel, Georg (1950 [1911]) 'The field of sociology', in *The Sociology of Georg Simmel*, ed. Kurt H. Wolff, New York: Free Press, pp. 3–9.

—— (1955 [1908]) 'Conflict', in *Conflict and the Web of Group-Affiliations*, ed. Kurt H. Wolff, New York: Free Press, pp. 3–17.

—— (1989 [1890]) *Über soziale Differenzierung: soziologische und psychologische Untersuchungen: Gesamtausgabe*, Vol. 2, Frankfurt am Main: Suhrkamp.

—— (1992 [1908]) *Soziologie: Untersuchungen über die Formen der Vergesellschaftung: Gesamtausgabe*, Vol. 11, Frankfurt am Main: Suhrkamp.

Siverson, Randolph M., and Harvey Starr (1990) 'Opportunity, willingness and the diffusion of war, 1816–1965', *American Political Science Review* 84: 46–67.

Skinner, Quentin (2000 [1985]) 'Introduction: the return of Grand Theory', in Quentin Skinner, ed., *The Return of Grand Theory in the Human Sciences*, Cambridge: Cambridge University Press, pp. 1–20.

Skocpol, Theda, ed. (1984) *Vision and Method in Historical Sociology*, Cambridge and New York: Cambridge University Press.

Skrbina, David (2003) 'Panpsychism as an underlying theme in Western philosophy', *Journal of Consciousness Studies* 10(3): 4–46.

Slovic, Paul (1995) 'The construction of preference', *American Psychologist* 50(5): 364–71.

Smith, Quentin (2003) 'Why cognitive scientists cannot ignore quantum mechanics', in Quentin Smith and Aleksandar Jokic, eds, *Consciousness: New Philosophical Perspectives*, Oxford: Clarendon Press, pp. 409–46.

Smith, Steve (1997) 'New approaches to international theory', in John Baylis and Steve Smith, eds, *The Globalization of World Politics*, Oxford: Oxford University Press, pp. 165–90.

—— (2000) 'Wendt's world', *Review of International Studies* 26(1): 151–63.

Sober, Elliott, and David Sloan Wilson (1998) *Unto Others: The Evolution and Psychology of Unselfish Behavior*, Cambridge, MA: Harvard University Press.

'Special issue on the origins of the national interest' (1999) *Security Studies* 8(2–3).

Spruyt, Hendrik (1994) *The Sovereign State and its Competitors: An Analysis of Systems Change*, Princeton, NJ: Princeton University Press.

Stapp, Henry (1996) 'The hard problem: a quantum approach', *Journal of Consciousness Studies* 3(3): 194–210.

Stein, Arthur A. (1990) *Why Nations Cooperate: Circumstance and Choice in International Relations*, Ithaca, NY: Cornell University Press.

Strange, Susan (1990) 'The Name of the Game', in N. Rizopoulos, ed., *Sea-Changes: American Foreign Policy in a World Transformed*, New York: Council on Foreign Relations Press, pp. 238–74.

Stubbs, Richard, and Geoffrey Underhill, eds (1994) *Political Economy and the Changing Global Order*, New York: St Martin's Press.

Suganami, Hidemi (1996) *On the Causes of War*, Oxford: Clarendon Press.

—— (2001) 'Alexander Wendt and the English School', *Journal of International Relations and Development* 4(4): 403–23.

—— (2002) 'On Wendt's philosophy: a critique', *Review of International Studies* 28(1): 23–37.

Sylvan, David, and Barry Glassner (1985) *A Rationalist Methodology for the Social Sciences*, Oxford: Blackwell.

Tegmark, Max (2000) 'Importance of quantum decoherence in brain processes', *Physical Review E* 61(4): 4194–206.

Teller, Paul (1986) 'Relational holism and quantum mechanics', *British Journal for the Philosophy of Science* 37: 71–81.

Tenbruck, Friedrich (1985) 'George Herbert Mead und die Ursprünge der Soziologie in Deutschland und Amerika: ein Kapitel über die Gültigkeit und Vergleichbarkeit soziologischer Theorien', in Hans Joas, ed., *Das Problem der Intersubjektivität: neuere Beiträge zum Werk George Herbert Meads*, Frankfurt am Main: Suhrkamp, pp. 179–243.

Tilly, Charles (1978) *From Mobilization to Revolution*, New York: McGraw-Hill.

—— (1995) 'To explain political processes', *American Journal of Sociology* 100(6): 1594–610.

Todorov, Tzvetan (1984) *The Conquest of America*, New York: Harper.

Tönnies, Ferdinand (1957) *Community and Society*, East Lansing, MI: Michigan State University Press.

Turner, John C. (1987) *Rediscovering the Social Group: A Self-Categorization Theory*, Oxford: Blackwell.

US Department of Commerce (1977) *Proceedings of the Colloquium on the Science Court*, Washington, DC: Commerce Technical Advisory Board.

Van Evera, Stephen (1999) *Causes of War: The Structure of Power and the Roots of War*, Ithaca, NY: Cornell University Press.

Vasquez, John A. (1983) *The Power of Power Politics: A Critique*, London: Frances Pinter.

Velmans, Max (2002) 'How could conscious experiences affect brains?', *Journal of Consciousness Studies* 9(11): 3–29.

'Vertrag über die abschließende Regelung in bezug auf Deutschland' (1993) repr. in *Grundgesetz für die Bundesrepublik Deutschland*, 51st edn, Munich: C. H. Beck: 107–14.

Viale, Riccardo (2000) 'The mind–society problem', *Mind and Society* 1(1): 3–24.

Vitiello, Giuseppe (2001) *My Double Unveiled: The Dissipative Quantum Model of Brain*, Amsterdam: John Benjamins.

von Wright, Georg Henrik (1971) *Explanation and Understanding*, Ithaca, NY: Cornell University Press.

Vovelle, Michele (1982) *Idéologies & mentalités*, Paris: François Maspero.

—— (1988) 'L'histoire de la longue durée', in Jacques Le Goff, ed., *La Nouvelle Histoire*, Paris: Éditions Complexe, pp. 77–108.

Wæver, Ole (1996) 'The rise and fall of the inter-paradigm debate', in Steve Smith, Ken Booth and Marysia Zalewski, eds, *International Theory: Positivism and Beyond*, Cambridge: Cambridge University Press, pp. 149–84.

—— (1997) 'Figures of international thought: introducing persons instead of paradigms', in Iver B. Neumann and Ole Wæver, eds, *The Future of International Relations: Masters in the Making?*, London and New York: Routledge, pp. 1–37.

Walker, R. B. J. (1993) *Inside/Outside: International Relations as Political Theory*, Cambridge: Cambridge University Press.

Wallace, Alan B. (2000) *The Taboo of Subjectivity: Towards a New Science of Consciousness*, Oxford: Oxford University Press.

Walt, Stephen M. (1987) *The Origins of Alliances*, Ithaca, NY: Cornell University Press.

Waltz, Kenneth N. (1979) *Theory of International Politics*, Reading, MA: Addison-Wesley.

Weber, Cynthia (1998) 'Performative states', *Millennium: Journal of International Studies* 27(1): 77–95.

Weber, Max (1962) *Basic Concepts in Sociology*, London: Peter Owen.

—— (1980 [1921–2]) *Wirtschaft und Gesellschaft: Grundriss der Verstehenden Soziologie*, Tübingen: J. C. B. Mohr (Paul Siebeck).

Weiner, Myron (1971) 'The Macedonian syndrome: an historical model of international relations and political development', *World Politics* 23: 665–83.

Wendt, Alexander (1987) 'The agent–structure problem in International Relations', *International Organization* 41(3): 335–70.

—— (1991) 'Bridging the theory/meta-theory gap in international relations', *Review of International Studies* 17(4): 389–92.

—— (1992a) 'Anarchy is what states make of it: the social construction of power politics', *International Organization* 46(2): 391–425.

—— (1992b) 'Levels of analysis vs. agents and structures: part III', *Review of International Studies* 18(2): 181–5.

—— (1994) 'Collective identity formation and the international state', *American Political Science Review* 88: 384–96.

—— (1995) 'Constructing international politics', *International Security* 20(1): 71–81.

—— (1996) 'Identity and structural change in international politics', in Yosef Lapid and Friedrich Kratochwil, eds, *The Return of Culture and Identity in IR Theory*, Boulder, CO, and London: Lynne Rienner, pp. 47–64.

—— (1998) 'On constitution and causation in International Relations', *Review of International Studies* 24(special issue): 101–17.

—— (1999) *Social Theory of International Politics*, Cambridge: Cambridge University Press.

—— (2000) 'On the via media: a response to the critics', *Review of International Studies* 26(1): 165–80.

—— (2001) 'Driving with the rearview mirror: on the rational science of institutional design', *International Organization* 55(4): 1019–49.

—— (2003) 'Why a world state is inevitable', *European Journal of International Relations* 9(4): 491–542.

—— (2004) 'The state as person in international theory', *Review of International Studies* 30(2): 289–316.

—— (n.d.) 'Quantum mind and social science', book manuscript in preparation.

Wendt, Alexander, and Raymond Duvall (1989) 'Institutions and international order', in Ernst-Otto Czempiel and James Rosenau, eds, *Global Changes and Theoretical Challenges: Approaches to World Politics for the 1990s*, Lexington, MA: Lexington Books, pp. 51–74.

White, Harrison C. (1992) *Identity and Control*, Princeton, NJ: Princeton University Press.

Wight, Colin (1996) 'Incommensurability and cross-paradigm communication in International Relations theory: "what's the frequency Kenneth?"', *Millennium: Journal of International Studies* 25(2): 291–319.

—— (1999) 'They shoot dead horses don't they? Locating agency in the agent–structure problematique', *European Journal of International Relations* 5(1): 109–42.

—— (2002) 'Philosophy of social science and International Relations', in Walter Carlsnaes, Thomas Risse and Beth A. Simmons, eds, *Handbook of International Relations*, London: Sage, pp. 23–51.

Wight, Martin (1966) 'Why is there no international theory?', in Herbert Butterfield and Martin Wight, eds, *Diplomatic Investigations*, Cambridge: Cambridge University Press, pp. 17–34.

—— (1977) *Systems of State*, Leicester: Leicester University Press.

—— (1991) *International Theory: The Three Traditions*, Leicester: Leicester University Press.

Wolf, Fred A. (1998) 'The timing of conscious experience: a causality-violating, two-valued, transactional interpretation of subjective antedating and spatial–temporal projection', *Journal of Scientific Exploration* 12(4): 511–42.

Wolfers, Arnold (1962) *Discord and Collaboration: Essays on International Politics*, Baltimore, MD and London: Johns Hopkins University Press.

Wolff, Kurt H. (1950) *The Sociology of Georg Simmel*, New York: Free Press.

Zak, Michail (2000) 'Quantum decision-maker', *Information Sciences* 128(3–4): 199–215.

Zaller, John (1992) *The Nature and Origins of Mass Opinion*, Cambridge: Cambridge University Press.

Zehfuß, Maja (1998) 'Sprachlosigkeit schränkt ein. Zur Bedeutung von Sprache in konstruktivistischen Theorien', *Zeitschrift für Internationale Beziehungen* 5(1): 109–37.

Zehfuss, Maja (2001) 'Constructivisms in International Relations: Wendt, Onuf and Kratochwil', in Knud-Erik Jørgensen and Karin M. Fierke, eds, *Constructing International Relations: The Next Generation*, Armonk, NY: M. E. Sharpe, pp. 54–75.

Ziman, John (1991) *Reliable Knowledge: An Exploration of the Grounds for Belief in Science*, Cambridge: Cambridge University Press.

Zohar, Danah, and Ian Marshall (1994) *The Quantum Society: Mind, Physics, and a New Social Vision*, New York: Quill.

Zukav, Gary (1979) *The Dancing Wu Li Masters: An Overview of the New Physics*, New York: Quill.

Index

situate   jettisoned
embed
unpack

Made in the USA
San Bernardino, CA
16 October 2015